Forgery in Musical Composition

Forgery in Musical Composition

Aesthetics, History, and the Canon

FREDERICK REECE

OXFORD
UNIVERSITY PRESS

Oxford University Press is a department of the University of Oxford.
It furthers the University's objective of excellence in research, scholarship,
and education by publishing worldwide. Oxford is a registered trade mark of
Oxford University Press in the UK and in certain other countries.

Published in the United States of America by Oxford University Press
198 Madison Avenue, New York, NY 10016, United States of America.

© Oxford University Press 2025

All rights reserved. No part of this publication may be reproduced, stored in a retrieval system, transmitted, used for text and data mining, or used for training artificial intelligence, in any form or by any means, without the prior permission in writing of Oxford University Press, or as expressly permitted by law, by license or under terms agreed with the appropriate reprographics rights organization. Inquiries concerning reproduction outside the scope of the above should be sent to the Rights Department, Oxford University Press, at the address above.

You must not circulate this work in any other form
and you must impose this same condition on any acquirer

Library of Congress Cataloging-in-Publication Data
Names: Reece, Frederick, author.
Title: Forgery in musical composition : aesthetics, history, and the canon / Frederick Reece.
Description: [1.] | New York, NY : Oxford University Press, 2025. |
Includes bibliographical references and index. |
Identifiers: LCCN 2024055853 (print) | LCCN 2024055854 (ebook) |
ISBN 9780197618301 (hardback) | ISBN 9780197618332 |
ISBN 9780197618325 (epub)
Subjects: LCSH: Mozart, Wolfgang Amadeus, 1756–1791—Forgeries. |
Music—18th century—History and criticism.
Classification: LCC ML410.M9 R46 2025 (print) |
LCC ML410.M9 (ebook) |
DDC 780.9/034—dc23/eng/20241204
LC record available at https://lccn.loc.gov/2024055853
LC ebook record available at https://lccn.loc.gov/2024055854

DOI: 10.1093/9780197618332.001.0001

Printed by Marquis Book Printing, Canada

The Publisher gratefully acknowledges support from the AMS 75 PAYS Fund
of the American Musicological Society, supported in part by the National
Endowment for the Humanities and the Andrew W. Mellon Foundation.

For Annie

Contents

List of Music Examples	ix
List of Figures	xi
List of Tables	xiii
Preface	xv
Acknowledgments	xxi
Introduction: The Van Meegeren Syndrome	1

PART I. ROMANTIC CULTURES OF FORGERY, 1791–1945

1. Mozartian Swan Songs	39
2. Kreislerian Fantasies	78

PART II. MODERN CULTURES OF FORGERY, 1945–2000

3. Schubert's Untrue Symphony	121
4. Haydn's Missing Link	164
Epilogue	201
Bibliography	207
Index	223

Music Examples

P.1 Henri Casadesus, "Handel" Viola Concerto in B minor. Solo part. Allegro moderato (mvt. i), mm. 7–13, here renumbered as mm. 1–7 — xvi

1.1 W. A. Mozart, Requiem in D minor, K. 626, in the traditional completion by F. X. Süssmayr. Piano-vocal score by Friedrich Brissler. Lacrimosa, mm. 10–19 — 60

1.2 W. A. Mozart, Requiem in D minor, K. 626, in the traditional completion by F. X. Süssmayr. Piano-vocal score by Friedrich Brissler. Sanctus, mm. 1–8 — 63

1.3 W. A. Mozart, Minuet in D Major, K. 355 (594a, 576b), completed (?) by Maximilian Stadler — 74

2.1 Fritz Kreisler, "Louis Couperin" La Précieuse, mm. 99–105 — 107

2.2 Fritz Kreisler, "Vivaldi" Violin Concerto in C Major. Violin-piano score. Andante doloroso (mvt. ii), mm. 11–35 — 108

2.3 Albert Lavignac, Cours d'Harmonie: Théorique et Pratique (Paris: Henry Lemoine & Co., 1909), fig. 102, p. 122 — 109

2.4a Fritz Kreisler, "Pugnani" Praeludium and Allegro, mm. 1–23 — 111

2.4b Fritz Kreisler, "Pugnani" Praeludium and Allegro, mm. 1–17, voice-leading analysis — 112

2.5 Fritz Kreisler, "Pugnani" Praeludium and Allegro, mm. 119–150 — 113

3.1a Gunter Elsholz, "Schubert" Symphony in E Major (Gmunden), "D. 849." Andante molto—Allegro—Andante molto (mvt. i), mm. 1–8 — 141

3.1b Franz Schubert, Octet in F Major, D. 803. Andante molto—Allegro—Andante molto—Allegro (mvt. vi), mm. 1–7 — 142

3.2a Gunter Elsholz, "Schubert" Symphony in E Major (Gmunden), "D. 849." Andante molto—Allegro—Andante molto (mvt. i), mm. 27–34 — 147

3.2b Franz Schubert, Fantasy in C Major (Wanderer), D. 760 (op. 15), mm. 197–200 — 148

3.2c Franz Schubert, Der Wanderer, D. 489 (op. 4, no. 1), mm. 22–30 — 149

3.3a Gunter Elsholz, "Schubert" Symphony in E Major (Gmunden), "D. 849." Scherzo: Un poco agitato (mvt. ii), mm. 53–60 — 150

3.3b Franz Schubert, Symphony No. 9 in C Major (Great), D. 944. Scherzo: Allegro vivace (mvt. iii), mm. 143–50 — 151

X MUSIC EXAMPLES

3.4a Gunter Elsholz, "Schubert" Symphony in E Major (Gmunden), "D. 849."
Andante molto—Allegro—Andante molto (mvt. i), mm. 137–68   154

3.4b Franz Schubert, Symphony No. 9 in C Major (Great), D. 944. Andante
con moto (mvt. ii), mm. 245–56   158

4.1 Winfried Michel, "Haydn" Sonata in D Minor, "Hob. XVI:2a." Moderato
(mvt. i), mm. 1–11   188

4.2 Winfried Michel, "Haydn" Sonata in D Minor, "Hob. XVI:2a." Moderato
(mvt. i), mm. 62–78   189

4.3 W. A. Mozart, *Idomeneo*, K. 366. Piano reduction by Richard Metzdorff.
Overture, mm. 156–64   191

4.4 Winfried Michel, "Haydn" Sonata in B Major, "Hob. XVI:2c." Allegro
Moderato (mvt. i), mm. 14–24   192

4.5 Winfried Michel, "Haydn" Sonata in B♭ Major, "Hob. XVI:2d." Allegretto
(mvt. i), Michel's "completion," mm. 74–82   197

Figures

I.1 Han van Meegeren with *Christus in de Tempel* (1945). Photograph
by Koos Raucamp. Nationaal Archief, The Hague. CC0   2

1.1 W. A. Mozart, *Requiem* (Leipzig: Breitkopf & Härtel, 1800), Title Page.
Allen A. Brown Collection of Music, Boston Public Library   56

1.2 Draft score of the Lacrimosa in Mozart's hand with Eybler's additions
circled by Stadler. Mus. Hs. 1756ib, fol. 33v, Österreichische
Nationalbibliothek, Musiksammlung. © ÖNB Vienna   69

1.3 Delivery score for the Requiem with Süssmayr's forgery of Mozart's
signature. Mus. Hs. 1756ia, fol. 1r, Österreichische Nationalbibliothek,
Musiksammlung. © ÖNB Vienna   70

2.1 Fritz Kreisler (second from left) and Arnold Schoenberg (seated at the cello)
as members of a Schrammelmusik Quintet. Reichenau, July 8, 1900.
PH1386, A5, C1, Arnold Schönberg Center Bildarchiv. Private Collection   91

2.2 Henry Wallis, *The Death of Chatterton*, Tate Version (1855)   97

4.1 H. C. Robbins Landon holding photocopies of the "rediscovered"
manuscripts. © Denzil McNeelance, News UK & Ireland Limited,
14 December 1993   165

4.2 John Cooke, *Piltdown Gang* (1915)   172

4.3a Westphalian Manuscript, Title Page. From the H. C. Robbins Landon
Collection (Box 78; Folder 11), Howard Gotlieb Archival Research Center
at Boston University   181

4.3b Westphalian Manuscript, First Page of Forged Sonata in D minor,
"Hob. XVI:2a." From the H. C. Robbins Landon Collection (Box 78;
Folder 11), Howard Gotlieb Archival Research Center at
Boston University   183

4.4 Westphalian Manuscript, page 37. From the H. C. Robbins Landon
Collection (Box 78; Folder 11), Howard Gotlieb Archival Research Center
at Boston University   196

Tables

2.1 Kreisler's Forgeries with Dates of Publication and Confession of Authorship   79

3.1 Grove's Chronology of Schubert's Symphonies adapted from
A Dictionary of Music and Musicians, Vol. 3 (1883)   129

4.1 Chronologies of Haydn's Early Solo Keyboard Works from Hob. XVI   166

Preface

Forgery in Musical Composition is perhaps in danger of seeming a willfully obscure title. To be sure, the idea of forging paintings, sculptures, or literary works by skillfully emulating historical styles is familiar enough: one has only to think of Han van Meegeren's "Vermeer" canvases (from the twentieth century), Giovanni Bastianini's "Renaissance" busts (from the nineteenth century), or William Henry Ireland's "Shakespeare" plays (from the eighteenth century) to get something of the general idea. Broadly recognizable as these types of art forgery may be, technical notions of authenticity are notoriously difficult to transpose from one medium to another, and the substance of musical composition is not generally thought to be quite like that of painting, sculpture, or literature, at least in any simple sense. Indeed, as the most abstract, intangible, and immaterial of the arts, music's capacity for truth content, for cultural durability, and for financial value has often been called into question in ways that might superficially appear to render the category of forgery nonsensical. If music is taken to be hermeneutically inscrutable, historically impermanent, and economically insignificant by its very nature, there might seem to be little compelling reason to bother faking it in the first place.

And yet forged compositions are far more common within the culture of classical music than most people realize. In the course of the long nineteenth century, new generations of listeners became increasingly disposed to intertwine music with non-verbal meaning, with documentary historical truth, and with emergent notions of the authorial self in ways that served to galvanize both the production and the unmasking of compositional forgeries at scale. The critic's goal in confronting such works has generally been to restore order by asserting that any attempt at forgery will inevitably be betrayed, in the fullness of time, by certain clearly discernible "tells"—i.e., evidential details of source or style that allow the connoisseur to reliably distinguish real from fake. *Forgery in Musical Composition* maintains that there is a great deal to be learned and achieved through such rigorous engagement with musical evidence of authorship as such. Yet the book also stresses the historical fact that artistic authentication and attribution have often been disappointingly messy, provisional, and divisive in practice. New documents and insights can readily turn up unbidden to flip the script on a seemingly well-reasoned academic judgment, dramatically reversing the fortune of a fake thought to be an authentic work or an authentic work thought to be a fake, sometimes quite literally overnight. The intellectual arms races

Example P.1 Henri Casadesus, "Handel" Viola Concerto in B minor. Solo part. Allegro moderato (mvt. i), mm. 7–13, here renumbered as mm. 1–7

that frequently develop between criticism and its "criminal sibling" forgery appear unwinnable in any enduring historical sense precisely because so many of the skills and techniques needed to authenticate artistic sources and styles are readily readapted to the act of simulation.[1] And, in the final analysis, there is simply no getting around the brute fact that "we can only talk about the bad forgeries" in studies such as this, since—as Metropolitan Museum of Art curator Theodore Rousseau once wisely observed—"the good ones are," by definition, "still hanging on the walls."[2] With all this practical complexity and difficulty in mind, it is easy to become paranoid about the philosophical viability of music's authenticity in general, an uncomfortable reality that has occasionally lent compositional forgery a starring role in certain post-Enlightenment critical attempts to demonstrate that music-as-truth is, in itself, little more than a romantic fiction.

Like many fledgling music students, I first became tentatively aware of compositional forgery and the issues that it raises long before I had words for the phenomenon. Perhaps the crucial moment came the summer before college, when a revered teacher deposited an unfamiliar score on my stand: a 1924 Max Eschig edition of a Viola Concerto in B Minor, the cover of which was emblazoned with the familiar authorial name "G. F. Händel." Further down the page and in smaller font, a supplemental—and, seemingly, unremarkable— paratextual notice typical of early music publications from the era was printed in French: "thoroughbass realization and orchestration by Henri Casadesus."[3] Scanning the opening of the concerto in my lesson, I drew bow to string and haphazardly sightread the passage reproduced in example P.1.

---

[1] On this reciprocal "sibling" relationship between forgery and criticism, see Anthony Grafton, *Forgers and Critics: Creativity and Duplicity in Western Scholarship* (London: Collins & Brown, 1990), 127.

[2] Theodore Rousseau, "The Stylistic Detection of Forgeries," *Metropolitan Museum of Art Bulletin* 26, no. 6 (1968): 247–52, at 247.

[3] "Réalisation de la basse et orchestration par Henri Casadesus." [Henri Casadesus] G. F. Händel, *Concerto en si mineur pour alto avec accompagnement d'orchestre* (Paris: Max Eschig, 1924).

PREFACE   xvii

The phrase had an oddly angular beauty that I found immediately striking. Most obviously, its first cadence fell asymmetrically, and earlier than I had expected, at the downbeat of the solo part's m. 7. Indeed, for the sight-reader, the entire passage had a disorienting syncopated quality. The first two eighth notes in my part (F♯–B, or $\hat{5}$–$\hat{1}$) gave the surprising impression of a harmonic downbeat on the final quarter-note beat of m. 1, while the double neighbor figure (E–C♯) embellishing D on the true downbeat of m. 2 obscured any sense of a corresponding new beginning there, such that the overall beat groupings in the first two bars appeared to be 3 + 2 + 3, across the printed measure line, as marked in example P.1.[4] I hasten to add that none of this was aesthetically unappealing. Yet it reminded me, in a nagging way, of the deliberately jagged and unpredictable approach to rhythm, phrase, and cadence I had occasionally wrestled with in neo-classical works from the 1920s and 1930s by the likes of Paul Hindemith and Igor Stravinsky. Once I had finished playing my teacher seemed to confirm the truth of this musical observation when she uttered a sentence that imprinted itself on my memory as if chiseled in stone: "I don't think it's actually by Handel, but it's a good piece."

Of course, she wasn't wrong. In graduate school years later I stumbled across an academic source that confirmed that Henri Casadesus (1879–1947)—a celebrated violist and founding member of the Parisian *Société des instruments Anciens*—had composed the entire concerto from scratch, knowingly performing and publishing it under Handel's name in what can only accurately be described as an act of compositional forgery.[5] With the veil of deception now decisively removed, the unnerving experience of confusion in that long-ago musical encounter with the "Handel" concerto made a strange kind of retrospective musicological sense. As an imitation of eighteenth-century music published in the 1920s, the work's neo-classical metrical qualities could be reinterpreted as evidence of the forger's unwitting and anachronistic musical presence in his own composition, a monumental shift in perspective that seemingly transfigured the exposed fake into an authentic document of latter-day stylistic mishearing. The realization that forged musical works such as this existed soon led me to become preoccupied with the question of how many more fakes might be lurking elsewhere in dark corners of the repertory. Before long, a history of forgery in musical composition appeared inevitable.

---

[4] Violists will recognize this phrasing from foundational recordings of the work issued by Casadesus's contemporaries. See, for example, William Primrose (viola), *Handel Concerto in B Minor*, RCA Victor Red Seal Records, DM1131, 1946, shellac discs.

[5] Henri Casadesus's widow confessed as much in 1963 correspondence documented in Walter Lebermann, "Apokryph, Plagiat, Korruptel oder Falsifikat?," *Die Musikforschung* 20, no. 4 (1967): 413–25, at 422. This notably contradicts both the published Max Eschig edition and the testimony provided three decades earlier in M. Casadesus, "Handel Concerto en si Mineur Pour Alto Avec Accompagnement d'Orchestre," *Notes* 1 (1934): 9.

xviii PREFACE

I recount this initial first-person encounter with compositional forgery at the risk of appearing unduly self-indulgent in part because I suspect that its autobiographical contours will be at least vaguely familiar to classical musicians of many different stripes. One often hears vocalists telling similar stories about formative moments of music-historical unease with the aria *Pietà, Signore!*, a widely sung composition attributed to Alessandro Stradella (1639–1682) in such prominent published editions as G. Schirmer's immortal student anthology *Twenty-Four Italian Songs and Arias*, but to pioneering music scholar François-Joseph Fétis (1784–1871) in the authoritative *Répertoire International des Sources Musicales* (RISM) following a critical tradition dating back at least to the final decade of the nineteenth century.[6] In the realm of choral music, suspicions of inauthenticity are not infrequently aroused in relation to the unfailingly popular four-part chanson *Mon cœur se recommande à vous*, a work widely circulated under the name of Orlando di Lasso (1532–1594) since its appearance in the 1853 early music anthology *Échos du temps passé*, but more plausibly composed—according to current musicological consensus—by that collection's editor, Jean-Baptiste Weckerlin (1821–1910).[7] For their part, cellists are often familiar with a Girolamo Frescobaldi (1583–1643) Toccata first published in 1925 and now widely believed to have been composed by its self-identified arranger, Gaspar Cassadó (1897–1966).[8] And it is difficult to find a classically trained violinist who has not played the Praeludium und Allegro by acclaimed concert soloist Fritz Kreisler (1875–1962), even if many present-day musicians are unaware that Kreisler published and performed it as a rediscovered work by Gaetano Pugnani (1731–1798) for decades until dramatically confessing his own authorship of the composition on the front page of the *New York Times* in February 1935.[9] Guitarists engaged in conversation on this topic tend to bring up a similar spate of works published under the names of Silvius Leopold Weiss (1687–1750) and

---

[6] The work is also familiar to many under the title *Se i miei sospiri*. Compare Alessandro Stradella, "Pietà, Signore!," in *Twenty-Four Italian Songs and Arias of the Seventeenth and Eighteenth Centuries* (New York: G. Schirmer, 1894) and François-Joseph Fétis (conjectural), *Se i miei sospiri*, Brussel, (B-Br) MS Fétis 7328 C Mus (A/II; RISM ID no. 700007075). On this aria's history, see in particular Sarah Hibberd, "Murder in the Cathedral? Stradella, Musical Power, and Performing the Past in 1830s Paris," *Music & Letters* 87, no. 4 (2006): 551–79, esp. 554–63.

[7] Daniel R. Melamed, "Who Wrote Lassus's Most Famous Piece?," *Early Music* 26, no. 1 (1998): 6–26; Katharine Ellis, *Interpreting the Musical Past: Early-Music in Nineteenth-Century France* (New York: Oxford University Press, 2005), 115–16.

[8] Walter Schenkman, "Cassado's Frescobaldi: A Case of Mistaken Identity or Outright Hoax," *American String Teacher* 28, no. 22 (1978): 26–29; Elizabeth Cowling, *The Cello* (London: Charles Scribner's Sons, 1975), 214; Gabrielle Kaufman, *Gaspar Cassadó: Cellist, Composer and Transcriber* (Abingdon: Routledge, 2017), 14, 111, 139, 198–200; Nathaniel Jacob Chaitkin, "Gaspar Cassadó: His Relationship with Pablo Casals and His Versatile Musical Life" (DMA diss., University of Maryland, 2001), 24–31.

[9] Kreisler's forgeries are evaluated at length in this book's second chapter. His front-page confession can be found in Olin Downes, "Kreisler Reveals 'Classics' as Own; Fooled Music Critics for 30 Years," *New York Times*, 8 February 1935, 1.

PREFACE   xix

Alessandro Scarlatti (1660–1725) in numerous mid-twentieth-century editions, but in fact written for virtuoso soloist Andrés Segovia's use by Manuel Ponce (1882–1948) in the 1920s and 1930s.[10] And in the classical recording industry, compositions such as the "Albinoni" Adagio in G minor (by Remo Giazotto) and the "Caccini" Ave Maria (by Vladimir Vavilov) have risen to considerable prominence on anthology discs marketed with such implicitly historicizing and aggrandizing titles as *Baroque Masterpieces*, thus ironically becoming iconic of what generically Baroque music sounds like in the public imagination despite being nothing of the sort.[11]

For those who know where to look for them, compositional forgeries such as these appear endemic.[12] Yet when any individual fake is encountered in isolation it is all too easily dismissed as a quirky repertorial oddity marginal to the academic canon and thus unworthy of appreciable intellectual consideration as such.[13] *Forgery in Musical Composition* was written to challenge this presumption by contending that compositional forgeries arise not as discrete aberrations of the classical canon but rather as characteristic by-products of its own internal logic. As the case studies explored in this book suggest, classical music can be

[10] John W. Duarte, "Weiss—Fiction and Fact," *BMG: Banjo, Mandolin, Guitar* 67, no. 785 (1970): 386–87; Peter Kun Frary, "Ponce's Baroque Pastiches for Guitar," *Soundboard* 14, no. 3 (1987): 159–63; Kevin R. Manderville, "Manuel Ponce and the Suite in A minor: Its Historical Significance and an Examination of Existing Editions" (DMA diss., Florida State University College of Music, 2005).

[11] The title "Baroque Masterpieces" comes from various artists, *Baroque Masterpieces*, Sony Classical, 2110992, 2002, compact disc, the liner notes of which describe the Adagio in G Minor as Albinoni's "most beloved and deeply moving work." Vavilov's "Caccini" *Ave Maria* appears under Caccini's name alone on such chart-topping vocal anthology discs as Andrea Bocelli (tenor), *Sacred Arias*, Philips Records, 462-600-2, 1999, compact disc; and Charlotte Church (soprano), *Voice of an Angel*, Sony Classical, B000000I9CF, 1998, compact disc. A detailed account of these compositions can be found in Frederick Reece, "Baroque Forgeries and the Public Imagination," in *The Oxford Handbook of Public Music Theory*, edited by J. Daniel Jenkins (New York: Oxford University Press, 2021).

[12] A useful list of such works can be found in Charles L. Cudworth, "Ye Olde Spuriosity Shoppe, or, Put It in the *Anhang* (Conclusion)," *Notes* 12, no. 4 (1955): 533–53. For documentation of selected additional musical forgeries not discussed in my text or Cudworth's, see, for example, Marica S. Tacconi, "Three Forged 'Seventeenth-Century' Venetian Songbooks: A Cautionary Tale," *Journal of Seventeenth-Century Music* 27, no. 1 (2021), https://sscm-jscm.org/jscm-issues/volume-27-no-1/three-forged-seventeenth-century-venetian-songbooks/; Erin Elizabeth Smith, "Mozart, Pergolesi, Handel?: A Study of Three Forgeries" (MA Thesis, University of Maryland, 2014); Richard Macnutt, "Berlioz Forgeries," in *Berlioz: Past, Present, Future–Bicentenary Essays*, edited by Peter Anthony Bloom (Rochester: University of Rochester Press, 2003): 173–92; Philippe Lescat, "'Il pastor Fido,' une œuvre de Nicolas Chédeville," *Informazioni e studi vivaldiani* 11 (1990): 5–19; Martin Staehelin, "'Dank sei Dir, Herr': Zur Erklärung einer Händel-Fälschung des frühen zwanzigsten Jahrhunderts," in *Göttinger Händel-Beiträge*, II, edited by Hans Joachim Marx (Kassel: Bärenreiter-Verlag, 1986): 194–206; Frank Walker, "Two Centuries of Pergolesi Forgeries and Misattributions," *Music & Letters* 30, no. 4 (1949): 297–320.

[13] On recent critiques of quirk historicism in music research, see Nicholas Mathew and Mary Ann Smart, "Elephants in the Music Room: The Future of Quirk Historicism," *Representations* 132 (2015): 61–78. The distinction between the "repertory canon" and the "academic teaching canon" is developed in Marcia J. Citron, *Gender and the Musical Canon* (Urbana: University of Illinois Press, 1993), 22–41.

seen to conform to broader anthropological trends in which forgeries appear most abundantly wherever art's value is closely tethered to its perceived historical and authorial pedigree. With this in mind, compositional forgeries can readily be examined as evidence of the things that a culture of authenticity centered in post-Enlightenment ideas about history, identity, and the self does to music when we are not looking. Here, inauthentic works reward serious analysis not despite but precisely because of the fact that they are not what they appear.

It should go without saying that attending to forgeries in this manner need not involve comprehensively dismantling classical hierarchies or else iconoclastically claiming that there is no difference whatsoever between authentic works and fakes. Indeed, those who earnestly seek to contain forgeries should find the practical incentives for rigorously documenting them especially obvious. Patterns of deception are more easily recognized by those with long memories. And there is thus a sense in which amnesia about the reality of compositional forgery aids no one so much as the aspiring forgers of the present and future. In the end, I maintain that one does not have to choose between treating forgers and forgeries either as cultural irrelevancies to be banished and forgotten or as idols of anti-canonic transgression to be actively revered. Perhaps the middle path is best. For, in truth, the inner logic of creative falsification is just as difficult to grasp from a position of straightforward condemnation as it is from one of contrarian celebration. An excessive fixation on the (im)morality of fakes risks obscuring the more subtle and ambiguous roles that forgery has always played in mediating contested symbolic relationships between self and expression, appearance and essence, beauty and truth.[14] In these rarefied contexts the persistence of forgery suggests that music's authenticity remains all too real not least because it must constantly be renegotiated and reconstructed as fiction.

---

[14] In this way art forgers can be seen to resemble the archetypal tricksters who populate world mythology. As Lewis Hyde's evocative account has it, the boundary-crossing (and, thus, boundary-defining) stories of Coyote, Eshu, Hermes, Loki, Raven et al. can be understood collectively to demonstrate an important truth about human creativity. Namely, that—as Hyde puts it—"the origins, liveliness, and durability of cultures require that there be space for figures whose function is to uncover and disrupt the very things that cultures are based on." See Lewis Hyde, *Trickster Makes This World: Mischief, Myth, and Art* (New York: Farrar, Straus and Giroux, 1998), 9.

Acknowledgments

Forgery in Musical Composition is a meditation on creative deception and mistrust, written—at least primarily—in academic seclusion. Much as I enjoyed the process, such paranoid intellectual work has its occupational hazards. It is not easy to make a home for oneself in a mirror world of fakes where no one can be believed without reservation and no firm ground of certainty exists on which to rest one's feet. And yet, from my perspective, this manuscript has indeed been a curious home of sorts for the better part of a decade, shared at various times with a great many guests, colleagues, friends, and sponsors to whom I am now pleased to owe my thanks. In laying down my pen, it is deeply gratifying to turn from forgery's manifold illusions toward these final pages of acknowledgment. Here, generic tradition demands that all pretense be banished. Only the most earnest and straightforward of approaches will do.

The ideas explored in *Forgery in Musical Composition* first took substance in my doctoral dissertation. My advisor Alexander Rehding and my committee members Suzannah Clark, Emily Dolan, and Christopher Hasty helped cultivate that project from its earliest origins, shaping and reshaping my thinking and writing in fundamental ways. Everything that follows owes something of import to their formative guidance and mentorship at Harvard and thereafter.

The book took its final form on the opposite side of the United States, at the University of Washington in Seattle, where I now teach. The academic community at the UW has left more imprints on my work than I could hope to adequately account for here. My music history department colleagues Mark Rodgers, Stephen Rumph, and Anne Searcy are a constant source of stimulation and professional support. Our late friend and department chair JoAnn Taricani believed in this project with a depth of understanding that encouraged me to keep writing. The Walter Chapin Simpson Center for the Humanities and the UW School of Music generously furnished resources for a book symposium on the topic of forgery in musical composition, which allowed me to rehearse key aspects of this publication's argument among colleagues before delivering the manuscript for publication; I am particularly indebted to Kathleen Woodward, to Caitlin Palo, to Jenifer Moreland, and to Joël-François Durand for making that event a reality. Across campus, Katie Beisel Hollenbach offered much wisdom, friendship, and solidarity in matters musicological, and Peter Nicolas has been an invaluable interdisciplinary interlocutor on issues of musical authorship, ethics, and law. My students at the UW and elsewhere have consistently provoked and surprised me

xxii ACKNOWLEDGMENTS

in the best senses of those words. Many of them have tested and refined the ideas in this book directly in pedagogical contexts, clarifying and strengthening my thinking in ways I could scarcely have imagined on my own. Finally, a quarter of research leave for junior faculty development at the UW provided me with the time and resources necessary to finish this book.

Before coming to the Pacific coast, my perspectives on compositional forgery deepened considerably during an idyllic year spent as postdoctoral resident scholar and visiting assistant professor in music theory at Indiana University (Bloomington). I am profoundly grateful to the Department of Music Theory at IU—including Kyle Adams, Jay Hook, Gretchen Horlacher, Eric Isaacson, Roman Ivanovitch, Blair Johnston, Marianne Kielian-Gilbert, Andrew Mead, and Frank Samarotto—for supporting my work at this critical juncture in my career. Despite proudly wearing my music theory cap in Indiana, I was pleased to be greeted with great warmth by inspiring colleagues across the hall at IU's Department of Musicology, many of whom became valued interlocutors on research and other matters. For their particular kindness toward me during my year in Bloomington I wish to thank J. Peter Burkholder, Phil Ford, Halina Goldberg, Daniel Melamed, Kristina Muxfeldt, Devon Nelson, and Jill Rogers.

Academic grants and fellowships from a variety of institutions allowed me to complete key research and writing work on this project at various stages of development. Significant costs involved in the book's publication were defrayed by the AMS 75 PAYS Fund and the General Fund of the American Musicological Society, supported in part by the National Endowment for the Humanities and the Andrew W. Mellon Foundation. I further gratefully acknowledge the support of the Alvin H. Johnson AMS 50 Dissertation Fellowship and Harold Powers World Travel Grant from the American Musicological Society (AMS), the Richard F. French Fellowship from the music department at Harvard University, and a research scholarship from the German Academic Exchange Service (DAAD). For graciously hosting me during my time in Germany as a DAAD fellow I am deeply indebted to Christian Thorau and to the University of Potsdam. And for their warm collegiality during my time on dissertation fellowship leave in Miami (and in the course of my subsequent formative year of teaching at the highly acclaimed Frost School of Music) I owe sincere thanks to David Ake, Melvin Butler, Marysol Quevedo, and Brent Swanson.

Numerous friends and colleagues not already mentioned here have generously given their time to read and comment on various drafts and excerpts from this book. At a late stage of development James Currie and Melanie Lowe reviewed the manuscript in its entirety and provided extensive feedback, which allowed me to understand the project anew. Abigail Fine offered additional wise suggestions concerning key sections as I prepared for publication. Earlier in the writing process I received invaluable commentary on various chapter drafts from Michael Beckerman, Katie Callam, Hayley Burton Richards, Joseph Fort, William O'Hara, Kay Kaufman Shelemay, W. Dean Sutcliffe, Michael Uy, and Daniel Walden, among others. The finished book would be far weaker were it not for their careful engagement with my work in progress.

Many of the sources for *Forgery in Musical Composition* were made accessible to me through the expertise and guidance of librarians and archivists in a wide range of locations I have had the privilege of visiting in the last decade. In this context I wish especially to thank the staff at the Berlin State Library (Staatsbibliothek zu Berlin), the Austrian National Library (Österreichische Nationalbibliothek), the British Library, the Library of Congress, the Boston Public Library, the Howard Gotlieb Archival Research Center at Boston University, the Loeb Music Library at Harvard University, the Marta and Austin Weeks Music Library at the University of Miami, the William and Gayle Cook Music Library at Indiana University, and the University of Washington Music Library. For their kind correspondence and assistance in locating sources remotely I am grateful to Armin Raab at the Haydn Institute in Cologne and Susanne Eckstein at the Neue Schubert-Ausgabe in Tübingen.

My editor at Oxford University Press, Norman Hirschy, has stewarded this work into print with unfailing enthusiasm, professionalism, and attention to detail, shaping the publication in many insightful ways while responding to my occasionally rambling emails with uniformly breathtaking speed and accuracy. Earlier in the writing process I received sage advice on academic publishing from Suzanne Ryan, who generously discussed the project with me over Pop-Tarts during our overlap in Bloomington. My anonymous peer reviewers cannot be mentioned by name here, but I owe them an enormous debt of gratitude for improving the quality of *Forgery in Musical Composition* through their judicious and encouraging commentaries on prior drafts of my manuscript. For making the finished product more beautiful than I could have hoped I owe special thanks to Bob Geiger, who engraved the music examples.

I am pleased to acknowledge that excerpts from *Forgery in Musical Composition* have previously appeared in the following publications: "Composing Authority in Six Forged 'Haydn' Sonatas," *Journal of Musicology* 35, no. 1 (2018): 104–43; and "Baroque Forgeries and the Public Imagination," in *The Oxford Handbook of Public Music Theory*, edited by J. Daniel Jenkins (New York: Oxford University Press, 2021).

My family I thank for their patience and support. Anna and Graham, my mother and father, have made everything in my life possible. I could never thank them enough. My mother-in-law Margaret, my father-in-law Bill, my sister-in-law Michelle, my brother-in-law Christopher, and my nieces Elizabeth and Kate have welcomed me into their family with open arms and supported me in good times and bad. More broadly, my many friends, colleagues, and mentors within

xxiv ACKNOWLEDGMENTS

and beyond the worlds of academia and music have been a source of great intellectual stimulation and spiritual renewal during the long and sometimes arduous processes of research and writing. Among those individuals not already mentioned by name here, special thanks go to Suzanne Aspden, Lynne Baker, Jonathan Barritt, Richard Beaudoin, Ralph Berry, James Blasina, Jon Bradshaw, Monica Burns, Alex Cowan, Jon Curtis-Brignell, Kristin Franseen, John Gabriel, Josh Gailey, Daniel Grimley, Paul Harper-Scott, Monica Hershberger, Jo Hicks, Anne Holzmüller, Sarah Jessop, En Liang Khong, Zuzana Keckesova, Shigehisa Kuriyama, Carrie Lambert-Beatty, Frank Lehman, Olivia Lucas, Andrew Littlejohn, Emily MacGregor, Alana Mailes, Peter McMurray, Emerson Morgan, Caleb Mutch, Brooke Okazaki, Samuel Parler, Christine Peralta, Reuben Phillips, Steffi Probst, Norie Sato, Caitlin Schmid, Naomi Waltham-Smith, Judy Tsou, Etha Williams, Gavin Williams, and Abi York.

Finally, I thank Annie, who has been with me at every stage of this project, high and low. Her encouragement, wisdom, and grace power every word I have written. I dedicate this book to her.

Introduction
The Van Meegeren Syndrome

For a philosopher to say, "the good and the beautiful are one," is in-
famy; if he goes on to add, "also the true," one ought to thrash him.
Truth is ugly. We possess *art* lest we *perish of the truth.*

Friedrich Nietzsche[1]

In his widely read 1966 article for *High Fidelity* magazine, "The Prospects of
Recording," pianist Glenn Gould describes Han van Meegeren, the most notorious art forger of the twentieth century, as someone "who for a long time has
been high on my list of private heroes."[2] Gould's admiration stemmed from van
Meegeren's 1945–47 detention and trial, an international media event during
which the Dutch artist was put in the bizarre position of having to prove that
he had in fact forged a series of Vermeer portraits sold to high-ranking Nazis,
including Hermann Göring.[3] During the early months of his incarcera-
tion, van Meegeren quite literally saved his neck by painting a new "Vermeer,"
Christus in de Tempel [Christ in the Temple] (figure I.1) live under observation, thereby demonstrating that the priceless national treasures he stood accused of expropriating were nothing more or less than his own original works.
In this absurdist courtroom turn the artist became a legendary figure, escaping
the death sentences associated with collaboration and treason in the very act of
incriminating himself as a forger.

Since 1945, philosophical aesthetics has never quite gotten over van
Meegeren, and for good reason. In one moment, his paintings were historical
objects so incalculably precious as to be worth killing for, at least in the eyes

---

[1] Friedrich Nietzsche, *The Will to Power*, edited by Walter Kaufmann, translated by Walter
Kaufmann and R. J. Hollingdale (New York: Vintage Books, 1968), aphorism 822. Emphasis from
original text.

[2] Glenn Gould, "The Prospects of Recording," in *The Glenn Gould Reader*, edited by Tim Page
(New York: Alfred A. Knopf, 1984): 331–53, at 341; first published in *High Fidelity*, April 1966.

[3] Van Meegeren's sensational story has been told and retold many times. For a classic academic
account, see Hope B. Werness, "Han van Meegeren *fecit*," in *The Forger's Art: Forgery and the
Philosophy of Art*, edited by Denis Dutton (Berkeley: University of California Press, 1983): 1–57.

Forgery in Musical Composition. Frederick Reece, Oxford University Press. © Oxford University Press 2025.
DOI: 10.1093/9780197618332.003.0001

Figure I.1 Han van Meegeren with *Christus in de Tempel* (1945). Photograph by Koos Raucamp. Nationaal Archief, The Hague. CC0

of his accusers. In the next, the very same artworks were transfigured into reprehensible forgeries for which the creator was to be imprisoned. Crucially, all this transpired without any detail of the works themselves having changed, which—as Gould and many others have pointed out—raises some troubling questions.[4] For a start, it is by no means universally obvious that the moral stain of van Meegeren's falsehood should undermine the reality of his achievements on canvas. Nor should it be taken as given that human experiences of beauty are contingent on knowing when that beauty was created, and by whom. In the moment of undeceiving, the revealed forgery suggests an unutterable suspicion that threatens to undermine the stability of canonical hierarchies, the possibility of hermeneutic knowledge, and the legitimacy of contextual discourse about art itself. What if beautiful things hold no truth content or moral value whatsoever? Like the totems smashed by the iconoclasts of old, such false impressions of authenticity are "dangerous to unmask" because, as in Jean Baudrillard's well-known formulation, they appear to "dissimulate the fact that there is nothing behind them."[5] No authorial or historical truth. No identity or moral worth. Just exquisite sound, signifying nothing beyond itself.

---

[4] See in particular Glenn Gould, "Forgery and Imitation in the Creative Process," in *The Art of Glenn Gould: Reflections of a Musical Genius*, edited by John P. L. Roberts (Toronto: Malcolm Lester Books, 1999): 204–221.

[5] Jean Baudrillard, *Simulacra and Simulation*, translated by Sheila Faria Glaser (Ann Arbor: University of Michigan Press, 1994), 5; first published as *Simulacres et Simulation* (Paris: Éditions Galilée, 1981).

INTRODUCTION 3

This book is an attempt to grapple with these and other such issues from an explicitly musical perspective. At its core are four in-depth examinations, in the chapters to follow, of what I call compositional forgery—i.e., the deliberate misattribution of one's own work to someone else, often, but not necessarily, a figure from the historical past. More specifically, I am concerned with musical compositions that fall into the category philosopher Jerrold Levinson has termed "inventive" forgery.[6] For Levinson, inventive forgeries are newly created works falsely attributed to an existing author or artist, as opposed to direct copies of authentic artworks—paintings, for example—intended to be passed off as originals, a phenomenon Levinson calls "referential" forgery.[7] Crucially, Levinson's two categories of forgery should further be differentiated from plagiarism, that somewhat more familiar cousin with which forgery, in music, is often confused. In fact, forgery and plagiarism are better understood as opposites: whereas forgery involves attributing one's own work to somebody else, plagiarism instead entails taking credit for someone else's work. Naturally plagiarists are widely condemned for plundering the fruits of another's creative labor. Yet it should be remembered, in what follows, that forgery's acts of misappropriation are arguably no less transgressive, their object consisting—however intangibly—in identity itself.

These basic features of forgery raise important questions of motivation. Juxtaposed with the obvious potential for material profit in musical plagiarism, the forger's habitual refusal to take creative credit can superficially appear to undermine any clear financial reason for one to pursue imposture in an allographic medium like musical composition, where the work in question is by definition not a unique physical object of potentially immense monetary value.[8] But to presume that nobody has bothered to forge musical works because compositional forgery must not pay well enough underestimates the human appetite for deceit while simultaneously ignoring straightforward methods of monetizing forgery in publication—for example, by securing a copyright and royalties as the "editor" or "arranger" (not composer) of a rediscovered work. All this being said, the

[6] Jerrold Levinson, *Music, Art, and Metaphysics: Essays in Philosophical Aesthetics* (Oxford: Oxford University Press, 2011), 103.

[7] Umberto Eco independently drew similar distinctions as early as 1987, proposing the terms "forgery ex-nihilo" and "downright forgery" for what Levinson later called "inventive" and "referential" forgery. See Umberto Eco, "Fakes and Forgeries," in *The Limits of Interpretation* (Bloomington: Indiana University Press, 1990): 174–201, at 182–88; first published as "Tipologia della falsificazione," *Fälschungen im Mittelalter* 33, no. 1 (1987): 69–82.

[8] Nelson Goodman defines "allographic" art forms as those in which a single work can have any number of distinct authentic tokens (for example, recordings of a symphony or print copies of a poem), effectively rendering the work in question unforgeable in Levinson's referential sense. The situation is different in "autographic" art forms such as painting and sculpture, where each work is considered to have only one authentic token, a state of affairs that in turn makes referential forgery possible. See Nelson Goodman, *Languages of Art: An Approach to a System of Symbols* (Indianapolis: Bobbs-Merrill, 1968), 112–13.

4 INTRODUCTION

received misconception that forgery belongs exclusively to autographic media such as painting is likely one significant reason for the relative lack of explicit musicological commentary on the topic during the last century, a state of affairs that has largely persisted into the present despite Guido Adler's assurance—in one of the field's foundational texts—that while issues of "authenticity and forgery . . . do not play such a prominent role in music history as in art history, where there are often material motivations for forgery," they "nonetheless come up in our field, too."[9]

Musicians forget this reality at their peril. The stories presented in this study suggest that forgery may be more widespread in musical practice than even Adler imagined, a fact that in turn invites scholars from across the arts to reconsider the cultural implications of authorial falsification in general from the vantage of a medium in which "material motivations"—as Adler calls them—are not always the most obvious cause. It is particularly regrettable in this context that when compositional forgery has come up for discussion in the musicological literature since Adler's day, it has often been under such well-intentioned but ultimately misleading headings as "spuriosity," "mystification," and "hoax": vague umbrella terms and polite euphemisms which themselves betray a certain disciplinary discomfort with the more weighty and often unsavory cultural implications of the f-word favored here for its terminological clarity, interdisciplinary currency, and ethical heft alike.[10] For clarity's sake, forgery must likewise be strictly distinguished from the related but wholly inoffensive (and even academically dignified) phenomenon Bruce Haynes terms "period composition"—i.e., the practice of making "correctly attributed" works in historical styles.[11] The factual and ethical trespasses associated with actual authorial imposture are of the essence of compositional forgery in its genuine—i.e., incorrectly attributed—sense. For these and other reasons, "The concept of forgery is"—as philosopher Alfred Lessing points out—"a normative one," connoting a crucial "absence or negation

---

[9] "In der Musikgeschichte spielt Echtheit und Fälschung (Unechtheit, allerdings nicht gleichbedeutend mit Fälschung) nicht eine solche Rolle wie in der Kunstgeschichte, in der vielfach materielle Interessen zur Fälschung die Veranlassung sind. Immerhin kommt sie auch bei uns vor." Guido Adler, *Methode der Musikgeschichte* (Leipzig: Breitkopf & Härtel, 1919), 57.

[10] The catch-all "spuriosity"—a portmanteau of "spurious" and "curiosity" sometimes used to refer to forged, plagiarized, pseudonymous, misattributed, and otherwise doubtful compositions en masse—was introduced into musicological parlance in a 1954 essay by Charles Cudworth, who reports that the word was originally coined by Otto Erich Deutsch, apparently as a "little joke." See Charles L. Cudworth, "Ye Olde Spuriosity Shoppe, or, Put It in the *Anhang*, Part 1," *Notes* 12, no. 1 (1954): 25–40, at 25, and Otto Erich Deutsch, "Unfortunately Not by Me (Musical Spuriosities)," *Music Review* 19, no. 1 (1958): 305–310.

[11] Bruce Haynes, *The End of Early Music: A Period Performer's History of Music for the Twenty-First Century* (Oxford: Oxford University Press, 2007), 210. Unlike forgery, what Haynes calls period composition has long been openly acknowledged as a central feature of the academic study of music: pedagogical exercises in historical counterpoint, scholarly reconstructions of fragmentary works from the distant past, et al., can all be considered under the banner of "correctly attributed" stylistic anachronism.

of value" that goes beyond the merely descriptive.[12] To invoke it is unavoidably to engage with a host of prescriptive judgments about the way art ought to be, implicitly separating the musically "authentic" from what Richard Taruskin once memorably dubbed its "invidious antonym" with the kind of moralizing force that demands critical interrogation.[13]

Gould's heroic vision of van Meegeren the forger is characteristically provocative in no small part because it neatly upends this conventional binary opposition, willfully celebrating the artistically inauthentic as such in ways that cannot help but call the ideology of authenticity itself into question. If Gould's 1966 prediction is to be believed, the success of van Meegeren's forgeries was not only an implicit challenge to mid-twentieth-century cultural orthodoxies about the value of canonical art but also the omen of an oncoming "time-transcending" revolution in aesthetic culture which, aided by electronic communications technologies, will serve to liberate pure forms from the "tyranny of appraisaldom" based on "chronological evidence."[14] Tellingly, in "The Prospects of Recording," Gould chooses to dub this shift away from the default "determination of the value of a work of art according to the information available about it"—and thus, arguably, from the prevailing authenticity culture of "post-Renaissance" modernity writ large—"the van Meegeren syndrome" in honor of the forger who, as he puts it, was "martyred for a reluctance to be bound by the hypocrisy of this argument."[15] Only "when the forger is done honor for his craft and no longer reviled for his acquisitiveness," writes Gould, will "the arts . . . have become a truly integral part of our civilization."[16]

Postmodern intellectual panegyrics to art forgery in this vein have become increasingly widespread in the cultural criticism of recent decades.[17] Nonetheless, Gould's proposal that the van Meegeren syndrome might be an "entirely appropriate" depiction of "the aesthetic condition of our time" remains a bitter pill to swallow for many.[18] In the early stages of the twenty-first century, the search for personal and aesthetic authenticity alike is still routinely described—in alternately mocking and earnest tones—as a form of "spiritual quest" or "struggle,"

---

[12] Alfred Lessing, "What Is Wrong with a Forgery?," *Journal of Aesthetics and Art Criticism* 23, no. 4 (1965): 461–71, at 461, reprinted in *The Forger's Art: Forgery and the Philosophy of Art*, edited by Denis Dutton (Berkeley: University of California Press, 1983).

[13] Richard Taruskin, "The Pastness of the Present and the Presence of the Past," in *Authenticity and Early Music: A Symposium*, edited by Nicholas Kenyon (New York: Oxford University Press, 1988), 137–210, at 137.

[14] Gould, "The Prospects of Recording," 341.

[15] Gould, "The Prospects of Recording," 341.

[16] Gould, "The Prospects of Recording," 343.

[17] See, for example, Jonathon Keats, *Forged: Why Fakes Are the Great Art of Our Age* (New York: Oxford University Press, 2013), and Blake Gopnik, "In Praise of Art Forgeries," *New York Times*, 3 November 2013, 5.

[18] Gould, "The Prospects of Recording," 343.

6   INTRODUCTION

perhaps precisely because "the authentic" itself is so widely believed to have accumulated an outsized scarcity value in modern life.[19] To be sure, intellectual alarmism about the decline of authenticity is at least as ancient as Plato, whose philosophical investment in music's truth content against the grain of modern times was emphatic as early as the fourth century BCE.[20] Yet, from a contemporary perspective colored by the industrial revolution and its long cultural aftermath, there is little point in denying that attitudes toward the arts have been fundamentally reshaped, in the course of these last two centuries, by the pervasive mood David Shields names "reality hunger."[21] In a climate of escalating technological mediation, unfettered resource extraction, and widespread social alienation driven by an all-consuming instrumental rationality, authentic modes of being and expression alike have been felt to dwindle in an unprecedented and even apocalyptic manner, diminishing, like the earth's coal and oil reserves, to a terminally depleted short supply. It is in this near-midnight context that Gould's prophecy of an unabashedly atemporal and anachronistic age of forgery emerges as a defiantly optimistic techno-utopian counternarrative. If commentators such as Jonathon Keats are correct in noting that "the cultivated angst evoked by legitimate [modern] art" has more than a little in common with "the shock of getting duped" by a fake, it may—as Gould suggests—be time to seek insight and creative renewal in a rigorous confrontation with the aesthetic reality of forgery.[22]

THE AGE OF INAUTHENTICITY

Forgery in Musical Composition can be read as a narrative reflection on the anxieties of authorship in classical music culture between the twilight of the eighteenth century and the dawn of the new millennium, a period culminating in what is sometimes called "the age of authenticity."[23] From a musicological perspective, it makes good sense to begin an exploratory account of compositional forgery here: as Michael Talbot has written, it was during "the years between 1780 and 1820" that music's authorship emerged as a matter of paramount intellectual, ethical, and aesthetic concern under the auspices of an ascendent culture

---

[19] Consider the radically contrasting uses of this language of "quest" and "struggle" in—for example—Charles Taylor, *The Ethics of Authenticity* (Cambridge, MA: Harvard University Press, 1991), 120, and Andrew Potter, *The Authenticity Hoax: How We Get Lost Finding Ourselves* (New York: HarperCollins, 2010), 3.

[20] Poets who had begun to assert that "music has no truth, and, whether good or bad, can only be judged of rightly by the pleasure of the hearer" are rebuked in Plato, *Laws*, 700–701c.

[21] David Shields, *Reality Hunger: A Manifesto* (New York: Vintage Books, 2011).

[22] Keats, *Forged*, 4.

[23] See, for example, Charles Taylor, *A Secular Age* (Cambridge, MA: Harvard University Press, 2007), esp. 473–504.

of "composer-centredness."[24] In the course of this transitional period, it became increasingly normal—as Talbot asserts—to sort music "primarily according to composer, and not, as previously, according to genre . . . or performer."[25] Crucially, by foregrounding the identity of the composer behind the work, the paradigm of composer-centeredness also served to elevate the cultural significance, in music, of what Denis Dutton has termed "nominal authenticity."[26] For Dutton, "nominal authenticity" is simply "the correct identification of the origins, authorship, or provenance" of an artwork.[27] In theory these nominal qualities should in turn be distinguished from an artwork's "expressive authenticity," which Dutton capaciously describes as its "character as a true expression of an individual's or a society's values and beliefs."[28] When *The Harvard Dictionary of Music* defines authenticity first and foremost as "the nature and validity of the link between a composer and a work that bears his or her name," it might superficially be seen to highlight the nominal, rather than expressive, sense of the term.[29] Yet, in implying a "link" between composer and work the "nature and validity" of which can presumably involve more than the merely propositional act of naming, the *Harvard Dictionary*'s definition also evokes the composer-centered tendency to fold expressive authenticity into nominal authenticity, entangling authorial identity and musical aesthetics in a manner that served to galvanize both the production and the unmasking of compositional forgeries in the post-Enlightenment era. Here a musical work's expressive authenticity came to lean heavily on its nominal authenticity precisely because authenticity as self-expression cannot be rightly judged without knowledge of the authorial self being expressed.

I contend that this composer-centered culture of authenticity functioned as a key condition of possibility for the emergence of a newly heated discourse surrounding compositional forgery in the course of the long nineteenth century. Indeed, many of the intellectual and material developments behind this cultural shift are already well established in the musicological literature. Philosophically speaking, it was in the 1790s and 1800s that a host of influential thinkers began to adopt the novel belief that instrumental music can tell the truth about the contours of the human subject precisely by virtue of the medium's apparent

[24] Michael Talbot, "The Work-Concept and Composer-Centredness," in *The Musical Work: Reality or Invention?*, edited by Michael Talbot (Liverpool: Liverpool University Press, 2000): 168–86, at 172.

[25] Talbot, "Composer-Centredness," 172.

[26] Denis Dutton, "Authenticity in Art," in *The Oxford Handbook of Aesthetics*, edited by Jerrold Levinson (New York: Oxford University Press, 2003): 258–74, at 259.

[27] Dutton, "Authenticity in Art," 259.

[28] Dutton, "Authenticity in Art," 259.

[29] Don Michael Randel, ed., *The Harvard Dictionary of Music* (Cambridge, MA: Belknap Press, 2003), s.v. "Authenticity."

8   INTRODUCTION

semantic imprecision.[30] In the more practical realm of music publishing and intellectual property the 1777 Bach v Longman case saw the rights of the author set out in the Statute of Anne successfully litigated with respect to music for the first time.[31] And it was during this same period that the scholarly enterprise of documenting, reviving, and celebrating "ancient" or "classic" music by figures drawn from more than a decade or two in the past was pioneered in the antiquarian discourse of England.[32] Considered in tandem, the long-term significance of these disparate late eighteenth-century trends in establishing a historicist culture of composer-centeredness is difficult to overstate: in one memorably pithy assessment Carl Dahlhaus went so far as to assert that the musical culture of the nineteenth century can most fundamentally be distinguished from what came before it by reference to "the overpowering presence of earlier music, a presence that has apparently become irrevocable in [the twentieth] century."[33] A wealth of recent scholarship has rendered the romantic tendency to recirculate and reinscribe historical musical works under the banner of cultural authenticity in sharp canon-critical relief.[34] Yet the overarching structural effects of the new composer-centered approach to music remain clear enough: throughout the 1800s and 1900s individuals and institutions became increasingly disposed to elevate a select group of compositions by a limited pantheon of outstanding creators to the status of documentary artifacts worthy of repeated performance, of meticulous archival preservation, and of intensive academic study within the bounds of what Lydia Goehr, in an inspired riff on Franz Liszt, has dubbed "the imaginary museum of musical works."[35]

The chapters to follow make the case that these familiar trends in the history of classical music culture have long been deftly exploited through acts of compositional forgery. In the course of the study, I will endeavor to demonstrate, by example, that the imaginary museum's sublimated contingency on

[30] Mark Evan Bonds, *Music as Thought: Listening to the Symphony in the Age of Beethoven* (Princeton: Princeton University Press, 2006).

[31] David Hunter, "Music Copyright in Britain to 1800," *Music & Letters* 67, no. 3 (1986): 269–82, esp. 278–80.

[32] William Weber, *The Rise of Musical Classics in Eighteenth-Century England: A Study in Canon, Ritual, and Ideology* (Oxford: Oxford University Press, 1992). On issues of musical authenticity in antiquarian circles, see in particular Devon R. Nelson, "The Antiquarian Creation of a Musical Past in Eighteenth-Century Britain" (PhD diss., Indiana University, 2020).

[33] Carl Dahlhaus, *Nineteenth-Century Music,* translated by J. Bradford Robinson (Berkeley: University of California Press, 1989), 22; first published as *Die Musik des 19. Jahrhunderts* (Wiesbaden: Athenaion, 1980).

[34] See, for example, Katherine Bergeron, *Decadent Enchantments: The Revival of Gregorian Chant at Solesmes* (Berkeley: University of California Press, 1998); Katharine Ellis, *Interpreting the Musical Past: Early-Music in Nineteenth-Century France* (New York: Oxford University Press, 2005); Alexander Rehding, *Music and Monumentality: Commencement and Wonderment in Nineteenth-Century Germany* (New York: Oxford University Press, 2009).

[35] Lydia Goehr, *The Imaginary Museum of Musical Works: An Essay in the Philosophy of Music* (New York: Oxford University Press, 1992), 205.

the inauthentic works it excludes becomes readily apparent if one is willing to take the unusual step of treating forgeries with the kind of close academic attention that has generally been denied to them as soon as they are exposed as such. Indeed, the book proceeds from a belief that the lies that cultures choose to tell about themselves should be taken seriously, not least because they have a disquieting tendency to reveal deeper truths that might otherwise remain unspoken. In precisely this manner, compositional forgeries can be seen to spotlight with unusual clarity the internal tensions and contradictions underlying such seemingly monolithic music-historical paradigms as composer-centeredness. To be sure, the long nineteenth century can accurately be considered an age of authenticity and musical historicism governed by an intense ethical allegiance to the author concept, to the regime of intellectual property, and to the sanctity of canonical works. Yet, as forgeries are apt to demonstrate, this very same period was also an age of inauthenticity that sought out acts of fraudulence with a near obsessive critical fascination while habitually fantasizing the vaunted canonical pasts held forever tragicomically out of reach by an all-too-earnest fidelity to the notion of an enduring and historically embedded compositional self. If authenticity cultures tend to be haunted by their spectral inauthentic others in this dialectical manner, I propose—following pioneering art-historical and literary scholarship by Aviva Briefel, Margaret Russett, and others—that the shadow-side of musical romanticism and its long canonical aftermath remains ripe for renewed examination from an aberrant perspective centering compositional forgery.[36] As Briefel succinctly puts it, a close analysis of romantic aesthetic culture suggests that "without forgery... there might be no identity at all."[37]

In documenting this largely uncharted music-historical territory, an uncommonly wide horizon spanning more than two centuries has been chosen for two loosely connected reasons. In the first place, there is an important sense in which the inalienably time warping and transhistorical qualities of art forgery demand a correspondingly expansive and flexible approach to issues of narrative chronology from anyone attempting to come to grips with the subject. The artistic fake always belongs both to its authentic point of origin and to the illusory past it projects, with the two competing temporal contexts—real and imaginary—overlapping in the forgery's aesthetic space like an art-historical palimpsest. In this sense, accurately describing works of "Haydn" and "Schubert" forged toward the end of the 1900s (in the latter half of this book) necessitates a panoramic perspective on the long nineteenth century made very long indeed. To avoid any potential confusion that might arise from the peculiar untimeliness

---

[36] Aviva Briefel, *The Deceivers: Art Forgery and Identity in the Nineteenth Century* (Ithaca, NY: Cornell University Press, 2006); Margaret Russett, *Fictions and Fakes: Forging Romantic Authenticity, 1760–1845* (Cambridge: Cambridge University Press, 2006).

[37] Briefel, *The Deceivers*, 179.

10   INTRODUCTION

of such forgeries, all subsequent chapters have been ordered in a strictly sequential fashion—i.e., solely according to the true date of composition for the forged
works discussed, and not the false dates that forgery feigns for itself. Thus, it is
not out of any inattentiveness or scholarly caprice that material on fake Schubert
from the 1970s in chapter 3 precedes material on fake Haydn from the 1990s
in chapter 4. Ultimately, any attempt to write a history of forgery as forgery is
likely to entail a certain retrograde counterfactual approach of this ilk wherein
familiar canonical timelines—for example, Haydn-before-Schubert—are deliberately if momentarily unmoored so as to better bring fakes into the discursive
foreground.

In the second place, a bird's-eye bicentennial scope bisected by van
Meegeren's arrest in 1945 makes it possible to establish long-range connections
between the evolving practice of compositional forgery and the broader intellectual paradigms of musical authenticity treated in this book's two large parts.
In clarifying the implications of these two subsections—organized, respectively,
around what I call "romantic" (1791–1945) and "modern" (1945–2000) cultures
of forgery—Lionel Trilling's *Sincerity and Authenticity* remains an indispensable
interdisciplinary touchstone. The central claim is deceptively simple: in essence,
Trilling observes that the worldview that flourished between the Enlightenment
and the mid-twentieth century envisioned behaviors, utterances, and artworks
alike as "authentic" insofar as they were understood to be underwritten by inner
truths, derived subjectively, from the self.[38] In this sense Trilling further contends
that the culture of authenticity should be distinguished from a rather older but
related paradigm of "sincerity" in which expressions were (and are) justified not
through any introspective appeal to the self for its own sake but rather in reference to the self's reciprocal harmony with outer truths derived from a public
sphere occupied by others.[39] Thus it was during the post-Enlightenment period
that a work of art's capacity to speak the truth came increasingly to be judged not
only in terms of its objective formal and mimetic qualities but also by virtue of
its confessional veracity in depicting the internal identity of the artist.[40] A mar-
velous music-culinary analogy concocted by Robert Gjerdingen is instructive in
illustrating the distinction: for much of the eighteenth century, as Gjerdingen has
it, "the notion that a sad piece by the court composer was about the composer's
sadness would have seemed just as strange as the idea that a tart sauce prepared
by the court chef was about the chef's tartness."[41] In an impish mood one could

[38] Lionel Trilling, *Sincerity and Authenticity* (Cambridge, MA: Harvard University Press, 1973),
6–12.
[39] Trilling, *Sincerity and Authenticity*, 1–6.
[40] On this point, see M. H. Abrams, *The Mirror and the Lamp: Romantic Theory and the Critical
Tradition* (New York: Oxford University Press, 1953).
[41] Robert O. Gjerdingen, *Music in the Galant Style* (New York: Oxford University Press, 2007), 7.

INTRODUCTION   11

correspondingly argue that the idea of a forged musical composition would hardly have been more intellectually coherent or ethically concerning under these conditions than the idea of a forged bordelaise or cheese béchamel.[42] Not so in the transition to the increasingly composer-centered 1800s, when music, unlike sauce making, was elevated to exalted status among the romantic fine arts.[43] Mark Evan Bonds summarizes the effects with characteristic long-range elegance: in the first half of the nineteenth century a paradigm of "objective expression" in which composers were thought of as artful orators operating within a "framework of rhetoric" came to be usurped by a newly dominant paradigm of "subjective expression" wherein composers were cast as sublime oracles at the center of a "framework of hermeneutics."[44] Whereas the composer orators of objective expression "sought to persuade," the composer oracles of subjective expression "used the intrinsically abstract, opaque medium of instrumental music to utter truths" in ways that quite understandably led "consumers" to desire "to know with certainty that a published work by Mozart—or Haydn, or Beethoven—was indeed what it claimed to be."[45]

Of course, Gould considered these historical developments a travesty. In "The Prospects of Recording" the pianist celebrates the possibility of reversing the romantic notion of subjective expression and returning to a culture of timeless, anonymous, and ecstatic creative reiteration made manifest by the van Meegeren syndrome and its aesthetic idealization of art forgery.[46] Here Gould and Bonds make for compelling intellectual counterpoint on a number of levels. For a start, the apparent coincidence that Bonds styles the long nineteenth-century ascendancy of subjective expression "the Beethoven syndrome" after the archetypal composer of romantic selfhood is strikingly reminiscent of Gould's own medical (and quasi-pathological) "syndrome" terminology applied, in his case, to the name of the twentieth-century's preeminent art forger.[47] In terms of historical chronology, one could moreover reasonably conclude that Gould's van

---

[42] Talbot effectively asserts this point when he observes that "the lack of any overriding interest in the authorship of a composition is betrayed, equally, by the general public tolerance extended before 1800 to the appropriation by one composer of the music of another." See Talbot, "Composer-Centredness," 178. In a similar vein, Mark Evan Bonds argues that "the many works falsely marketed under Haydn's name during his lifetime" were evidence of the belief among eighteenth-century audiences that "certain names . . . promised a higher quality of music" while maintaining that such audiences "did not attend a concert or buy a new work of published music anticipating a revelation of the announced composer's inner self." See Mark Evan Bonds, *The Beethoven Syndrome: Hearing Music as Autobiography* (New York: Oxford·University Press, 2019), 145.

[43] On the emergence of the concept of fine art in this period, see Larry Shiner, *The Invention of Art: A Cultural History* (Chicago: University of Chicago Press, 2001).

[44] Bonds, *The Beethoven Syndrome*, 2–4.

[45] Bonds, *The Beethoven Syndrome*, 97, 118.

[46] Gould, "The Prospects of Recording," 341–43.

[47] Specifically, Bonds defines the Beethoven syndrome as "the inclination of listeners to hear composers *in* their music." See Bonds, *The Beethoven Syndrome*, 1. Emphasis from original text.

12 INTRODUCTION

Meegeren syndrome picks up more or less where Bonds's Beethoven syndrome definitively recedes—i.e., toward the time of van Meegeren's trial, at the twentieth century's midpoint. Indeed, while Bonds's study maintains that the ideal of subjective expression never disappeared entirely (persisting "particularly in the realm of popular music"), he nevertheless argues that the fortunes of the Beethoven syndrome declined precipitously in classical music culture during the 1900s, "beginning with the New Objectivity of the interwar years and running through the high modernism of mid-century."[48] By this stage, Bonds has it that "many leading composers and critics returned to an outlook that openly acknowledged expression—and art in general—as an artifice," a significant shift in cultural perspective which, in my analysis, can be seen to have had marked effects on both the production and the reception of compositional forgeries.[49] Consider Igor Stravinsky's well-known 1936 formalist provocation that "music is, by its very nature, essentially powerless to express anything at all," let alone the composer's authentic innermost self.[50] Roland Barthes's seemingly definitive 1967 declaration of "the death of the author" should not be forgotten as the apotheosis of such ideas, tellingly appearing the year after Gould's "Prospects of Recording": here, Barthes famously observed that "writing" had long since been reconfigured as "the destruction of every voice, of every point of origin," effectively obsolescing older forms of criticism "tyrannically centered on the author" in which audiences were implicitly required to presume that "Baudelaire's work is the failure of Baudelaire the man, Van Gogh's his madness, Tchaikovsky's his vice."[51] By the mid-twentieth century, open intellectual hostility to the ideal of subjective expression—and, relatedly, to the so-called intentional fallacy among critics—had begun to assert its own form of orthodoxy in certain artistic circles on the basis of beliefs such as these, diversely rooted in the anti-romantic new objectivity of the 1920s, the new-critical formalism of midcentury arts scholarship, and the coming tide of post-structuralism already visible on the intellectual horizon.[52] As we shall see, these new cultural currents in turn had a marked effect on fakes: with the influence of Bonds's Beethoven syndrome waning by midcentury, a correspondingly modern culture of forgery aligned with Gould's van Meegeren syndrome emerged with new targets, motives, and methods explored in the course of this book's second part.

A rigorously cultural and historical perspective on these issues is important in no small part because the topic of forgery enmeshes seemingly unworldly and

[48] Bonds, *The Beethoven Syndrome*, 3.

[49] Bonds, *The Beethoven Syndrome*, 3.

[50] Igor Stravinsky, *An Autobiography* (London: Simon and Schuster, 1936), 53.

[51] Roland Barthes, "The Death of the Author," in *Image, Music, Text* (New York: Hill and Wang, 1977): 142–48, at 142, 143; first published in *Aspen* 5–6 (1967).

[52] On the intentional fallacy, see W. K. Wimsatt Jr. and M. C. Beardsley, "The Intentional Fallacy," *Sewanee Review* 54, no. 3 (1946): 468–88.

INTRODUCTION   13

abstruse metaphysical claims about art's truth and falsehood with comparatively familiar, down-to-earth matters of human psychological, interpersonal, and professional concern. Indeed, with no less than the integrity of the self at stake, there can be small wonder that deep-rooted personal qualms about identity, authenticity, and social status have a way of bubbling to the surface whenever fakes come up for discussion. Even when deliberately misattributed compositions do not lead to financial damages and the criminal proceedings that are so often associated with them in such autographic forms as sculpture and oil painting, the fact remains that art lovers tend not to enjoy the experience of having been unduly deceived by the objects of their affection, nor the pangs of anxiety, guilt, and shame that ensue once the veil is lifted. This host of negative emotions sheds considerable light on the grisly fates of some exposed forgeries in corporeal media, which include incineration and crushing by industrial crane.[53] The polite legal rationale for such material carnage is generally a prophylactic strike against economic fraud: by removing counterfeits from the market, the financial value accrued by authentic works is protected from dilution, or so the argument goes. Be that as it may, it is hard not to regard the destructive burning, smashing, or melting of an alleged forgery as an unnecessarily elaborate ceremonial act: as Mary Douglas observes on a sweeping anthropological scale in *Purity and Danger*, rituals "separating, purifying, demarcating and punishing transgressions" in this manner "have as their main function to impose system on an inherently untidy experience."[54] Whether or not it is sponsored by the state, anti-inauthenticity iconoclasm can thus reasonably be seen to aspire to something of the violence of retributive justice, itself barely distinguishable from revenge.[55] In flagrantly disproportionate and theatrically destructive responses to forgery such as these the defense of the real, as manifested in art's accumulation of capital, becomes total.

It would be easy to avoid writing about such ungainly emotional reactions to forged artworks in an account such as this, where dispassionate surgical intervention is the norm. Yet there is a danger that the historian's "painstakingly constructed carapace of academic expertise"—ice cold, pristinely rational, and

[53] Dalya Alberge, "The Man Whose 'Real Chagall' Could Now Be Burnt as a Fake," *The Observer*, 1 February 2014, accessed July 2023, https://www.theguardian.com/artanddesign/2014/feb/01/chagall-could-be-furnt-fortune-or-fake; *Wine Spectator*, "Rudy K's Fake Wines Get the Death Penalty," 10 December 2015, accessed July 2023, https://www.winespectator.com/articles/rudy-ks-fake-wines-get-the-death-penalty-52489. Eerie footage of Rudy Kurniawan's forged wines being crushed by an industrial crane at a waste disposal facility in Austin, Texas, can be viewed at https://www.youtube.com/watch?v=AJqGbfzDE5o, accessed July 2023.
[54] Mary Douglas, *Purity and Danger: An Analysis of Concepts of Pollution and Taboo* (London: Routledge, 2002 [1966]), 5.
[55] This analogy can be taken further: like capital punishment meted out against human beings, the destruction of forged artworks—judicial or otherwise—is difficult to defend as a general policy not least because it is irreversible in cases where the initial judgment is refuted by new evidence.

14 INTRODUCTION

unimpeachably objective—leaves certain important aspects of the topic un-examined.[56] Art forgery is apt to dissolve the ego-defensive outer armor of the hard-nosed connoisseur, not infrequently exposing a soft, tender, and all-too-human underbelly. This is especially the case for career academics because, as Regina Bendix has eloquently pointed out, the very act of declaring some-thing "authentic" not only "legitimate[s] the subject declared authentic" but also serves—in a potent reciprocal fashion—to "legitimate the authenticator."[57] Whether we scholars like it or not, there is much truth to the idea that our acts of authentication authenticate us in turn. And it is by the same token that a forgery mistaken for an original threatens to delegitimate its unwary advocate, seem-ingly demonstrating, as in H. C. Andersen's classic fable, that the emperor has no clothes. Thus Reinhold Brinkmann freely admits, in an important musico-logical essay on the subject, that "it is possible to become trapped" by forgery in ways that "undermine your confidence in the trustworthiness of your own discipline, of scholarship in general."[58] Musicology "is a dangerous field," adds Brinkmann—seemingly only half in jest—with "traps, abysses, everywhere."[59] Indeed, occupational anxieties of the kind discussed by Bendix and Brinkmann are common enough when the topic of forgery is raised in any serious way across the arts and humanities. Here fakes appear as fatal snares of hubris, hedonism, and appetite, simultaneously beguiling and deadly as the serpent's apple or siren's song.

For these reasons among others, *Forgery in Musical Composition* maintains that technical approaches to artistic authenticity cannot be fully understood when divorced from concerns about truth, falsehood, and the self that manifest in broader cultural, psychological, and philosophical domains. The history of exposed forgeries is inevitably a tale of human deceit, shame, and disappoint-ment as much as objective falsification, which makes a certain degree of com-passion and empathy for those involved indispensable. In the experiences of scholars and art devotees as much as anyone, the intense reactions forgery tends to provoke are precisely the kinds of discomforting, self-directed social feelings that, as Elspeth Probyn aptly puts it, have a way of getting "to the heart of who we think we are."[60]

---

[56] Benjamin Walton, "Quirk Shame," *Representations* 132 (2015): 121–29, at 121.

[57] Regina Bendix, *In Search of Authenticity: The Formation of Folklore Studies* (Madison: University of Wisconsin Press, 1997), 7.

[58] Reinhold Brinkmann, "The Art of Forging Music and Musicians," in *Cultures of Forgery: Making Nations Making Selves*, edited by Judith Ryan and Alfred Thomas (New York: Routledge, 2003), 111–25, at 112.

[59] Brinkmann, "The Art of Forging Music and Musicians," 116.

[60] Elspeth Probyn, *Blush: Faces of Shame* (Minneapolis: University of Minnesota Press, 2005), x.

SOURCES, STYLES, SELVES

In this spirit of introspection, it is well to begin at home. And, for music historians, there is simply no evading the fact that authentication and attribution—i.e., the processes of establishing who wrote what, and when—number among the very oldest and most venerable of all disciplinary techniques, functioning, in effect, as the field's methodological first principles. Such foundational concerns may appear archaic in contemporary academic contexts where much has changed and a certain adversarial distaste for one's "positivist" institutional forebears has broadly become the norm, expected from scholars as a matter of good moral hygiene.[61] Nonetheless, I contend that the early intellectual origins of musical authentication and attribution continue to pull with considerable weight on discourse about music's truth and falsehood in the present, often in ways that remain poorly understood. To return to Gould's framing of the issue in "The Prospects of Recording," the act of finding "a predetermined historical niche in which to lock the object of [one's] analysis" is still all but indispensable for the musicologist, not least because it is impossible to contextualize music historically or culturally without first knowing when and where in history and culture that music should be placed on a basic factual level.[62] With disinformation and the ethics and politics of identity once again at the forefront of present-day humanistic concerns, the ever-present possibility of misattribution and outright forgery is particularly apt to demonstrate the extent to which authenticity still functions as a vital Archimedean point anchoring complex historical and cultural interpretations of music that would all too readily unravel if the perceived self behind the work were to change in some fundamental way.[63] With all this in mind, there is a compelling sense in which attribution will always matter to musicologists both old and new, not least because the authenticity of music's relationships to history, culture, and the self constitutes the fundamental matter of what is permitted as knowledge within the field's distinctive regime of truth.[64]

---

[61] See, for example, Joseph Kerman, *Contemplating Music: Challenges to Musicology* (Cambridge, MA: Harvard University Press, 1985).

[62] Gould, "The Prospects of Recording," 341.

[63] Recent high-profile musical reattributions from Felix Mendelssohn to Fanny Hensel, from "Keiko Yamada" to Larry Clark, and from Mamoru Samuragochi to Takashi Niigaki can be seen to demonstrate something of the high drama with which such self-unraveling can occur in cases where scholarly misunderstanding or deliberate imposture crosses lines of gender, race, or disability. See Angela Mace Christian, "The *Easter Sonata* of Fanny Mendelssohn (1828)," *Journal of Musicological Research* 41, no. 3 (2022): 182–209; Jennifer Jolley, "The Curious Case of Keiko Yamada," *New Music USA*, 7 November 2019, https://newmusicusa.org/nmbx/the-curious-case-of-keiko-yamada/, accessed August 2023; Roland Kelts, "The Unmasking of 'Japan's Beethoven,'" *New Yorker*, 2 May 2014, https://www.newyorker.com/culture/culture-desk/the-unmasking-of-japans-beethoven, accessed August 2023.

[64] On regimes of truth, see Michel Foucault, *Discipline and Punish: The Birth of the Prison*, translated by A. Sheridan (New York: Vintage Books, 1977), 30ff; first published as *Surveiller et punir: Naissance de la prison* (Paris: Gallimard, 1975).

16   INTRODUCTION

Of course, the question of precisely how music should be dated and attributed has been a subject of significant controversy since the beginning. As Friedrich Blume put it in an influential 1961 essay to which I shall return in subsequent chapters, the arbitration of musical authenticity problems has generally boiled down to what is, in the end, "a question of method of historical music-research": "source-philology or style criticism?"[65] Blume himself notes that this dialectical source/style perspective on the issue is at least somewhat "oversimplified" and that the two approaches to musical evidence should ultimately be made "to complement each other" in some form of methodological synthesis.[66] Be that as it may, the cases of compositional forgery explored in subsequent chapters of this book suggest that many of the most entrenched critical conflicts concerning musical authenticity have indeed hinged on an underlying ideological tension between the two basic methodological positions identified by Blume. Time and again dispute arises when an individual who values the apparent immediacy and musicality of style evidence as manifested in the "internal" qualities of the composition itself is confronted with a disciplinary counterpart who instead values the apparent objectivity and methodological transparency of source evidence as manifested in the "external" qualities of the documents through which music is transmitted. In practice, scholarly attempts to resolve the resulting clash of perspectives with regard to any particular work's contested status as authentic or otherwise frequently spiral into relitigation of the basic machinery of musical proof and thence to intractable metaphysical concerns about music's ability to speak the truth (or not) on its own terms. While this makes the tension between source philology and style criticism all but impossible to resolve as a general principle, the chapters to follow demonstrate that there have indeed been periods of history during which critical perceptions of the relative legitimacy of source and style as evidence have shifted dramatically because of evolving cultural beliefs about the broader nature of musical authenticity as such.

Within musicology, Guido Adler remains by far the most influential proponent of style-critical evidence for authentication and attribution. In the opening paragraphs of his 1885 paper outlining musicology's "Scope, Method, and Aim"—a text widely considered to be one of the field's most important founding documents—Adler describes how, once confronted with an unknown "work of art," the scholar of music should arrive, before all else, at "the important definitive decision about the period of origin" through systematic examination of notation, rhythm, harmony

---

[65] Friedrich Blume, "Requiem but no Peace," translated by Nathan Broder, *Musical Quarterly* 47, no. 2 (1961): 147–69, at 169, reprinted in German as "Requiem und kein Ende," in *Syntagma musicologicum*, edited Martin Ruhnke (Kassel: Bärenreiter, 1963): 714–34.
[66] Blume, "Requiem but no Peace," 169.

INTRODUCTION 17

and counterpoint, text setting, and instrumentation.[67] The imagined scenario in Adler's opening gambit in which the researcher is faced with an unattributed composition in need of an author and date is broadly characteristic of much early musicological activity in the nineteenth century, when pioneering scholars were frequently tasked with establishing a chronological, geographical, and authorial identity for unfamiliar works found in unprocessed primary sources.[68] Yet crucially, in proposing foundational methodological solutions to the pressing problems of attribution and dating, Adler makes it abundantly clear, from the outset, that not all musical evidence of authorship and date is of equal value to the musicologist. In short, musical attributions should, in Adler's view, be made through an examination not simply of external details of handwriting, paper, provenance, or source filiation, but rather through rigorous engagement with purely musical qualities evident in the notes themselves in ways that only the musicological specialist can reliably discern.[69] "In thus referring a work of art to its time and place, in defining its author"—writes Adler, with characteristically unflinching authority—"we avail ourselves of all outwards helps (among them paleography and semiography); we make use of the single criteria; we fix the limits of the style-periods."[70]

This dogmatically internalist style-critical approach to authentication and attribution explicitly extends, in Adler's account, beyond benignly unattributed and undated works to pastiches, misattributions, and outright forgeries.[71] To his credit, Adler readily acknowledges that compositions constructed with the intent to deceive might well include deliberately misleading stylistic features apt to trip up the aspiring connoisseur.[72] Yet, even in the face of such knowing deception, Adler continues to emphasize that, when examining a piece of music which

[67] Guido Adler and Erica Mugglestone, "Scope, Aim, and Method of Musicology (1885): An English Translation and Historico-Analytical Commentary," *Yearbook for Traditional Music* 13 (1981): 1–21, at 6, 7; first published as Guido Adler, "Umfang, Methode, und Ziel der Musikwissenschaft," *Vierteljahrsschrift für Musikwissenschaft* 1 (1885): 5–20.

[68] Adler's German terms for these various tasks are "Zeitbestimmung," "Ortsbestimmung," and "Autorbestimmung," respectively. These three subtypes of musical attribution are treated at length in "Part B" of Adler, *Methode der Musikgeschichte*, 146–81.

[69] Mozart's *Requiem* was a particularly important example for Adler on this issue. The various authenticity disputes involving the *Requiem* are so convoluted and methodologically taxing to approach that, for Adler, they can only adequately be arbitrated in strictly music-historical (i.e., style-critical) terms. See Adler, *Methode der Musikgeschichte*, 5.

[70] Guido Adler and W. Oliver Strunk, "Style-Criticism," *Musical Quarterly* 20, no. 2 (1934): 172–76, at 174.

[71] Adler, *Methode der Musikgeschichte*, 57

[72] It should be mentioned that, practically speaking, Adler did not always find it easy to avoid being tripped up by problems of authenticity himself. In 1888, for example, he upheld a misattribution of the first movement of Jan Josef Rösler's Piano Concerto No. 1 in D Major, op. 15 to Beethoven on the basis of an incomplete set of orchestral parts, noting that "neither external nor internal evidence speaks against it." See Guido Adler, "Ein Satz eines unbekannten Klavierkonzertes von Beethoven," *Vierteljahrschrift für Musikwissenschaft* 4 (1888): 450–70. The attribution was corrected in Hans Engel, "Das angebliche Beethovensche Klavierkonzertsatz," *Neues Beethoven Jahrbuch* 2 (1925): 167–82.

18 INTRODUCTION

"originated at a time to which, according to its nature, it no longer belongs," the ideal musicologist should be capable of noticing "particular features in the work which betray that, despite the outward analogous characteristics, it yet does not wholly correspond to the spirit of the age to which it belongs by virtue of its structure and texture."[73] Whereas style-critical evidence was often sufficient to provide definitive proof for Adler, external source-philological methods "can, or should, never be the sole support of an attribution."[74] To the contrary, sound musicological judgments about authorship are ultimately to be "achieved through the observation of lines of inner style-critical argument to which external circumstances provide" only "a test and a corroboration."[75]

During the decades following the end of the Second World War, a growing disciplinary consensus would turn Adlerian musicology's characteristic hierarchical emphasis on style over source on its head. In his landmark study *The Haydn Tradition* (1939), Jens Peter Larsen now asserted, contra Adler, that "only source criticism can provide a secure basis for research by identifying a corpus of documentably authentic works."[76] Far beyond the domain of Haydn studies proper, Larsen's influential statements of priority on the subject of authentication and attribution set the groundwork for a fundamental midcentury revision of inherited evidentiary norms in the increasingly professionalized culture of academic music research.[77] In the first place Larsen proposed that the practice of using source criticism as a means of establishing a secure corpus for further authentications was necessary to solve the problem of infinite regress that would arise from a purely style-critical model of musical authenticity in which misattributions could otherwise unknowingly be used as bogus stylistic precedents with which to authenticate other misattributions.[78] This

---

[73] Adler and Mugglestone, "Scope, Aim, and Method," 7.

[74] "[Äußere Quellen] allein können oder sollen nie die einzige Stütze der Zuerkennung sein." Adler, *Methode der Musikgeschichte*, 171–72.

[75] "Aus den beobachteten Gliedern der inneren stilkritischen Argumentation soll sich in Berücksichtigung und Prüfung der äußeren Umstände die Erkenntnisreihe bis zur Feststellung des Hauptzieles dieser Untersuchung, der Autorbestimmung erheben." Adler, *Methode der Musikgeschichte*, 171–72.

[76] "Eine ganz sichere Grundlage der Forschung vermag nur die Quellenprüfung durch die Ausscheidung der authentisch bestätigten Werke zu schaffen." Jens Peter Larsen, *Die Haydn-Überlieferung* (Copenhagen: Ejnar Munksgaard, 1939), 17. Translation from John Spitzer, "Style and the Attribution of Musical Works," in *Rückkehr des Autors: Zur Erneuerung eines umstrittenen Begriffs*, edited by Fotis Jannidis et al. (Tübingen: Max Niemeyer Verlag, 1999): 495–510, at 498.

[77] For a detailed assessment of Larsen's contributions in this regard, see, in particular, Spitzer, "Style and the Attribution of Musical Works."

[78] "Every examination of authenticity must proceed from a basis secured by undisputed authentic sources. Style analysis alone provides no basis for judgment, but only style comparison. Such a comparison cannot be initiated before there is a basis of verified source material, and this can only be obtained through the evidence of the sources." Jens Peter Larsen, "Problems of Authenticity in Music from the Time of Haydn to Mozart," in *Handel, Haydn, & the Viennese Classical Style*, translated by Ulrich Krämer (Ann Arbor: UMI Research Press, 1988): 123–35, at 131; first published as "Über die Möglichkeit einer musikalischen Echtheitsbestimmung für Werke aus der Zeit Haydns und Mozarts," *Mozart-Jahrbuch 1971–72* (1973): 7–18.

INTRODUCTION   19

epistemological problem is particularly germane to the threat of forgery, since—in Umberto Eco's analysis—there is a self-evident sense in which "the original cannot be used as a parameter for unmasking its forgeries unless we blindly take for granted that what is presented to us as the original is unchallengeably so."[79] Yet even beyond this foundational issue of infinite style-critical regress, Larsen valued source-critical evidence highly for its apparent objectivity, transparency, and aesthetic detachment by comparison to style criticism, a method that Larsen and his followers contrastingly regarded as inherently subjective in its inalienable association with aesthetics and thus with unaccountable and culturally contingent value judgments concerning relative compositional quality.[80] While the style-critical method "permits a rough triage" in cases where source-based evidence is unavailable or inconclusive, its application to questions of authenticity ultimately rests on shaky terrain in Larsen's account, since the attempt "to establish authenticity . . . on grounds of an evaluation of quality" is tantamount to "abandoning objectivity entirely."[81]

Of course, Adler would surely have rejected Larsen's characterization of style-criticism as subjective out of hand. For Adler, "scientifically recognizable style criteria" are absolutely distinct from "the criterion of aesthetic beauty," and it is "only those stylistic judgments [made] without aesthetic evaluation and without aesthetic theory" that "stand on the firm ground of academic research."[82] Be this as it may, Larsen and his followers had good reasons for believing that in practice style-critical authentication was never as objective nor as scientific as Adler had

---

[79] Eco, "Fakes and Forgeries," 199. Nelson Goodman terms the stylistic features that distinguish a particular artist's corpus its "precedent class," noting (apropos van Meegeren) that "every time a Van Meegeren was added to the corpus of pictures accepted as Vermeers, the criteria for acceptance were modified thereby; and the mistaking of further Van Meegerens for Vermeers became inevitable." See Goodman, *Languages of Art*, 111. Michael Talbot makes a similar point about the exclusion of authentic works distorting an artist's precedent class, arguing that "the logical problem with making stylistic analysis a decisive criterion of authenticity is that the process of argument is circular. What constitutes the composer's personal style is determined by examining the works that have *already* been accepted into the canon. If, for whatever reason, genuine works are excluded from the canon at an early stage, their later admission is made difficult by the fact that they have not contributed to the overall picture of the composer's style, which may be more diverse than previously imagined." See Michael Talbot, "The Genuine and the Spurious: Some Thoughts on Problems of Authorship Concerning Baroque Compositions," in *Vivaldi Vero E Falso: Problemi di Attribuzione*, edited by Antonio Fanna and Michael Talbot (Florence: Leo S. Olschki, 1992): 13–24, at 19–20. Emphasis from original text.

[80] Larsen, "Problems of Authenticity," esp. 129–30.

[81] "Wo die Quellenprüfung keine Anhaltspunkte für die Echtheitsbestimmung gewährt, ermöglicht die Stiluntersuchung wohl eine Einteilung in großen Zügen." Larsen, *Die Haydn-Überlieferung*, 17. Translation from Spitzer, "Style and the Attribution of Musical Works," 498. Larsen, "Problems of Authenticity," 134. Translation amended.

[82] "Das Kriterium des Ästhetisch-Schönen ist ein schwankendes, nur relative geltendes Merkmal, dessen Aufstellung in der Zeiten Lauf wechselt, während die wissenschaftlich erkannten Stilkriterien für sich bestehen . . . allein auf dem positiven Boden der wissenschaftlichen Forschung stehen nur Stilbestimmungen ohne Schönheitswertung und ohne Schönheitslehre der Ästhetik." Adler, *Methode der Musikgeschichte*, 121–22.

20   INTRODUCTION

claimed. For a start, Eco's observation about the possibility of an infinite regress in which forgeries are unwittingly used as precedents with which to authenticate further forgeries evokes something of the fatally circular quality inherent in the project of prescriptively pruning back a repertory to fit music-stylistic norms given that music-stylistic norms are themselves inevitably determined, descriptively, by the repertory to be pruned.[83] In this sense the characteristic rules and regulations of style-compositional music-theory pedagogy can all too easily take on a life of their own when uncritically recontextualized as analytical tools for style-critical authentication to be turned against contested works in place of student exercises. As Paula Higgins rightly points out, such style-analytical approaches often end up enforcing a Procrustean regime of authenticity in which "authenticity and perfection ... become mutually constitutive" to such an extent that attributions are wantonly banished from a composer's corpus on the grounds of any perceived technical blemish with little if any thought for the collateral damage that might result from treating free composition with the kind of inflexible scrutiny generally reserved for academic counterpoint.[84] On this issue, Larsen himself observed that the attempt to demolish an attribution to a canonical composer on the basis of some apparently unprecedented stylistic feature often falls prey to fundamental problems of inductive inference, not least because "it belongs to the royal prerogatives of genius that he must be able to create unbounded by traditions, even his own."[85] And it should be added in this context that successful compositional forgeries have often been apt to exploit the presumed "royal prerogatives" of the "genius" in just the opposite direction, too: as subsequent chapters of *Forgery in Musical Composition* will demonstrate, skilled forgers are generally well aware that deviations from stylistic norms are all too readily rehabilitated as hallmarks of inspired ingenuity and creative foresight rather than incompetence or anachronism by analysts consciously or subconsciously inclined to uphold a contested attribution to a famous historical figure. For all these reasons, Larsen ultimately maintained that "the very nature of style criticism makes it impossible to consider an attribution which has been established in this manner as secure or even as relatively secure," a critical perspective which his younger colleague H. C. Robbins Landon effectively echoed and redoubled when he noted in an important 1957 paper on matters of musical authenticity that "internal, i.e., stylistic evidence" for authorship is "a very

---

[83] On the important historical distinction between prescriptive theories of music (also called "practical" or "regulative") and descriptive music analysis, see Thomas Christensen, introduction to *Cambridge History of Western Music Theory*, edited by Thomas Christensen (Cambridge: Cambridge University Press, 2002), 1–22, at 13–14.

[84] Paula Higgins, "The Apotheosis of Josquin des Prez and Other Mythologies of Musical Genius," *Journal of the American Musicological Society* 57, no. 3 (2004): 443–96, at 467.

[85] Larsen, "Problems of Authenticity," 134.

INTRODUCTION 21

subjective and ... limited criterion" which "almost invariably leads to the wrong conclusion."[86]

The belief that style analysis is too unscientific to justify claims of authorship without supporting source-historical evidence led mid-twentieth-century scholars to a demanding practical question: How should contested attributions be resolved when no extant sources can reliably be traced back to the alleged composer in the first place? Forgers are often wont to exploit the unfortunate reality that history does not always preserve her documentary sources as well as scholars bent on source-philological authentication might hope. And, in the absence of a robust style-critical fallback, the aura of uncertainty surrounding contested works lacking substantial documentary traditions became increasingly bothersome for a number of musicologists operating in the wake of Larsen's disciplinary interventions. In the aforementioned 1957 paper, Landon—a figure who will play a central role in the final chapter of this book—went so far as to propose a novel solution to this perceived problem, positing that, instead of remaining agnostic about the authenticity of undocumented works, "musicology should" instead "reverse the common law, and judge a doubtful work guilty until it is proved beyond doubt to be innocent."[87] Some years later, Joshua Rifkin effectively harmonized with Landon's strikingly skeptical legalistic proposition, asserting—in a landmark publication on issues of authenticity in Josquin studies—that while "the presumption of innocence until proved guilty ... makes for humane justice ... it also makes for weak scholarship."[88] And Georg Feder states the issue even more frankly in a reflection on his editorial work as director of the Joseph Haydn Institute, boldly pointing out that "banishing an authentic work to the appendix or supplement" of a complete works edition might well be considered the "lesser" of "two evils" when compared to the act of mistakenly "accepting an inauthentic one into the main part."[89] Feder, Landon, and Rifkin had substantially divergent ideas about the utility of style-critical evidence. Yet,

[86] "Infolge des ganzen Charakters der Stilprüfung wird es aber nicht möglich sein, die Echtheit der nur auf diesem Weg zu bestätigenden Werke als gesichert oder bloß annähernd gesichert anzusehen." Larsen, Die Haydn-Überlieferung, 17. Translation from Spitzer, "Style and the Attribution of Musical Works," 498. H. C. Robbins Landon, "Problems of Authenticity in Eighteenth-Century Music," in Instrumental Music: A Conference at Isham Memorial Library, May 4, 1957, edited by David G. Hughes (Cambridge, MA: Harvard University Press, 1959): 31–56, at 36.

[87] Landon, "Problems of Authenticity," 37.

[88] Joshua Rifkin, "Problems of Authorship in Josquin," in Proceedings of the International Josquin Symposium Utrecht 1986, edited by Willem Elders (Utrecht, 1991): 45–52, at 46–47.

[89] "Vielleicht sollte man eher ein echtes Werk in den Anhang oder einen Supplementband verbannen als ein unechtes in den Hauptteil aufnehmen. Denn ein unechtes Werk, als Haydn gespielt, verfälscht das Haydn-Bild und kann dem Ansehen des Komponisten schaden. Das Fehlen eines echten Werkes im Hauptteil macht das Haydn-Bild zwar ärmer, verfälscht es aber nicht. Man muß hier zwischen zwei unvermeidlichen Übeln das kleinere wählen." Georg Feder, "Die Echtheitskritik in ihrer Bedeutung für die Haydn-Gesamtausgabe," in Opera incerta: Echtheitsfragen als Problem musikwissenschaftlicher Gesamtausgaben, edited by Hanspeter Bennwitz et al. (Stuttgart: F. Steiner, 1991): 71–112, at 102.

22   INTRODUCTION

tellingly, all three scholars consider the prospect of a "false positive" in which an authentic work is cast out of the canon as collateral damage to be considerably less concerning than the contrary case—i.e., a hypothetical or actual "false negative," wherein an inauthentic work seizes an illegitimate cultural position for itself by effectively passing as authentic. In the chapters to follow I shall call this widespread if often unspoken late twentieth-century musicological doctrine that treats attributions as doubtful until they are demonstrated to be otherwise "presumptive inauthenticity" in contradistinction to a preceding long nineteenth-century norm of what might contrastingly be termed "presumptive authenticity." These two respective paradigms are significant in what follows, not least because they correspond chronologically to *Forgery in Musical Composition*'s two large subsections: while romantic cultures of forgery might be said to reflect a climate that presumed musical attributions to be authentic until they were definitively proven inauthentic, modern cultures of forgery stem from an altogether more skeptical age in which attributions to historical figures came to be regarded with default suspicion until shored up by predominantly source-philological evidence interrogated by the professional scholars who, increasingly, served as the classical canon's de facto gatekeepers.

The achievements of the post-war regime of musical authentication and attribution are so imposing as to need little introduction here. Monumental thematic catalogues with now-iconic numerical identifiers for J. S. Bach (BWV), Schubert (D.), and Haydn (Hob.) appeared in swift succession in 1950, 1951, and 1957 just as ambitious *Urtext* complete works editions were founded for J. S. Bach (1954), Mozart (1955), Haydn (1958), and Schubert (1964) in the aspiration of upholding newly authoritative standards of authenticity and text-critical rigor. Yet even as such Herculean feats of scholarship and publishing were being conceived, the apparent neutrality of source-philological methods of attribution was once again called into question by a growing number of musicologists dissatisfied with the notion of authenticity by purely external means. In a paper on musical authentication published in 1973, Georg von Dadelsen lamented that "Bach, Mozart, and Haydn research" had, in preceding decades, "threatened to become an arcane archival science" in which researchers "interested purely in the work of art itself had no place" and "the only things that can be considered genuine are those established as such by writing implements, watermarks, ink pigmentation . . . and the editorial institute's seal of authenticity."[90] Feder, who

---

[90] "Bach-, Mozart, und Haydn-Forschung drohten zu einer Geheimwissenschaft der Archivkundigen zu werden. Der allein am Kunstwerk selbst interessierte Forscher konnte hier nicht mithalten." "Als echt kann nur gelten, was durch Schreiber, Wasserzeichen, durch Tintenfarbe und Löschsand sowie durch das Echtheitssiegel des Editionsinstituts als authentisch ausgewiesen ist." Georg von Dadelsen, "Methodische Bemerkungen zur Echtheitskritik," in *Musicae scientiae collectanea: Festschrift Karl Gustav Fellerer zum 70. Geburtstag* (1973): 78–82, at 78.

served as Larsen's successor as director of the Joseph Haydn Institute after 1960, might well have agreed at least in part, admitting—at the 1972 Congress of the International Musicological Society—that whether style-critical or source-philological in method, "a judgment about musical authenticity is," after all, "in essence a value judgment."[91] With the authenticating project's inalienable association with value judgment duly acknowledged, specifically style-critical authentication remained "now as ever a desideratum" for Feder as for many of his contemporaries and successors who similarly felt "the inescapable necessity of also being convinced by the music itself."[92] As John Spitzer deftly surmises, there is a sense in which the fundamental qualities that "make Haydn's music worth preserving and performing" in such accounts "are not Haydn's handwriting, the color of his ink or the way he notated appoggiaturas," but rather "musical qualities" that "ought to be audible." Indeed, "If people cannot tell by listening whether a symphony is by Haydn or by Carlos Ordoñez, then an attribution based on external evidence seems beside the point."[93] The tentative resurgence of the idea that adequate proof of musical authenticity can and perhaps should be in the pudding where possible is perhaps most precociously and pithily summed up by a Q&A response to Landon's 1957 paper by Oliver Strunk, who—as Spitzer points out—asserted, contra Landon, that "if the study of internal evidence almost invariably leads us to the wrong conclusions, something is wrong with our methods."[94] To pronounce judgment on issues of authenticity while foreswearing the epistemological significance of the music itself is to sever aesthetics and history at the bone, an act that—in Strunk's profoundly evocative analogy—risks putting music scholars in the position of the kind of snob who proudly "says 'I smoke only Camel cigarettes,' but who cannot tell a Camel from a Chesterfield unless he looks at the brand on the package."[95]

Gould would surely encourage us to take Strunk's musicological line of reasoning a step further by asking why one should bother with names and brands and packaging at all if the thing at issue in music's authenticity is ultimately its aesthetic value as music. In outlining the van Meegeren syndrome's effects in "The Prospects of Recording" the pianist contends that acts of forgery expose an underlying sense in which "we have never really become equipped to adjudicate

---

[91] "Das musikalische Echtheitsurteil ist also im wesentlichen ein Werturteil." Georg Feder, "Die Bedeutung der Assoziation und des Wertvergleichs für das Urteil in Echtheitsfragen," in *Report of the 11th Congress of the International Musicological Society, Copenhagen 1972*, vol. 1, edited by Henrik Glahn et al. (Copenhagen: Hansen, 1974): 365–77, at 370.

[92] "Diese Tatsache und unser unabweisliches Bedürfnis, uns auch von der Musik selbst überzeugen zu lassen, macht die musikalische Echtheitskritik nach wie vor zu einem Desideratum." Feder, "Die Bedeutung der Assoziation und des Wertvergleichs," 365.

[93] Spitzer, "Style and the Attribution of Musical Works," 496.

[94] Oliver Strunk quoted in Landon, "Problems of Authenticity," 53. See Spitzer, "Style and the Attribution of Musical Works," 495.

[95] Strunk quoted in Landon, "Problems of Authenticity," 53.

24   INTRODUCTION

music per se" precisely because "our value judgments" insist that we ground any "determination of the value of a work of art" merely in "the information available about it," thereby seemingly elevating the dreary supplemental clutter of brand and package over the vivid pleasures of the cigarette aflame.[96] Gould's first-person-plural "we" and "our" might need some interrogation here: after all, beyond the world of academia, the broader public is not infrequently skeptical of excessive nominal contextualization in ways that can occasionally make forgers seem more sympathetic than the individuals who pursue them. Cambridge University music librarian Charles Cudworth—one of the twentieth century's most perspicacious writers on issues of musical authenticity—captures this reality with characteristic satirical flare:

> Oddly enough, the public doesn't hate or despise the forger for his forgery; on the contrary, it often has a sneaking admiration for him, as one who has managed to hoodwink the experts, those dastardly enemies of the common man. The experts themselves, of course, are usually regarded with grave suspicion; for one thing, they have specialized knowledge, ever a matter of deep distrust; and, furthermore, for some strange reason musicological experts seem to be generally regarded as inimical to the music itself.[97]

Is the reasoning Cudworth attributes to the public really so strange? Surely one cannot be blamed for regarding with "grave suspicion" a class of experts who would happily denigrate a painting or a musical composition as a forgery on contextual or material grounds while refusing to evaluate the aesthetic content of the art object as such.

In raising this question I am by no means suggesting that scholars should abdicate their responsibility to speak the truth about who wrote what and when, bitterly difficult as that process might sometimes be. Nor should anything I am asserting here be confused with a normalization of forgery to the point of uncritical acceptance or incitement. Nonetheless, the act of repudiating a work's aesthetic content on the basis of its source tradition alone can be seen to reveal key internal inconsistencies both in the mid-twentieth-century's unsustainable high-modernist anxieties about music's connections to subjectivity and in the subsequent and countervailing contextualist tendency toward what Lawrence Kramer once described as "a musicology without music," arguably no less abhorrent of the aesthetic for all its high-flown ethical aspirations.[98]

From this perspective it is no coincidence that the fundamental epistemological problem of attribution is scarcely mentioned in today's Anglophone

[96] Gould, "The Prospects of Recording," 342, 341.

[97] Cudworth, "Ye Olde Spuriosity Shoppe," 40.

[98] Lawrence Kramer, "Music Criticism and the Postmodernist Turn," *Current Musicology* 53 (1993): 25–35, at 27.

musicological mainstream. This is not because that problem has in any sense been solved but rather because it was actively abandoned and forgotten.[99] As has been widely discussed, the post-war era of the van Meegeren syndrome encompasses precisely the period during which "music theory" emphatically severed itself from music history in no small part by defining the theoretical self against "what it perceived musicology as being: manuscript study, watermarks . . . and worst of all, the study of style and stylistic change," a process that barely predates the so-called new musicology's wholesale rejection of many of these very same practices under the allied banners of anti-positivism (manuscript study) and anti-formalism (score analysis).[100] With music history and music theory thus duly balkanized at an institutional level in much of the English-speaking world, the methodological divides between style and source and between aesthetics and history can be seen to have become so insurmountably wide that the basic factual problem of music's authorship has in many cases fallen from the edge of the map, relegated to a once central intellectual territory now mutually abandoned by both theory and history. That this happened precisely at the moment when (historical) musicology began to reinvest itself in neo-romantic notions of subjectivity and the self toward the end of the twentieth century is perhaps the deepest irony of all. And it is in such contexts that I propose that the work of the forger serves as a vital and inevitable reminder of the ways in which the aesthetic experience of music both constructs and tears asunder the identities and contexts that are imagined to stand within and behind it. In James Currie's luminously haunting phrasing (echoing Strunk, from a distance), here as always "the 'music itself,' with seeming indifference to our concerns regarding how she might be misused and abused, remains with cigarette in hand, seated at the table she has been asked to leave—a stain, indelible as a ghost."[101]

MUSIC AS TRUTH

Much of the preceding discussion hinges on the implicit relationship between the practice of preparing musical editions and catalogues claiming to represent a composer's complete works and the corresponding if now rarely discussed musicological norm of consigning inauthentic pieces, including forgeries, to the ash

[99] In the 1980s, Rifkin made something like this point by implying (in a paraphrase of Oscar Wilde) that musicological approaches to authentication and attribution "went from barbarism to decadence without experiencing civilization in between." See Rifkin, "Problems of Authorship in Josquin," 45.

[100] Patrick McCreless, "Contemporary Music Theory and the New Musicology: An Introduction," *Journal of Musicology* 15, no. 3 (1997): 291–296, at 293–94.

[101] James Currie, "Music after All," *Journal of the American Musicological Society* 62, no. 1 (2009): 145–203, at 177.

26 INTRODUCTION

heap of history—or, at best, to the appendix of the complete works edition—as soon as they are exposed as such.[102] It must be acknowledged that compositional falsifications have a dangerously infectious quality in the completionist music-historical imagination, "corrupting our vision of the artist's work as a whole" in ways that can often feel deeply threatening.[103] Left unchecked, there is a real danger that beguiling modern forgeries will altogether eclipse the authentic achievements of the peripherally canonical figures with whom they have become associated in the public sphere: surely the most obvious example is the "Albinoni" Adagio in G Minor, a work that Albinoni did not write but which Michael Talbot—in the introduction to his magisterial academic study of the composer—feels called to address before any of Albinoni's authentic works, pointing out that, in fact, its "style is so totally unlike Albinoni's that it invites us to explore his music under false premises."[104] For musicologists in Talbot's position it can be genuinely disheartening to seek to preserve the authentic products of the musical past and see them discarded in preference for inauthentic works that nonetheless better conform to modern tastes and desires. And for these reasons among others, music scholars have long been in the habit of weeding out fakes from academic discourse with extreme prejudice, all the while seemingly confident in the self-assurance that—as Larsen once wrote—"forgeries of supposedly old musical works . . . have little to do with serious musical research."[105]

One can hardly blame Larsen for his contempt. If musicology's primary goal is to establish an authentic art-historical record within the aspirationally objective frameworks outlined above, then addressing exposed forgeries in any substantial way might indeed feel like a failure of serious musical research as such. In-depth studies of fakes are readily dismissed as little more than intellectual profligacy or perversion from this perspective, especially when so much real art remains unarchived, unstudied, and unloved. Yet just as the competent detective inevitably becomes a student of criminality, the very act of casting away and condemning fakes is also, unavoidably, to seek them out and fix our attention mercilessly upon them. As even a cursory reading of Larsen's own source-critical

---

[102] An overview of the role of authentication in these and other early historical editions can be found in Stanley Sadie, ed., *The New Grove Dictionary of Music and Musicians* (New York: Oxford University Press, 2001), s.v. "editions, Historical," by Sydney Robinson Charles, George R. Hill, Norris L Stephens, and Julie Woodward.

[103] Leonard B. Meyer, "Forgery and the Anthropology of Art," in *Music, the Arts, and Ideas: Patterns and Predictions in Twentieth-Century Culture* (Chicago: University of Chicago Press, 1967), 54–67, at 64; first published in *The Yale Review* 52, no. 2 (1963) and reprinted in *The Forger's Art: Forgery and the Philosophy of Art*, ed. Denis Dutton (Berkeley: University of California Press, 1983): 77–92.

[104] Michael Talbot, *Tomaso Albinoni: The Venetian Composer and His World* (Oxford: Clarendon Press, 1990), v. For more on this work, see Frederick Reece, "Baroque Forgeries and the Public Imagination," in *The Oxford Handbook of Public Music Theory*, edited by J. Daniel Jenkins (New York: Oxford University Press, 2021).

[105] Larsen, "Problems of Authenticity," 125.

INTRODUCTION   27

work or the Adlerian style criticism that preceded it demonstrates, (in)authenticity and (mis)attribution have been at the core of the music-historical enterprise from the very start. Nowadays, the inauthentic tends to lurk just beneath the surface as a barely concealed Derridean supplement—or Taruskinesque "invidious antonym"—to its more desirable counterpart, ever-present if rarely named as such.[106] And it could thus be asserted that scholars who still claim to defend the associated values of truth, identity, and history in music are duty bound to develop an intimate understanding of falsehood, imposture, and anachronism, beginning their inquiries with the kind of radical epistemic doubt that casts the van Meegeren's of music not as Gouldian "heroes," but rather as Cartesian demons whose remarkable powers of deception force us to establish that which is beyond even the most hard-boiled academic skepticism.[107]

Of course, there will also be those more sympathetic to Gould for whom such skepticism is not nearly skeptical enough, and for whom all such unabashed talk of music's truth and falsehood itself appears markedly archaic if not ideologically tainted. As far back as 1985, Joseph Kerman was already writing of the days when musicologists "dealt mainly in the verifiable, the objective, the uncontroversial, and the positive" using the polemical past tense.[108] In another widely read disciplinary intervention published some two decades after Kerman's, Carolyn Abbate posits that "conjuring authority out of beautiful noise involves a ruse," notably adding that the strategy of "giving music the capacity to convey the best truth remains a romantic cliché and need not be accepted at face value."[109] A still more recent panoptic critique of musicology's disciplinary bad habits rendered in explicitly ethical terms by William Cheng sums up the fallout of these now dominant attitudes by perceptively noting that "the word [truth] itself is taboo" in much contemporary discourse, all before further warning readers that "pursuits of truth have dark sides"—the "uncomfortable," the "injurious," and the "coerced."[110]

To speak of truth too loudly and unapologetically at this late hour is indeed to risk a host of unflattering associations. For one thing, breaking the unspoken taboo on truth identified by Cheng can be regarded as an indecent flirtation not only with the old-guard Adlerian brand of positivism so successfully provincialized by

---

[106] On the supplement see Jacques Derrida, *Of Grammatology*, translated by Gayatri Chakravorty Spivak (Baltimore: John Hopkins University Press, 2016), esp. 144–45. For a related and highly influential interpretation of the archive as a site defined by exclusion and forgetting (as well as inclusion and remembrance) see Jacques Derrida, *Archive Fever: A Freudian Impression*, translated by Eric Prenowitz (Chicago: University of Chicago Press, 1996).

[107] René Descartes, *Meditations on First Philosophy*, translated and edited by John Cottingham (Cambridge: Cambridge University Press, 1996), 15.

[108] Kerman, *Contemplating Music*, 42.

[109] Carolyn Abbate, "Music—Drastic or Gnostic?," *Critical Inquiry* 30, no. 3 (2004): 505–536, at 522.

[110] William Cheng, *Just Vibrations: The Purpose of Sounding Good* (Ann Arbor: University of Michigan Press, 2016), 46–47.

28   INTRODUCTION

Kerman and his followers, but also with the more metaphysical and ever divisive Adornian brand of music-as-truth, which maintains with unapologetically elitist swagger that "authentic compositions unfold their truth-content ... in a temporal dimension through the law of their form" while other, inauthentic works simply do not.[111] As Adorno's many critics have pointed out at exhaustive length, this aesthetic formalist conception of truth often masquerades as factual historical truth (and vice versa) under the cloak of "cultural authenticity," an endlessly slippery ideal all-too-easily co-opted to lend unexamined biases about art the rhetorical weight of cold hard fact.[112] More withering still is the widespread contention (derived, foundationally, from the work of Pierre Bourdieu) that any putatively high-minded concern about art's authenticity must ultimately boil down to little more than a sublimated form of class or status anxiety that can readily be made to vanish in a puff of cultural capital.[113] Small wonder that truth and authenticity have themselves been rendered intellectually hypothetical for so many of us, at worst reduced to artifacts of the vulgar "musical moralism" that Andrew Durkin accuses of promoting "aesthetic arrogance and even brutality" once "followed to its logical extreme."[114] Truth lingers with a guilty conscience in discourse about music when it appears at all, frozen in the ironizing scare quotes of fading romantic superstition and thereby ineluctably "linked," as all things must now be, "in a circular relationship with systems of power which produce and sustain it."[115]

Listening closely to compositional forgeries in this belated intellectual landscape leads one to ask some unsettling questions about how and why we continue to make meaning and history out of music in general. Tarnished and bloodstained as truth's dark sides may be, a perspective that includes fakes and forgeries suggests that there might be good reasons to avoid turning radical mistrust of so hoary a concept as music-as-truth against the newer musicological shibboleths of identity, subjectivity, and cultural context in turn when the stakes are high. To be sure, the idea that music has no meaning beyond what we arbitrarily construct for it, that no artist is more or less disingenuous than any other,

[111] Theodor W. Adorno, "Bach Defended Against His Devotees" in *Prisms*, translated by Samuel and Shierry Weber (Cambridge, MA: MIT Press, 1995): 135–46, at 143. In outspoken support of musical truth content, see, for example, Kofi Agawu, "How We Got Out of Analysis and How to Get Back in Again," *Music Analysis* 23, nos. 2–3 (2004): 267–86, esp. 271–73.

[112] Trevor Wishart, for example, argues that Adorno's "use of the words 'authentic' and 'true' simply imply an evaluative position for [him] as critic which transcends the social situation," thereby obscuring the deeper fact that "all appeals to culturally transcendent values, truth, or authenticity are spurious." See Trevor Wishart, "On Radical Culture," in *Whose Music? A Sociology of Musical Languages*, edited by John Shepherd et al. (New Brunswick: Transaction Books, 1977): 233–56, at 235.

[113] Pierre Bourdieu, *Distinction: A Social Critique of the Judgment of Taste*, translated by Richard Nice (Cambridge, MA: Harvard University Press, 1987); first published as *La Distinction: Critique sociale du jugement* (Paris: Les Éditions de minuit, 1979).

[114] Andrew Durkin, *Decomposition: A Music Manifesto* (New York: Pantheon Books, 2014), 116.

[115] Michel Foucault, "Truth and Power," in *Power/Knowledge: Selected Interviews and Other Writings, 1972–77*, edited by Colin Gordon (New York: Pantheon Books, 1980): 109–133, at 133.

INTRODUCTION 29

and that we should in fact be celebrating forgers as "the foremost artists of our age" remains palatable in the cloistered realm of the Gouldian sound studio.[116] Yet when the foundational values of authorship and authenticity are given up in the name of disciplinary progress away from positivism and value judgment, it is worth taking the time to consider the possibility that some version of those ideals and of the values associated with them might now be precisely what is needed to defend the autonomy of persons and musics excluded from the nineteenth century's canon-building projects. From this perspective, music scholars casting a critical eye over the van Meegeren syndrome as a phenomenon rooted in the culture of the late twentieth century would be well justified in questioning whether there could be something more than pure coincidence to the fact that, historically speaking, it is "just when women and minority peoples have become visible as subjects [that] individual subjectivity is being questioned."[117] Withering deconstructive doubt about such issues is one thing in the magic circle of academic discourse, but quite another when applied to what Bruno Latour has dubbed "matters of concern" outside—i.e., to forms of knowledge "whose import will no longer be to debunk but to protect and care," and which ultimately call for "the cultivation of a *stubbornly realist attitude*."[118]

CANONICAL TEMPORALITIES

Van Meegeren's arrest, trial, and sentencing mark a world-historical threshold in Gould's analysis of forgery. According to his 1966 *High Fidelity* article, the affair was nothing less than a "magnificent morality play" that "perfectly epitomizes the confrontation between those values of identity and of personal-responsibility-for-authorship which post-Renaissance art has until recently accepted and those pluralistic values which electronic forms assert."[119] Boldly prophetic and historically sweeping as this statement may appear, in the broader intellectual context of the late 1960s Gould was far from alone in positing that the forms of authorship established by post-Renaissance modernity were disintegrating.[120] As if not to be outdone by

[116] Keats, *Forged*, 3–4.

[117] Marion Guck, "Music Loving, or the Relationship with the Piece," *Journal of Musicology* 15, no. 3 (1997): 343–52, at 351.

[118] Bruno Latour, "Why Has Critique Run Out of Steam? From Matters of Fact to Matters of Concern," *Critical Inquiry* 30 (2004): 225–48, at 232, 231, italics original.

[119] Gould, "The Prospects of Recording," 341.

[120] In proposing that the "electronic age" will be a radical cultural break from the "age of movable type" (i.e., the era of "post-Renaissance" ideology) Gould echoes a highly influential argument made by his sometime collaborator Marshall McLuhan in *The Gutenberg Galaxy* (Toronto: University of Toronto Press, 1962). On the pivotal role of the 1960s in the philosophy of authorship writ large, see, for example, Séan Burke, ed., *Authorship: From Plato to the Postmodern* (Edinburgh: Edinburgh University Press, 1995).

30 INTRODUCTION

Roland Barthes's and Michel Foucault's subsequent diagnoses that "the reign of the author" was ultimately a temporary artifact of movable type's long cultural aftermath in "English empiricism, French rationalism, and the personal faith of the Reformation," the pianist—in his precocious analysis of sound recording's effects on music—takes things a step further still, heralding nothing less than a utopic new dark age of anonymous and atemporal "electronic culture" for which "the role of the forger, of the unknown maker of unauthenticated goods, is emblematic."[121]

The forger's workshop and the sound studio are bound together in this elaborate conceptual analogy above all by Gould's underlying concern with time, that elusive aspect of human phenomenology that governs not only moment-to-moment experiences of music as such but also many narrative accounts of aesthetic culture's large-scale historical unfolding. From this perspective, Gould argues that recordings should be understood to have a promethean "time-transcending objective" in our society, effectively liberating the experience of musical sound from its temporal origins in the unrepeatable acoustic moment of performance just as forgeries purport to liberate aesthetic forms from their origins in linear art-historical chronology.[122] This rhapsodic praise for the untimely qualities of recording was inspired in no small part by Gould's affection for magnetic tape's "non-linear cultural techniques," as Andrea Bohlman and Peter McMurray have called them: revolutionary time-warping technologies of "looping," "dubbing," and "rewind[ing]" that flourished alongside the "splendid splice" in the post-war decades, demolishing once and for all the old phonographic idea that sound recordings—like signed and finished works of art—must in any way "provide documentation pertaining to a specific date."[123] The fact that studio recordings—Gould's exclusive mode of performance after 1964—came to be coded as inauthentic post-facto simulations of something original, live, or real in much the same terms as forgeries during this period was much to the point for the pianist.[124] By attempting to rewind art history itself, the phony works of van Meegeren and those like him functioned, in Gould's view, as a particularly

---

[121] Barthes, "The Death of the Author," 147, 143; Michel Foucault, "What Is an Author?," in *Textual Strategies: Perspectives in Post-Structuralist Criticism*, edited by Josué V. Harari (Ithaca, NY: Cornell University Press, 1979): 141–60; first published as "Qu'est-ce qu'un auteur?" *Bulletin de la Société française de philosophie* 63, no. 3 (1969): 73–104; Gould, "The Prospects of Recording," 343.

[122] Gould, "The Prospects of Recording," 340.

[123] Andrea F. Bohlman and Peter McMurray, "Tape: Or, Rewinding the Phonographic Regime," *Twentieth-Century Music* 14, no.1 (2017): 3–24, at 8–9. Gould, "The Prospects of Recording," 337–40.

[124] Gould's much-discussed decision to withdraw from concert performance and focus exclusively on studio recording after 1964 has itself often been understood, at least in part, as a form of anti-romantic, anti-authenticity "protest" in this vein. See, for example, Tim Hecker, "Glenn Gould, The Vanishing Performer and the Ambivalence of the Studio," *Leonardo Music Journal* (2008): 77–83, and Nicholas Mathew, "Gould and Liberace, or the Fate of Nineteenth-Century Performance Culture," *Journal of Musicological Research* (2020): 1–15.

laudable form of "protest" in the context of a technophobic culture that will "be able to express the agelessness of the aesthetic impulse" only when definitively "freed from the conformities that time imposes" and thus also "freed from the conformity that we have permitted history to impose" on musical performance, on composition, and on sound itself.[125]

It is difficult to imagine a more radically destabilizing vision for the future of the arts. Clearly, taking Gould's views on forgery and authorship seriously would have seismic consequences for conventional models of classical music's historical value and the canon of authentic works that undergirds it. As composer-theorist and philosopher Leonard B. Meyer puts it in his own 1960s meditation on the topic, "forgeries are banished to the basement" for good reason in such traditions, above all because "they are in conflict with our most fundamental beliefs" not only about art, but also "about the nature of human existence: beliefs about causation and time, creation and freedom."[126] Any "watertight separation between aesthetic criteria and cultural beliefs" of the type Gould might seem to propose is "mistaken and misguided" from this perspective, a point that Meyer illustrates by means of his own musical analogy to melodic reprise.[127] "In simple folk tunes as well as great symphonies," says Meyer, "a sequence of tones stated early in the piece sometimes returns toward the end," a fact that, in Meyer's view, fundamentally changes the nature of the former with respect to the latter no matter how precise the repetition.[128] The ontology of any object or experience must, after all, include not only the thing in itself, but also "our knowledge, whether correct or not, of how it came into being" in time. For Meyer, this reality ultimately renders the proposal that forgeries are in any way as valuable as authentic works little more than "a pretentious form of inverted snobbery."[129] As he puts it:

> Because our fundamental beliefs influence our sensations, feelings, and perceptions, *what* we know literally changes our responses to a work of art. Thus once we *know* that a work is a forgery our whole set of attitudes and resulting responses are profoundly and necessarily altered. It is pointless to say that it is all in the mind. Our beliefs are our beliefs and we can no more change them than we can breathe in a vacuum.[130]

In the course of this breathtaking paragraph, Meyer (like Gould) can be seen to universalize attitudes toward authenticity from the panoptic first-person-plural

---

[125] Gould, "Forgery and Imitation in the Creative Process," 209, 221.
[126] Meyer, "Forgery and the Anthropology of Art," 67.
[127] Meyer, "Forgery and the Anthropology of Art," 58.
[128] Meyer, "Forgery and the Anthropology of Art," 63.
[129] Meyer, "Forgery and the Anthropology of Art," 63, 56, 57.
[130] Meyer, "Forgery and the Anthropology of Art," 57. Emphasis from original text.

32   INTRODUCTION

perspective of "we" and "our," assuming an authoritative position that appears to leave little if any room for a meaningful human diversity of "feelings" and "perceptions," much less (in Meyer's case) the possibility that "cultural beliefs" can, and do, change. Ultimately, the blunt tautology that "our beliefs are our beliefs" is a telling rhetorical capstone in an argument that audaciously attempts to collapse time and identity as if to raise the ethical and aesthetic rejection of forgery to the status of an immutable and incontrovertible natural law.

Here one encounters an impasse central to this book between two seemingly incompatible ways of listening not just to forgeries but to music in general. For Gould, composition is aesthetic in an almost pre-rational sense, beautiful and therefore valuable for reasons rooted in ancient human impulses toward "myth" and "religio[n]" that have no necessary connection to the unartful virtues of historical truth and moral goodness, much less to such changeable and intangible cultural ideas as "originality" and "authenticity."[131] Meyer, on the other hand, hears in music a kind of socio-temporal document embedded, as he puts it, in "the history of culture, the history of art, and the history of the artist," ideas that unavoidably raise the normative ethical specters of unoriginality and inauthenticity.[132] In Meyer's view, loving forgeries is ultimately a kind of sickness or pathology, far more pernicious than Gould's van Meegeren syndrome because it trespasses against the natural order of things, much like insisting that one can "breathe in a vacuum." These two attitudes have a long and fraught history in critical thought on music. And the uncomfortable ideological dissonance between them will in turn play a significant role in the structure of this book. For now, suffice it to say that the tensions between Gould's and Meyer's opposing attitudes toward music and its value—the aesthetic and the historical, as I shall often imperfectly call them, following Dahlhaus's influential dialectical formulation—will appear time and again in the chapters that follow even as the names of their various advocates change.[133] Crucially, the consequence of adopting Meyer's attitude is the belief that music can lie, and—perhaps more important—that it should matter when it does. This in time results in the rigorously historicized canon to which classical musicians have grown accustomed, populated by works that have been—as Kerman puts it—"authorized in some way for contemplation, admiration, interpretation, and the determination of value": not merely beautiful, but good and true, too.[134]

---

[131] Gould, "Forgery and Imitation in the Creative Process," 208, 210, 216.

[132] Meyer, "Forgery and the Anthropology of Art," 63, 57.

[133] Dahlhaus's account of this issue can be found in Carl Dahlhaus, *Foundations of Music History*, translated by J. B. Robinson (Cambridge: Cambridge University Press, 1983), 19–33; first published as *Grundlagen der Musikgeschichte* (Cologne: Musikverlag Hans Gerig, 1977).

[134] Joseph Kerman, "A Few Canonic Variations," *Critical Inquiry* 10, no. 1 (1983): 107–125, at 107.

INTRODUCTION   33

Embracing the van Meegeren syndrome and forgery against the grain of hundreds of years of tradition would surely have substantial side effects, including the abandonment of an extended order of canonical values that many of us depend upon to process our experiences with art. To begin with, the still-widespread Bloomian modernist view that creativity should be understood as an agonistic struggle between originality and influence—i.e., between "strong poets" and their "strong precursors"—would collapse once bereft of a viable authorial distinction separating anterior "influencing" texts on the one hand and posterior "influenced" texts on the other.[135] The same fate would befall the Enlightenment notion of artistic genius, famously described by Immanuel Kant as a phenomenon for which "originality" is the "foremost property"—i.e., "the talent to create something for which no determinate rule can be given [and] not . . . a skill for something that can be learned by following some rule or other."[136] Discriminating between "rule-giving" talent and "rule-following" skill only makes sense, after all, so long as the style-historical clock—itself a kind of chronometric canon—continues to tick ineluctably onward, transfiguring today's avant-garde technical innovation into tomorrow's derivative anachronism through reliable attribution and dating.[137]

It is easy to see how the paradoxical demands of such an oxymoronic tradition of originality might lead one to believe that we have arrived in history at a terminally late stage during which substantial new contributions to the arts are, at best, highly improbable. "When a great poet has lived," writes Meyer (here quoting T. S. Eliot), "certain things have been done once and for all and can never be done again."[138] From this vantage any attempt to return to the past in compositional practice evokes Renaissance-faire sentimentality at best and the insidious pseudo-classicist phantasmagoria of the *Zeppelinfeld* at worst, at least if Adorno and his followers are to be believed.[139] In Fredric Jameson's more recent

[135] Harold Bloom, *The Anxiety of Influence: A Theory of Poetry*, 2nd ed. (New York: Oxford University Press, 1997), 5.

[136] Immanuel Kant, *Critique of Judgment*, translated by Werner S. Pluhar (Indianapolis: Hackett, 1987), §46; first published as *Critik der Urtheilskraft* (Berlin: Lagarde und Friedrich, 1790).

[137] On the far-reaching influence of this phenomenon, see Jim Samson, "The Great Composer," in *The Cambridge History of Nineteenth-Century Music*, edited by Jim Samson (Cambridge: Cambridge University Press, 2001): 259–86.

[138] Meyer, "Forgery and the Anthropology of Art," 58. The passage Meyer cites is from T. S. Eliot, *Notes towards the Definition of Culture* (London: Faber and Faber, 1949), 114.

[139] Consider the association of "retrogressive" compositional styles with the cultural impulses toward authoritarianism and fascism in Theodor W. Adorno, "Stravinsky and Restoration," in *Philosophy of New Music*, translated by Robert Hullot-Kentor (Minneapolis: University of Minnesota Press, 2019), and "Gloss on Sibelius," translated by Susan H. Gillespie, in *Jean Sibelius and His World*, edited by Daniel M. Grimley (Princeton: Princeton University Press, 2011): 333–37.

34   INTRODUCTION

but no less pessimistic postmodern formulation, Gould's electronic age emerges not as an atemporal utopia freed from the constraints of the past, but rather as an unspeakably barren and uncreative paradigm doomed to repeat it in a purgatorial stupor driven only by the amnesiac instrumental rationality of unregulated capital: "a world in which stylistic innovation is no longer possible [and] all that is left is to imitate dead styles, to speak through the masks and with the voices of the styles in the imaginary museum."[140]

Van Meegeren's "Vermeers," sold for a fortune to buyers including prominent Nazis, do little to resist such critical attitudes toward art forgery, which root the phenomenon firmly in the psychological excesses of fascist nostalgia and capitalist greed. Yet there is also an unorthodox Gouldian perspective from which forgeries can appear to short-circuit all such belated professorial melancholia and political moralizing about the arts, suggesting, in a supreme aestheticist provocation, that the threefold canonizing metric of authenticity, originality, and genius might be little more than a temporary snare that modernity has laid in the unspeakably more ancient and irrevocable path of beauty itself.[141] In a remarkable passage, the pianist illustrates the implications of this last point through a thought experiment centered explicitly on forgery not in the visual arts, but in music:

> Imagine the critical response to an improvisation which, through its style and texture, suggested that it might have been composed by Joseph Haydn. (Let's assume it to be brilliantly done and most admirably Haydnesque.) If one were to concoct such a piece, its value would remain at par—that is to say, at Haydn's value—only so long as some chicanery were involved in its presentation, enough at least to convince the listener that it was indeed by Haydn. If, however, one were to suggest that although it much resembled Haydn it was, rather, a youthful work of Mendelssohn, its value would decline; and if one chose to attribute it to a succession of authors, each of them closer to the present day, then—regardless of their talents or historical significance—the merits of this same little piece would diminish with each new identification. If, on the other hand, one were to suggest that this work of chance, of accident, of the here and now, was not by Haydn but by a master living some generation or two before his time (Vivaldi, perhaps), then this work would become—on the strength of that daring, that foresight, that futuristic anticipation—a landmark in musical composition.[142]

[140] Fredric Jameson, "Postmodernism and Consumer Society," in *The Anti-Aesthetic: Essays on Postmodern Culture*, edited by Hal Foster (Seattle: Bay Press, 1983): 111–25, at 117.

[141] Gould's argument is, of course, easier to make in cases where forgery secures little financial profit, which serves to further highlight the limits of the van Meegeren example.

[142] Gould, "The Prospects of Recording," 342. This imagined Haydn forgery is likely framed as an improvisation and not a composition in the first sentence to avoid complicating the thought experiment with the question of source-historical authentication. For a similar thought experiment involving a modern "Beethoven" sonata, see Milan Kundera, *The Curtain: An Essay in Seven Parts*, translated by Linda Asher (New York: Harper Perennial, 2006), 4.

INTRODUCTION   35

A provocative line of argument. Yet, in "The Prospects of Recording," Gould overlooks the crucial fact that compositional forgery is no mere thought experiment, but a vivid cultural reality against which we can test the validity of his hypothesis, tracking changing perspectives on music's values and our own along the way.

PRÉCIS: MUSICA FICTA

No book could claim to offer exhaustive coverage of so long a historical period as that under discussion here. Instead, *Forgery in Musical Composition* presents a series of four case studies that have been selected for exploration with the aim of providing sufficient depth to illustrate key trends in detail while simultaneously establishing a framework for future research on this underexplored topic. To clarify important aspects of compositional forgery's development across historical time, the examples to follow have necessarily been organized chronologically according to the true date of composition for each forgery under analysis, momentarily laying such false dates of composition as are inherently characteristic of forgery to one side so as to more effectively reconstruct an authentic overarching narrative sequence.

Chapter 1, "Mozartian Swan Songs," centers on a re-examination of a much-discussed music-historical episode from romanticism's infancy: Franz Xaver Süssmayr's completion of the recently deceased W. A. Mozart's Requiem Mass, K. 626. Tellingly, this act has alternately been accepted as benign by some and decried as the archetypal compositional forgery by others with little sign of definitive consensus. Foundational methodological tensions between source and style as forms of musical evidence are explored in the context of historical debates about the authenticity of this and other posthumously published "Mozart" works that skeptics believed to be fraudulent completions or outright misattributions sold to publishers and patrons in the wake of Mozart's death, including the strikingly dissonant Minuet in D Major, K. 355 (576b). Ultimately, the chapter concludes with a meditation on the role of Mozart's widow in shaping her deceased husband's estate, and on the authenticating work done by musicologists as academic curators in the present.

Chapter 2, "Kreislerian Fantasies," turns to the early twentieth century, when romantic musical culture was in its twilight. On 8 February 1935, the *New York Times* ran a front-page article in which Austrian-born virtuoso violinist and composer Fritz Kreisler confessed that some seventeen pieces he previously claimed to have adapted from antique manuscripts by figures such as Vivaldi and Pugnani were, as he put it, "in every detail my original compositions." The revelation led to a heated debate between Kreisler and London *Sunday Times* music critic Ernest Newman, who claimed that the

36 INTRODUCTION

forgeries only appeared to have "fooled the experts" because "a vast amount of seventeenth- and eighteenth-century music was merely the exploitation of formulae" to begin with. Yet, curiously, pre-1935 critics had applauded the authenticity of Kreisler's "rediscoveries" on account of precisely those faux-Baroque features that strike modern audiences as egregiously anachronistic. In this sense, Kreisler's forgeries emerge as important documents of their time.

Chapter 3, "Schubert's Untrue Symphony," introduces key principles characteristic of modern cultures of forgery. In 1975, Swiss-born East German musicologist Harry Goldschmidt received a curious letter from a West German journalist and amateur musician named Gunter Elsholz claiming that Schubert's lost "Gmunden-Gastein" Symphony, D. 849, had been rediscovered after a century and a half in the wilderness. Institutions including the Neue Schubert-Ausgabe responded to Goldschmidt by using source criticism in an attempt to repudiate the composition. Yet, despite this evidence, the town-hall debate that preceded the symphony's 1982 premiere in Hanover concluded with the majority of lay listeners siding with Goldschmidt—i.e., in favor of Schubert's authorship—when asked to vote on the matter in an unprecedented act of public musicological judgment. The case of Schubert's Untrue Symphony was only resolved two years later when the Federal Institute for Materials Testing [Bundesanstalt für Materialprüfung], or BAM, in West Berlin used groundbreaking forensic technologies to test the ink and paper of the score itself. However, in the wake of this new historical development, the uncomfortable fact remained that it was laboratory analysis that had resolved the matter, and not the work's sources or its sounding structure as traditionally understood.

Chapter 4, "Haydn's Missing Link," considers modern cultures of compositional forgery in a still more recent historical context. On the morning of 14 December 1993, musicologist H. C. Robbins Landon stood before a crowded London press conference and announced that six lost Haydn keyboard sonatas (Hob. XVI:2a–e and 2g) had been rediscovered after more than 200 years. In this case, the works subsequently revealed as forgeries were compelling not only because they were based on four-measure phrases recorded in Haydn's *Entwurfkatalog* that correspond to lost works but also because the incipits dated from the crucial yet ill-documented 1767–70 period, long considered a stylistic "missing link" in the composer's development. This chapter explores how the forged sonatas functioned against the disciplinary and cultural background of the 1990s. Musical analyses are ultimately complemented by original correspondence with the forger, Winfried Michel, who—as if echoing Glenn Gould's provocative mid-century hypotheses about forgery—declares that our "obsession with 'authenticity' and 'famous names' is symptomatic of modern art reception" in which "what people choose to call academia hinders our appreciation of a work of art."

PART I

ROMANTIC CULTURES OF FORGERY, 1791–1945

1

Mozartian Swan Songs

What do poets praise more highly than the nightingale's enchantingly beautiful song in a secluded thicket on a quiet summer evening by the soft light of the moon? And yet we have cases where some jovial innkeeper, unable to find such a songster, played a trick—received with greatest satisfaction [initially]—on the guests staying at his inn to enjoy the country air, by hiding in a bush some roguish youngster who (with a reed or rush in his mouth) knew how to copy that song in a way very similar to nature's. But as soon as one realizes that it was all deception, no one will long endure listening to this song that before he had considered so charming; and that is how it is with the song of any other bird.

Immanuel Kant[1]

Wolfgang Amadeus Mozart died on 5 December 1791. It was some two months before his thirty-sixth birthday and a little more than a year after the first printing of Kant's lyrical meditation on the twilight song of the false nightingale reproduced in the epigraph at the beginning of this chapter. Mozart's premature death was, of course, a landmark event in musical culture. In the decades around 1800, it inspired a sprawling array of biographical and pseudo-biographical writing, from the legitimate to the literary-fictitious and the downright libelous.[2] Through the early accounts of Friedrich Schlichtegroll,[3] Franz Xaver Niemetschek,[4] and, in particular, Johann Friedrich Rochlitz,[5] Mozart the

---

[1] Immanuel Kant, *Critique of Judgment*, translated by Werner S. Pluhar (Indianapolis: Hackett, 1987), §42; first published as *Critik der Urtheilskraft* (Berlin: Lagarde und Friedrich, 1790).

[2] For an extensive examination of the biographical mythology surrounding Mozart's death see William Stafford, *Mozart's Death: A Corrective Survey of the Legends* (London: Macmillan, 1991).

[3] Friedrich Schlichtegroll, *Nekrolog auf das Jahr 1791* (Gotha, 1793).

[4] Franz Xaver Niemetschek, *Life of Mozart*, translated by Helen Mautner (London: Leonard Hyman, 1956); first published as *Leben des K. K. Kapellmeisters Wolfgang Gottlieb Mozart, nach Originalquellen beschrieben* (Prague: Herrlischen Buchhandlung, 1798).

[5] Rochlitz's twenty-seven *Verbürgte Anekdoten* were first published in the *Allgemeine musikalische Zeitung* between 1798 and 1801. An English translation with extensive critical commentary can be found in Maynard Solomon, "The Rochlitz Anecdotes: Issues of Authenticity in Early Mozart Biography," in *Mozart Studies*, edited by Cliff Eisen (Oxford: Clarendon Press, 1991): 1–59.

Forgery in Musical Composition. Frederick Reece, Oxford University Press. © Oxford University Press 2025.
DOI: 10.1093/9780197618332.003.0002

40 FORGERY IN MUSICAL COMPOSITION

man gradually began to merge with the now-familiar cultural image of "Mozart" as far more than a strikingly precocious and significant talent.[6] It was in the 1790s and the early 1800s, principally under the influence of the newly founded *AmZ* (*Allgemeine musikalische Zeitung*) and other publications like it, that the posthumous Mozart increasingly appeared as a defining example of artistic "genius,"[7] as nothing less than a spiritual embodiment of "the Beautiful" itself,[8] and— ultimately—as a world-historical figure "unable to find a place for himself during his lifetime"[9] who would, implicitly or explicitly, come to occupy that proper position only when "transfigured" in death.[10]

Recent scholarship has gone to considerable lengths to exorcise the excesses of this nineteenth-century Mozart tradition with its characteristically morbid fixation on the circumstances of the composer's demise and their purported metaphysical consequences.[11] This chapter in no way seeks to challenge or undermine such important revisionist work on the historical Mozart as such. Yet, from a perspective grounded in cultural criticism, I contend that romantic ideas about Mozart's genius, death, and transfiguration came to have a foundational impact on nineteenth-century conceptions of musical authenticity in ways that have yet to be fully unpacked.[12] Posthumous Mozartiana is particularly ripe for examination in this context, not least because the remarkable cornucopia of works printed soon after the composer's death immediately attracted widespread skeptical accusations of forgery and fraud in the first three decades of the nineteenth century. Indeed, the most intractable of these accusations have continued to haunt both the Mozart canon and the broader practice of music history ever since.

---

[6] On Rochlitz's influence on nineteenth-century Mozart reception, see Ulrich Konrad, "Friedrich Rochlitz und die Entstehung des Mozart-Bildes um 1800," in *Mozart: Aspekte des 19. Jahrhunderts*, edited by Hermann Jung (Mannheim: J & J, 1995): 1–22.

[7] Johann Friedrich Rochlitz, "Raphael und Mozart," *AmZ* 2, no. 37 (1800): 641–51, at 645.

[8] [Johann Friedrich Rochlitz?], "Das Reich der Harmonie," *AmZ* 12, no. 23 (1810): 353–67, at 365.

[9] "Aus diesem Werke sieht man, dass Mozart—wie so mancher große Mann—Zeit seines Lebens nicht an seinem Platze war." Johann Friedrich Rochlitz, "Anekdote aus Mozarts Leben," *AmZ* 1, no. 12 (19 December 1798): 177–80, at 178. In the original context of the anecdote from which this passage is frequently quoted, Rochlitz is most immediately referring to Mozart's composition of the Requiem and to his supposed plans, thwarted by an early death, to revive sacred music.

[10] Rochlitz, "Raphael und Mozart," 651.

[11] See, for example, Christoph Wolf, *Mozart at the Gateway to His Fortune: Serving the Emperor, 1788–1791* (New York: W. W. Norton, 2012).

[12] The influence of romantic "Kunstreligion" on "early nineteenth-century interest in the authorship of Mozart's Requiem" is highlighted in Elizabeth Kramer, "The Idea of Transfiguration in the Early German Reception of Mozart's Requiem," *Current Musicology* 81 (2006): 73–107, at 73. For an extensive examination of the role of art religion in canon formation, see Abigail Fine, *The Composer Embalmed: Relic Culture from Piety to Kitsch* (Chicago: University of Chicago Press, 2025).

OEUVRES COMPLETTES

Between 1791 and 1805, nearly twice as many new Mozart works appeared in print as had been published during the composer's lifetime.[13] Significantly, this figure includes the seventeen volumes of Breitkopf & Härtel's pioneering *Oeuvres complettes de Wolfgang Amadeus Mozart*, released beginning in 1798— i.e., the first serious attempt to publish a musical edition explicitly marketed as the "complete works" of a single composer.[14] Scholars including Maynard Solomon have pointed out that the *Oeuvres complettes de Mozart* was "one of the most profitable ventures in the early history of serious music publishing," a fact that hints at Breitkopf's sensitivity to, and influence on, broader cultural and economic trends.[15] Indeed, for Michael Talbot, Breitkopf's publication of the complete works of Mozart marks the onset not only of an influential new publishing paradigm but also of the "composer-centered" era of Western music history writ large.[16] As a printing and marketing strategy, the *Oeuvres complettes* succeeded so radically because the format played on a new way of conceptualizing and listening to music toward the end of the eighteenth century, fundamentally sorting it—as Talbot points out, and as was discussed in this book's introduction—"according to composer, and not, as previously, according to genre . . . or performer."[17] More than this, the novel attempt to assemble all of the authentic music that a single composer wrote—i.e., implicitly including the grandest of masterpieces alongside the slightest of juvenile and occasional works with relative indifference to repertory status and aesthetic quality—reveals a commitment to a certain historicist species of music-as-truth that was itself rapidly gaining currency in the decades after 1791.

Despite the undeniably remarkable achievement of publishing some 255 individual works by Mozart between 1798 and 1806, Breitkopf & Härtel's *Oeuvres complettes de Mozart* did not go quite this far in practice.[18] In 1799, the firm notably passed up the opportunity to purchase the entire collection of unpublished music manuscripts in Mozart's estate from the composer's widow, Constanze Mozart, née Weber, preferring to instead negotiate publishing rights

---

[13] The ratio is 1.85 to 1. See Gertraut Haberkamp, *Die Erstdrucke der Werke von Wolfgang Amadeus Mozart*, vol. 1 (Tutzing: Hans Schneider, 1986), 13.

[14] Samuel Arnold's pioneering collected edition of G. F. Handel's compositions begun in 1788 does not refer to the plural noun "works," which seems to have been a particular innovation of Breitkopf & Härtel. On this issue, see Michael Talbot, "The Work-Concept and Composer-Centredness," in *The Musical Work: Reality or Invention?*, edited by Michael Talbot (Liverpool: Liverpool University Press, 2000): 168–86, at 171.

[15] Solomon, "The Rochlitz Anecdotes: Issues of Authenticity," 56.

[16] In another measure of the project's success, Breitkopf's *Oeuvres complettes de Mozart* was followed in 1803 by the *Oeuvres complettes de Haydn* and *Oeuvres complettes de Clementi*. See Talbot, "The Work-Concept and Composer-Centredness," 172.

[17] Talbot, "The Work-Concept and Composer-Centredness," 172.

[18] Solomon, "The Rochlitz Anecdotes: Issues of Authenticity," 56.

42   FORGERY IN MUSICAL COMPOSITION

for individual compositions on a case-by-case basis. In her turn, Constanze did not flinch from selling the complete set of manuscripts to rival music publisher Johann Anton André of Offenbach, transferring the Mozart estate to him in an agreement of 8 November 1799 for the bulk sum of 3,150 Viennese gulden, or 700 ducats.[19] The following year, this landmark transaction furnished Constanze and André with a golden opportunity to turn the rhetoric of composer-centered authenticity—and, with it, the ideal of an *Oeuvres complettes de Mozart*—back against Breitkopf, most overtly by means of an open letter of landmark signifi-cance, signed by Constanze and dated 13 March 1800. The text, as printed pub-licly in the *Frankfurter Staats-Ristretto* on 4 April of that year, ran as follows:

> After I had passed on to Messrs. Breitkopf and Härtel in Leipsic against an hon-orarium some few original manuscripts of my late husband . . . for the better-ment of their edition, and after I had sold them the plates of the pianoforte concerto published by me, I voluntarily offered them my entire large collection for sale in one lot. The aforementioned gentlemen, who believed they could not evaluate them at this remove [i.e., from Leipzig], did not avail themselves of my offer. Herr André, who was enabled by his residence here [i.e., in Vienna] to judge the worth and richness of this estate, has since purchased it from me and thus become the sole legal possessor, not so much of a residue, as of an almost complete collection of absolutely accurate and absolutely authentic works in original manuscript from Mozart's earliest youth until his death.[20]

The message behind Constanze's letter is clear enough. André's forthcoming Mozart scores would constitute a "complete collection" of "absolutely accu-rate" and "absolutely authentic" material.[21] Breitkopf & Härtel's, by comparison, would not. Crucially, the latter firm would lack access to the original manuscript sources in the Mozart estate, which Constanze had furnished exclusively to André in November of 1799. As such, Breitkopf & Härtel simply would not be able to offer an *Oeuvres complettes* worthy of the name, spanning—as Constanze and André heavily implied that any such edition should—the years from the composer's "earliest youth until his death."[22]

Unsurprisingly, the insinuation that the *Oeuvres complettes de Mozart* was fated to remain inaccurate, inauthentic, and incomplete when measured against

---

[19] The contract is reproduced in Otto Erich Deutsch, *Mozart: A Documentary Biography*, translated by Eric Blom, Peter Branscombe, and Jeremy Noble (London: Adam & Charles Black, 1966), 490–91; first published as *Mozart: Die Dokumente seines Lebens* (Kassel: Bärenreiter, 1961).

[20] Constanze Mozart, "Erklärung über Mozarts musikalischen Nachlaß," *Frankfurter Staats-Ristretto*, 4 April 1800, 275–76, reprinted with translation in Deutsch, *Mozart: A Documentary Biography*, 495–96.

[21] Deutsch, *Mozart: A Documentary Biography*, 495–96.

[22] Deutsch, *Mozart: A Documentary Biography*, 495–96.

a new, rival Mozart edition explicitly endorsed by the composer's widow found considerable resistance in Breitkopf & Härtel's own house journal, the *AmZ*. In a public clarification written in response to Constanze's open letter, Breitkopf & Härtel themselves state that their firm had voluntarily and deliberately declined to purchase the estate in 1799, having made a considered judgment that "since it consisted primarily of Mozart's well-known or early compositions, we found little if anything that could be meaningful for our edition, or which we did not already possess among our extensive collection of impeccable Mozart works."[23] Breitkopf's central claim was that many if not all of the works in the Mozart estate had already been published or distributed elsewhere and that the few unpublished works exclusively documented in Constanze's manuscripts were "early compositions" [früheren Kompositionen] implied to be of comparatively little value.[24] Thus "Madame Mozart" was "very much in error" in asserting that "Herr André could become the *perfectly lawful* owner of such an *almost complete* collection only if he purchased this collection from *her*."[25] Yet even these lines of reasoning can be seen to contain a subtle confession. The *Oeuvres complettes de Mozart* would aspire to contain everything "meaningful" [bedeutend], everything "impeccable" [ungestochen] and, in short, everything that counted in Mozart's compositional work, at least in Breitkopf & Härtel's judgment. However, in omitting selected "early compositions" and other such supposedly marginal works, there is also an important sense in which the *Oeuvres complettes* could no longer claim to contain literally everything, from beginning to end, without Constanze's willing co-operation.

André is sometimes referred to as "the father of Mozart research" on the basis of the decisive difference in attitude embodied in his 1799 purchase—and not without reason.[26] In the early twenty-first century, an epistemic reverence for manuscript documentation is a basic requirement for anyone editing a serious musical edition. Yet around 1800, André's Mozart editions, the title pages of which proudly claimed to have been prepared "following the original manuscript" [nach dem Original-Manuscripte herausgegeben], put him markedly ahead of the curve with respect to his industry peers, at least when it came to

---

[23] ". . . wir . . . in ihrem obgleich starken Vorrathe von Manuscripten, da er meist aus bekannten oder früheren Kompositionen Mozarts bestand, wenig oder nichts fanden, was für unsere Ausgabe bedeutend gewesen wäre, oder was wir nicht schon unter unserer beträchtlichen Sammlung ungestochener Mozartscher Werke besitzen." Breitkopf & Härtel, "Mozarts Werke," *Intelligenz-Blatt zur Allgemeinen musikalischen Zeitung* 2, no. 12 (2 April 1800): 47–48, at 47.

[24] Breitkopf & Härtel, "Mozarts Werke," 47.

[25] "Hierbey scheint uns Madame Mozart sehr zu irren, wenn sie glaubt, dass Herr André nur dadurch *höchstrechtmäsiger* Besitzer einer solchen *fast vollständigen* Sammlung werden könne, dass er dieselbe von *ihr* erkauft hat." Breitkopf & Härtel, "Mozarts Werke," 47. Emphasis from original text.

[26] Stanley Sadie, ed., *New Grove Dictionary of Music and Musicians* (New York: Oxford University Press, 2001), s.v. "André family."

44   FORGERY IN MUSICAL COMPOSITION

assurances of authenticity.[27] Constanze's and André's claim to have assembled for publication "an almost complete collection of absolutely accurate and absolutely authentic works in original manuscript from Mozart's earliest youth until his death" marks a similar turning point toward an ideal of authenticity centered on the provision of an unabridged and uncorrupted record of an individual composer's works.[28]

Only a few decades before Mozart's death, it would not have been obvious that such a collection would constitute a desirable product, even if it were technically feasible. Yet the ideal of unabridged authenticity has been highly influential. By placing the humorous divertimento *Ein musikalischer Spaß* and the infamously vulgar six-voice canon *Leck mich im Arsch* in an unbroken series that also includes the op. 10 "Haydn" Quartets and *Don Giovanni*, an exhaustive complete works edition or thematic catalogue would seem to assert that each of these compositions has an indispensable part to play in constructing an accurate composite image not just of Mozart's music but also of Mozart himself. Works assembled in such a collection can be seen to aspire to the status of music-historical documents, implicitly inviting one to trace the composer's creative persona and stylistic development throughout the series with the promise that the assembled totality will reveal more than the sum of its parts. Crucially, there is a sense in which the relative aesthetic value of individual works within the complete works edition can be seen to fade into the background when measured against the documentary and biographical truth content that emerges synthetically from a composer's personal canon once considered as a whole. In the completionist imagination, the integrity and authenticity of the collection can thus be understood to transcend the particularity of any individual object within it, no matter how "meaningful" or "impeccable" such objects might appear to be on their own terms.

The emergence of this collective historicist attitude regarding dead composers and their works toward the end of the eighteenth century raised a host of new authenticity problems, both philosophical and practical, as the publishing skirmishes involving Mozart's estate are apt to illustrate. For one thing, it is often maddeningly difficult to determine where a posthumous record that aspires to be both maximally exhaustive and maximally authentic should end. As Foucault elegantly points out in a passage from "What Is an Author?" that could quite easily have been written about Mozart,

> Even when an individual has been accepted as an author, we must still ask whether everything that he wrote, said, or left behind is part of his work. The

---

[27] The most obvious example of this scholarly commitment to authenticity is André's landmark 1827 edition of Mozart's Requiem, with its lengthy editorial preface and use of the initials "M." and "S." to indicate Mozart's and Süssmayr's respective authorship within the score itself.

[28] Constanze Mozart, "Erklärung," 275–76.

problem is both theoretical and technical. When undertaking the publication of Nietzsche's works, for example, where should one stop? Surely everything must be published, but what is "everything"? Everything that Nietzsche himself published, certainly. And what about the rough drafts for his works? Obviously. The plans for his aphorisms? Yes. The deleted passages and the notes at the bottom of the page? Yes. What if, within a workbook filled with aphorisms, one finds a reference, the notation of a meeting or of an address, or a laundry list: is it a work, or not? Why not? And so on, ad infinitum. How can one define a work amid the millions of traces left by someone after his death? A theory of the work does not exist, and the empirical task of those who naively undertake the editing of works often suffers in the absence of such a theory.[29]

This chapter chronicles early musical attempts to navigate the questions raised by Foucault in the months and years following Mozart's death. Inevitably, the narrative centers to a significant extent on the surviving widow Constanze, an enduringly enigmatic if widely discussed character once described by H. C. Robbins Landon as "perhaps the most unpopular woman in music history."[30] Yet, in organizing her late husband's estate and liaising with such presses as Breitkopf, André, and others during the 1790s and 1800s, Constanze did not act alone. She was aided by her second husband, Georg Nikolaus von Nissen, and by a number of Mozart's musical friends, students, and assistants, a group prominently including Abbé Maximilian Stadler and Franz Xaver Süssmayr. Notably, Stadler helped to catalogue the Mozart estate in 1798–99, providing completions of numerous fragmentary manuscripts for publication.[31] When the extent of Süssmayr's compositional contributions to Mozart's Requiem became an international cause célèbre in the 1820s and 1830s, it fell to Stadler to defend the authenticity of the work in print based on his extensive knowledge of Mozart's unpublished manuscripts, not least since Süssmayr—who might have had more definitive answers to such questions—had himself died in 1803.[32]

It bears repeating that Constanze and her various musical advisors have long been figures of ill repute in some quarters of classical music culture. This aura

[29] Michel Foucault, "What Is an Author?," in *Textual Strategies: Perspectives in Post-Structuralist Criticism*, edited by Josué V. Harari (Ithaca, NY: Cornell University Press, 1979): 141–60, at 143–44; first published as "Qu'est-ce qu'un auteur?" *Bulletin de la Société française de philosophie* 63, no. 3 (1969): 73–104.

[30] H. C. Robbins Landon, *Mozart's Last Year, 1791* (New York: Schirmer Books, 1988), 182.

[31] See Deutsch, *Mozart: A Documentary Biography*, 529.

[32] Stadler's contributions to the dispute can be found in Abbé [Maximilian] Stadler, *Vertheidigung der Echtheit des Mozart'schen Requiem* (Vienna: Ben Tendler und von Manstein, 1826); Abbé [Maximilian] Stadler, *Nachtrag zur Vertheidigung der Echtheit des Mozart'schen Requiem* (Vienna: Ben Tendler und von Manstein, 1827); Abbé [Maximilian] Stadler, *Zweyter und letzter Nachtrag zur Vertheidigung der Echtheit des Mozart'schen Requiem* (Vienna: Ben Tendler und von Manstein, 1827).

46 FORGERY IN MUSICAL COMPOSITION

of contempt stems in no small part from the fact that the managers of Mozart's estate are so widely believed to have gone about "defin[ing] a work amid the millions of traces left by someone after his death" irresponsibly.[33] They stand accused of promoting the inauthentic publication under Mozart's name of fragmentary compositions finished posthumously by other often unacknowledged, and presumably inferior, hands. As we shall see, such alleged deception has often been branded "forgery" in ways that necessitate further explanation in the context of this study of that phenomenon and its rise to prominence in the years around 1800.[34]

INAUTHENTICITY, DISTINCT AND INDISTINCT

In what follows, I will focus my analysis on two of the "Mozart" works from the first wave of posthumous publication whose authenticity and compositional quality have been most aggressively called into question: the Requiem Mass in D Minor, K. 626, completed by Süssmayr, and the Minuet and Trio in D Major, K. 355 (576b), completed by Stadler. The radically contrasting genre, compositional scale, and repertory status of the two works in question should be immediately apparent. Indeed, the odd pairing has been selected in part because it is illustrative of two distinct kinds of musical authenticity problem outlined by Wolfgang Plath, one of the leading editorial directors of the Neue Mozart-Ausgabe. In the first place, the Minuet in D Major poses what might be considered an "indistinct authenticity problem" [unspezifische Echtheitsfrage] which, in Plath's terminology, concerns "the periphery of the tradition."[35] Significantly, while Plath freely admits that indistinct authenticity problems at the canon's outer reaches are "numerous," he also finds them "uninteresting" precisely by virtue of that marginal position, ultimately arguing that indistinct authenticity problems pose "no real problem in the true sense."[36] The Requiem, on the other hand, is perhaps the clearest imaginable example of what Plath calls a "distinct authenticity problem" [spezifische Echtheitsfrage], lying—as he explains—at "the *center* of the tradition."[37] In Plath's view, distinct authenticity

[33] Foucault, "What Is an Author?," 144.
[34] See, for example, William Watson and C. B. Oldman, "An Astounding Forgery," *Music & Letters* 8, no. 1 (1927): 61–72; H. C. Robbins Landon, *Mozart's Last Year, 1791* (New York: Schirmer Books, 1988), 163.
[35] "Es gibt Echtheitsfragen an der *Peripherie* der Überlieferung." Wolfgang Plath, "Zur Echtheitsfrage bei Mozart," *Mozart-Jahrbuch 1971/72* (1973): 19–36, at 19.
[36] ". . . sie sind zahlreich, aber uninteressant und stellen kein Problem im eigentlichen Sinne dar." Plath, "Zur Echtheitsfrage bei Mozart," 19.
[37] ". . . die *spezifischen*, nämlich solche, die zumeist im *Zentrum* der Überlieferung liegen." Plath, "Zur Echtheitsfrage bei Mozart," 19. Emphasis from original text.

MOZARTIAN SWAN SONGS   47

problems can thus be identified insofar as they "have a clearly recognizable relationship to Mozart, to the special individuality of his creative process, to his tradition, etc."[38]

For students of compositional forgery, Plath's differentiation between distinct and indistinct authenticity problems has a good deal of explanatory power. There is a reason the authorship of Mozart's Requiem has remained one of the most hotly contested and extensively documented of all music-historical issues over the last two centuries while comparatively little attention has been devoted to similar doubts concerning the authenticity of the Horn Concerto in D Major, K. 412 + 514 (= 386b), the E♭ Major Sinfonia Concertante for Four Winds, K. 297b (Anh. C 14.01), or—for that matter—the Minuet and Trio in D Major, K. 355 (576b).[39] To understand why, one only has to reflect on the stakes. For Rochlitz and for many who have followed him, the Requiem in D Minor is not simply another Mozart work filling out the *Oeuvres complettes* but rather one of art's great "monuments for eternity" [Denkmähler für die Ewigkeit].[40] Imagine the consequences if Jacob Gottfried Weber had been demonstrably correct when he attempted to argue—in an infamous 1825 polemic—that the Requiem can in fact "hardly be called a work of Mozart at all."[41] A host of cherished cultural ideas about the composer and his music would need to be demolished at ground level in order to accommodate the Requiem's absence in ways that would quite frankly be unnecessary for any number of more peripheral works. As Christoph Wolff remarks of the 1825–39 Requiem dispute [Requiemstreit] in which Weber was a key player, there is a compelling sense in which "Nothing less . . . than the integrity of Mozart's genius was at stake" on both sides of the debate.[42] For this reason, no piece of classical music has had its authenticity questioned so extensively, enduringly, and vehemently as Mozart's Requiem while simultaneously maintaining such a central position in

[38] "Sie zeichnen sich dadurch aus, daß sie einen klar erkennbaren Bezug zu Mozart, zu den ganz speziellen Eigentümlichkeiten seiner Schaffensweise, Überlieferung usw. haben." Plath, "Zur Echtheitsfrage bei Mozart," 19.

[39] The first two of these works did attract a spate of significant studies in the 1980s, a decade that saw a marked revival of interest in issues of authenticity and attribution. On the D Major Horn Concerto, see Alan Tyson, *Mozart: Studies of the Autograph Scores* (Cambridge, MA: Harvard University Press, 1987), 246–61. On the E♭ Major Sinfonia Concertante, see John Spitzer, "Musical Attribution and Critical Judgment: The Rise and Fall of the Sinfonia Concertante for Winds, K.297b," *Journal of Musicology* 5, no. 3 (1987): 319–56, and Robert D. Levin, *Who Wrote the Mozart Four-Wind Concertante?* (Hillsdale, NY: Pendragon Press, 1988).

[40] Rochlitz, "Raphael und Mozart," 651.

[41] Jacob Gottfried Weber, "Über die Echtheit des Mozartschen Requiem," *Cäcilia* 3, no. 11 (1825): 205–29, at 205.

[42] Christoph Wolff, *Mozart's Requiem: Historical and Analytical Studies, Documents, Score*, translated by Mary Whittall (Berkeley: University of California Press, 1994), 11; first published as *Mozarts Requiem: Geschichte—Musik—Dokumente—Partitur des Fragments* (Kassel: Bärenreiter Verlag, 1991).

48   FORGERY IN MUSICAL COMPOSITION

the canon and repertory alike, a paradox effectively rendering it the distinct authenticity problem par excellence.

Be all this as it may, there is an important sense in which an uncritical acceptance of Plath's apparent dismissal of indistinct authenticity problems as "uninteresting" would go too far.[43] Under the logic of the complete works edition, it is never truly safe to ignore the inauthenticity of a composition, no matter how insignificant the piece may appear when compared to other elements of a composer's canon. This is especially the case when indistinct authenticity problems are allowed to accumulate in large numbers on the outskirts of a tradition, since a key strength of the complete works edition lies in the utility of a large corpus for comparative authentication. As the body of works used to establish the parameters of a particular composer's style grows, so too does the evidentiary power of acts of authentication made on the basis of those parameters. Nelson Goodman calls any such empirically determined set of hallmarks for understanding an artist's style a "precedent-class," noting that the wrongful adoption of forgeries into a canon often poses an unacknowledged danger—i.e., a corpus that degrades exponentially as forgeries are mistakenly authenticated on the basis of the apparent stylistic "precedent" set by earlier undiscovered forgeries.[44] To be sure, there is a more profound philosophical sense in which any comparative approach to authentication is inescapably circular in any case. Yet, even leaving such imponderable problems of infinite epistemic regress to one side, the danger of indistinct authenticity problems snowballing out of control remains significant. This is particularly clear in the case of the Minuet, K. 355 (576b) to be discussed later in this chapter, a work of small scale in a modest genre that nevertheless appears to constitute one of Mozart's boldest exercises in "outrageous dissonance," relating—for Scott Burnham—"to more normative dance movements of the period as cubist painting relates to conventional portraiture."[45]

For contemporary commentators in the 1790s and 1800s, cultural anxieties about the authenticity of Mozart's posthumously published works often centered precisely on what might now be considered indistinct authenticity problems at the more marginal corners of the tradition. Niemetschek's landmark 1798 account of Mozart's life, for instance, complains that the composer had become a popular target for compositional forgers, being "saddled with many spurious works quite unworthy of his genius."[46] Particular ire is reserved for those "incompetent adapters" who would "patch together piano pieces from his larger works

[43] Plath, "Zur Echtheitsfrage bei Mozart," 19.
[44] Nelson Goodman, *Languages of Art: An Approach to a Theory of Symbols* (Indianapolis: Bobbs-Merrill, 1968), 111.
[45] Scott Burnham, *Mozart's Grace* (Princeton: Princeton University Press, 2013), 92.
[46] Niemetschek, *Life of Mozart*, 79.

MOZARTIAN SWAN SONGS   49

and sell them as though they were originals," even though—so Niemetschek claims—such works "are obviously not in the same class as his genuine piano compositions."[47] Ironically, though Constanze was the principal source of information for Niemetschek's biography and would likely have been pleased to discredit works printed by firms other than André after 1799, the managers of Mozart's estate were themselves hardly above publishing such patchwork pieces as original works. The trio that has always accompanied the Minuet in D, K. 355 (576b)—an addition supplied by Stadler under his own name for the first publication in 1801—might initially have been thought of as a more honest approach to such posthumous completion, though the Neue Mozart-Ausgabe's editorial report regards as "plausible" the thesis that Stadler composed a substantial section of the minuet too, adapting the work from a fragment originally intended not for the keyboard, but for string quartet.[48] Still less transparent was the 1797 publication of Mozart's Piano Trio in D Minor, K. 442, in an edition printed by André which, crucially, failed to disclose the fact that the purported "piano trio" was in reality comprised of three unrelated compositional fragments finished by Stadler after Mozart's death.[49] Similar criticisms could be leveled against the first published edition of Mozart's Violin Sonata, K. 402, which in 1801 appeared as "Sonata I" in Breitkopf's *Oeuvres complettes de Mozart* with no indication that this, too, was nothing more or less than a Mozartian fragment completed posthumously by Stadler. Numerous other such posthumously completed works, finished by Stadler and others, could be mentioned from the same era.[50] In Niemetschek's assessment, written less than a decade after the composer's death, the net result was a situation in which "absolute havoc is now being wrought with [Mozart's] works."[51]

It was not only learned critics such as Niemetschek and Weber who took umbrage with the apparent wave of phony "Mozart" publications that appeared in the wake of the real Mozart's untimely death. Composers who discovered that their own works were being printed and sold under Mozart's name without their consent were equally keen to object, if for somewhat different reasons. For example, in July and August of 1798, Anton Eberl—a Viennese musician then

---

[47] Niemetschek, *Life of Mozart*, 79.

[48] Ulrich Konrad, Neue Mozart-Ausgabe X/30/4 (Kassel: Bärenreiter Verlag, 2002), 276. The 1801 first printing by T. Mollo of Vienna is RISM A/I, M 7158.

[49] For extensive details on the manuscript sources and publication history for this work, see Wolf-Dieter Seiffert's preface and critical report to the Henle Urtext edition in W. A. Mozart, *Drei Sätze für Klaviertrio: Fragmente KV 442* (Munich: G. Henle Verlag, 2019), V–VIII, 91–100.

[50] For an account of Stadler's contributions specifically, see Ludwig Finscher, "Maximilian Stadler und Mozarts Nachlaß," *Mozart-Jahrbuch 1960/61* (1961): 168–72. Perhaps the most famous Stadler completion of a Mozart fragment is the Fantasy in C Minor, K. 396 (385f); first published in 1802, once more under Mozart's name alone. On this Mozart fragment and Stadler's completion of it, see Richard Kramer, *Unfinished Music* (New York: Oxford University Press, 2008), 317–22.

[51] Niemetschek, *Life of Mozart*, 79.

50 FORGERY IN MUSICAL COMPOSITION

employed abroad in St. Petersburg—had a letter published in several North German newspapers in which he complained that "3 works composed by myself," i.e., two sets of variations for the pianoforte and a Sonata in C Minor, "have already appeared in various music-shops under the name of the unforgettable Mozart."[52] Acts of plagiarism of this ilk naturally put Eberl and others like him in the doubly difficult position of losing out on the financial royalties and the notoriety of authorship that might have been gained from his music. "[H]owever flattering it may be for me that even connoisseurs were capable of judging these works to be the products of Mozart, I can"—writes Eberl, having made all due deference—"in no wise allow the musical public to remain under this delusion."[53]

There were, as we have seen, good reasons for these concerns expressed by Niemetschek, Weber, and Eberl. By the 1790s, artificially inflating a supply of compositions to meet increased demand after a composer's death by passing off posthumously completed fragments, forgeries, and even outright plagiarized works as unadulterated originals was nothing new; the practice can be dated back some three centuries through Pergolesi and Josquin to the origins of music printing itself.[54] Nonetheless, several important new contextual factors led to significant changes in musical authenticity culture in the decades following 1791. It is no mere coincidence that posthumously published Mozart works were so frequently called into question in the 1790s and 1800s, nor that—in the 1820s and 1830s especially—the Requiem in D Minor became "the first work" by any composer "to be subject in our modern sense to a most rigorous scrutiny regarding both sources and style" in ways which, for Christoph Wolff, remain "intimately related ... to the origins of our discipline."[55]

One undeniably significant element was the burgeoning public discourse of music criticism carried out in such journals as the *AmZ* (founded 1798), and— somewhat later—*The Harmonicon* (founded 1823), the *Berliner musikalische Zeitung* (founded 1824), *Cäcilia* (founded 1824), and the *Revue musicale* (founded 1827). Many of these specialized outlets furnished authors with the novel opportunity to publish examples set in staff notation alongside their prose, thus providing a large forum in which the authenticity of musical compositions could be contested in close analytical terms. Indeed, all of these journals published substantial essays on the Requiem's authenticity during the height of the *Requiemstreit*, from 1825 to 1839. Another important factor, already alluded

---

[52] Anton Eberl, "Suum cuique," *Allgemeiner litterarischer Anzeiger* no. 136, 28 August 1798, col. 1373–75, at 1373–74. Reprinted from *Hamburger unpartheyischer Correspondent* No. 118, 15 July 1798. English translation in Deutsch, *Mozart: A Documentary Biography*, 487. The Sonata in C Minor was subsequently republished, with the correct attribution, as Eberl's opus 1.

[53] Eberl, "Suum cuique," col. 1374.

[54] See, for example, Kate van Orden, *Music, Authorship, and the Book in the First Century of Print* (Berkeley: University of California Press, 2014).

[55] Christoph Wolff, "Review," *19th-Century Music* 15, no. 2 (1991): 162–65, at 165.

to, was the broader turn toward composer-centeredness in the first quarter of the nineteenth century. This is vital in part because, when combined with a broad cultural fascination with the ideal of genius and an escalating sacralization of great works of art, composer-centeredness increasingly led commentators to frame compositional misattribution and forgery not merely as unsavory business practices but also as profoundly immoral acts bordering, in some cases, on the sacrilegious.

Consider the aforementioned Anton Eberl's 1798 warning about the publication of his own compositions under Mozart's name. While Eberl's original letter studiously avoids pointing the finger at any parties guilty of misattributing his works, passing up the opportunity to speculate about the intentions that might have led such persons to an act that occurred "either inadvertently or for other reasons unknown to me," the tone of the commentary supplied to the wronged composer's missive for the Leipzig reprint by the editorship of the *Allgemeiner litterarischer Anzeiger* is not nearly so diplomatic:

> We emphasize this intelligence . . . in the express hope that sundry persons may . . . be moved to pursue further these thefts, the more so as . . . Mozart's widow has so little respect for her late husband's ashes that she not only willingly offers her support to all such unlawful dealings, but moreover was not ashamed to make similar proposals to a famous composer in Leipsic.[56]

The casual, unsubstantiated implication that Constanze may have been responsible not only for the theft of Eberl's intellectual property but also for many similar such acts of compositional plagiarism reveals a great deal about how negatively she came to be perceived in the years following Mozart's death. No evidence about the "famous composer in Leipsic" supposedly propositioned by "Mozart's widow" to lend compositions to her deceased husband is provided. And the manner in which Constanze's behavior in publishing putatively inauthentic works under Mozart's name is equated with a lack of appropriate widowlike respect "for her late husband's ashes" clearly suggests that more than just publishing rights are at stake in the complaint. For some commentators in the decades after Mozart's death, Constanze's power over the Mozart estate and reasonable desire to profit from it were at odds with an increasing tendency to regard Mozart's compositions not as ephemeral commodities, but rather—to return to Rochlitz's phrasing—as "monuments for eternity."[57]

---

[56] Eberl, "Suum cuique," col. 1374–75.
[57] Rochlitz, "Raphael und Mozart," 651.

52 FORGERY IN MUSICAL COMPOSITION

ROCHLITZ'S VISIONARY MOZART

This monumental attitude toward the authenticity, durability, and cultural significance of Mozart's compositions owes much to a particular set of nineteenth-century beliefs about how his works were created. The document most emblematic of this issue is a letter from the composer to an unnamed baron and musical amateur published posthumously, on 23 August 1815, in the *AmZ*, which Rochlitz edited.[58] In the century following its publication, the letter to the anonymous baron became, in Otto Erich Deutsch's words, "the most frequently quoted of all Mozart's letters."[59] As early as 1824 Goethe and Zelter discuss the "golden" letter "from Mozart to the baron" in their correspondence.[60] Thereafter, the text was cited as evidence of Mozart's creative process by commentators as diverse as German philosopher of the unconscious Eduard von Hartmann, American Quaker theologian Rufus M. Jones, and Austrian music theorist Heinrich Schenker.[61] The interest provoked by the *AmZ* letter is not difficult to understand when one considers its content, since, in the most widely circulated excerpt, Mozart appears to provide unusually detailed and lucid first-person commentary on his compositional process. Eschewing substantial reference to techniques of harmony, counterpoint, orchestration, and other such workaday composerly disciplines, the Mozart letter instead harps at length on a moment of ineffable inspiration followed by a process of unconscious imaginative elaboration:

> When I am, as it were, completely myself, entirely alone, and of good cheer; say travelling in a carriage, or walking after a good meal, or during the night, when I cannot sleep; it is on such occasions that my ideas flow best and most abundantly. *Whence* and *how* they come I know not, nor can I force them. Those ideas that please me, I retain in my memory, and am accustomed, as I have been told, to hum them to myself. If I continue in this way, it soon occurs to me, how I may turn this or that morsel to account, so as to make a good dish of

---

[58] [Johann Friedrich Rochlitz?], "Schreiben Mozarts an den Baron von . . ," *Allgemeine musikalische Zeitung* 17, no. 34 (1815): 561–66.

[59] Otto Erich Deutsch, "Spurious Mozart Letters," *Music Review* 25, no. 2 (1964): 120–23, at 121.

[60] Gerhard Fricke, ed., *Briefwechsel zwischen Goethe und Zelter* (Nürnberg: H. Carl, 1949), letter from Zelter dated December 1824.

[61] Eduard von Hartmann, *Philosophie des Unbewußten*, 10th ed. (Leipzig: Wilhelm Friedrich, 1897), 248; Rufus M. Jones, *Studies in Mystical Religion* (London: Macmillan, 1909); Heinrich Schenker, *Free Composition*, vol. 1, translated and edited by Ernst Oster, with commentary by Oswald Jonas (Hillsdale, NY: Pendragon Press, 1977), 129; first published as *Der freie Satz* (Vienna: Universal Edition, 1935). Extensive documentation of the many reprints and citations of the letter—including those listed here—can be found in Deutsch, "Spurious Mozart Letters," 121–22, and Joseph Heinz Eibl, "Ein Brief Mozarts über seine Schaffensweise?," *Österreichische Musikzeitschrift* 35 (1980): 578–93, at 581.

it, that is to say, agreeably to the rules of counter-point, to the peculiarities of the various instruments, &c. All this fires my soul, and provided I am not disturbed, my subject enlarges itself, becomes methodized and defined, and the whole, though it be long, stands almost finished and complete in my mind, so that I can survey it, like a fine picture or a beautiful statue, at a glance. Nor do I hear in my imagination the parts *successively*, but I hear them, as it were, all at once (*gleich alles zusammen.*) What a delight this is I cannot tell! All this inventing, this producing, takes place, as it were, in a pleasing lively dream.... What has been thus produced I do not easily forget, and this is, perhaps, the best gift I have my Divine Maker to thank for.[62]

This literary depiction of Mozart's artistic process makes for compelling reading in no small part because the *AmZ* letter is so rich in metaphor. Having broached the possibility of a musical equivalent to the totalizing atemporal conceptions of artistic form familiar in such visual arts as painting and sculpture, the letter's author can be seen to play on the ideals of intuitive imagination and organic unity of design that became cornerstones of romantic and modernist aesthetic cultures in the nineteenth century and thereafter. A genius of Mozart's caliber is understood to envision a work almost pre-compositionally in this context, as if given the music in its germinal stage by nature or divinity in a manner reminiscent of Schenker's "fundamental structure" [Ursatz], or what Arnold Schoenberg would term the "lightning-strike idea" [blitzartige Einfall].[63] Crucially, for the Mozart of the *AmZ* letter, there is little need for conscious development, editing, or revision of musical material after the initial flash of inspiration. Even the process of making "a good dish" with respect to "the rules of counter-point, the peculiarities of the various instruments, &c" happens in a largely unconscious fashion, before the composer's pen has touched parchment, as if still inhabiting "a pleasing, lively dream."[64] What remains, at the end of things, is the merely mechanical necessity of setting the notes down on the staff, something which can inevitably be accomplished at significant speed, since "every thing is ... already finished; and it rarely differs on paper, from what it was in my imagination."[65]

In the original *AmZ* issue the letter appeared with an editorial foreword which telegraphs its authenticity, hinting at the existence of an autograph source by claiming that "something of this nature must be printed with diplomatic

---

[62] [Johann Friedrich Rochlitz?], "Letter of W. A. Mozart, to the Baron V—," translated by J. R. S[chult]z, *Harmonicon* 3, no. 35 (1825): 198–200, at 199; first published as "Schreiben Mozarts an den Baron von ...," *Allgemeine musikalische Zeitung* 17, no. 34 (1815): 561–66.

[63] Arnold Schoenberg, "Inspiration," translated by Wayne Shoaf, *Serial: Newsletter of the Friends of the Arnold Schoenberg Institute* 1, no. 1 (1987): 3, cont. 7.

[64] [Rochlitz?], "Letter of W. A. Mozart," 199.

[65] [Rochlitz?], "Letter of W. A. Mozart," 199.

54 FORGERY IN MUSICAL COMPOSITION

precision, or not at all."[66] The foreword to the 1825 English reprint in the *Harmonicon* goes further, alluding to the existence of both stylistic and source-based evidence for authenticity: an explicit reference to the "original" copy is made before the editor adds that "the letter itself" bears "such strong interval evidence of its being Mozart's [that] there cannot remain the slightest doubt on the subject."[67] Yet, evocative and influential as this letter may be, the uncomfortable academic consensus today is that the publication was and remains a literary forgery, with the supposed "Mozart" text very likely produced by Rochlitz himself.[68] Of the numerous scholars to reach this conclusion, Deutsch supplies an impeccably clear and concise summary of the evidence:

> The letter gives itself away by the use of words and expressions that are definitely Saxon: the writer is not up to Viennese or Salzburg dialects. He calls Mozart's wife Constanze "Männerl," which Mozart would never have done: he claims to have asked her father for her hand in marriage whereas in fact the father was no longer alive: for Barbara he writes Bärbel instead of Betty, *etc*. It is probable, almost certain, that the letter is an invention of Rochlitz's, and what he says about Mozart's manner of composition does him much credit.[69]

Deutsch's debunking of spurious music-historical sources is exemplary. Yet there is something puzzling about this final sentence. While the first clause declares one of the most widely cited documents in early Mozart biography to be a literary forgery, the second seamlessly pivots to applaud the creditability of the suspected forger's fabulations about Mozart's creativity. Strikingly, the dialectical tension between the two sides of the central comma is passed over in silence. Oswald Jonas makes a similarly abrupt pivoting maneuver in defending the forged letter's prominence in Schenker's explanation of fundamental structure, noting—in the commentary supplied for the revised English edition of *Free Composition*—that although the 1815 *AmZ* publication "is generally thought to be a forgery by Rochlitz," the "content and manner of expression point toward the possibility that it may record words spoken by Mozart."[70] Here Jonas

---

[66] "So etwas muß mit diplomatischer Genauigkeit gedruckt werden, oder gar nicht." [Rochlitz?], "Schreiben Mozarts," 561.

[67] [Rochlitz?], "Letter of W. A. Mozart," 199.

[68] Deutsch, "Spurious Mozart Letters," 121; Eibl, "Ein Brief Mozarts über seine Schaffensweise?," 584–85; Maynard Solomon, "On Beethoven's Creative Process: A Two-Part Invention," *Music & Letters* 61, nos. 3–4 (1980): 272–83, at 275–77. It should be added that in 1828, the letter was already filed as "apocryphal" in Georg Nikolaus von Nissen, *Biographie W. A. Mozart's* (Leipzig: Breitkopf & Härtel, 1828), appendix XXI. Moreover, Otto Jahn questioned the authenticity of the letter as early as the 1850s but stopped short of calling it a forgery in its totality, clarifying: "I do not assume that the whole letter is forged; probably at its basis was a Mozart letter which was reworked." See Otto Jahn, *W. A. Mozart*, vol. 3 (Leipzig: 1856–59), 496–505.

[69] Deutsch, "Spurious Mozart Letters," 121.

[70] Commentary to Schenker, *Free Composition*, vol. 1, 129, n3.

is significantly more moderate than Schenker himself, who went to great lengths to defend the *AmZ* text's authenticity in a characteristically fervent 1931 article, claiming, "All doubts as to the authenticity of the letter must give way to the certainty that this divine message is neither forged nor revised, that it can stem from no other than Mozart himself!"[71] As Nicholas Cook aptly points out, for Schenker "the letter *must* be authentic because what it says is true."[72] Yet, even commentators fully aware of the document's inauthenticity have shown a surprising willingness to regard the forged *AmZ* letter almost as a music-historical version of the infamous "noble lie" at the heart of Plato's *Republic*.[73] While the letter itself may be false, the foundational vision it supports is often taken to be true and good enough that the deception can be brushed aside or otherwise politely overlooked.

Maynard Solomon is perhaps the greatest exception in this regard, suggesting outright that the motive for Rochlitz's numerous biographical falsifications was, at least in part, pecuniary. It is no mere coincidence that Breitkopf & Härtel, the first press to attempt to print the complete works of Mozart, was also the publisher of the *AmZ* and hence of both the forged 1815 letter and Rochlitz's *Verbürgte Anekdoten*, a series of documents in which, for Solomon, "biographical truth became a casualty of commercial enterprise and editorial vanity."[74] In his frank estimation, both "the circulation of Mozart's works and the financial health of Breitkopf & Härtel were well served" by Rochlitz's biographical campaign, not least because the *AmZ*'s Mozart anecdotes often functioned to discredit other presses, whose Mozart editions are not infrequently described within Rochlitz's anecdotes as both "worthless" and "unauthentic."[75]

This stance of editorial superiority is clearly present in Rochlitz's 1801 *AmZ* review of the first published edition of the Requiem in D Minor—i.e., Breitkopf & Härtel's 1800 printing of the score under Mozart's name alone.[76] The press's decision to present the Requiem as a work completed by Mozart and only Mozart— as suggested by the paratexts reproduced in figure 1.1—was wholly in line with Rochlitz's biographical assertion, in his *AmZ* anecdote published 19 December 1798, that Mozart had brought this "perfect work [the Requiem] to completion" in life; as the anecdote has it, "even before the four weeks were over [i.e., the deadline given by the gray messenger who brings Mozart the commission

---

[71] Heinrich Schenker, "Ein verschollener Brief von Mozart und das Geheimnis seines Schaffens," *Der Kunstwart* 44 (July 1931): 660–66, at 666. Translation from Nicholas Cook, *The Schenker Project: Culture, Race, and Music Theory in Fin-de-siècle Vienna* (New York: Oxford University Press, 2007), 68.

[72] Cook, *The Schenker Project*, 68. Emphasis from original text.

[73] Plato, *Republic*, Book 3, 414ff.

[74] Solomon, "The Rochlitz Anecdotes: Issues of Authenticity," 59.

[75] Solomon, "The Rochlitz Anecdotes: Issues of Authenticity," 59, 57.

[76] W. A. Mozarti, *Missa pro defunctis Requiem* (Leipzig: Breitkopf & Härtel, 1800).

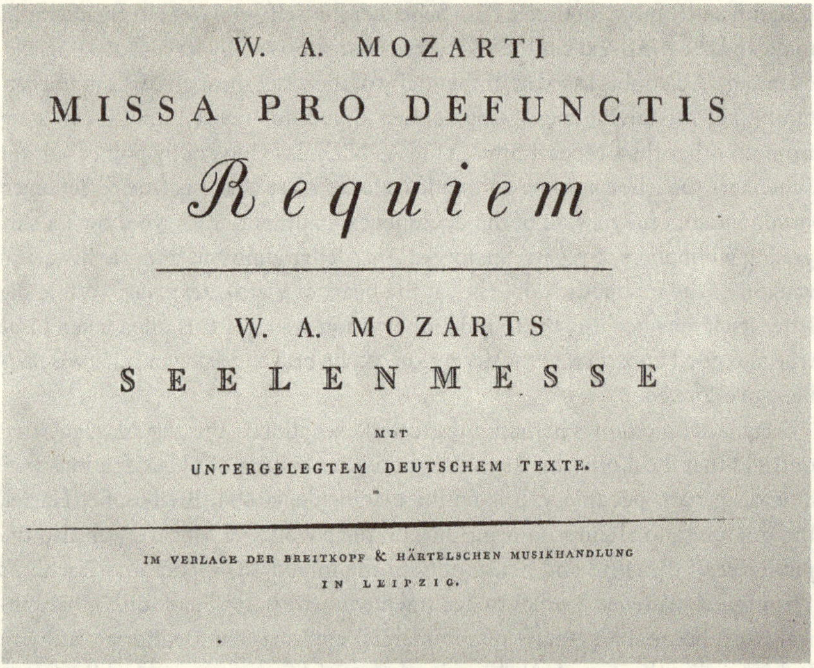

56 FORGERY IN MUSICAL COMPOSITION

Figure 1.1 W. A. Mozart, *Requiem* (Leipzig: Breitkopf & Härtel, 1800), Title Page. Allen A. Brown Collection of Music, Boston Public Library

for the Requiem in Rochlitz's account], he [Mozart] was finished, but he had also passed away."[77] Yet Rochlitz's widely circulated version of events was itself a marked departure not only from Niemetschek's 1798 biography but also from Schlichtegroll's extended obituary of 1793, both of which describe the Requiem as incomplete at the time of Mozart's death.[78] Readers of these conflicting biographical accounts who came across Breitkopf's publication of the Requiem in 1800 would have been well justified in wondering which story was true. For one thing, if Niemetschek and Schlichtegroll were correct that death had snatched the pen from Mozart's hand, then the exclusive attribution to him, as shown in figure 1.1, could not possibly be wholly what it appeared. With this in mind, Rochlitz's forged letter of 1815—with its insistence on Mozart's visionary ability to create unified works made "almost finished and complete in [his] mind" before committing them to paper—retrospectively illuminates the author's earlier

[77] Johann Friedrich Rochlitz, "Anekdote aus Mozarts Leben," *AmZ* 1, no. 12 (19 December 1798): 177–80, at 178. For a full English translation of the anecdote with critical commentary see Solomon, "The Rochlitz Anecdotes: Issues of Authenticity," 33–36.
[78] Niemetschek, *Life of Mozart*, 42–5; Schlichtegroll, *Nekrolog*, 108.

statements, from the 1798 anecdote and 1801 review, about the compositional integrity of the Requiem.[79]

Significantly, Rochlitz's review, co-authored with Christian Schwenke, was the first venue in which Süssmayr's letter to Breitkopf & Härtel, clarifying his role in the composition at their request, was published, thus bolstering with specific musical evidence the idea that Mozart had left the Requiem incomplete.[80] Given that this new evidence came from the self-proclaimed completer himself, it is unsurprising that Rochlitz—still absolutely committed to the idea that Mozart finished the Requiem with the possible exception of minor details of orchestration—devotes substantial space and energy to debunking Süssmayr's missive. The letter from Süssmayr, cited extensively in Rochlitz and Schwenke's review, opens in a strikingly confessional and self-deprecatory tone:

> I owe too much to the teaching of that great man to stand by silently and allow a work to be published as his, when the greater part of it is mine, for I am convinced that my work is unworthy of his great name. Mozart's oeuvre is so unique and, I venture to say, so far beyond the reach of the great majority of living composers that any imitator, and especially one who claimed Mozart as the author of his work, would cut an even worse figure than the notorious raven which dressed itself in peacock's feathers.[81]

Just as the roguish youth impersonates the song of the nightingale in Kant's third critique, so too does the self-described "raven" Süssmayr impersonate the "peacock" Mozart in this analogy. Aesop's well-known fable of envy and imposture is elegantly evoked in response to the prospect of Breitkopf's publication of the Requiem as a finished work by Mozart despite it being, in Süssmayr's own view, "unworthy of his great name."[82] Indeed, there is a compelling sense in which Süssmayr's strange task of arguing that he had composed music of which he was thought incapable mirrors the forger van Meegeren's task of demonstrating that he was capable of painting works previously attributed to Vermeer, as discussed in the introductory chapter of this book.

---

[79] [Rochlitz?], "Letter of W. A. Mozart, to the Baron V—," 199.

[80] [Johann Friedrich Rochlitz and Christian Schwenke], "Recension: W. A. Mozarti Missa pro Defunctis Requiem," *AmZ* 4, no. 1–2 (1801): 1–11, cont. 23–31.

[81] Franz Xaver Süssmayr, "Letter to Breitkopf & Härtel, February 8, 1800," in Christoph Wolff, *Mozart's Requiem: Historical and Analytical Studies, Documents, Score*, translated by Mary Whittall (Berkeley: University of California Press, 1994), 145–46, at 145; first published in [Rochlitz and Schwenke], "Recension," 2–3.

[82] While the object of imposture in the tale is always a peacock, the humble bird doing the imitating differs depending on which version of Aesop one consults. In the most influential English-language edition, folklorist Joseph Jacobs indexes the fable in question as No. 21, under the title "The Jay and the Peacock." See Joseph Jacobs, ed., *The Fables of Æsop* (London: Macmillan, 1894).

58   FORGERY IN MUSICAL COMPOSITION

Providing specifics about the extent of his work on the composition, Süssmayr claims to have finished the orchestration for "the 'Requiem' [Introit] with Kyrie, 'Dies irae' [sequence], and 'Domine Jesu Christe,'" for which Mozart completed just "the 4 vocal parts and the figured bass," leaving "only the motivic idea here and there" for the remaining instrumental parts.[83] Additionally, Süssmayr goes on to assert that in the "Dies irae" [sequence], it fell to him to complete not only the instrumental parts, but the entirety of the music after the line "qua resurget ex favilla" [in fact, one line later, from after "judicandus homo reus"]—i.e., in effect, everything after m. 8 of the Lacrimosa movement until the beginning of the Domine Jesu.[84] Finally, the sections of the Requiem that Mozart did not begin to write down in the surviving scores now known to us—namely, the settings of the "Sanctus, Benedictus, and Agnus Dei"—were, as Süssmayr puts it, "wholly composed by me" [ganz neu von mir verfertigt].[85]

The mainstream of modern scholarship has endorsed the basic outline of Süssmayr's own statements about his role in the composition of the Requiem, albeit with some notable exceptions and disputes concerning points of detail.[86] For Christoph Wolff, Süssmayr's letter of 1800 is "rightly" regarded as "the most important and most reliable testimony to [his] part in the Requiem," while Simon Keefe writes that the document is able "in general to stand the test of scrutiny" based on "what we now know for certain."[87] Alfred Einstein was even more accepting of Süssmayr's account of the extent of his role in the composition.[88] Yet, in their original 1801 commentary on Süssmayr's letter, Rochlitz and Schwenke make it absolutely clear from the outset that they consider the document to be highly suspect, primarily for musical reasons rooted in the composition itself.

[83] Süssmayr, "Letter to Breitkopf & Härtel, February 8, 1800," 146.

[84] Süssmayr, "Letter to Breitkopf & Härtel, February 8, 1800," 146.

[85] Süssmayr, "Letter to Breitkopf & Härtel, February 8, 1800." Süssmayr's final statement about his apparent authorship of the Sanctus, Benedictus, and Agnus Dei has been a subject of considerable academic debate. The translation into English of this last phrase, "ganz neu von mir verfertigt," is particularly fraught, since it is difficult to preserve the precise semantic ambiguities of Süssmayr's text once rendered out of his original German. The verb "verfertigen" can mean "to compose," in the sense that Süssmayr wrote those movements entirely from scratch. But "verfertigen" can also mean "to put together" in a more general sense, which might instead suggest that Süssmayr assembled the Sanctus, Benedictus, and Agnus Dei based on a collection of unpreserved Mozart sketches or oral instructions received either directly from the composer or indirectly via his widow. In defense of this latter interpretation of Süssmayr's letter, see, for example, Friedrich Blume, "Requiem but No Peace," translated by Nathan Broder, *Musical Quarterly* 47, no. 2 (1961): 147–69, at 159.

[86] In the twentieth- and twenty-first centuries as in the nineteenth, skeptics of Süssmayr's testimony have included both those who claim he wrote far less of the Requiem than he confessed in 1800, and those who claim, by contrast, that he wrote far more of it. Friedrich Bloom, for whom "not Süssmayr but Mozart must be considered in essentials the composer of the Sanctus with *Pleni*, Benedictus, and *Osanna* as well as the Agnus," is perhaps the most influential among the former group. See Blume, "Requiem but No Peace," 159.

[87] Wolff, *Mozart's Requiem*, 16. Simon P. Keefe, *Mozart's Requiem: Reception, Work, Completion* (Cambridge: Cambridge University Press, 2012), 176.

[88] Alfred Einstein, ed., *Chronologisch-Thematisches Verzeichnis Sämtlicher Tonwerke W. A. Mozarts,* 3rd ed. (Ann Arbor: J. W. Edwards, 1947), 808ff.

In Rochlitz and Schwenke's eyes, Süssmayr simply could not "have played a larger role" in the Requiem's creation than providing the "at times highly faulty instrumental accompaniment."[89] To be sure, the pair of *AmZ* reviewers considered apparent shortcomings in the orchestration—including m. 20 in the Tuba Mirum; mm. 32–43 in the Domine Jesu; mm. 4–5, m. 20, m. 41, and m. 50 in the Hostias; m. 5 in the Sanctus, "and many others"—as in themselves sufficient to demonstrate that "not everything flowed from M[ozart]'s quill exactly as it appears on the page."[90] Yet, leaving issues of deficient instrumentation to one side, the idea that Süssmayr had completed a Lacrimosa that had been left wholly unfinished by Mozart after m. 8 was highly implausible as far as Rochlitz and Schwenke were concerned. In their review, the pair find the latter part of that movement to be especially praiseworthy, above all singling out its achingly chromatic "modulation to F Major"—i.e., the radiant relative partner of the home key of D minor—across mm. 15–19, as illustrated by example 1.1.[91] Rochlitz and Schwenke go on to write that they consider this section to be "very beautiful, picturesque, and expressive of pious sensibility" in its hushed, *piano* setting of the text "Huic ergo parce Deus, Pie Jesu Domine" [Spare, O God, in mercy spare him, Lord all pitying, Jesu blest].[92]

Listening closely to the passage in example 1.1, it is not difficult to understand what Rochlitz and Schwenke meant in their favorable assessment of 1801. On the downbeat of m. 15, a maximally ambiguous diminished seventh chord built above the tonic pitch, D, begins the anguished plea to the father for mercy, at "Huic." By the end of m. 16 (at "Deus"), this chord has been transfigured— through a process of chromatic voice exchange—into what will soon come to function as an augmented sixth sonority in the oncoming relative key of F major. It is left to the music of mm. 17–19 to resolve the augmented sixth chord and lock the emerging F major tonal center into place, a modulatory process in which the textual turn toward Christ, "Pie Jesu Domine," is elegantly aligned with the movement's first major-mode perfect authentic cadence (PAC) at m. 19. The realization of this seamless transition between poignant chromatic unease (mm. 15–16) and the comfort of eternal salvation (mm. 17–19) far transcends the cliché madrigalist techniques that one might expect from a mediocre composer seeking to modulate to the relative major at this moment in the Requiem setting. Presumably it is passages such as this that Rochlitz and Schwenke find to be

---

[89] [Rochlitz and Schwenke], "Recension," 4.

[90] [Rochlitz and Schwenke], "Recension," 3.

[91] [Rochlitz and Schwenke], "Recension," 25.

[92] "S. 92, Takt 4 und S. 93 befindet sich wieder eine sehr schöne, mahlerische, ganz die fromme Empfindung ausdrückende Modulation nach f dur." [Rochlitz and Schwenke], "Recension," 25. The pagination and measure numbering here and in subsequent citations refer to the specific 1800 edition under review.

60 FORGERY IN MUSICAL COMPOSITION

Example 1.1 W. A. Mozart, Requiem in D minor, K. 626, in the traditional completion by F. X. Süssmayr. Piano-vocal score by Friedrich Brissler. Lacrimosa, mm. 10–19

Example 1.1 Continued

62 FORGERY IN MUSICAL COMPOSITION

Example 1.1 Continued

Example 1.2 W. A. Mozart, Requiem in D minor, K. 626, in the traditional completion by F. X. Süssmayr. Piano-vocal score by Friedrich Brissler. Sanctus, mm. 1–8

64   FORGERY IN MUSICAL COMPOSITION

Example 1.2 Continued

"unreachable not only for the majority of composers now living, but perhaps all of them," Süssmayr included.[93]

In Rochlitz and Schwenke's assessment, Süssmayr's claim to have "wholly composed" the "Sanctus, Benedictus, and Agnus Dei" is just as far beyond belief as his assertion that he had provided the aforementioned conclusion to the Lacrimosa. Consider, for instance, the Sanctus: a movement frequently attacked by critics who believe it to have been written by Süssmayr, but which the original *AmZ* reviewers nonetheless describe as "a true relic, full of elevated innocence, splendor, and dignity."[94]

Rochlitz and Schwenke's comments on this movement are best illustrated with reference to example 1.2, which reproduces an excerpt from the Sanctus's famous D-major opening section. In their *AmZ* review of 1801, the pair single out the bass C♮ on the downbeat of m. 6 as an especially praiseworthy and creative way to begin setting the new phrase "Pleni sunt Caeli et terra gloria tua" [Heaven and earth are full of Thy glory]. Technically speaking, this downbeat chromatic inflection on "Pleni" [full, abundant] follows hard on the heels of the phrase-ending tutti half cadence (HC) in m. 5, in which the terminal dominant chord is sung on the word "Sabaoth." Entering in soli unisono, the basses abruptly cancel the diatonic leading tone, C♯, proclaimed by the tenors in the preceding bar, thereby wrenching the music in rich new contrapuntal directions that transcend the unison D-major pomp of the Sanctus's opening five measures. "Which mortal," ask Rochlitz and Schwenke, "has announced the peace of the undying one and his immeasurable magnificence more powerfully than is achieved with the C in m. 6 and what follows?"[95]

Yet, for all their rapturous praise of the passage in example 1.2, Rochlitz and Schwenke decline to comment in detail on the Sanctus's infamous registrally accented parallel fifths, G–D, F♯–C♯, E–B, D–A, emerging from the curious leaping figuration of the linear first-inversion sonorities in the instrumental parts underscoring "Dominus Deus" in m. 4, just two bars before the "powerful" and "magnificent" bass C♮ annunciation on "Pleni."[96] Beckmesserish ridicule of this apparent contrapuntal faux pas has echoed down the centuries since Rochlitz's contemporary Frederik Samuel Silverstolpe first commented on it explicitly, writing—in a memoir composed within the same year that Breitkopf's score and the *AmZ*'s

[93] "Dass Mozarts Komposition zum Requiem einzig und eine ähnliche nicht nur dem grösten Theile, sondern vielleicht allen jezt lebenden Tonsetzern unerreichbar seyn möge, glaubt Rec. Vollkommen." [Rochlitz and Schwenke], "Recension," 3.

[94] ". . . ein wirkliches Heilig, voll hoher Einfalt, Pracht und Würde." [Rochlitz and Schwenke], "Recension," 28.

[95] "Welche Sterbliche hat die Ruhe des Unendlichen und seine unermessliche Fülle kräftiger verkündet, als es hier durch das im Einklange verstärkte C S.130, Takt 3 und weiter—geschieht?" [Rochlitz and Schwenke], "Recension," 28.

[96] The page and measure numbers are, however, listed in Rochlitz and Schwenke's long opening catalogue of "error-ridden instrumental accompaniment."

66 FORGERY IN MUSICAL COMPOSITION

review were published—"For my part, I cannot think of any reason why Mozart should have introduced these solecisms."[97] Naturally in subsequent accounts it has been Süssmayr, and not Mozart, who is the target of such critical remarks. Ultimately, as Rochlitz and Schwenke's review concludes: "It is highly plausible that a substantial part of the instrumental accompaniment must be attributed to Herr Süssmayer [sic]; yet the compositions we already know under Herr Süssmayer's name make a powerful rebuke against the idea that he could have played a larger role in this great work."[98]

For Rochlitz and for many of the commentators who have written about the Requiem since 1801, the relative plausibility of Süssmayr's involvement in the composition hangs not only on the perceived quality of the work itself but also on a set of beliefs about how Mozart's music was written. Geniuses of his species are imagined to create unified, flawless works "almost finished and complete in [the] mind" before so much as setting quill to parchment.[99] This in turn renders highly implausible the idea that a work could have been left incomplete (save perhaps for minor details of instrumentation), even when one is presented with the prospect of a compositional process interrupted by sudden fatal illness. Of course, the irony that Rochlitz himself supported these beliefs about how Mozart wrote music through the publication of a forged biographical document in 1815 should be self-evident, even if we believe the thesis behind the phony letter to ring true in its poetic description of certain aspects of Mozart's compositional process.

In reflecting on the various attacks on and defenses of the Requiem's technical and aesthetic qualities in 1801 and thereafter, it is well to remember an extraordinarily prescient observation made in response to the emerging Requiem controversy initiated by Gottfried Weber in 1825. The author of this passage is Adolf Bernhard Marx, an important theorist and critic who, five years later, would take up the first supernumerary professorship of musicology at a German university:

> Were the only effect of our estimable Gottfried Weber's aforementioned essay to liberate us from the authority of Mozart's name so that we might begin to examine and understand his Requiem impartially: then, we would see it as highly

---

[97] ". . . was soll man dann wohl von den vier Quintenfolgen im vierten Takt, G–D, Fis–Cis, E–H und D–A sagen? (Siehe die 130ste Seite dieser Partitur.) Möge ein jeder davon denken was er will. Für meinen Teil kann ich keinen Grund dafür erraten, weshalb Mozart diese Mißklänge angebracht haben soll." C. G. Stellan Mörner, "F. S. Silverstolpes im Jahr 1800 (oder 1801) in Wien niedergeschriebene Bemerkungen zu Mozarts Requiem," in *Festschrift Alfred Orel zum 70. Geburtstag*, edited by Hellmut Federhofer (Vienna: Rudolf M. Rohrer Verlag, 1960): 113–19, at 117. An English translation of the relevant excerpt is given in Wolff, *Mozart's Requiem*, 146–47.

[98] "Dass übrigens ein grosser Theil der Instrumentalbegleitung dem Hrn. Süssmayer [sic] zugerechnet werden müsse, ist sehr wohl möglich; nur unterwerfen die bereits bekannten Kunstprodukte des Herrn Süssmayer die Behauptung eines wesentlichern Antheils an diesem grossen Werke einer ziemlich strengen Kritik." [Rochlitz and Schwenke], "Recension," 4.

[99] [Rochlitz?], "Letter of W. A. Mozart," 199.

commendable. There is nothing more impotent and hollow than this orthodoxy about the name associated with a work. Therein lies the death of all independent thought and feeling; and the master himself must regard those who treat him with such reverence not as loving and devoted friends, but rather as timid slaves who would tear his work to pieces without hesitation or else discard it altogether were it not supported by credible attribution to a celebrated author.[100]

Marx's words echo through every chapter of this book. Time and again, unusual musical features judged to be brilliant and ingenious in a piece assumed to be by a well-known master become evidence of technical incompetence when those very same unusual musical features are reattributed to a relative nobody. The opposite scenario is equally possible when a piece long assumed to have been by an obscure figure is suddenly reattributed to an artist of unquestionable prestige, thus duly transfiguring many a perceived compositional blemish into the hallmark of unbridled visionary creativity.[101]

As Marx perceptively realized with reference to Mozart's Requiem as early as 1825, a healthy suspicion of misattribution and forgery has significant potential to free music criticism from the "orthodoxy" and circularity imposed by composer-centered attribution, a musical value system which risks, for Marx, "the death of all independent thought and felling."[102] In many respects, Marx's sentiment recalls Glenn Gould's perspective on forgery and the van Meegeren syndrome from the introduction, and we will hear not dissimilar opinions from such latter-day critics as Ernest Newman and Michael Beckerman in chapters to come. Yet, crucially, it is profoundly difficult to imagine Marx's opinion being expressed long before the early nineteenth century, when the ideal of composer-centered authenticity collided with professionalized music criticism for the first time in Western cultural history.

Mozart's Requiem is an important part of this story not least since the uniquely messy situation surrounding its composition arose at a time when ideas about what it might mean for music to be authentic were changing dramatically. Before continuing further with that tale, it is well to pause and assess the true story of the Requiem's composition as it is understood today. As we shall see, that complex tale illustrates common problems of authorship (and types of forgery) with unusual clarity.

---

[100] Adolf Bernhard Marx, "Nachschrift des Redakteurs," *Berliner Allgemeine musikalische Zeitung* 2, no. 46 (1825): 371–72, at 371.

[101] Perhaps the best-known example of this in music is Haydn's Cello Concerto No. 2 in D, Hob. VIIb: 2, which was mistakenly attributed to Anton Kraft for much of the first half of the twentieth century until Haydn's autograph manuscript was rediscovered in 1951. On the reception of this piece, see John Spitzer, "Authorship and Attribution in Western Art Music" (PhD diss., Cornell University, 1983), 1ff.

[102] Marx, "Nachschrift des Redakteurs," 371.

68 FORGERY IN MUSICAL COMPOSITION

DI ME W. A. MOZART MPPA. 1792

Mozart's untimely demise left his widow, Constanze, to face a series of grueling practical dilemmas. The exact details of the family's finances are contested, yet the fact remains that, with two young children, no independent income, and a series of debts left by her late husband, Constanze was in urgent need of funds in the weeks and months following 5 December 1791.[103]

During his final illness, Mozart had been at work on a setting of the Requiem mass commissioned by an anonymous patron. Acting through a clerk romantically described by Mozart's early biographers as a "gray messenger" (though most likely the lawyer Dr. Johann Nikolaus Sortschan), this unknown individual had, reportedly, offered to pay a 100 ducat (450 florin) fee for the score, with 50 d. paid in advance and the second 50 d. paid upon delivery.[104] This amount, 100 d., or 450 fl., was a substantial sum equal to the amount Artaria had paid Mozart for the publication rights to the six "Haydn" String Quartets, op. 10, in 1785, and half of Mozart's reported 200 d. fee, after 1789, for writing such operas as *Così fan tutte* and *La clemenza di Tito* for performance at the Viennese Imperial Theaters.[105] Yet, at the time of Mozart's passing, the Requiem remained incomplete, as the fragmentary score of the Lacrimosa in figure 1.2 illustrates, its final dominant chord, on "reus," poignantly unresolved. Musical fragments were not easily marketable products in the 1790s. Thus Constanze's dilemma: how best to capitalize on the substantial musical material that her late husband had left behind?

Some two months after Mozart's death, on 4 March 1792, Count Franz von Walsegg of Stuppach—the anonymous aristocrat who had commissioned the Requiem—received a complete copy of the work in a 200-page full score.[106] It was inscribed, on the top right-hand corner of the first folio, with the following Italian paratext (figure 1.3): "di me W. A. Mozart mppa. | 1792" [by me W. A. Mozart in my own hand | 1792].

---

[103] For an assessment of the Mozart family's finances, see Julia Moore, "Mozart in the Market-Place," *Journal of the Royal Musical Association* 114, no. 1 (1989): 18–42.

[104] This fee for the Requiem, and Sortschan's identity, are quoted in Anton Herzog, "True and Detailed History of the Requiem by W. A. Mozart, from its inception in the year 1791 to the present period of 1839," reprinted in Wolff, *Mozart's Requiem*, 131–38, at 133. Much confusion and debate has revolved around the precise extent of this fee and the amount given as an advance. Maynard Solomon, for example, argues that "actually, Mozart was paid between 30 and 50 ducats as an advance; and, after his death, Constanze Mozart negotiated for herself a fee of 100 ducats, which reportedly was received from Count Walsegg upon delivery of the Requiem on 4 March 1792." See Solomon, "The Rochlitz Anecdotes: Questions of Authenticity," 35.

[105] Julia Moore, "Mozart in the Market-Place," 21, 24–25. Moore notes that "probably Mozart's 100 d. fee for the six 'Haydn' Quartets was an unusually generous one." On Mozart's fees at the Imperial Theaters, see also Deutsch, *Mozart: A Documentary Biography*, "A Note on Currency." The accuracy of reports that Mozart received 200 d. for *Così fan tutte* and *La clemenza di Tito* is questioned in Andrew Steptoe, *The Mozart–Da Ponte Operas* (New York: Oxford University Press, 1988), 59–60.

[106] The manuscript, sometimes referred to as the "delivery score," is currently housed in the Austrian National Library (Österreichische Nationalbibliothek) under the shelf mark Mus. Hs. 1756ia. It has been digitized and is available for consultation online at http://data.onb.ac.at/rec/AC14016779.

Figure 1.2 Draft score of the Lacrimosa in Mozart's hand with Eybler's additions circled by Stadler. Mus. Hs. 1756ib, fol. 33v, Österreichische Nationalbibliothek, Musiksammlung. © ÖNB Vienna

Figure 1.3 Delivery score for the Requiem with Süssmayr's forgery of Mozart's signature. Mus. Hs. 1756ia, fol. 1r, Österreichische Nationalbibliothek, Musiksammlung. © ÖNB Vienna

MOZARTIAN SWAN SONGS   71

Each of the three factual statements asserted by this formula is a lie. Despite appearances, the Requiem was not entirely by Mozart in any simple sense. Nor was the score written substantially in his own hand. Perhaps most glaringly, Mozart certainly did not complete the work or anything else in 1792, having died the previous December. As has been discussed elsewhere in this chapter, the Sanctus, Benedictus, and Agnus Dei, as well as large parts of the sequence from the Dies Irae onward were written into the delivery score, at Constanze's request, by Mozart's pupil, copyist, and amanuensis Franz Xaver Süssmayr.[107] How much of what Süssmayr wrote may have been based on lost sketch material or oral instructions from Mozart remains a matter of significant debate. Regardless, in signing the manuscript with the deceased composer's name, Süssmayr committed what Christoph Wolff, H. C. Robbins Landon, and many others have since referred to as a deliberate act of "forgery."[108]

The convoluted saga illustrates important technical distinctions between different kinds of misattribution with remarkable clarity. Consider the finished score of Mozart's Requiem delivered to Count Walsegg early in 1792. In this case, Süssmayr unambiguously committed an act of forgery in that he falsely attributed his own work to Mozart, even signing the deceased composer's name to the score. In a compelling coincidence, Count Walsegg's mysterious anonymous commission was in fact motivated by a contrasting desire to plagiarize Mozart's work. A keen musical enthusiast, Walsegg employed a number of musicians to give concerts at his stately home at Stuppach each Tuesday and Thursday. He also indulged in the eccentric habit of enlisting composers, including such well-known figures as Franz Hoffmeister, to ghostwrite new works for performance at these bi-weekly events, where they were routinely passed off as Walsegg's own original works.

Even in the context of such dishonest behavior, the true story of the Requiem commission is something special—far stranger, indeed, than the urban legends and romantic fictions that have been associated with it since the first decades following Mozart's death. On 14 February 1791, the count's wife, Anna von Walsegg, had died, quite suddenly, at the age of just twenty. Stricken with grief, Walsegg commissioned the sculptor Johann Martin Fischer to construct a magnificent marble and granite memorial for her, reportedly costing over 3,000 florins.[109] More unusually, he also engaged Mozart to write a requiem mass that

---

[107] No substantial records remain concerning Süssmayr's studies with Mozart, though it is true that Süssmayr self-identified as Mozart's student when he confessed, in his letter to Breitkopf & Härtel, that he owed much to "the teaching of that great man." On Mozart's students see also Heinz Wolfgang Hamann, "Mozarts Schülerkreis: Versuch einer chronologischen Ordnung," *Mozart-Jahrbuch 1962/63* (1964): 115–39.

[108] Johannes Dalchow, Gunther Duda, and Dieter Kerner, *Mozarts Tod 1791–1971* (Pohl: Hohe Warte, 1971). Christoph Wolff, *Mozart's Requiem: Historical and Analytical Studies, Documents, Score* (Berkeley: University of California Press, 1994), 17. On Süssmayr's actions as "forgery," see also William Watson and C. B. Oldman, "An Astounding Forgery," *Music & Letters* 8, no. 1 (1927): 61–72; C. A. Moberg, "Äkthets Frågor i Mozarts Requiem," *Acta universitatis upsaliensis* 4 (1960): 5–75, at 75; H. C. Robbins Landon, *Mozart's Last Year: 1791* (New York: Schirmer Books, 1988), 163.

[109] This fee is given in Herzog, "True and Detailed History," 133.

72   FORGERY IN MUSICAL COMPOSITION

he could have recopied and performed under his own name each year as an outsourced sounding monument.[110]

One key difference between Walsegg's plagiarism and Süssmayr's forgery is that, while plagiarism involves taking credit for somebody else's work—what might be thought of as a kind of authorial greed—forgery is the act of giving someone else credit for your own labor. As was alluded to in this book's introduction, it is difficult to overstate the significance of this observation for any serious examination of the ethics and legality of forgery when compared to other forms of misattribution. The practice of plagiarism, for example, is widely treated as immoral, illegal, or both in part because the associated motives and effects are so obviously analogous to those of more generic forms of theft. This association is even borne out by the word's etymology: plagiarism is derived from the Latin noun *plagiārius*, which literally translates as "plunderer" or "kidnapper."[111] For most modern commentators, taking credit for another person's intellectual property is not so very different from plundering money from their pockets. As Roland Barthes put it, the importance of the author's "person" is underpinned by "positivism, resume and the result of capitalist ideology."[112] When authorial credit is understood to be rooted in financial credit in this manner, the plagiarist and the pickpocket are, in effect, one and the same.

By contrast, there is often thought to be a puzzling kind of authorial humility to forgery in that, by definition, forgers must renounce their authorial claims, effectively refusing—at least temporarily—to take credit for their own work. Be that as it may, it is well to remember that Constanze and Süssmayr also stood to gain something by assuming the deceased Mozart's authorial identity. To begin with, they took Walsegg's commission, which clearly wasn't nothing as far as Constanze was concerned. Yet financial cost and benefit is not the end of the story. Identity theft is still rightly conceptualized as a form of theft even if the assumed identity does not result in direct profit. In the most extreme cases forgers can be seen to deprive the figures whose names they appropriate of something more valuable than mere coin.

THE MINUET IN D MAJOR, K. 355

In a fascinating 1966 article, Ernst Oster modeled an analytical process similar to the one to which the Requiem was subjected in microcosm using the Minuet in

---

[110] The last such memorial concert was given on Saint Valentine's day, 1794—the third anniversary of Anna von Walsegg's death—at a small pilgrimage church outside the Lower Austrian town of Semmering. Anton Herzog gives an account of this performance in a manuscript suppressed by the Viennese censorship office: see "True and Detailed History," 136.

[111] T. F. Hoad, ed., *Oxford Concise Dictionary of English Etymology* (Oxford: Oxford University Press, 1996), s.v. "plagiary." Appropriately, the English "forgery" has a more creative origin: it is derived from the Latin noun *fabrica* meaning (as in the vernacular) both skilled artisanship in general and a smith's workshop—where metal is literally "forged"—in particular.

[112] Roland Barthes, "The Death of the Author," in *Image, Music, Text* (New York: Hill and Wang, 1977): 142–48, at 143.

D Major, K. 355. From a source-historical perspective, we know next to nothing about the work's documentary tradition, as Oster's article is quick to remind us. No autograph manuscript exists, and—like Mozart's Requiem—the piece was first published posthumously, in 1801, when it was grafted onto a trio composed by Maximilian Stadler. Except that, in Oster's analytical opinion, Stadler's contributions go much further than just the trio. According to Oster, the entire reprise of the minuet after m. 33 is nothing more or less than Stadler's botched completion of an experimental work that Mozart left unfinished.

To see what Oster means, compare the opening five measures of the A section and the compositional treatment of the same material reprised in mm. 29–33, reproduced in example 1.3. A prominent surface characteristic of the Minuet, K. 355 is the use of augmented triad sonorities, including in accented metrical positions. The "forte" chord that lands on the downbeat of m. 5 in the A section and at m. 33 in the reprise is a good example. In the A section, m. 5 marks the beginning of a sequential passage in which the music modulates away from the home key toward the dominant. Recognizing this, whoever completed the minuet clearly decided to transpose everything from m. 5's augmented triad onward up by a perfect fourth. This way, the reprise lands in the tonic rather than the dominant key, with no recompositional effort involved in completing the piece beyond the simple act of transposition.

Of course, verbatim transposition of a modulating A section is a common enough compositional strategy on its own. Oster's problem with the procedure in this case is that while the apparent "augmented triad" in m. 5 is easily explained as the result of a linear accented passing tone prepared and resolved in the inner voice, the augmented triad in m. 33 seems to appear as if from nowhere, with the inner-voice D♯ sounding as an unprepared augmented fifth above the bass. In the second half of m. 32, the left hand's neighboring motion around A is effectively stranded, serving no obvious contrapuntal purpose in relation to what follows. In his article, Oster ultimately refuses to believe that—at this crucial point in the composition—Mozart would have "settled for such a pseudo-solution as this, which only circumvents the real problem."[113] The analytical hypothesis is that Stadler contributed all of the material after m. 32, publishing the minuet as a complete work by Mozart in an act of Frankensteinian editorial forgery. In positing this, Oster turns to the implications of this type of work for analysis in general, ultimately writing:

> It is not enough to furnish a purely descriptive analysis. . . . Ideally, analysis should advance to the point where it can show to what degree the composer was able to realize the nature of his art. It will then be possible for analysis to

---

[113] Ernst Oster, "Analysis Symposium: Mozart Menuetto in D Major for Piano (K. 355)," *Journal of Music Theory* 10, no. 1 (1966): 18–52, at 50.

74 FORGERY IN MUSICAL COMPOSITION

Example 1.3 W. A. Mozart, Minuet in D Major, K. 355 (594a, 576b), completed (?) by Maximilian Stadler

Example 1.3 Continued

76   FORGERY IN MUSICAL COMPOSITION

distinguish between good and bad, and also, whenever necessary, to distinguish between authentic compositions and spurious ones.[114]

One striking feature of this approach is its blurring of the traditional divide between music theory's "regulative" and "analytic" modes, to adapt Carl Dahlhaus's influential taxonomy.[115] Where "analytic theory" is typically descriptive and concerns the musical work as it is, "regulative theory" tends toward the prescriptive, setting standards for what a musical work should be. In the classroom, regulative theory is frequently used to correct student counterpoint exercises, hunting forbidden parallels, illegally resolved leading tones, and unprepared augmented triads. Rarely if ever is the same critical scrutiny applied to music encountered in the analysis seminar, where any score held up for discussion is generally assumed—albeit tacitly—to be a Great Work from the outset. When analytic theory discovers an irregularity in the repertory, it is generally interpreted not as evidence of technical incompetence or inauthenticity but rather as a moment of inspiration, the very hallmark of compositional genius. For this reason, analyzing a suspected forgery often feels uncannily akin to grading a counterpoint assignment. The function is not necessarily one of appreciation, but rather of evaluative authentication, stemming from a mood of fundamental skepticism. As A. B. Marx suggested with reference to the Requiem in 1825, it may be worth considering whether such skepticism about authorship could liberate aesthetic experience and understanding alike from the constraints of composer-centered authenticity.

CONSTANZE, CANONS, CAPITAL

These philosophical questions have serious practical implications for how we, as scholars, choose to maintain the musicological canon today. Here we should return to history's often-severe judgments of the role Constanze played in curating her own husband's musical legacy, above all when it comes to the thorny ethical and editorial issues associated with the Requiem. In a backhanded comment that is typical of much literature on the topic, Heinz Gärtner writes: "It would be unfair to expect Constanze to become the devoted guardian of her late husband's immortal music" because, "from her limited perspective, his works were basically objects of material value, to be dealt with according to the laws of supply and demand."[116]

---

[114] Oster, "Analysis Symposium: Mozart Menuetto in D," 50–51.

[115] For a more extensive summary of this distinction in English see Thomas Christensen, introduction to *Cambridge History of Western Music Theory*, edited by Thomas Christensen (Cambridge: Cambridge University Press, 2002), 1–22, at 13–14.

[116] Heinz Gärtner, *Constanze Mozart: After the Requiem*, translated by Reinhard G. Pauly (Portland, OR: Amadeus Press, 1991), 17; first published as *Mozarts Requiem und die Geschäfte der Constanze M.* (Munich: Langen Müller, 1986).

Without fully unpacking the psycho-sexual undertones of Gärtner's heavily gendered "devoted guardian" ideal, the association of the Requiem forgery with a kind of editorial infidelity through economic materialism speaks volumes.[117] The implication is that in revealing the unspoken exchange value of the Requiem, Constanze's act of forgery also adulterates the work's putative status as a bounded, single-authored, autonomous abstraction. Her conduct is so provocative not because she lacked perspective about "her late husband's immortal music"—as Gärtner puts it—but rather because she so unromantically reminds us of what any good source historian already knows. Even the most death-driven and spiritual of musical utterances attains "immortality" only though networks of material objects that can be bought, sold, and, indeed, falsified.

With all this in mind, one might well ask what a dutiful academic guardian of Mozart's music should do with K. 626 today. Do we expurgate Süssmayr's compositional insertions in publications and performances? Or else let them stand in spite of the potential historical, aesthetic, and ethical taint of forgery? And if we do take the bold step of deleting Süssmayr's contributions, how should we fill the yawning music-historical chasm that such an action would create? The fact is that, unlike Bach's *Art of Fugue*, the Requiem refuses to break off all at once to form a conveniently performable romantic fragment. And while some academics might consider a modern-day completion ethically or aesthetically superior to an eighteenth-century forgery, performers and audiences remain broadly resistant to the idea that anyone alive today could surpass Süssmayr's genuine canonical fake.

It should be pointed out that in the modern history of compositional forgery, Mozart's Requiem is an exceptional case. The remainder of this book is devoted to twentieth-century forgeries, which tend to be composed hundreds of years after the deaths of their supposed authors, not mere weeks. Nonetheless, K. 626's editorial afterlife serves as a compelling reminder of forgery's tacit presence at the very heart of the musicological canon. To think seriously about forgery's history—and our judgments of figures such as Constanze, Süssmayr, and Stadler—is to ask what sort of curators we should aspire to be in the here and now.

---

[117] In Gärtner's account, Constanze's supposed "editorial" infidelity was accompanied by sensationalist speculation about sexual infidelity. With no substantial evidence, Gärtner suggests not only that Constanze had an affair with Süssmayr but also that Süssmayr could be the true father of Constanze's second child, Wolfgang Xaver Mozart. The obvious psychoanalytic reading of this story is that, for Gärtner, Constanze must have adulterated her marriage because she adulterated Mozart's work, and vice versa. See Gärtner, *Constanze Mozart: After the Requiem*, 40.

2

Kreislerian Fantasies

The artist is the creator of beautiful things. To reveal art and conceal the artist is art's aim.

Oscar Wilde[1]

I am a collector—a collector of everything you can imagine.

Fritz Kreisler[2]

On 8 February 1935 the *New York Times* ran an article at the top of its front page that would turn the world of music criticism on its head.[3] Telegramming from Europe between concert appearances, sixty-year-old Austrian-born virtuoso violinist and composer Fritz Kreisler confessed to the *Times*'s chief music critic Olin Downes that a group of some seventeen pieces he previously claimed to have adapted from antique manuscripts were, as he put it, "in every detail my original compositions."[4]

With the exception of a single full-length concerto, these pieces were, as summarized in table 2.1, brief violin-and-piano miniatures that Kreisler had passed off as his arrangements and transcriptions from old sources gathered in the libraries, palaces, and monasteries of Europe.[5] In fact, Kreisler had been performing them in public under the names of seventeenth- and eighteenth-century

---

[1] Oscar Wilde, *The Picture of Dorian Gray* (London: Ward, Lock, 1891), v.

[2] *New York Times*, "How Kreisler Finds Musical Novelties," 8 November 1909, 7.

[3] Olin Downes, "Kreisler Reveals 'Classics' as Own; Fooled Music Critics for 30 Years," *New York Times*, 8 February 1935, 1, 26.

[4] While Kreisler's telegram confession of 1935 contains a list of just fourteen compositions (including three not marketed as *Classical Manuscripts*), he adds that "the entire series labeled 'classical manuscripts' [in published editions]" are his own work. It is not clear why Nos. 8, 9, and 17 in the *Classical Manuscripts* series—marked as "implicit" confessions in the rightmost column found in table 2.1—were excluded from Kreisler's own 1935 list. See Downes, "Kreisler Reveals 'Classics' as Own," 26.

[5] Table 2.1 collates information from numerous existing catalogues of Kreisler's works. These include: Louis Lochner, *Fritz Kreisler* (St. Clair Shores, MI: Scholarly Press, 1951), "Compositions, Transcriptions, and Arrangements," 403–12; Amy Biancolli, *Fritz Kreisler: Love's Sorrow, Love's Joy* (Portland, OR: Amadeus Press, 1998), "Appendix B," 344–53; and Edmond T. Johnson, "Revival and Antiquation: Modernism's Musical Pasts" (PhD diss., University of California, Santa Barbara, 2011), "Figure 3.9," 132.

Forgery in Musical Composition. Frederick Reece, Oxford University Press. © Oxford University Press 2025.
DOI: 10.1093/9780197618332.003.0003

Table 2.1 Kreisler's Forgeries with Dates of Publication and Confession of Authorship

Attribution	Work Title	Classical Manuscripts No.	Date of Publication	Date of Confession
W. F. Bach (1710–1784)	Grave	17	1910	1935 (implicit)
Luigi Boccherini (1743–1805)	Allegretto	8	1910	1935 (implicit)
Jean Baptiste Cartier (1765–1841)	La Chasse (Caprice)	16	1910	1935
Louis Couperin (1626–1661)	Aubade Provençale	15	1910	1935
	Chanson Louis XIII and Pavane	1	1910	1935
	La Précieuse	4	1910	1935
Karl D. von Dittersdorf (1739–1799)	Scherzo	7	1910	1935
Fransçois Francoeur (1698–1787)	Sicilienne et Rigaudon	6	1910	1935
[Joseph Lanner (1801–1843)] "Alt-Wiener Tanzweisen"	Liebesfreud	10	1910	1910?
	Liebesleid	11	1910	1910?
	Schön Rosmarin	12	1910	1910?
Padre [G. B.] Martini (1706–1784)	Andantino	2	1910	1935
	Preghiera	13	1910	1935
Niccolo Porpora (1686–1768)	Menuet	3	1910	1935
	Allegretto in G minor	—	1913	1935
Gaetano Pugnani (1731–1798)	Praeludium and Allegro	5	1910	1935
	Tempo di minuetto	14	1910	1935
Giuseppe Tartini (1692–1770)	Variations on a Theme by Corelli	9	1910	1935 (implicit)
Anton Stamitz (1750–c.1800)	Study on a Choral	—	c.1930?	1935
Antonio Vivaldi (1678–1741)	Violin Concerto in C Major "RV Anh. 62"	—	1927	1935

80 FORGERY IN MUSICAL COMPOSITION

musicians for at least a decade before B. Schott's Söhne of Mainz succeeded in securing the publication rights in 1910. The firm soon released seventeen of the misattributed works in a numbered series (table 2.1), giving them the suggestive collective title "Klassische Manuskripte" [Classical Manuscripts].[6] Kreisler later claimed that they paid him "ten dollars" apiece.[7] In any case, it turned out to be a profitable deal for Schott: one year later, the publisher proudly announced that 75,000 copies of Kreisler's sheet music had been sold to the public.[8]

In the twenty-five years that would elapse between this 1910 first edition and Kreisler's grand confession of 1935, many of the so-called *Classical Manuscripts* became staples on violin recital programs around the world.[9] Kreisler himself featured the works on his extensive tours of Europe, the United States, and— in the 1923 concert season—Japan and China. During this same period the *Classical Manuscripts* appeared no fewer than five times on 78s released by the RCA Victor "Red Seal" imprint known for promoting such stars of early commercial sound recording as Mischa Elman and Enrico Caruso.[10] The net result of all this publishing, touring, and recording was that—whether on commercial phonographs, in the domestic music room, or on stage—Kreisler's forgeries were all but inescapable in the classical music culture of the early twentieth century. Indeed, unlike the other, more modern forgeries discussed in the second part of this book, many of Kreisler's pieces maintain a conspicuous place in the repertory to this day, appearing frequently on violin recital programs and performance examination syllabi, albeit—in most cases—under the true author's name.[11] If Joseph Kerman was right in observing that "repertories are determined by performers, canons by critics," the stubborn persistence of Kreisler's

---

[6] The *Classical Manuscripts* series includes three works—*Liebesfreud*, *Liebesleid*, and *Schön Rosmarin*—for which Kreisler asserted he had already claimed authorship by 1910. In recitals given prior to that year *Liebesfreud*, *Liebesleid*, and *Schön Rosmarin* were performed under false pretenses as Kreisler's adaptations of waltzes by the nineteenth-century Austrian composer and violinist Joseph Lanner. Although published editions from after 1910 make no mention of Lanner, they do list these three compositions with the curious folkloric paratext "Alt-Wiener Tanzweisen" [Old-Viennese Dance Tunes] in place of the name of the author.

[7] Louis Biancolli, "The Great Kreisler Hoax," *Etude* 69 (1951): 8, 56, at 56.

[8] On the early sales figures for Kreisler's *Classical Manuscripts*, see Biancolli, *Love's Sorrow*, 339.

[9] Galina Kopytova, for example, notes in her biography of Jascha Heifetz that "[the forged] 'baroque' miniatures . . . became integral to the repertoire of almost every Russian violinist" following Kreisler's 1910 tour to St. Petersburg. See Galina Kopytova, *Jascha Heifetz: Early Years in Russia*, translated by Dario Sarlo and Alexandra Sarlo (Bloomington: Indiana University Press, 2013), 68.

[10] Kreisler himself attributed the success of his 1923 tour of Japan and China to the global reach of these Victor recordings, which included, for example, the 78s catalogued as Victor 64142; Victor 64292; Victor 64315; Victor 74172; and Victor 64202. See Eric Wen's comprehensive discography of Kreisler's recordings printed in Biancolli, *Love's Sorrow*, "Appendix C," 354–420. On Kreisler's experiences in Asia, see Lochner, *Fritz Kreisler*, 205–20.

[11] The "Martini" Andantino, for example, appeared on list B of the Grade 6 violin syllabus for 2020–2023 set by the Associated Board of the Royal Schools of Music under the title now used by Schott: "Andantino in the style of Martini." See Associated Board of the Royal Schools of Music, *Violin Exam Pieces: ABRSM Grade 6, 2020–2023* (London: ABRSM, 2019).

KREISLERIAN FANTASIES   81

forgeries at the core of the violinist's concert literature in spite of their demonstrably deceptive origins should give pause to music scholars and practitioners alike.[12] Nearly a century after they were publicly and irrevocably revealed to be elaborate historical fakes Kreisler's mendacious *Classical Manuscripts* endure unquestioned as music, their extra-compositional involvement in past critical controversies all but forgotten.

It is singularly appropriate in this context that the front-page confession of 1935 was prompted not by an independent academic inquiry, but by one of the many violin recitals featuring Kreisler's forgeries. On the evening of 8 February 1935—the day the *New York Times* story was ultimately released—the eighteen-year-old prodigy Yehudi Menuhin was scheduled to perform works including what was then known as Kreisler's arrangement (for violin and piano) of the eighteenth-century Italian composer Gaetano Pugnani's "Praeludium and Allegro" as part of a recital series Olin Downes ran at the Brooklyn Academy of Music.[13] Himself something of a celebrity on New York City's cultural scene, Downes was to supplement the young Menuhin's performance by expounding on edifying musical and historical details connected to the day's program in what was then a rather novel didactic innovation: the lecture recital. Yet, in researching his presentation, Downes was surprised to find himself at a loss to locate any meaningful information about the original eighteenth-century sources for Kreisler's "Pugnani" arrangement. It seemed that nobody before him had put much effort into checking. In a certain sense, this was unsurprising. The historical details behind violin recital programs were rarely subject to any serious musicological attention during Kreisler's youth. Downes, however—as part of a new generation of academically minded music critics that had risen to prominence in the 1920s and 1930s—considered it his "business," as a lecturer, "to find out what the differences were between the supposedly original composition and its arrangement by Kreisler."[14] Published reference books failed to mention Pugnani ever having sketched such a work, and Downes's scholarly inquiries with colleagues at the research libraries of New York City and Washington, D.C. left him unable to substantiate even the most basic facts of provenance for Kreisler's sources.[15] Frustrated, Downes decided to tackle the issue directly by simultaneously telegramming the violinist and his American publishers, Carl Fischer, Inc., to request an explanation, point blank.

[12]   Joseph Kerman, "A Few Canonic Variations," *Critical Inquiry* 10, no. 1 (1983): 107–125, at 112.
[13]   *New York Times*, "Kreisler's Secret Kept by Musicians," 9 February 1935, 17.
[14]   Olin Downes, "Kreisler's 'Classics': Story of Their Authorship—Some Rumors and Interpretations of His Course," *New York Times*, 3 March 1935, X5.
[15]   According to Louis Lochner, Downes engaged Harold Spivacke—then assistant chief of the music division at the Library of Congress—to do detailed research work on the Pugnani question on his behalf. Lochner, *Fritz Kreisler*, 294. For Downes's own account of his research in preparation for the Brooklyn recital, see Downes, "Kreisler's 'Classics,'" X5.

82 FORGERY IN MUSICAL COMPOSITION

Once confirmed by Fischer, the frank confession that Kreisler wired back from his tour across the Atlantic on 6 February provided Downes and the *Times* with a story that would continue to provoke heated debate for decades to come. It is hard to imagine that Kreisler fully comprehended the weight of his actions when he telegrammed: "Your assumption absolutely correct. The entire series labeled Classical Manuscripts are my original compositions."[16] Within forty-eight hours the contents of this message were plastered on the front page of the *New York Times*. After some thirty-five years in Kreisler's performances and twenty-five years of distribution in print and on record, the works listed in table 2.1 had been unmasked as compositional forgeries in a single stroke.

UGLY APPELLATIONS

The word "forgery" is striking in its absence from Downes's original article and most of the press coverage that followed. Since I will nonetheless continue to insist that it is the only truly appropriate word we have to describe the case, a point of terminological clarification is in order. In this book's introduction, I defined compositional forgery as "the deliberate misattribution of one's own work to someone else"—just as Kreisler misattributed his compositions to Vivaldi, Pugnani, and the other seventeenth- and eighteenth-century composers listed in table 2.1. Why then, given its conceptual clarity, is the term absent from even the most critical period discussions of Kreisler's actions?

There are a number of reasons. One undeniably important factor is the long-standing and radical under-theorization of forgery in music prior to the controversy unleashed by Kreisler's disclosure. Unlike forgery in the visual arts or in literature, musical forgery simply had not been a subject of widespread public discussion before Downes's article hit the front page of the *New York Times*. As a result, commentators around the globe struggled—and often failed—to find appropriate vocabulary with which to describe what had happened. A second significant element that should be considered is the extraordinary cult of celebrity surrounding Fritz Kreisler in the broader cultural landscape of the 1930s. This was an era of burgeoning mass communication in which classical musicians—such as Kreisler's peers Jascha Heifetz, Enrico Caruso, and Sergei Rachmaninov—commanded a degree of global public recognition that would have been broadly unthinkable in the nineteenth century. But even by these lofty standards, Kreisler was something special. He packed out concert halls across Europe, the Americas, and Asia. His recordings and sheet music sold tens of thousands of copies worldwide. Newspapers and magazines sought—and

---

[16] Downes, "Kreisler's 'Classics,'" X5.

printed—his opinions on contemporary cultural issues well beyond the realm of music, from war to divorce.[17] He was profiled in arts journals and gentlemen's lifestyle magazines alike; *Esquire*, for example, boldly declared that "no artist of our time—with the possible exceptions of Paderewski and Toscanini—has inspired such adoration from audiences throughout the world as Kreisler."[18] And they were not wrong. As Amy Biancolli knowingly surmises in her 1998 biography: "Had he *tried* [in the 1930s] to ruin his reputation or earn a scathing review the press and public would simply not have co-operated."[19]

While Kreisler's popularity served to expose musical forgery to the mass-media limelight for the first time, it also, ironically, prevented the phenomenon from being adequately contextualized or even named as such. Faced with a widely adored celebrity committing such an inscrutable and morally ambiguous act, the majority of contemporary writers allowed politeness to trump clarity of description, following Downes's example by settling on the word "hoax." The *Oxford English Dictionary* defines this term as "a humorous or malicious deception."[20] Tellingly, it was often placed in scare-quotes that bespeak a certain degree of semantic discomfort if not outright embarrassment.[21] Nonetheless, with respect to Kreisler's unmasked *Classical Manuscripts*, the word has stuck.[22]

This is particularly ironic given that many of Kreisler's contemporaries—including Downes himself—were well aware that the "hoax" formulation was in some sense serving as a fig leaf with which to shield the violinist from the more troubling connotations wrapped up in the unspeakable f-word forgery. An editorial by Paul Kempf in the American Magazine *The Musician* remarked: "In the sister arts—painting, sculpture, drama and literature—there are *ugly appellations* for those who profess classic authorship for their own brain children."[23] Without daring to commit any of these ugly appellations to print, Kempf made his tacit analogy to forgery in the visual arts perfectly clear: "The case of the painter who steeps himself in the spirit and technical methods of Corot and then offers his own products as those of the French master is not unlike that of the musician who composes a concerto in C major and causes it to be published as a work of Vivaldi."[24]

[17] For a summary of some of these interviews, see Biancolli, *Love's Sorrow*, 158.
[18] David Ewen, "L'Amico Fritz," *Esquire*, August 1935, 64, 148.
[19] Biancolli, *Love's Sorrow*, 159. Emphasis from original text.
[20] *Oxford Dictionaries Online*, s.v. "hoax." See https://en.oxforddictionaries.com/definition/hoax. Accessed 15 January 2018.
[21] See, for example, Paul Kempf (editorial), "The Kreisler 'Hoax,'" *The Musician*, February 1935, 3.
[22] The two major biographies of Kreisler—written at the mid- and endpoints of the twentieth century, respectively—both favor this term. See Lochner, *Fritz Kreisler*, chapter 25, "Confession of an Old Hoax"; and Biancolli, *Love's Sorrow*, chapter 7, "Hoaxes All: Pugnani, Vivaldi, Martini, and Kreisler."
[23] Kempf, "The Kreisler 'Hoax,'" 3. My Emphasis.
[24] Kempf, "The Kreisler 'Hoax,'" 3.

84 FORGERY IN MUSICAL COMPOSITION

Despite so unambiguously invoking the charge of forgery, Kempf—like most of his contemporaries—ultimately gave Kreisler a pass in the face of his extraordinary artistic achievements. He surmised: "Aside from the ethical considerations one cannot escape the conclusion that the violin literature has been precisely richened by this music which has brought unmeasured happiness to thousands of listeners."[25] While refusing to condemn his colleague, Ukrainian-American concert violinist Mischa Elman was somewhat more critical, euphemistically remarking: "It is indeed a surprise . . . that one who stands so high for all that is beautiful, pure and true in art as Kreisler should have resorted to *such means* . . . when these composers are unable to enjoy the plaudits or endure the criticisms which these compositions may or may not evoke."[26] Meanwhile, in another tacit allusion to forgery in painting and sculpture, Downes himself defended Kreisler by asserting that, in this case, no composer of the past had "lost royalties or reputation by *a device which has again and again been employed in the history of art*, and nowhere more harmlessly than in the present instance."[27] The ominous identity of Kreisler's artistic "device" (for Downes)—like the implicitly untrue and impure "means" to which he resorted (for Elman)—is left to the reader's imagination. Alongside Kempf's "ugly appellation" it remains implicitly familiar and yet, tellingly, unutterable.

Of course, the "ethical considerations" raised by ugly unspoken words like forgery are not so lightly brushed aside. If the "unmeasured happiness" of aesthetic enrichment does not excuse a forged Corot, one is surely well justified in questioning the grounds on which so many critics insisted—often without any rational explanation—that a forged Vivaldi should be judged more leniently. And while there is surely a certain extent to which this knee-jerk leniency hinges on the status of music as an art form in general, it is also profoundly contingent—in this singular case—on the unique artistic persona of Fritz Kreisler in particular.

TALL TALES AND TRUE FICTION

There can be no doubt that Kreisler was profoundly gifted both as a violinist and as a composer. Yet the unprecedented fame he enjoyed by the 1930s and throughout the rest of his life must also in part be attributed to his worldly geniality, his charm as a raconteur, and, perhaps above all, his mastery of creative self-fiction. Fused with his antiquarian aesthetic affinity for things past, Kreisler's utter indifference toward questions of historical and biographical truth

---

[25] Kempf, "The Kreisler 'Hoax,'" 3.
[26] *New York Times*, "Kreisler's Secret Kept by Musicians," 17. My emphasis.
[27] Downes, "Kreisler's 'Classics,'" X5. My emphasis.

KREISLERIAN FANTASIES   85

fits the paradigmatic psychological profile of the art forger to perfection. As Amy Biancolli surmises, Kreisler was a man who "saw the truth not as a collection of literal details but as something more liter*ary*, lacking in accuracy but abundantly rich in meter and metaphor."[28]

Put rather less generously, Kreisler was in the habit of lying about himself, again and again, beautifully and unabashedly. While the fictional origins of the *Classical Manuscripts* are among the most egregious and controversial of his deceptions, they were by no means unique. Making an admirable effort to expurgate such infelicities from the biographical record established in part by Louis Lochner's authorized (and thus itself heavily Kreislerized) 1950 account, Biancolli recites a litany of the most compelling and widely repeated anecdotes.[29] There are the typical apocryphal stories, à la Paganini, of superhuman virtuosity overcoming a self-imposed—and utterly gratuitous—technical handicap (the "I once played with a bow covered with soap" tale).[30] There are the undocumented and often perilous encounters with folkloric character archetypes in far-flung corners of the globe (the "I once played for a sultan" tale; the "a cowboy held me at gunpoint" tale).[31] And then there are the shamelessly ornamented—and occasionally outright fictionalized—accounts of Kreisler's bohemian youth and subsequent loss of innocence in the Austrian military (the "I went to art school in Paris tale"; the "My leg was seriously wounded in an attack by the Russians during World War I" tale).[32]

These autobiographical fragments are the stuff of myth-building. Unserious as many of them sound—a recital with a bow covered in soap? a revolver-toting American frontiersman demanding to hear solo Bach?—their broader point, considered in aggregate, is of crucial importance. Behind the impressive corpus of Kreislerian tall tales lies a man determined to fashion a distinctive identity for himself as an ambassador for old-world romanticism in an increasingly global and unromantic age. It was not enough for the violinist to be a "great musician" in the artisanal sense in which contemporary figures such as Jascha Heifetz— widely considered the polar foil to Kreisler, both technically and personally— came to define consummate musicianship for early twentieth-century string players. (One struggles to imagine Heifetz interacting with belligerent cowboys or absentmindedly dripping soap on his bow.) While younger generations of elite concert artists chose, increasingly, to present themselves as hyper-disciplined

---

[28] Biancolli, *Love's Sorrow,* 151. Emphasis from original text.

[29] As Biancolli put it: "Even Kreisler's earnest (but ultimately wan) efforts at correction in Louis Lochner's *Fritz Kreisler* had little effect, mainly because he balanced those corrections with a stunning collection of fresh new yarns." Biancolli, *Love's Sorrow,* 135.

[30] Biancolli, *Love's Sorrow,* 139–41.

[31] Biancolli, *Love's Sorrow,* 143–46.

[32] Biancolli, *Love's Sorrow,* 136–39.

86   FORGERY IN MUSICAL COMPOSITION

Olympians, Kreisler deliberately cultivated an aesthetic of artful artlessness, or "sprezzatura," even up to the point of repeatedly stating—apparently in earnest—that he did not practice much because "I have hypnotized myself into the belief that I do not need it, and therefore I do not."[33] Like all the anecdotes Kreisler concocted about himself, this biographical detail ultimately serves to suggest that he was no mere concert violinist but also a talented painter, a tragic war hero, a jilted lover, an intrepid adventurer, and, at the heart of it all, a teller of stories.

If the claims he made appear implausible or even unhinged, that is precisely the point. As an archetypal trickster, Kreisler aspired to transgress otherwise impassable boundaries—between past and present, high and low culture, fiction and reality—with characteristic audacity and humor. This perhaps goes some way toward explaining why his forgeries were brushed aside as mere "hoaxes" by sympathetic commentators such as Downes and Kempf. Deriving many of his pseudo-autobiographical anecdotes from the tropes of romantic fiction, Kreisler aspired to belong as much to the Hoffmannesque dreamscapes of his literary namesake Johannes as to twentieth-century modernity. And, by and large, audiences loved him for it.

Yet, even by the standards of the dozens of apocryphal tales Kreisler told about himself, his pre-1935 accounts of the provenance of his so-called *Classical Manuscripts* were brazen. For one thing, the violinist characteristically failed to keep his story straight, offering at least two mutually contradictory accounts of how he had come by his antique sources. In the first version, printed in an October 1909 interview for *The Musician*, Kreisler claimed that he had "discovered a collection of manuscript music in the possession of the monks who inhabit one of the oldest monasteries in Europe."[34] Without giving a name or specific location for the monastery, Kreisler stated that he was so keen to have the works for himself that—in an act of flagrant archival misdemeanor—he "copied one of the pieces on his shirt cuff."[35] When the monks objected to this, he reported that he had purchased the whole collection "for a considerable sum of money."[36]

In November of 1909, a mere month after the publication of his interview with *The Musician*, Kreisler reported a second rediscovery narrative to the *New York Times*. This time, the setting changes from "one of the oldest monasteries in Europe" to "a certain palace" in Italy where the violinist had been invited to indulge his passion for antiques.[37] While "admiring the objets d'art," he noticed

---

[33]   W. E. B., "Fritz Kreisler," *The Musician* 14 (1909): 453.
[34]   W. E. B., "Fritz Kreisler," 453.
[35]   W. E. B., "Fritz Kreisler," 453.
[36]   W. E. B., "Fritz Kreisler," 453.
[37]   *New York Times*, "How Kreisler Finds Musical Novelties," 7.

several musical manuscripts "in a glass display case," and attempted to memorize one particularly eye-catching melody (as in the first version of the narrative) "with the aid of some notes . . . made on my cuff."[38] But, upon returning to his hotel and trying out the little piece on his violin, Kreisler concluded that his hasty shirt-cuff transcription had failed to capture its charm. He would need another look. Yet he discovered to his dismay the next day that "the owner," evidently displeased by his attempts at transcription, "had put a cover over the pile of music."[39] Luckily for Kreisler—in another echo of the monastery version of the narrative—"the family who owned the collection was poor, and I finally managed to buy the manuscript." "This," he claimed, "was the beginning of my collection."[40]

CURATION AND CONNOISSEURSHIP

It was less than one year after telling these elaborate discovery narratives to *The Musician* and the *New York Times* that Kreisler published seventeen of the works in question, as listed in table 2.1, with B. Schott's Söhne. Each edition of the *Classical Manuscripts* containing one or more of these supposed transcriptions bore the following prefacing "notice"—printed in German and French, as well as English—on its inside cover:

> The original Manuscripts used for these transcriptions are the private property of Mr. Fritz Kreisler and are now published for the first time; they are moreover so freely treated that they constitute, in fact, original works. Further transcriptions of any of these compositions will therefore constitute an infringement of copyright. When played in public, Mr. Kreisler's name must be mentioned on the programme.[41]

The exact implications of this terse and rather obfuscatory paratextual statement became a subject of intense debate in 1935.[42] Its fundamental ambiguity

---

[38] *New York Times*, "How Kreisler Finds Musical Novelties," 7.

[39] *New York Times*, "How Kreisler Finds Musical Novelties," 7.

[40] The second version of the story does include an additional nod to the first, with Kreisler stating: "Other pieces I discovered in an old convent in the South of France." (Note, however, the switch from monastery to convent, and the newly elaborated geographic detail). *New York Times*, "How Kreisler Finds Musical Novelties," 7.

[41] [Fritz Kreisler] Luigi Boccherini, *Allegretto* (Mainz: B. Schott's Söhne, 1910). The English text used here is original to Schott's editions; their German and French versions of the notice (printed alongside the English) are near identical, allowing for minor idiomatic differences in language.

[42] For an overview of the concept of "paratext" see Gérard Genette, *Paratexts: Thresholds of Interpretation*, translated by Jane E. Lewin (Cambridge: Cambridge University Press, 1997); first published as *Seuils* (Paris: Éditions du Seuil, 1987).

88 FORGERY IN MUSICAL COMPOSITION

arises from the following contradiction: in the first place, the prefacing notice does hint, heavy-handedly, that the transcriptions were "so freely treated that they constitute, in fact, original works"; yet, in a crucial turn, it also deceptively maintains that they were based on "original manuscripts" that were Kreisler's "private property."[43]

Practically speaking, this clarification served a dual purpose. First, it protected Kreisler, Schott, and Carl Fischer from rival publishers who wished to produce their own arrangements of the works. (The notice itself confirmed that nobody except Kreisler had access to the supposed original manuscripts, and that the violinist's adaptations of them were protected by copyright as derivative works.) Second, the paratext allowed Kreisler to defend himself from the more academic accusation that he had manipulated the antique sources without due editorial transparency. Any "Kreislerisms" that were discovered in the music were to be chalked up to the arranger, not the composer, which was a particularly useful defense given that Kreisler himself was unwilling to give away where one ended and the other began.

From a modern academic perspective, these rediscovery narratives—with their romantic settings and illicit shirt-cuff scrawling—might well appear charmingly naïve. Yet there remain important senses in which, in the early-twentieth century, musicological standards of evidence and editorial practice were still relatively far removed from the modern regimes of authenticity discussed in this book's second part. The monumental thematic catalogues that can reliably be found in the reference sections of academic music libraries—Wolfgang Schmieder's *Thematisch-systematisches Verzeichnis der Werke Joh. Seb. Bachs* (1950), Otto Erich Deutsch's *Schubert: A Thematic Catalogue of all his Works in Chronological Order* (1951), and Anthony van Hoboken's *Joseph Haydn: Thematisch-bibliographisches Werkverzeichnis* (1957), for example—would appear *en masse* only at the twentieth century's midpoint, bringing with them numeric references such as "BWV," "D.," and "Hob."[44] The historical irony is that while Kreisler was claiming to have abducted non-existent old manuscripts from the archives, Schmieder, Deutsch, Hoboken, and their ilk were conducting painstakingly meticulous research to provide the general public with reliable information about who really did compose what and when.

This was one of the key points of ethical objection raised against the forgeries by Kreisler's most persistent and articulate antagonist in the press, long-serving London *Sunday Times* music critic Ernest Newman. Like Olin Downes at the

---

[43] [Fritz Kreisler] Luigi Boccherini, *Allegretto* (Mainz: B. Schott's Söhne, 1910).

[44] Wolfgang Schmieder, *Thematisch-systematisches Verzeichnis der Werke Joh. Seb. Bachs* (Leipzig: Breitkopf & Härtel, 1950); O. E. Deutsch, *Schubert: A Thematic Catalogue of All His Works in Chronological Order* (London: J. M. Dent, 1951); Anthony van Hoboken, *Joseph Haydn: Thematisch-bibliographisches Werkverzeichnis* (Mainz: B Schott's Söhne, 1957). Köchel's Mozart catalogue, first published in 1862, is an outlier here.

New York Times—in many senses his American opposite number—Newman was at the vanguard of a new generation of star music critics whose learned and belletristic prose commentary became a defining feature of the cultural land-scape of the 1930s and 1940s.[45] In addition to writing for the *Sunday Times* for the best part of forty years, Newman authored more than two dozen books on music, often drawing on extensive original research.[46] Throughout his volumi-nous critical and scholarly writings, the hyper-literate Newman—a Lancastrian tailor's son, born William Roberts—consistently advocated for forward-thinking cultural ideas rooted in rigorous intellectual principles of skepticism and ration-alism, both within and beyond the arts.[47] In this sense, apocryphal reports that he adopted his pen name as a "new man in earnest" can be seen to endure be-cause they are an efficient if undocumented means of capturing the essence of the Newman prose persona in biographical anecdote—i.e., a literary demeanor of pugnacious progressive idealism fused with iron-wrought intellectual fastid-iousness and the brutalizing observational wit of the unflinchingly honest.[48] If there is any truth to the old adage that character is destiny, an explosive confron-tation between the punctilious rationalist Newman and the silver-tongued fabu-list Kreisler was all but inevitable. Indeed, when Kreisler responded to Newman's harsh indictment of his *Classical Manuscripts* deception by recriminating the critic—that "venerable grumbler" and "irate public prosecutor of artists"—in a letter to the editor of the *Sunday Times*, the two men became embroiled in a pro-tracted dispute that exposes the frictions between romantic and modern modes of thinking about authenticity and musical value with exceptional clarity.[49]

In an open letter back to Fritz Kreisler printed on 17 March 1935, Newman put it to the violinist that while "the practice hitherto has been to assume that when an 'editor' claimed to have in his possession an original manuscript of the work he was speaking the truth.... You [Fritz Kreisler] have unfortunately shown us that in this connection words do not always, or entirely, mean what they say."[50] Consider, once again, the publisher's preface printed in the sheet music of Kreisler's forgeries, which boldly states that "the original manuscripts used ... are so freely treated that they constitute, in fact, original works."[51] Kreisler

---

[45] For a detailed account of Newman's life and criticism, see Paul Watt, *Ernest Newman: A Critical Biography* (London: Boydell & Brewer, 2017).

[46] His monumental four-volume biography of Richard Wagner may be his most influential musi-cological work. See Ernest Newman, *The Life of Richard Wagner*, 4 vols. (New York: Alfred A. Knopf, 1933–46).

[47] For Newman's early manifesto in anti-romantic skepticism, see [Ernest Newman] Hugh Mortimer Cecil, *Pseudo-Philosophy at the End of the Nineteenth Century* (London: University Press, 1897).

[48] On Newman's pseudonyms and associated anecdotes, see Watt, *Ernest Newman*, 10ff.

[49] Fritz Kreisler, "Mr. Kreisler's Defence," *Sunday Times* (London), 10 March 1935, 15.

[50] Ernest Newman, "An Open Letter to Fritz Kreisler," *Sunday Times* (London), 17 March 1935, 7.

[51] [Fritz Kreisler] Luigi Boccherini, *Allegretto* (Mainz: B. Schott's Söhne, 1910).

90 FORGERY IN MUSICAL COMPOSITION

insisted that his authorship was "in a measure confessed" by such words, yet Newman begged to differ, insisting that these prefaces were "simply a formula to ensure copyright."[52] "All this," he shot back at Kreisler, "has nothing whatever to do with the ethical point at issue . . . *you* gave the public to understand that what you had done was to operate upon an *original manuscript . . .* when as a matter of fact *there was no such manuscript.*"[53] Even to say "that 'they are so freely treated as to,' etc.,"—as Newman damningly concludes—"is equivalent to affirming that there *was* an original to be so treated."[54]

DUSTY, OLD, FORGOTTEN CLOAKS

In the wake of the *New York Times* revelations, Kreisler insisted that he had adopted the names of "old masters" only because he found it "inexpedient and tactless to repeat [his] name endlessly on the programs."[55] There is an element of truth to this: when Kreisler first started incorporating the forged works into performances around 1900 he was a touring violinist in his mid-twenties who had just completed a two-year stint in the military. While not unknown, he was by no means the beloved grandfatherly authority figure that he would become by 1935. Olin Downes was probably not wrong when he defended the actions of his informant by claiming that "neither the public, the press, nor Mr. Kreisler's colleagues would have taken as kindly to these compositions had they been designated as being merely the creations of a living violinist."[56]

When Kreisler launched his career at the dawn of the twentieth century, the outlook for anyone wishing to be taken seriously as both a violinist and a composer was becoming increasingly bleak. As the respective technical aspirations of both performance and composition became ever more rarefied, cross specialization dwindled, leading to an increasingly stark division of labor—what Leon Botstein has called a "separation of functions"—between musical authors, on the one hand, and their instrumental and vocal agents, on the other.[57] It did not help that aspirationally serious composers were expected to forsake genres foregrounding individual virtuoso soloists as an implicitly low-brow distraction from the strictures of abstract musical structure under a regime of what might be considered a heightened form of composer-centeredness.

---

[52] Fritz Kreisler, "Kreisler Aroused by Critics' Taunts," *New York Times*, 18 February 1935, 19. Newman, "An Open Letter to Fritz Kreisler," 7.

[53] Newman, "An Open Letter to Fritz Kreisler," 7. Emphasis from original text.

[54] Newman, "An Open Letter to Fritz Kreisler," 7. Emphasis from original text.

[55] Quoted in Downes, "Kreisler Reveals 'Classics' as Own," 1.

[56] Downes, "Kreisler's 'Classics,'" X5.

[57] Leon Botstein, "Music of a Century: Museum Culture and the Politics of Subsidy," in *The Cambridge History of Twentieth-Century Music*, edited by Nicholas Cook and Anthony Pople (Cambridge: Cambridge University Press, 2008): 40–68, at 50.

In his unwillingness to put down the violin for the composer's pen as much as his stubbornly anti-modernist embrace of tonality, Kreisler asserted the appearance—like so many forgers throughout history—of a man born two centuries too late. His public persona was, as discussed above, designed in no small part to complement this anachronistic image with biographical tropes echoing the heroic age of the virtuoso composer. Despite growing up in the same city as his contemporary and occasional collaborator Arnold Schoenberg (figure 2.1), Kreisler openly rejected modernist aesthetics, maintaining a self-consciously old-Viennese preference for tunefulness, nostalgia, and easy-going charm reflected in every element of his image down to the elaborate three-piece suits and impeccably groomed mustache.

Tellingly, when Kreisler turned to forgery, the very masks that he chose to wear—in names like Pugnani, Cartier, and Vivaldi—harkened back to a prelapsarian performer-centered culture in which a virtuoso could be considered to have written important music without the advantage of being deceased. Edmond T. Johnson has recently speculated that Kreisler may have chosen these names in part because they lay ready to hand in recently published reference books on

Figure 2.1 Fritz Kreisler (second from left) and Arnold Schoenberg (seated at the cello) as members of a Schrammelmusik Quintet. Reichenau, July 8, 1900. PH1386, A5, C1, Arnold Schönberg Center Bildarchiv. Private Collection

92   FORGERY IN MUSICAL COMPOSITION

the history of violin playing.[58] The suggestion is compelling not least because many of the names in question (with the possible exception of Vivaldi) would have been unfamiliar to all but the most academic of contemporary audiences. On this point Kreisler's own explanation of his choice of names—published in response to Newman's critiques and including an explicit reference to "musical reference books"—is worth quoting at length:

> The names I carefully selected were, for the most part, strictly unknown. Who ever had heard of a work by Pugnani, Cartier, Francoeur, Porpora, Louis Couperin, Padre Martini or Stamitz before I began to compose in their names? They lived exclusively as paragraphs in musical reference books, and their work, when existing and authenticated, lay mouldering in monasteries and old libraries. Their names were no more than empty shells, dusty, old, forgotten cloaks, which I borrowed to hide my identity.[59]

This is an astonishing metaphor. Let us leave to one side the work that has since gone into publishing serious performing editions and musicological criticism addressing the "mouldering" music that Kreisler so brashly dismisses out of hand. His specification that he selected the names with "care" (presumably to make sure that they really were "strictly unknown") does nothing to mitigate the closing comparison of actual historical figures—Pugnani, Cartier, Francoeur, Porpora, Louis Couperin, Padre Martini, and Stamitz—to "dusty, old, forgotten cloaks."[60] From a critical perspective this remarkable phrasing can be seen to reduce real human beings to objects of use. Like items of clothing, their identities are, in Kreisler's eyes, inanimate things to be picked up and discarded at will, especially when they have the misfortune of being judged "dusty," "old," and "forgotten."

In the wake of the authorship scandal, Kreisler protested that he never intended to publish the works when he began composing and performing them around the turn of the century. "In the course of years, however, I was put under pressure . . . by my colleagues" who, Kreisler tells us, "claimed that for selfish reasons I was monopolizing the selections."[61] When he finally released the *Classical Manuscripts* with Schott in 1910 (purportedly under peer pressure), Kreisler claimed that the compositions "had meanwhile become so

---

[58] Johnson suggests the following three sources by way of example: James M. Fleming, *The Fiddle Fancier's Guide* (London: Haynes, Foucher, 1892); A. Ehrlich, *Berühmte Geiger der Vergangenheit und Gegenwart* (Leipzig: A. H. Payne, 1893); and T. L. Phipson, *Famous Violinists and Fine Violins* (London: Chatto & Windus, 1903). See Johnson, "Revival and Antiquation: Modernism's Musical Pasts," 106.

[59] Fritz Kreisler, "A Letter from Fritz Kreisler," *Sunday Times* (London), 31 March 1935, 7.

[60] Kreisler, "A Letter from Fritz Kreisler," 7.

[61] Kreisler, "Kreisler Aroused by Critics' Taunts," 19.

KREISLERIAN FANTASIES   93

popular under the assumed names given them that there was no possibility of rechristening them."[62]

Taken at face value, this is a familiar, all-too-human story. Lies beget more lies. Deception hardens and deepens through elaboration, slowly snowballing out of all proportion and control. And yet, despite Kreisler's professed belief that it would have been impossible to correct his misattributions by 1909, the original 1910 *Classical Manuscripts* series did, in fact, take the opportunity to do just that. Three of Kreisler's earliest forgeries—the waltzes "Liebesfreud," "Liebesleid," and "Schön Rosmarin" ["Love's Joy," "Love's Sorrow," and "Beautiful Rosemary"]—were reattributed in publication under the ambiguous subtitle "Alt-Wiener Tanzweisen" [Old-Viennese Dance Songs] in place of an authorial name. Suggestive as "Alt-Wiener Tanzweisen" may be, the fact remains that all three pieces had originally been penned—and were explicitly performed in Kreisler's concerts—under the name of the composer-violinist Joseph Lanner, a lesser-known rival of Johann Strauss I. In published versions of the *Classical Manuscripts*, Lanner's name is nowhere to be found.

According to a story that Kreisler repeated frequently during the authorship scandal of 1935, the violinist confessed to composing the three "Lanner" works in a 1910 confrontation with the German music critic Dr. Leopold Schmidt of the *Berliner Tageblatt*.[63] As Kreisler had it, Schmidt had upbraided him for arrogantly including the "Caprice Viennois," a work of his own composition, on "the same program as the dances of Lanner [i.e., "Liebesfreud" and "Liebesleid"], these delightful genre creations filled with Schubertian melos and reflecting the Vienna of pre-March days."[64] In numerous interviews given after 1935, Kreisler gleefully recounts how he had sent a letter to Schmidt, explaining: "If the Lanner pieces were 'worthy of Schubert,' then I was Schubert, because I had written them!"[65] It was a matter of disbelief, for Kreisler, that "musical experts did not stumble upon the truth [about the *Classical Manuscripts*] immediately" given that, as he put it, "the [Schmidt] incident ought to have taught them a lesson."[66] In his biography of the violinist, Lochner supports this position, summarizing the "Alt-Wiener Tanzweisen" affair by declaring: "As a young man of thirty-five, [Kreisler] had tried in vain to set musicologists on the scent of his 'forgeries.'"[67]

Clearly, there is another way of looking at this. Given that Kreisler saw fit to confess to the three "Lanner" forgeries in 1910, even striking the composer's name from the published editions in favor of the vague and folkloric subtitle "Alt-Wiener Tanzweisen," why not do the same with the other fourteen *Classical*

[62] Kreisler, "Kreisler Aroused by Critics' Taunts," 19.
[63] Kreisler, "Kreisler Aroused by Critics' Taunts," 19.
[64] Quoted in Kreisler, "Kreisler Aroused by Critics' Taunts," 19.
[65] Quoted in Louis Biancolli, "The Great Kreisler Hoax," 56.
[66] Kreisler, "Kreisler aroused by Critics' Taunts," 19.
[67] Lochner, *Fritz Kreisler*, 292.

94 FORGERY IN MUSICAL COMPOSITION

Manuscripts? Kreisler's 1909 interview with the *New York Times* about the provenance of the works holds a clue. In this article, Kreisler is quoted as claiming: "I have altogether fifty-three manuscripts of this sort in my possession."[68] "Five of them," he added, "are more or less valueless," but "[f]orty-eight of them are gems."[69] Subtracting the "nineteen" that the violinist admitted had already found their way onto his programs by 1909 (including the seventeen *Classical Manuscripts* published in 1910), Kreisler was left with a total of twenty-nine such "gems" that he could arrange, debut, and publish at will later in his career. In other words, Kreisler harbored no genuine intention of ceasing to forge new compositions for himself after rebranding the "Lanner" works, as the three additional forgeries published under false attributions to Stamitz, Porpora, and Vivaldi after 1910 (see table 2.1) clearly demonstrate.

CHATTERTONS AND DOSSENAS

Ethically speaking, forgery is more complex and ambiguous than other forms of allonymy, including, for example, plagiarism and pseudonymity. As previous chapters have explored, plagiarism is widely considered to be morally objectionable above all because it involves what might be thought of as authorial greed, since plagiarists are fundamentally in the business of stealing labor from others. Contrastingly, forgery is sometimes thought to involve a kind of authorial humility in that, by definition, the forger must temporarily refuse to take credit for his or her own work. As the *Chicago Daily Tribune*'s music columnist Edward Moore sardonically remarked in defense of Kreisler's actions, "What other composer has there ever been since the first note was written down on paper who was unwilling to take all the credit he could get?"[70]

This defense is particularly compelling in cases of inventive forgery, where an entirely new artwork is created and falsely attributed to an existing author.[71] Unlike both plagiarism and referential forgery (i.e., the act of passing off a copy as an original), inventive forgery is end-positive. This is to say that it does not appropriate the existing structure or authorship of an artwork already made but rather adds an entirely new artwork to the world. The ethical and economic

---

[68] *New York Times*, "How Kreisler Finds Musical Novelties," 7.

[69] *New York Times*, "How Kreisler Finds Musical Novelties," 7.

[70] Edward Moore, "Kreisler Gives His Name to Classic Music," *Chicago Daily Tribune*, 17 February 1935, E3. Of course, Moore's statement about musicians having consistently demanded to take credit for their work since "the first note was written down on paper" might be considered rather ironic given that the earliest notated music sources in the European tradition are, overwhelmingly, anonymous.

[71] On "referential" and "inventive" categories of forgery, see the introduction of this book and Jerrold Levinson, *Music, Art, and Metaphysics: Essays in Philosophical Aesthetics* (Oxford: Oxford University Press, 2011), 103.

implications of this argument led Downes, for example, to assert that because "no composer of the past . . . lost royalties" through Kreisler's actions, the deception was "harmless"—in other words, a victimless crime.[72] The money Kreisler made from the *Classical Manuscripts* was not stolen to the detriment of other rightful authors but rather was earned through an original act of creation. Or so the argument goes.

The logic of this defense is, of course, deeply capitalist-materialist, relying on an autonomous view of musical works as pure exchange value in which authorship and identity has no bearing. Thus Downes conceptualizes "harm done" exclusively in terms of pecuniary damages—i.e., the "loss of royalties"—with no thought to the symbolic violence involved in identity theft, historical defamation, and abuse of trust. Even economically speaking, the implication is that appropriating a name provides no undue advantage so long as the compositional labor is the forger's own. Fundamentally, this assumes that the market for musical works is—or, at least, should be—a meritocracy in which composers earn only in proportion to the inherent, objective, and immutable qualities of the sounding structure itself. Kreisler expressed such views frequently enough throughout his career, above all when he complained of the scourge of the modern artistic "snob"—a favorite term of insult with which to recriminate his critics.[73] In a February 1935 *New York Times* article written to defend his actions, the violinist rails against those "who judge merely by name" and "draw on musicians' lexicons for their enthusiasm," ultimately warning readers that "so long . . . as there is snobbism in us, so long will there also be Chattertons and Dossenas."[74]

In this last reference, Kreisler provides us with some compelling examples with which to interrogate his claims. The Italian sculptor Alceo Dossena had become a subject of public fascination as recently as 1928 when it was revealed that works that had ended up in the Boston Museum of Fine Arts, the Cleveland Museum, and New York City's Metropolitan Museum of Art—including a fifteenth-century "Mino da Fiesole" sarcophagus and an "ancient-Greek" statue of Athena dated to the fifth century BCE—were, in fact, his own original creations.[75] Crucially, Dossena claimed that he had always believed he was inventing entirely new works in historical styles for sale as such. It was his crooked dealers, Alfredo Fasoli and Romano Palesi, who had sold his pieces as genuine antiques without his knowledge or consent. "The truth," Dossena

---

[72] Downes, "Kreisler's 'Classics,'" X5.

[73] In 1909, for example, he complained at length about how "snobbishness in music is making it difficult for the giver of concerts." *New York Times*, "How Kreisler Finds Musical Novelties," 7.

[74] Kreisler, "Kreisler Aroused by Critics' Taunts," 19.

[75] The sarcophagus was purchased by the Boston Museum of Fine Arts for $100,000 while the Cleveland Museum paid $120,000 for the statue of Athena. See Jonathon Keats, *Forged: Why Fakes Are the Great Art of Our Age* (New York: Oxford University Press, 2013), 51 and 56.

professed, "is that I have never made any [sic] but original things, modeling them from nature in an antique character and style."[76]

Given that Dossena subjected many of these "original things" to elaborate acid baths and sandblasting in an apparent attempt to create the illusion of natural ageing, his pleas of innocence might sound rather farfetched. Yet there are good economic reasons to take the artist seriously. In the 1920s, his dealers, Fasoli and Palesi, often made hundreds of thousands of dollars from a Dossena piece sold to a prominent museum or private collector as the work of an old master. In aggregate, their profits from the scam have been estimated at over $2 million.[77] Yet Dossena, who claimed to have had no idea that American museums were exhibiting his works as genuine antiques, reportedly saw less than a 1 percent share of this princely sum. As Jonathon Keats surmises, Fasoli and Palesi were paying one of the most technically masterful—and financially lucrative— sculptors of the early twentieth century what amounted to "a good wage for an accomplished stonemason."[78] If Dossena was in on the scam, it is difficult indeed to imagine that he was motivated by greed.

After his forgeries were unmasked in 1928, Dossena received enough publicity to be openly exhibited under his own name in Paris, Berlin, Vienna, and London. Yet, poignantly, he failed to recapture anything resembling the economic success that Fasoli and Palesi had achieved in selling his works under false pretenses. When thirty-nine of Dossena's "authentically fake" pieces of renaissance and antique sculpture were auctioned off in the ballroom of New York City's Plaza Hotel in 1933, the highest price paid—for a marble relief of the Madonna and child in the style of Mino da Fiesole—was $675.[79] This is a paltry sum compared, for example, to the $225,000 that Helen Clay Frick had parted with less than a decade earlier for a similar "fourteenth-century" annunciation scene by Dossena.[80] Four years after the botched auction, the artist died in Rome, a poor man.

Unlike Dossena, Kreisler certainly could not plead ignorance that his antique-style *Classical Manuscripts* had been misattributed. Yet the mere comparison underscores Kreisler's appeal to authorial humility by aligning him with a famous forger widely regarded as a tragic outsider figure. Moreover, by intentionally disguising his works with the names of old masters, Kreisler claimed to be casting off the antiquarian shackles of authenticity, attunement, and tyrannical high-brow snobbery under which Dossena and those like him had suffered. In doing so, he not only won a kind of vicarious revenge but also proved—as he insisted to Newman—that when "the name changes, the value remains."[81]

[76] Keats, *Forged*, 61.
[77] Keats, *Forged*, 54.
[78] Keats, *Forged*, 54–55.
[79] Keats, *Forged*, 64.
[80] Keats, *Forged*, 55.
[81] Kreisler, "Mr. Kreisler's Defence," 15.

Figure 2.2 Henry Wallis, *The Death of Chatterton*, Tate Version (1855)

The violinist's reference to Chatterton serves a similar purpose. Having failed to secure patronage after attempting to disguise his works as the writings of a fictional fifteenth-century monk named "Thomas Rowley," the seventeen-year-old poet Thomas Chatterton famously went on to take his own life by poisoning himself with arsenic in 1770.[82] The cult of romanticism subsequently recast Chatterton as a hero condemned to die young and penniless on the altar of art in ways aptly evoked by Henry Wallis's classic pre-Raphaelite depiction of his death, shown here in figure 2.2. Kreisler's point in bringing up all this was to appeal to the idea that forgers are humble folk who conceal their identities in the face of professional adversity. The implication is that they are not so much criminals as victims of a brutally unappreciative art world too shot through with snobbery to value a living poet as much as a dead one.

Of course, there was a key ethical difference between Chatterton's poetry and Kreisler's compositions. While Chatterton invented "Thomas Rowley" from scratch, Kreisler took the names of real historical figures—Cartier, Pugnani, Vivaldi, and the rest—and ascribed his own works to them. In this sense, Chatterton's poems are acts of high-pseudonymity (the attribution of your own works to an invented, fictional figure), while Kreisler's *Classical Manuscripts* remain forgeries. The distinction was not lost on contemporary observers. When

---

[82] For Chatterton's poems, see *Poems, supposed to have been written at Bristol, by Thomas Rowley, and others, in the Fifteenth Century* (London: T. Payne and Son, 1777).

98 FORGERY IN MUSICAL COMPOSITION

Kreisler attempted to argue that he had misattributed his compositions out of the sheer "necessity" of shielding his identity, Newman—himself an experienced user of literary pseudonyms—responded trenchantly:

> I can understand a composer wishing certain works of his to appear under another name than his own. But what is this "necessity"—more dire, surely, than anything ever conceived by the imagination of a Greek tragedian!—that compels [you] to choose, out of the million possible names offered . . . Vivaldi, Pugnani, Porpora, Martini, Couperin, Cartier, Dittersdorf, Francoeur, and Stamitz?[83]

The analogy to Chatterton, Newman proceeds, is thus "transparently false."[84] Clearly, the parallel to Kreisler's own conduct "would have been for Chatterton to have published his inventions under the names of well-known poets of the fifteenth century."[85] The *Musical Times* made a similar objection, noting that there was no reasonable necessity that could have prevented Kreisler from simply "using a *nom de guerre*" in place of the names of real historical figures.[86] The crucial ontological and ethical boundary here—between Chatterton's pseudonym and Kreisler's forgery—goes well beyond mere money. As the magazine *Musical America* argued, the grievance against Kreisler's actions was rooted in trust and historical fidelity: "A departed musician who cannot speak for himself is being made a party to a deception and is being given a false musical front before the world."[87]

THE BROTHERS CASADESUS

There is a sense in which Kreisler's forgeries also, paradoxically, made him a man of his time. Fin de siècle aesthetic culture often took considerable liberties in its pursuit of the antique: in many ways, this was a hangover from prevailing editorial attitudes to pre-classical music in the nineteenth century, when, as Harry Haskell surmises, many composers and arrangers "felt no qualms about touching up another artist's work; in fact, they felt they were doing the old masters a favor by bringing their music up to date," perhaps above all in the soloistic genres where performer-centeredness persisted the most tenaciously.[88]

---

[83] Newman, "An Open Letter to Fritz Kreisler," 7.
[84] Newman, "An Open Letter to Fritz Kreisler," 7.
[85] Newman, "An Open Letter to Fritz Kreisler," 7.
[86] *Musical Times*, "Kreisleriana," March 1935, 251.
[87] *Musical America*, "L'Affaire Kreisler," 25 February 1935, 17.
[88] Harry Haskell, *The Early Music Revival: A History* (London: Thames and Hudson, 1988), 86. On performer-centeredness (as opposed to composer-centeredness), see this book's introduction and Michael Talbot, "The Work-Concept and Composer-Centredness," in *The Musical Work: Reality or Invention?*, edited by Michael Talbot (Liverpool: Liverpool University Press, 2000): 168–86.

In their editions of the chaconne from J. S. Bach's Partita in D Minor for Solo Violin, BWV 1004, published, respectively, in 1847 and 1854, both Felix Mendelssohn and Robert Schumann, for example, took the liberty of adding an entirely new piano accompaniment to Bach's already contrapuntally complex solo texture. Today the majority of mainstream performers and audiences would surely consider these adaptations to be distasteful examples of editorial over-reach. Yet, for much of the latter half of the nineteenth century, Mendelssohn's and Schumann's interventions into Bach's text were widely thought to be favorable compositional modernizations to the point of becoming the default performing versions of the "solo" chaconne.[89] One 1889 treatise on instrumentation argues that one should "prefer a performance of the Chaconne with the very appropriate piano accompaniment by Felix Mendelssohn" because, in the original version, "it is not possible to suppress the notion that . . . we miss an accompaniment by lower voices, and particularly a complementary and secure bass line."[90] As if to sum up this editorial attitude, no less a figure than Eduard Hanslick was quoted as declaring that the artist who cuts, adapts, and arranges old compositions "seems more righteous in the interest of the work than those purists, who would rather sacrifice the living effect for the sake of philological faithfulness to the letter."[91]

In some cases, this lack of editorial transparency extended to outright deception. Consider the Parisian *Société des instruments Anciens*, a performing group founded in 1901 by the violist Henri Casadesus and his siblings Marius Casadesus, on violin; Marcel Casadesus, on cello and viola da gamba; and Régina Patorni-Casadesus, on keyboard instruments. With Camille Saint-Saëns as its patron, the *société* toured widely across Europe, the Middle East, and North America, where it played a key role in introducing early twentieth-century concert audiences to instruments such as the viola d'amore, the quinton, and the harpsichord. Compellingly, the Casadesuses also claimed to be reviving historical repertory, including works by the likes of Giovanni Battista Borghi, Antonio Bruni, Jean-Joseph Mouret, and the evidently not-so-dusty-and-forgotten François Francoeur.[92] Yet, much like Kreisler's *Classical Manuscripts*, these compositions were not what they seemed. Hinting at this fact, the noted early twentieth-century

---

[89] See Georg Feder, "History of the Arrangements of Bach's Chaconne," in *The Bach Chaconne for Solo Violin: A Collection of Views*, edited by Jon F. Eiche, translated by Egbert M. Ennulat (Athens, GA: American String Teachers Association, 1985): 41–61; first published as "Geschichte der Bearbeitung von Bachs Chaconne," in *Bach-Interpretationen, Walter Blakenburg zum 65. Geburtstag* (Göttingen: Vandenhoeck & Ruprecht, 1969): 168–89.

[90] Salomon Jadassohn, *Lehrbuch der Instrumentation* (Leipzig: Breitkopf & Härtel, 1889), 136.

[91] Cited in Friedrich Chrysander, "Was Herr Prof. Hanslick sich unter 'Kunstzeloten' vorstellt," *Leipziger allgemeine musikalische Zeitung* 3 (1869): 387. Translation in Alexander Rehding, *Music and Monumentality: Commemoration and Wonderment in Nineteenth-Century Germany* (New York: Oxford University Press, 2009), 148.

[92] Haskell, *The Early Music Revival*, 51.

100   FORGERY IN MUSICAL COMPOSITION

Italian composer and keyboard player Alfredo Casella—by no means an anti-Hanslickian "purist" when it came to the transcription of old compositions—once stated that he had ceased associating with the family and their *société* because "almost all of the music played was either apocryphal or had at least been cleverly 'retouched' by [Henri] that talented and sympathetic rascal of a Casadesus."[93]

Casella didn't know the half of it. The "rascal" Henri was, in reality, the composer of works including two forged viola concertos attributed to J. C. Bach and G. F. Handel, the latter of which was discussed in passing in this book's preface.[94] Henri's brother Marius, meanwhile, authored the Violin Concerto in D Major supposedly written by the ten-year-old Mozart in dedication to Louis XV's eldest daughter, princess Adélaïde of France. As if to pin down a biographical provenance for the concerto's existence, Marius's published edition of the work—released with Schott in 1933, two years after the violinist had premiered the work in concert—even included an invented letter of dedication from Mozart to Adélaïde dated 1766.[95] The English version of this preface, translated from "Mozart's" original French, is reproduced in full, below:

> Madame,
> In accepting the homage which my poor strains render to your great talent, you overwhelm me once more with your favour. If your august eyes have watched over my work, your indulgence and your goodness have greatly facilitated it. And if the name of Adelaide will grace these modest efforts, it will remain to all eternity graven on my heart.
> With the most profound respects, I remain your most humble, most obedient and very small servant,
> J. G. Wolfgang Mozart,
> Versailles, May 26th 1766[96]

The editorial preface goes on to state that the work was likely composed before Adélaïde's eyes and in a controlled span of time as a means for the child Mozart

[93] Alfredo Casella, *Music in My Time*, translated by Spencer Norton (Norman: University of Oklahoma Press; 1955), 226.

[94] For Henri Casadesus's wife's confession, see Walter Lebermann, "Apokryph, Plagiat, Korruptel oder Falsifikat?," *Die Musikforschung* 20 (1967): 413–25, at 422.

[95] [Marius Casadesus] Wolfgang Amadeus Mozart, *Violinkonzert in D* (Adelaide-Konzert), edited and arranged by Marius Casadesus (Mainz: B. Schott's Söhne, 1933).

[96] The French text attributed to Mozart reads: "En agréant l'hommage de mon faible savoir à Votre grand talent, Vous me comblez une fois de plus de Vos bienfaits. Si Vos yeux augustes ont présidé à mon travail, Votre indulgence et Votre bonté l'ont singulièrement facilité, et si le nom d'Adélaïde veut bien étendre sa protection sur ces modestes essais il restera à tout jamais gravé dans mon cœur. Je suis, avec le plus profond respect, Madame, Votre très humble, très obéissant et très petit serviteur." Some of the wording in this dedication was surely inspired by—if not directly lifted from—the child Mozart's "op. 1" (i.e., K. 6 and K. 7), published in Paris in 1764 with a remarkably similar dedication to Princess Victoire of France.

KREISLERIAN FANTASIES   101

to demonstrate his precocious compositional abilities for potential aristocratic patrons. Eighteenth-century audiences, it claims, "often doubted the astonishing talent of the young artist and therefore set him a task that had to be performed in the presence of those giving the commission."[97] The original manuscript, now housed "in a private collection in France . . . which was not unknown to experts," was reportedly written in short score, with "the upper [staff] containing the solo violin part as well as the tutti and the lower the bass part."[98] While the lower staff of the original manuscript was in E major, the upper staff—including the solo part—was written down in D, reflecting the princess's apparent preference for playing a pochette (or "lady's violin," as Marius calls it) tuned a whole step up. The implication of this elaborate narrative was that—like Kreisler's "freely treated" *Classical Manuscripts*—the performing version of the "Adélaïde" concerto for soloist and orchestra was the result of a considerable amount of editorial retouching on Marius Casadesus's part. Crucially, this ensured that his copyright in the arrangement could be maintained as a derivative work, beyond the public domain despite the age of "Mozart's" alleged original composition.

On 3 November 1934, one year after Schott's publication of the concerto, the Hungarian violinist Jelly d'Arányi gave Casadesus's "Adélaïde" its British premiere. In response, the Mozart scholar and critic Alfred Einstein published an article in the *Daily Telegraph* provocatively subtitled "A Question or Two for Marius Casadesus."[99] Einstein protested that according to Leopold Mozart's travel diaries, the family had not been in Versailles on 26 May 1766; in fact, they arrived two days later, on 28 May. The "Adélaïde" concerto was, moreover, excluded from Leopold's 1768 *Verzeichnis* of his son's works, which catalogues even the smallest of the young Wolfgang's compositions to that date in meticulous detail, right down to the informal sketchbooks. Could the dispositionally fastidious Leopold Mozart really have neglected to make any formal record of such a substantial work dedicated to a royal patron? Given that eighteenth-century dedications were customarily appended only to published works, would it not moreover have been a grievous faux pas for the child Mozart to write a letter of dedication to accompany an unpublished manuscript for a concerto in short score? There was little hope of Camille Saint-Saëns or Jean-Baptiste Weckerlin—the two musical experts who supposedly knew the original source manuscript—speaking up on these points, since they were both deceased by the time Schott published the "Adélaïde" concerto in 1933.[100] As such, Einstein's article ends with an open challenge, effectively inviting Marius to prove his case

---

[97] [Casadesus] Mozart, *Violinkonzert in D*.

[98] [Casadesus] Mozart, *Violinkonzert in D*.

[99] Alfred Einstein, "The 'Adelaide' Concerto—A Question or Two for Marius Casadesus," *Daily Telegraph* (London), 3 November 1934, 9.

[100] Alfred Einstein, "Mozart's 'Adelaide' Concerto," in *Essays on Music* (New York: W. W. Norton, 1956), 233–36 at 234.

102 FORGERY IN MUSICAL COMPOSITION

by delivering the source-critical goods: "Mr. Casadesus is in a position to satisfy all these doubts if he will only circulate a photostat of the manuscript. By doing so he can dispel our apprehensions and turn a doubting Thomas into the most faithful of all Mozart disciples."[101]

Of course, Marius never provided Einstein with the requested photographic evidence. Nor did he take the opportunity to respond with a confession which, in 1934, might have beaten Kreisler to the international headlines by a year. The story was that the owner of the manuscript source wished to remain anonymous at all costs, refusing any request for photography or for public viewing.[102] (As subsequent chapters will demonstrate, the invention of an uncooperative owner who wishes to remain anonymous while refusing access to original manuscripts became a consistent stalling tactic used by modern musical forgers who wish to avoid producing a "historical" document that will be subjected to expert scrutiny.) When Einstein's monumental revision of the Köchel catalogue was published in 1937, the "Adélaïde" concerto was thus filed as K. Anh. 294a, under the *Anhang* or "appendix" reserved for doubtful and misattributed works. Einstein's editorial comments for the revised Köchel conclude that given the extensive list of problems with the concerto's provenance, "proceeding to analyze the work's 'inner evidence' would be superfluous."[103] Writing more bluntly in 1945, he referred to "the so-called 'Adelaide' concerto" as nothing more than "a piece of mystification à la Kreisler."[104]

With a little help from new media, the "Adélaïde" concerto had become popular enough to maintain a life of its own despite Einstein's best efforts to repudiate the work. In 1934, the teenage prodigy Yehudi Menuhin—whose Brooklyn recital would put Olin Downes on Kreisler's scent the following year—made a recording of the concerto for HMV that would soon prove immensely commercially successful. (Paul Webster, for example, would later call it "one of the world's best selling classical records.")[105] As a result, HMV's growing market of home listeners were reassured that they were hearing a concerto by W. A. Mozart, "edited and arranged by Marius Casadesus." In sheer breadth of reach, no scholarly reclassification in a thematic catalogue could compete with an LP cover. It is particularly ironic, then, that the unprecedented success of Menuhin's recording would ultimately prove the forged concerto's undoing.

The problem came in 1976, when Pathé-Marconi, the French arm of EMI, absorbed HMV's old catalogues. As a result of the merger, Marius Casadesus's

---

[101] Einstein, "Mozart's 'Adelaide' Concerto," 236.

[102] *Der Spiegel*, "Schwindel in D," 24 July 1977, 139–40, at 139.

[103] Ludwig Ritter von Köchel, *Chronologisch-thematisches Verzeichnis sämtlicher Tonwerke Wolfgang Amade Mozarts*, edited by Alfred Einstein (Michigan: J. W. Edwards, 1947 [1937]), 908.

[104] Alfred Einstein, *Mozart: His Character, His Work*, translated by Arthur Mendel and Nathan Broder (New York: Oxford University Press, 1945), 278.

[105] Paul Webster, "Mozart's First Concerto Was a Fiddle," *Guardian*, 16 July 1977, 1.

royalties for Menuhin's recording—owed to him as the "Adélaïde" concerto's registered editor and arranger—were stopped.[106] As if adding insult to injury, Pathé then reissued the Menuhin LP with a redesigned front cover that failed to mention anything about an "arranger" or "editor," implicitly attributing the work to Mozart alone. Marius, now aged eighty-four, responded the following July by beginning a legal action against Pathé that cast the forger not as defendant but as plaintiff. His goal was not only to recover lost royalties to the tune of 50,000 francs (or about $10,000 US in 1977), but also, more fundamentally, to assert his authorial rights as the sole composer of the "Adélaïde" concerto, setting the record straight after some four decades of deception.[107]

On 22 July 1977, the head of the Paris tribunal that heard the case ruled that while he was unable to transfer the concerto's registered authorship, Pathé would have to refund Marius's royalties for every copy of the Menuhin LP that had been sold without crediting his orchestration and harmonization.[108] A substantial payout followed. Yet, in the subsequent press fallout, Marius—like Kreisler before him—was keen to represent himself as a tragic Faustian figure who had, in old age, become the victim of his youthful ambitions. "I was a young man back then, 37 or 38 years old," he wrote.[109] "Everybody was playing the concerto and I was receiving credit as the man who orchestrated it. After a certain point, it was too serious an affair to disabuse my friends and colleagues."[110] Of course, the violinist makes scant reference to the question of the 50,000 franc indemnity or of his decades of royalties earned from Menuhin's recording and Schott's sheet music. Nor does he mention the missed opportunity to confess to Einstein following his London *Daily Telegraph* rebuke of 1934. At the tribunal itself, the question of how much extra revenue Marius gained by falsely associating his concerto with Mozart seems not to have come up for discussion.

MUSICAL VALUES

In his dealings with Kreisler, Ernest Newman was not so forgiving. The article that set in motion the public dispute between these two men closes with Newman wondering what would happen "if someone were to claim damages from Kreisler

---

[106] Webster, "Mozart's First Concerto Was a Fiddle."

[107] *Le Monde*, "Qui a conçu 'Adélaïde'?," 23 July 1977, 13. *New York Times*, "Marius Casadesus Suing over Concerto 'by Mozart,'" 16 August 1977, 40.

[108] *Le Monde*, "La paternité d'Adelaïde," 25 July 1977, 13. The issue of the attribution would have to be taken up with SACEM, the French "Society of Musical Authors, Composers, and Editors" [Société des auteurs, compositeurs, et éditeurs de musique] where Marius himself had registered the concerto as his edition and orchestration of a work by Mozart in 1931.

[109] *New York Times*, "Marius Casadesus Suing over Concerto 'by Mozart,'" 16 August 1977, 40.

[110] *New York Times*, "Marius Casadesus Suing," 40.

and his publishers."[111] "Presumably," he quips, such a person "would at least be entitled to have his money back."[112] Two years into Roosevelt's "New Deal," with UK and US unemployment levels still well above 15 percent, it is appropriate enough that the linchpin of Newman's critique was that greatest of all romantic taboos: the question of profit.[113] His article's secondary headline, "Debit and Credit," exposes the deeply unromantic bond between the latter word's financial and authorial meanings in a sharp bit of wordplay. Put simply, Kreisler may have refused to take composerly credit for the *Classical Manuscripts*, but as a self-declared arranger he certainly enjoyed no shortage of credit when it came to the matter of royalties, just like Marius and Henri Casadesus.

To Edward Moore's facetious aforementioned defense of Kreisler's forgeries—"what other composer has there ever been ... who was unwilling to take all the credit he could get?"—Newman might well have responded that it depends on what sort of credit is meant.[114] Even when their works are distributed under false authorial names, forgers such as Fritz Kreisler and Marius Casadesus are ultimately still in a position to receive a substantial amount of financial credit, so long as they are credited as arrangers and editors: thus Marius's litigious response when his paratexts and royalties for the "Adélaïde" concerto were unceremoniously stripped by Pathé-Marconi. Yehudi Menuhin's father, Moshe, may not have appreciated the double-meaning when he told the *New York Times*: "There is no question that this [group of forged compositions] is one of the most *creditable* things that Kreisler has done."[115] In defending himself from Newman, Kreisler himself insisted that while "the name changes, the value remains."[116] Where and in what form that value accumulates is arguably another matter altogether.

Back in New York, Olin Downes was keen to rebuff the charges of false advertising leveled by Newman. For one thing, Downes hastened to clarify that Kreisler's US publisher, Carl Fischer, had in fact offered a refund to anyone who wanted it. But, according to Downes, Newman's unsatisfied customers never materialized—quite to the contrary, Fischer was experiencing something of "an extra demand for printings of the old editions as souvenirs."[117] Historical ignorance is aesthetic bliss, a sentiment that Downes echoed by asking Kreisler's critics whether "the man who has kissed the wrong girl in the dark [should]

[111] Ernest Newman, "The Kreisler Revelations: Debit and Credit," *Sunday Times* (London), 24 February 1935, 5.

[112] Newman, "The Kreisler Revelations," 5.

[113] Bureau of Labor Statistics, *Historical Statistics of the United States from Colonial Times to the 1970*, Part I (US Government Printing Office, 1975), Series D 85-86 Unemployment: 1890–1970, 135. James Denman and Paul McDonald, "Unemployment Statistics from 1881 to the Present Day," *Labour Market Trends* 104, no. 1 (1996): 5–18, at 6.

[114] See Moore, "Kreisler Gives His Name to Classic Music," E3.

[115] *New York Times*, "Kreisler's Secret Kept by Musicians," 17. My emphasis.

[116] Kreisler, "Mr. Kreisler's Defence," 15.

[117] Downes, "Kreisler's 'Classics,'" X5

condemn the practice of kissing."[118] Cringe-inducingly dated as this 1930s take on illicit eroticism may sound today, Downes's philosophical point is dead serious. Unlike conventional compositions, forgeries put us at liberty to experience music as pure sensuous pleasure—a kiss in the dark, signifying nothing, no strings attached.

As such, forged works of art can be seen to serve a useful didactic purpose by driving out the aesthetic prejudices bound up with authorship and history. If only on this single issue, Newman was in total agreement with Downes and Kreisler. The difference was that, for Newman, the forgeries were not a means to elevate Kreisler to the status of his historical predecessors but rather a way of making the public recognize the crushing mediocrity of most authentically old music. If Kreisler's forgeries had succeeded, Newman claimed it was only because a vast amount of seventeenth- and eighteenth-century music was "merely the exploitation of formulae" in the first place.[119] "In so far as Bach and Handel . . . sat down in perfectly cold blood and ground out their morning's ration of music-according-to-the-recipe," he writes, they "produced well-sounding stuff that anyone of any intelligence to-day could turn out by the handful."[120]

From "formulae" and "exploitation" to the insipid grinding out of a "morning's ration," Newman's language maps a host of depression-era Fordist anxieties about mass production onto the act of musical composition. The comparison would not have been lost on Newman's near contemporary Max Friedländer—a pioneering scholar of authentication in the fine arts—for whom "an original resembles an organism; a copy, a machine."[121] Yet crucially, for Newman, it is not only the forgery as copy that is machine-like. Seventeenth- and eighteenth-century pastiche is so often successful, he claims, because much of the authentic material from that era was already mechanical in its reliance on the kinds of stock formulae and patterns normalized within a pre-romantic culture that conceived of music primarily in terms of combinatoric rhetoric and what Mark Evan Bonds has called objective expression.[122] Significantly, organic masterworks were exempt from Newman's iconoclastic assault. While he argued that it was perfectly possible to imitate the workaday mechanics of an unremarkable Bach chorale or Mozart minuet, one does not simply "grind out" the spirit and texture of a

---

[118] Downes, "Kreisler's 'Classics,'" X5

[119] Newman, "The Kreisler Revelations," 5.

[120] Newman, "The Kreisler Revelations," 5.

[121] Max J. Friedländer, *On Art and Connoisseurship*, translated by Tancred Borenius (Boston: Beacon Hill, 1960), 236; first published as *Von Kunst und Kennerschaft* (Berlin: Bruno Cassirer, 1942).

[122] On objective expression as conceptually distinct from subjective expression, see this book's introduction and Mark Evan Bonds, *The Beethoven Syndrome: Hearing Music as Autobiography* (New York: Oxford University Press, 2019).

St. *Matthew Passion* or a *Don Giovanni*. "The first-rate work of the first-rank classics" remains, he assures us, "inimitable."[123]

Newman's insistence on cultivating connoisseurship may strike many modern readers as willfully elitist. Yet, rightly or wrongly, the critic envisioned his task as a form of demystification and democratization in service of ordinary music lovers. "It has long been my contention"—writes Newman, impatiently—"that the musical public is too much influenced in its judgements by names: it will accept admiringly the most ordinary composition if only it bears the name of a classical composer."[124] In this sense, the scandal of the Kreisler forgeries was of such fascination because it provided an ideal opportunity to promote vigilance about aesthetic quality by lifting the scales from the eyes of the laity.

THE EXPLOITATION OF FORMULAE

For his part, Kreisler vigorously denied having followed compositional formulae, insisting—in the *New York Times*—that he had "made no endeavor whatever to stick closely to the style of the period from which [the *Classical Manuscripts*] were alleged to date."[125] This was in stark contradiction to a rather ham-fisted statement made by a representative from Carl Fischer, who not ten days earlier had written that the *Classical Manuscripts* were in fact "faithful to the style of these masters."[126]

Today, musicians might justifiably wonder whether the music itself bears out Newman's, Kreisler's, or Fischer's positions. There is indeed a sense in which the melodic profiles and large-scale forms of the *Classical Manuscripts* conform to seventeenth- and eighteenth-century precedents: for example, most of the miniatures adhere to a simple small ternary structure, generally totaling between 46 and 120 measures in length. Yet some of the harmonies, particularly in the piano accompaniments, flirt with late-romantic techniques that are wholly out of style for the earlier period in ways consistent with Kreisler's 1909 pre-confession explanation that—in transcribing and arranging the works that became the *Classical Manuscripts*—he had "made a few minor changes in the melodies, and . . . modernized the accompaniments to some extent" while trying to "retain the spirit of the original compositions."[127]

Consider the closing measures of *La Précieuse*, a work originally attributed to Louis Couperin, reproduced here in example 2.1. The piece's final dominant chord progresses to the tonic on the downbeat of m. 100. Yet Kreisler consciously

---

[123] Newman, "The Kreisler Revelations," 5.
[124] Newman, "The Kreisler Revelations," 5.
[125] Kreisler, "Kreisler Aroused by Critics' Taunts," 19.
[126] *New York Herald Tribune*, "Publisher Tells Why Kreisler Hoaxed Public," 9 February 1935, 9.
[127] *New York Times*, "How Kreisler Finds Musical Novelties," 7.

Example 2.1 Fritz Kreisler, "Louis Couperin" *La Précieuse*, mm. 99–105

neglects to resolve the leading tone, $\hat{7}$ (i.e., C♯), in the piano part at the moment of cadential arrival, producing a major seventh chord that substitutes for the expected tonic triad. The hazy, pungent effect of the unresolved major seventh (C♯) above the tonic (D) evokes the sound world of the Belle Époque: while the chord at the downbeat of m. 100 functions as a tonic triad, the dissonant extension marks it as open and unstable at a structural moment where maximal closure and stability are expected. The overlapping contrary-motion parallel fifths that occupy the piano part during its plagal codetta from m. 100 (D–A rises to G–D, while F♯–C♯ simultaneously falls to E–B) only serve to exacerbate the sense of anachronism with respect to Louis Couperin, even if Kreisler probably conceived the prominent parallel fifths that frame *La Précieuse* quite deliberately, as characteristically fin-de-siècle markers of a hazy, quasi-medieval archaism—nostalgic for a time beyond time.

It is difficult to reconcile such passages with Carl Fischer's claim that Kreisler was "faithful to the style" of Louis Couperin and other composers of the seventeenth and eighteenth centuries, much less with Edmond Johnson's assertion that the violinist's forgeries are "ultra-conservative in their harmonic conception, with a nearly obsessive avoidance of anything more than a passing dissonance."[128] Indeed, such comments make still less sense of the forged "Vivaldi" violin concerto, which—by its very nature as a large-scale multi-movement work—admittedly remains the exception among Kreisler's forgeries. Yet, despite early reviews stating that "a century and a half of neglect ha[d] scarcely staled" Kreisler's supposedly rediscovered Vivaldi, this particular composition is also exceptional in the depth of its stylistic anachronisms.[129]

Example 2.2 shows mm. 11–35 from the concerto's slow movement. Authentic movements of this type generally modulate either to the dominant or the

---

[128] Johnson, "Revival and Antiquation," 122.
[129] *New York Times*, "Kreisler Soloist at Philharmonic," 5 January 1908, 11.

Example 2.2 Fritz Kreisler, "Vivaldi" Violin Concerto in C Major. Violin-piano score. Andante doloroso (mvt. ii), mm. 11–35

Example 2.3 Albert Lavignac, *Cours d'Harmonie: Théorique et Pratique* (Paris: Henry Lemoine & Co., 1909), fig. 102, p. 122

mediant. And, at first, Kreisler's forgery appears to be following this script, momentarily tonicizing III (C major) at mm. 16–17. Yet this plan seemingly breaks down in mm. 18–19, when the local V^7 chord that might otherwise have cemented C major into place as the subordinate key collapses in a deceptive progression that pulls the music back into the orbit of the global tonic, A minor. Here Kreisler gives up on the mediant entirely, continuing to downshift sequentially by third: in this manner, he tonicizes VI (F major) at m. 23, iv (D minor) at m. 31, and finally the non-diatonic ♭II (B♭ major) at m. 35, each time using a prominent perfect authentic cadence (PAC) to emphasize the new key. Attending closely to this passage, it is easy to see what Kreisler meant when he claimed, years after exposure, that while other features of the concerto may have been "Vivaldian," the slow movement's "harmonic changes" were "strictly Schubertian and Berliozian."[130] A neo-Riemannian theorist might even point out the symmetrical pattern of alternating minor and major thirds in Kreisler's root motion from C to A to F to D to B♭, which, fully extended as an RL chain, would cycle seamlessly through all twenty-four keys in the tonal system.

Yet, for all this, Newman was not entirely incorrect. Anachronistic as they may sound to our ears, Kreisler's forgeries are nothing if not formulaic. Example 2.3—taken from Albert Lavignac's *Cours d'Harmonie* of 1909—is apt to confirm that more modest sequences based on root motion by third have been a consistent feature of harmony textbooks for quite some time. This treatise is particularly relevant here because Lavignac was the Paris Conservatoire's professor of harmony in the 1880s and 1890s, when the school's students included Henri Casadesus, Marius Casadesus, and Fritz Kreisler. Like many French pedagogues of his era, Lavignac puts a heavy emphasis on the realization and ornamentation of hundreds of stock sequences and thoroughbass patterns modeled on the eighteenth-century classics. Speaking speculatively, it is not hard to picture an errant student of this system fantasizing a "baroque" style by expanding these faux-antique formulae to industrial proportions. In composing out Lavignac's sequence No. 102 as a series of tonicizations—for example—such a student would need only to flatten the B in m. 5 to avoid prolonging a dissonant diminished triad in order

---

[130] Biancolli, "The Great Kreisler Hoax," 56.

110   FORGERY IN MUSICAL COMPOSITION

to produce the symmetrical "Schubertian" or "Berliozian" tonal structure which Kreisler described in his forged Vivaldi slow movement.

A similar compositional strategy is at work in Kreisler's "Praeludium and Allegro" attributed to Gaetano Pugnani, the opening passage of which is reproduced in example 2.4a. As the comparative voice-leading sketch in example 2.4b shows, Kreisler's prelude begins with a strikingly austere open fifth sonority. From the opening measure the intervallic pairing of E and B is voiced as a verticality in the piano part while the violin oscillates between those same two pitch classes, skipping up to the registral stratosphere. Crucially, this rapid violinistic alternation of $\hat{1}$ and $\hat{5}$ remains modally ambiguous until it is filled in by the missing chordal third G ($\hat{3}$) that arrives only at the end of the piano's chromatic inner-voice descent from B at m. 6. With the tonic triad in E minor complete at last, successive prolongations of the bass scale-steps i–VII–VI–V–iv–III ensue across mm. 6–17. Here each new step in the E–G descending hexachord pattern is prepared by its dominant: D at m. 8 is prepared by A at m. 7, C at m. 10 is prepared by G at m. 9, and so on. It is only with the arrival of the true dominant in the home key of E minor at m. 12 that the consistent intervallic pattern 10–10–10–10–10 arising from the contrary motion leaps of a fifth between the outer voices can be heard to break. Just as the piano's linear expansion of the tonic triad in mm. 1–6 partitions the descending hexachord into two linear segments (i.e., E–B and B–G), so too does the sequential pattern in mm. 7–17 divide with the arrival of V at m. 12 before proceeding to a cadential reaffirmation of the tonic.

The beauty of this passage is not in question. Yet it is difficult to imagine an eighteenth-century composer writing anything quite like Kreisler's opening five measures, which direct the violin to see-saw dramatically from E to B and back across two octaves without any hint of a chordal third, thus creating a monumentally open sonority that resists modal classification. Nor was there much precedent in Pugnani's era for the Beethovenian retransitional dominant pedal on B which, later in the same piece, occupies an enormous span of 27 measures, or nearly a full minute in performance time, as shown in example 2.5. Yet, for all this, it should nonetheless be emphasized that the underlying structure of Kreisler's music—the formula being exploited in the "Pugnani" work's iconic opening passage shown in example 2.4—remains unmistakably Baroque: a linear descent through the octave used as a vehicle for the kind of arpeggiated, quasi-improvisational violin preluding that would have been eminently familiar, if not to Pugnani in the latter half of the eighteenth century, then at least to Corelli, Biber, and their contemporaries a generation or two earlier. If Kreisler's composing out of the sequential descent ultimately resembles a true Baroque prelude only in the same manner that a neo-Gothic cathedral can be said to resemble its medieval model, it is not so difficult to acknowledge that the semblance might have rung true on a certain expressive level between 1910

Example 2.4a Fritz Kreisler, "Pugnani" Praeludium and Allegro, mm. 1–23

Example 2.4b Fritz Kreisler, "Pugnani" Praeludium and Allegro, mm. 1–17, voice-leading analysis

and 1935. Indeed, even before the revelation of Kreisler's authorship, many of the most questionable technical elements of these fakes could be chalked up to his "arrangements" rather than the fabled "original manuscripts" on which they were supposedly based. Poetic license would, after all, supply Kreisler with the requisite plausible deniability for an accompaniment seasoned with a few tastefully modern harmonic twists.

While Kreisler's tendency to make romantic mountains out of pre-romantic molehills in these expansive passages may strike modern musicians as blatantly inauthentic, it is worth remembering just how unfamiliar most baroque and galant music was to early twentieth-century audiences, recalling, for example, the 1908 reviewer who applauded Kreisler's "resuscitated" Vivaldi concerto as "a strikingly strong and vigorous piece... which a century and a half of neglect has hardly staled."[131] Here, recognition of the fact that Kreisler's anachronisms may not have sounded anachronistic to his contemporaries recalls an important lesson on connoisseurship from Max Friedländer, the aforementioned pioneer of art authentication. "Forgeries," Friedländer aphoristically tells his readers, "must be served

---

[131] *New York Times*, "Kreisler Soloist at the Philharmonic," 11.

Example 2.5 Fritz Kreisler, "Pugnani" Praeludium and Allegro, mm. 119–150

Example 2.5 Continued

hot."[132] A forgery produced by a contemporary artist will often succeed, he writes, "precisely because something in it responds to our natural habit of vision; because the forger has understood, and misunderstood, the old master in the same way as ourselves."[133] Consider van Meegeren's phony oil paintings as discussed in this book's introduction and pictured in figure I.1, which have long since been perceptively analyzed by Denis Dutton and others as "influenced by photography [with] . . . sentimental eyes and awkward anatomy . . . more reminiscent of German expressionist works of the 1920s and 1930s than they are of the works of Vermeer."[134] Forgeries can be seen to encode historical habits of listening as well as seeing from this perspective precisely because they are anachronistic. And it is for this reason that their untimeliness becomes legible only as they go cold with time's passing.[135] With all this in mind, the forged works confined to art's cultural basements begin to appear like Dorian Gray's attic-bound picture: always already decaying beneath their unimpeachable surfaces, having purchased the illusion of timeless perfection by being, in effect, supremely of their time.

Dissecting forgeries in this Newmanesque manner can feel like dealing out a deeply satisfying kind of critical justice, seemingly proving that time will tell and thus, in a sense, that history itself abhors the ahistorical fake. Yet one should not get too excited. Critics might just as well remember Kreisler's defense that he "made no endeavor whatever" to stick closely to the style of Pugnani, et al.[136] Reluctant as one may be to take the violinist at his word, some level of intentional inventiveness would explain the Praeludium and Allegro's deviations from Baroque compositional formulae at least as neatly in this case as the infinitely more grandiose notion of a "test of time" meted out by some avenging spirit of history. It is important to remember that the pseudo-Baroque works discussed here were not necessarily designed with the permanent, unimpeachable deception of experts in mind. Often, in romantic cases of forgery such as these, it is the broader musical public, and not academic critics, that the forger seeks to seduce. And in this, Kreisler seems to have succeeded admirably.

INNOCENCE LOST

In many ways, the *Classical Manuscripts* controversy and its aftermath marks a turning point in the history of compositional forgery. Situated at the

[132] Friedländer, *On Art and Connoisseurship*, 261.
[133] Friedländer, *On Art and Connoisseurship*, 262.
[134] Denis Dutton, "Han van Meegeren," in *Encyclopedia of Hoaxes*, edited by Gordon Stein (Detroit: Gale Research, 1993): 26–28, at 28.
[135] On this issue, see also Anthony Grafton, *Forgers and Critics: Creativity and Duplicity in Western Scholarship* (London: Collins & Brown, 1990), 67–68.
[136] Kreisler, "Kreisler Aroused by Critics' Taunts," 19.

116 FORGERY IN MUSICAL COMPOSITION

twilight of romantic musical culture, Fritz Kreisler, Marius Casadesus, and their contemporaries belonged to the first generation of fakers to lock horns with a substantial professional class of musicologists embodied, in this chapter, by Ernest Newman and Alfred Einstein. The front-page media attention that Kreisler's compositional forgeries attracted in 1935 was similarly unprecedented in ways that clearly alarmed the day's critics: that year, the *Musical Times* went so far as to express concern that impressionable young musicians of the future might "follow Kreisler's example" by "making capital (in the most solid sense of the term) out of the names and reputations of composers beyond the protection of the law."[137] And while concrete instances of copycat forgery are difficult to substantiate in any objective or definitive sense, the Gaspar Cassadó, Manuel Ponce, and Remo Giazotto works discussed in this book's preface stand out as plausible candidates that can be seen to pointedly follow the model established by Kreisler's *Classical Manuscripts*.[138] In this context, Einstein's 1945 use of the phrase "mystification à la Kreisler" to describe the "Adélaïde" concerto forged by Marius Casadesus aptly illustrates the influence that Kreisler's actions came to have on public conversations about musical authenticity and inauthenticity in the mid-twentieth century.[139] Here, in an ironic twist, the violinist's name had itself begun to function as yet another euphemism for the "ugly appellation" of forgery in musical composition, effectively standing in for the phenomenon writ large.[140]

Standards of evidence among music publishers and critics sharpened considerably in the decades after the *Classical Manuscripts* scandal. And while this surely happened for a variety of interacting structural and academic reasons, Kreisler's forgeries served as a compelling example of the dangers inherent in lax documentary standards. As Olin Downes suggested, the Kreisler controversy of 1935 could reasonably be interpreted as "a commentary . . . on the manner in which all sorts of facts which should be promptly questioned are allowed to pass in this field."[141] "Outside of a very few leading figures," wrote Downes, "musicographers the world over are open to criticism for lack of scientific method and accurate classification of data."[142] Of course, Newman's response was that it had previously seemed unreasonable to expect some nameless musicological gatekeeper to "take the trouble . . . to spend months of his time trying to trace the source" every time a new edition claimed to bear some relationship

---

[137] *Musical Times*, "Kreisleriana," 251.

[138] On similarities between Kreisler's *Classical Manuscripts* and the "Albinoni" Adagio in G minor in particular, see Frederick Reece, "Baroque Forgeries and the Public Imagination," in *The Oxford Handbook of Public Music Theory*, edited by J. Daniel Jenkins (New York: Oxford University Press, 2021).

[139] Einstein, *Mozart: His Character, His Work*, 278.

[140] Downes, "Kreisler's 'Classics,'" X5.

[141] Downes, "Kreisler's 'Classics,'" X5.

[142] Downes, "Kreisler's 'Classics,'" X5.

to an unpublished antique document.[143] Yet, by claiming to have based his "transcriptions" on original manuscripts when in fact nothing of the sort existed, Newman asserted that Kreisler had effectively shattered the existing moral contract such that it could never be fully repaired.[144] The solution, instantiated in the Urtext culture of publishing and editing that rose to prominence following the Second World War, was an attitude of presumptive inauthenticity in which works attributed to historical figures in recent sources were presumed to be inauthentic until proven otherwise by musicological means. As this book's second part will illustrate, post-war compositional forgeries thus came to have a substantially different flavor to the *Classical Manuscripts* discussed here. In essence, the romantic Kreislerian model of forgery became increasingly untenable in a newly suspicious age.

With all this in mind, it might reasonably be presumed that Kreisler's forgeries also had a significant and enduring impact on his own legacy as a performing musician. In an *Esquire* profile penned some six months after the *Classical Manuscripts* controversy first broke, David Ewen admits—at the end of an otherwise glowing celebration of the violinist's outstanding artistic achievements and natural personal charisma—that "it is not beyond the realm of possibility that the name of Fritz Kreisler will be descended to posterity for a reason other than [that] he is the greatest violinist of our age."[145] "One can," he continues, "well imagine a musical dictionary of the twenty-first century referring to Kreisler in the following fashion: '. . . He is remembered today only because of a hoax which he perpetrated upon the entire world of music in his time.'"[146] Yet, looking back from a twenty-first-century perspective, Ewen's fears that the 1935 scandal would somehow eclipse the rest of Kreisler's career appear utterly unfounded. The dozens of sumptuous interpretations he committed to record during the first half of the twentieth century have rightly immortalized Fritz Kreisler as a defining figure in what is often called the golden age of violin playing. And many of his compositions have continued to enjoy a secure place at the center of the violin repertory in the twenty-first century even as the stories behind works like the "Praeludium und Allegro" have faded from public recollection.

In this context, it should be noted that Kreisler's biographers have often gone to great lengths to exonerate him from blame and to encourage selective amnesia about the true historical nature of the *Classical Manuscripts* among musicians. In his foundational authorized account of the violinist's life and work, Louis Lochner has little hesitation in letting Kreisler off the hook for the fact that "it took

---

[143] Newman, "An Open Letter to Fritz Kreisler," 7.
[144] Newman, "An Open Letter to Fritz Kreisler," 7.
[145] Ewen, "L'Amico Fritz," 148.
[146] Ewen, "L'Amico Fritz," 148.

thirty-odd years for the proper occasion for unburdening his mind to present itself," thereby seemingly implying both that Kreisler had harbored feelings of guilt and that a more prompt confession would somehow have been an unbearable inconvenience.[147] Amy Biancolli can be seen to go to even greater lengths to demonstrate Kreisler's innocence in her updated 1998 biography, tying herself in rhetorical knots by protesting that the violinist "did so very little to perpetuate the hoax beyond getting it started. He lit the fire and then walked away, clearly expecting someone to discover the flames and douse them before they turned into a genuine blaze."[148] Like Lochner's earlier apologia, Biancolli's analogy is a jaw-dropping study in self-contradiction and denial: clearly, the arsonist who starts a fire and walks away cannot expect his jury to be so accommodating as to believe that he was politely waiting for someone else to put out the inferno for him. To imply otherwise is to willfully cast aside the most basic notions of personal responsibility on Kreisler's behalf. And yet, even in appearing to do just this, Biancolli herself is ultimately compelled to admit, quite correctly, that "history has been lenient on Fritz Kreisler—lenient and forgetful."[149]

Nine decades after his confession, Kreisler's musically seductive acts of compositional forgery are worth remembering precisely because of the curious leniency and forgetfulness with which they have been treated. As antiquarian fantasy in the romantic mold the works remain highly compelling—their internal charm, like Kreisler's personal appeal, is not in question. Beyond these charismatic factors, the comparative lack of condemnation that the *Classical Manuscripts* have enjoyed since Kreisler's death has a great deal to do with the fact that he appropriated the identities of fellow virtuoso composer-violinists from an era in which performer-centeredness and objective expression were the norms, thereby seemingly earning a license to invoke pre-romantic performer-centered notions of authenticity himself. Figures like Pugnani and Louis Couperin were coincidentally drawn from the more obscure peripheries of the canon, effectively making it easier for audiences to regard their identities not as indices of the kind of composer-centered subjective expression allotted to Mozart in the nineteenth-century tradition discussed in chapter 1, but rather—in Kreisler's own words—as equivalent to "dusty, old forgotten cloaks," free for use and abuse at will. In this book's second part, we will encounter modern forgers who were not so modest in this respect and who thus directly engaged with increasingly professionalized institutions designed to safeguard the authenticity of centrally canonic figures like Schubert and Haydn from a skeptical Newmanesque perspective of presumptive inauthenticity after the Second World War.

---

[147] Lochner, *Fritz Kreisler*, 292.
[148] Biancolli, *Love's Sorrow*, 180.
[149] Biancolli, *Love's Sorrow*, 182.

PART II

MODERN CULTURES OF FORGERY, 1945–2000

3

Schubert's Untrue Symphony

On 14 February 1975, Swiss-born East German musicologist Harry Goldschmidt received an unsolicited letter of potentially monumental music-historical import. Writing from Kronberg near Frankfurt in West Germany to Goldschmidt in East Berlin, Gunter Elsholz—identifying himself as a journalist and amateur musician—claimed that relatives of his were in possession of a set of orchestral parts for what Elsholz believed to be a lost Symphony in E Major by Franz Schubert, dated 1825.[1] Crucially, what Elsholz professed to have access to was not simply a copy of the well-known fragmentary Symphony in E Major, D. 729, left in a substantial draft without any internally finished movements in 1821 and thereafter numbered as Schubert's "seventh" essay in the genre by George Grove.[2] On the contrary, the work in question was an entirely different symphony, in four completed movements. Still more tantalizing, Elsholz's set of parts appeared to correspond, in many important particulars, to what likely remains the single greatest archival holy grail in the history of musicology, relentlessly sought out by generations of Schubertians since Grove had first posited its existence in 1881: Schubert's missing "Gastein" Symphony, D. 849.[3]

But there was a catch. Elsholz explained that he was unable to retrieve the orchestral parts containing the symphony from his aunt's house in West Berlin, apparently because of a bitter family feud. Given that he was thus incapable of granting Schubert scholars such as Goldschmidt access to the antique historical manuscripts themselves, Elsholz instead proposed to surreptitiously copy out a full orchestral score from the inaccessible set of parts in a painstaking, movement-by-movement transcription process. In a letter to Goldschmidt from April of 1975, Elsholz projected that it would take at least two full years for him to deliver the symphony's four respective movements in this incremental manner.[4]

---

[1] Gunter Elsholz to Harry Goldschmidt, 14 February 1975. Staatsbibliothek zu Berlin, Mus. Nachl. H. Goldschmidt B.14.

[2] Gunter Elsholz to Harry Goldschmidt, 8 March 1975. Staatsbibliothek zu Berlin, Mus. Nachl. H. Goldschmidt B.14. On this numbering, see the foundational George Grove, ed., *A Dictionary of Music and Musicians*, 4 vols. (London: Macmillan, 1879, 1880, 1883, 1899), s.v. "Franz Peter Schubert," reprinted in George Grove, *Beethoven, Schubert, Mendelssohn* (London: Macmillan, 1951), 121–251 at 161.

[3] For a recording of this work, see Gerhard Samuel and the Cincinnati Philharmonia, *Franz Schubert, Symphony in E Major, "1825"* (Centaur CRC 2139, 2010, compact disc).

[4] Gunter Elsholz to Harry Goldschmidt, 7 April 1975. Staatsbibliothek zu Berlin, Mus. Nachl. H. Goldschmidt B.14.

Forgery in Musical Composition. Frederick Reece, Oxford University Press. © Oxford University Press 2025.
DOI: 10.1093/9780197618332.003.0004

122 FORGERY IN MUSICAL COMPOSITION

Despite the apparent necessity of such a lengthy wait and the impossibility of seeing the historical sources firsthand, Goldschmidt's curiosity was piqued, and—during the course of Elsholz's elaborate reconstruction and documentation process—the two men struck up a prolific epistolary relationship from opposing sides of the divided Germany.[5] Elsholz provided Goldschmidt with updates on his transcription efforts, detailing various setbacks and frustrations arising from the immense amount of time and energy invested in the project from month to month. And in turn, Goldschmidt questioned Elsholz at length about his family history, attempting to establish a provenance linking the set of orchestral parts rediscovered in Berlin back to Schubert and his immediate Viennese circles via a series of mysterious nineteenth-century documents that Elsholz had reportedly found preserved with the parts among his family's belongings. An unsigned letter dated 1832 and later speculatively attributed to Anna Fröhlich mentions one of Elsholz's ancestors by the name of "Wolff" before describing a Symphony "in E Major" which the recently deceased Schubert "wanted to have cared for like a child" after his untimely death, while a tantalizing pair of notes signed by "Joseph Kalkbrenner" and dated 1888 and 1894, respectively, recount favorable assessments of the symphony's score by two of the most imposing musical figures of the era: Pyotr Ilyich Tchaikovsky and Johannes Brahms.[6]

As Elsholz's and Goldschmidt's discussions expanded and proliferated in innumerable directions while these accompanying documents were investigated, the transcribed orchestral score slowly but surely began to materialize. Elsholz had already sent the scherzo by post in April 1975.[7] Four months later, he visited Goldschmidt in East Berlin, handing over the symphony's slow movement in person.[8] In March 1976, the first movement was delivered at another face-to-face meeting.[9] And the mammoth finale arrived last, in a thick packet containing over a thousand measures of orchestral score posted to East Berlin in July 1977, some two years and three months after the first installment, more or less as Elsholz had anticipated.[10] At each stage of this process Goldschmidt expressed strong

---

[5] The correspondence between Elsholz and Goldschmidt would ultimately span hundreds of letters written between 1975 and 1985, now archived in Staatsbibliothek zu Berlin, Mus. Nachl. H. Goldschmidt B.14.

[6] The three documents were published in full and discussed in Harry Goldschmidt, "Eine gefälschte Schubert-Sinfonie? Eine quellenkritische Gegendarstellung," in *Musica* 38 (1984): Beilage 1–15, at 14. For a skeptical evaluation of these sources, see Walther Dürr, "Eine gefälschte Schubert-Sinfonie," *Musica* 37, no. 2 (1983): 135–42.

[7] Gunter Elsholz to Harry Goldschmidt, 7 April 1975. Staatsbibliothek zu Berlin, Mus. Nachl. H. Goldschmidt B.14.

[8] Harry Goldschmidt to Gunter Elsholz, 18 August 1975. Staatsbibliothek zu Berlin, Mus. Nachl. H. Goldschmidt B.14.

[9] Gunter Elsholz to Harry Goldschmidt, 2 March 1976; Gunter Elsholz to Harry Goldschmidt, 22 April 1976. Staatsbibliothek zu Berlin, Mus. Nachl. H. Goldschmidt B.14.

[10] Gunter Elsholz to Harry Goldschmidt, 15 July 1977. Staatsbibliothek zu Berlin, Mus. Nachl. H. Goldschmidt B.14.

approval for the overall Schubertian quality of the music Elsholz sent him while nonetheless identifying numerous self-quotations alongside curious surface-level flaws in the symphony's figuration and orchestration which seemed to suggest that the parts may have been based on a fragmentary score posthumously completed and retouched by someone other than Schubert in much the same manner that Süssmayr had posthumously completed and retouched Mozart's Requiem.[11] Responding to these positive and negative critical comments, Elsholz took careful note of those aspects of the music deemed Schubertian or otherwise, simultaneously flattering Goldschmidt's self-image as a connoisseur by lavishly commending his sensitivity not only to historical facts, but also—and most emphatically—to the internal structural and expressive qualities of the music itself.[12] Nonetheless, as time went on, Goldschmidt became increasingly anxious to see even a few pages of Elsholz's historical source firsthand. Both men were well aware that the clock was ticking: 1978 was to be the 150th anniversary of Schubert's death, and the Austrian Society for Musicology was organizing an international conference in Vienna in June of that year to honor the occasion. As Goldschmidt had explained to an East German colleague as early as 1976, presenting a rediscovered Schubert symphony to the public at this event would be a major musicological coup, just so long as concerns about the work's authenticity could be cleared up in good time.[13]

Late in the summer of 1977, with the final installment of the symphony delivered and less than a year remaining before the sesquicentennial Schubert Congress, Goldschmidt continued to press Elsholz to bring samples of the original parts to Berlin so that they could be subjected to substantive analysis and material testing.[14] Crucially, these tests were to be carried out in collaboration with a paper expert who now insisted that a meaningful examination could only be carried out if Elsholz supplied each of the fourteen orchestral parts in its totality, rather than a selection of individual pages.[15] Perhaps predictably, Elsholz balked at this demand, abruptly adopting a strikingly defensive posture. Yet, in an apparent effort to placate Goldschmidt, he now noted that—under renewed pressure—his family had promised to let him have the orchestral parts, but only in five years (i.e., long after the Schubert Congress), by which

[11] Harry Goldschmidt to Gunter Elsholz, 20 May 1975. Harry Goldschmidt to Gunter Elsholz, 18 August 1975. Harry Goldschmidt to Gunter Elsholz, 15 August 1977. Staatsbibliothek zu Berlin, Mus. Nachl. H. Goldschmidt B.14.

[12] Gunter Elsholz to Harry Goldschmidt, 30 March 1975. Staatsbibliothek zu Berlin, Mus. Nachl. H. Goldschmidt B.14.

[13] Harry Goldschmidt to Wisso Weiß, 27 October 1976. Berlin State Library, Mus. Nachl. H. Goldschmidt B.15.

[14] Harry Goldschmidt to Gunter Elsholz, 15 August 1977. Staatsbibliothek zu Berlin, Mus. Nachl. H. Goldschmidt B.14.

[15] Wisso Weiß to Harry Goldschmidt, 18 August 1977. Berlin State Library, Mus. Nachl. H. Goldschmidt B.15.

124   FORGERY IN MUSICAL COMPOSITION

stage his disagreeable aunt would be too old to object, or so Elsholz presumed.[16] Whatever the reality, he appeared to be stalling. And, perhaps for this reason, Goldschmidt dramatically lost patience altogether, writing to Elsholz on 2 October 1977 that he had become extremely suspicious, and that—without the possibility of verifying the sources systematically—he was unprepared to pursue his investigations into the symphony any further.[17] The whole two-year saga might well have ended here. Yet, in a seeming compromise broached both with his paper expert and with Elsholz, Goldschmidt ultimately reconciled himself to assessing only a single page from each of the rediscovered symphony's orchestral parts.[18] In turn, Elsholz duly delivered source samples to a Berlin contact of Goldschmidt in December 1977, mere days before the beginning of the Schubert year.[19]

Six months later, on the afternoon of 5 June 1978, Goldschmidt stood before the Hobokensaal of the Austrian National Library's music collection and declared that the lost symphony for which musicologists had been searching since the 1880s had, in essence, been rediscovered.[20] Yet, having analyzed the work in full, he hastened to clarify his belief that the score in question was not, in fact, entirely by Schubert at all. To the contrary, Goldschmidt explained that the 2,014 bars of music brought before the congress was a posthumous completion of a particello draft left unfinished at the time of the composer's death. While Schubert had written the outer voices, much of the remaining orchestral material had been filled out by an inferior composer who had seemingly attempted to produce a performing version around the time that the two Kalkbrenner letters had been written in the final decades of the nineteenth century.[21] Crucially, this completed symphony had been transported to Elsholz's family's former residence in Strausberg near Berlin between the 1890s and 1930s, and was presumably copied into the set of orchestral parts ultimately rediscovered by Elsholz there sometime before the full score had gone "missing in the chaos of the first weeks following the Second World War."[22] With all this musical and source-historical complexity in mind, Goldschmidt surmised that the symphony painstakingly

[16] Gunter Elsholz to Wisso Weiß, 5 September 1977. Berlin State Library, Mus. Nachl. H. Goldschmidt B.15.
[17] Harry Goldschmidt to Gunter Elsholz, 2 October 1977. Berlin State Library, Mus. Nachl. H. Goldschmidt B.14.
[18] Harry Goldschmidt to Gunter Elsholz, 4 November 1977. Berlin State Library, Mus. Nachl. H. Goldschmidt B.14.
[19] Gunter Elsholz to Harry Goldschmidt, 1 December 1977. Berlin State Library, Mus. Nachl. H. Goldschmidt B.15.
[20] The paper was published as Harry Goldschmidt, "Eine weitere E-Dur-Sinfonie? Zur Kontroverse um die 'Gmunden-Gastein'-Sinfonie," in *Schubert-Kongreß Wien 1978*, edited by Otto Brusatti (Graz: Österreichischen Gesellschaft für Musikwissenschaft, 1979): 79–112.
[21] Goldschmidt, "Eine weitere E-Dur-Sinfonie?," 84.
[22] Goldschmidt, "Eine weitere E-Dur-Sinfonie?," 81.

SCHUBERT'S UNTRUE SYMPHONY   125

re-transcribed from the surviving orchestral parts by Elsholz in the 1970s could best be compared to "a deficiently and haphazardly restored painting" which—in his estimation—remained, unmistakably, "the work of a master."[23]

In conceptualizing the rediscovered symphony as a Schubert fragment concealed beneath layers of posthumous completion, Goldschmidt established a convenient analytical alibi with which to dismiss any technical compositional deficiencies found in Elsholz's score while simultaneously echoing the elevated romantic ideal of unfinished musical works as sites of untempered and unmediated originality too radical, in conception, to be closed off by anything but the ineffable abyss of the blank page.[24] Any peculiar musical details found within the Symphony in E Major could now readily be chalked up either to the technical incompetence of the scapegoated Süssmayeresque completer or—in a diametrically opposed alternative—to the visionary, formally unbounded creativity that has often been attributed to such existing large-scale Schubert fragments as the "Unfinished" Symphony, D. 759, and *Quartettsatz*, D. 703. And it is in this latter vein that the published version of Goldschmidt's Congress paper ultimately declares Schubert's widely revered "Great" Symphony in C Major "a step backwards and a compromise" by comparison to the more maverick but incomplete Symphony in E Major rediscovered, in a partially corrupted form, by Elsholz.[25]

Not everyone present at the Schubert Congress was so convinced that the find could be authentic, even in part. The claims made in Goldschmidt's paper were contested with vigor by Neue Schubert-Ausgabe editorial directors Walther Dürr and Arnold Feil, who asserted that the putatively rediscovered symphony was not a work by Franz Schubert at all. As Dürr and Feil revealed in a co-authored statement appended to Goldschmidt's paper in the published congress report, Elsholz had attempted to court the Neue Schubert-Ausgabe's interest in the "Gmunden" parts as early as 1974, having been put in direct communication with its editorial directorship after first contacting Henle Verlag about the supposed rediscovered symphony in 1973.[26] By the time Goldschmidt was first contacted about the case early in 1975 the Neue Schubert-Ausgabe had already ended its correspondence with Elsholz because it had become clear to Dürr and

---

[23] "Bei diesem unvollendeten Werk, in dem Zustand, in dem es uns nun überliefert vorliegt, handelt es sich um ein mangelhaft und willkürlich restauriertes Bild. Aber das Bild stammt von einem Meister." Goldschmidt, "Eine weitere E-Dur-Sinfonie?," 107.

[24] On this rich aesthetic tradition, see in particular Richard Kramer, *Unfinished Music* (New York: Oxford University Press, 2008).

[25] "Was Schubert 1823 zu Leopold Sonnleithner als seine Zielstellung bezeichnet—'eine neue Form zu erfinden' und 'vorwärts zu gehen'—wird in diesem Werk-Entwurf mit einer Radikalität verfolgt, an der gemessen die *Große C-Dur-Sinfonie* eine Zurücknahme, jedenfalls ein Einlenken darstellt." Goldschmidt, "Eine weitere E-Dur-Sinfonie?," 84–85.

[26] Walther Dürr and Arnold Feil, "Stellungnahme der Editionsleitung der Neuen Schubert-Ausgabe," in *Schubert-Kongreß Wien 1978*, edited by Otto Brusatti (Graz: Österreichischen Gesellschaft für Musikwissenschaft, 1979): 113–15, at 114.

126   FORGERY IN MUSICAL COMPOSITION

Feil that a photocopied "Schubert" autograph letter addressed to "Wolff" was a clumsy forgery and that Elsholz was moreover either unwilling or unable to provide access to his other supposed historical sources for closer consultation.[27] Only at this stage did Elsholz seemingly cut his losses and attempt to win critical academic legitimation elsewhere, turning to Goldschmidt in February of 1975 but replacing the forged "Schubert" letter with a series of newly rediscovered provenance documents that had conveniently turned up in his family's private archive since 1973, this time coincidentally attributed to obscure and anonymous nineteenth-century writers whose authorship would be more difficult to authenticate than Schubert's.[28] Recounting these events in their succinct but sobering co-authored congress report statement, Dürr and Feil duly declared the "source tradition" for the work to be "so dubious" that the editorship of the Neue Schubert-Ausgabe had long since come to regard Elsholz's symphony not as "the work of a master," but rather an act of "forgery" on a monumental scale.[29]

This open disagreement at the 1978 Schubert Congress marks the beginning of the twentieth century's most prolonged and deeply entrenched musicological dispute concerning the authenticity of a single rediscovered work. In the immediate wake of the congress the stark conflict between Goldschmidt and his international colleagues caused enough kerfuffle to be featured in the Viennese *Wochenpresse*, which described "heated" emotions among the assembled ranks of music scholars.[30] Yet, for all its academic melodrama and sprawling complexity of detail, the basic architecture of the "Schubert" controversy was in many ways entirely typical of the modern cultures of forgery discussed in the second half of this book.

In the first place, Elsholz's symphony was touted as a rediscovered work corresponding to a pre-conceived music-historical gap at the heart of the canon. This was not an original fantasy in a pseudo-antique style à la Kreisler but rather a self-conscious attempt to fill a void in formalized musicological notions of Schubert's output. In a move further characteristic of modern cultures of forgery, Elsholz had attempted to win the approval of gatekeepers associated with some of the major Urtext powerhouses of the post-war era—i.e., Henle Verlag and the Neue Schubert-Ausgabe—before turning, in rejection, to an alternative source of musicological authority in Goldschmidt. With newly strict documentary editorial norms established for the publication of classical music by institutions such as these, the fabrication of a work came to necessitate the production of historical sources and provenance documents in the mid-twentieth century to accompany

[27] Dürr and Feil, "Stellungnahme," 113, 115. The "Schubert" letter was betrayed, among other things, by objective orthographic anachronisms.
[28] Dürr, "Eine Gefälschte Schubert-Sinfonie," 136.
[29] Dürr and Feil, "Stellungnahme," 113. Goldschmidt, "Eine weitere E-Dur-Sinfonie?," 107.
[30] W. G., "Gefälscht?" *Wochenpresse* (Vienna), 7 June 1978, 7.

and legitimate forged music as such. In this vein, modern forgers targeting canonical composers have typically concocted phony latter-day manuscript copies more easily passed off as authentic than composer autographs, distributing these sources as photocopies or partial paper samples while keeping the supposed original documents as inaccessible as possible.

Finally, it should be remembered that the division between the two main academic camps involved in the dispute was underpinned, to a striking extent, by fundamentally divergent and opposing epistemologies of musical authenticity. Whereas Goldschmidt was inclined to treat style-critical evidence for authorship with a seriousness in keeping with his broader intellectual commitments to composer biography and hermeneutic analysis, Dürr and Feil followed the institutional and methodological norms of mid-century West German Urtext culture in regarding source philology as a far firmer and more objective test of attribution, decisively rejecting Elsholz's symphony as a forgery "independently of all style-critical reservations."[31] The unprecedented emphasis on Urtext complete-works editions granted source-critical methods a new institutional prestige in ways that dramatically reinvigorated source/style tensions in the era directly following the Second World War. Indeed, in the second half of the twentieth century, most high-profile compositional forgeries actively responded to this new status quo in ways aptly modeled by Schubert's "Untrue" Symphony.

THE GASTEIN MYTHOS

Elsholz's supposed rediscovery was seductive in no small part because it rested heavily on pre-existing musicological narratives about the Schubert canon and its lacunas. And, like many of the most persistent and influential ideas in Schubert studies, the notion of a missing "Gastein" Symphony can be traced back to Grove, who published an extended letter on the topic—titled "Another Unknown Symphony by Schubert"—in the *Times* of London in September 1881.[32] Here Grove reports that in working on the Schubert article for the first edition of his *Dictionary of Music and Musicians* he had uncovered striking evidence that a "10th" Schubert symphony as yet unknown to audiences was still waiting to be found in some dark and forgotten corner, perhaps not unlike "the complete Rosamunde music," which—as Grove evocatively reminds

---

[31] Dürr and Feil, "Stellungnahme," 113. On possible cold-war contexts for these differences in musicological method, see Anne Shreffler, "Berlin Walls: Dahlhaus, Knepler, and Ideologies of Music History," *Journal of Musicology* 20, no. 4 (2003): 498–525.

[32] George Grove, "Another Unknown Symphony by Schubert," *Times* (London), 28 September 1881, 7. A German-language summary of Grove's letter was subsequently published in Vienna as "Eine unbekannte Sinfonie Schuberts," *Neue freie Presse*, 1 October 1881, 2.

128 FORGERY IN MUSICAL COMPOSITION

readers—was "dragged by Mr. [Arthur] Sullivan and myself out of a cupboard in Vienna in 1867 in a large parcel an inch thick in dust which had all the appearance of not having been unpacked since the original performance in 1823."[33]

Grove's evidence for the existence of a lost tenth Schubert symphony stemmed from a history of the Viennese Gesellschaft der Musikfreunde published in 1871 by that institution's head archivist, Carl Ferdinand Pohl. In an internal report dated 9 October 1826 the society's committee had declared that Schubert—who had long wished to dedicate a symphony to the organization—would receive 100 silver florins C. M. without reference to any specific cause, but rather "simply in recognition of services rendered to the society and as further incitement and encouragement."[34] Pohl's book goes on to state that a brief letter from Schubert had been filed shortly thereafter—i.e., "between October 9 and 12"—in the records of the Gesellschaft der Musikfreunde.[35] In this highly important—but, critically, internally undated—note addressed directly "To the Committee of the Austrian Musical Society" Schubert can be seen to state the following in an apparent reply to the financial gift of 9 October 1826: "Convinced of the Committee of the Austrian Musical Society's noble intention to support any artistic endeavour as far as possible, I venture, as a native artist, to dedicate to them this, my Symphony, and to commend it most politely to their protection."[36]

Frustratingly, Schubert's brief covering letter of dedication offers no further details to assist subsequent generations of scholars in identifying the precise symphony at issue. In the absence of more substantive clues, the idea that Schubert's note had been submitted to the Gesellschaft der Musikfreunde in October of 1826—presumably with a finished score for "this, my Symphony"—took on serious musicological implications.[37] Crucially, the chronology of Schubert's works formalized in the first edition of Grove's *Dictionary of Music and Musicians* and summarized in table 3.1 simply does not fit with a symphony received with a dedication to the Gesellschaft der Musikfreunde in 1826.[38] Moreover, the autograph score of the "Great" Symphony in C Major, D. 944, contains no paratextual dedication and is seemingly dated by the composer himself to "March 1828"—i.e., two years too late to correspond to the work

---

[33] Grove, "Another Unknown Symphony by Schubert," 7.

[34] "Es wurde hierauf beschlossen, Schubert, ohne Bezug auf die Sinfonie, sondern blos in Anerkennung der um die Gesellschaft erworbenen Verdienste und zur ferneren Aneiferung und Ermunterung, eine Renumeration von 100 fl. A. C. ausfolgen zu lassen." Carl F. Pohl, *Die Gesellschaft der Musikfreunde des österreichischen Kaiserstaates und ihr Conservatorium* (Vienna: Wilhelm Braumüller, 1871), 16. See also Otto Erich Deutsch, *Schubert: A Documentary Biography*, translated by Eric Blom (London: J. M. Dent, 1946), 559.

[35] "Schubert sandte gleichzeitig zwischen 9. und 12. October seine Composition mit nachfolgendem Begleitungsschreiben ein." Pohl, *Die Gesellschaft der Musikfreunde*, 16.

[36] Deutsch, *Schubert: A Documentary Biography*, 559.

[37] Deutsch, *Schubert: A Documentary Biography*, 559.

[38] See Grove, "Franz Peter Schubert."

SCHUBERT'S UNTRUE SYMPHONY   129

Table 3.1 Grove's Chronology of Schubert's Symphonies adapted from *A Dictionary of Music and Musicians*, Vol. 3 (1883)

Work Title	Deutsch Number	Date (Grove 1)
Symphony No. 1 in D Major	D. 82	1813
Symphony No. 2 in B♭ Major	D. 125	1814–15
Symphony No. 3 in D Major	D. 200	1815
Symphony No. 4 in C minor (Tragic)	D. 417	1816
Symphony No. 5 in B♭ Major	D. 485	1816
Symphony No. 6 in C Major	D. 589	1817–18
Symphony No. 7 in E Major	D. 729	1821
Symphony No. 8 in B minor (Unfinished)	D. 759	1822
Lost Symphony (Gmunden-Gastein)	D. 849	c.1825–26
Symphony No. 9 in C Major (Great)	D. 944	1828

☐   missing work

referenced in Schubert's letter.[39] Significantly, Grove considered the remaining incomplete and juvenile symphonies unsuitable for dedication: Schubert, he writes, "was hardly likely to submit an inferior work to so important a society or to go back to one of his boyish compositions of 1817 or 1818."[40] And with all this in mind, Grove's letter to the *Times* duly concludes that the manuscript referred to in Schubert's dedication and in the records of the Gesellschaft der Musikfreunde must be some other, unknown work composed in 1825 or 1826, which "if it fortunately exists in some nook or corner of the society's collection or elsewhere ... will be a matter of extraordinary interest to the musical world."[41]

There was no shortage of corroborating evidence for this thesis. After lamenting his declining health and anguished emotional state in a frequently cited and deeply confessional letter to Leopold Kupelwieser dated 31 March 1824, Schubert goes on to explain a recent shift in his creative focus from "songs" to "instrumental works," stating: "I wrote two Quartets for violins, viola and violoncello [D. 804 and D. 810] and an Octet [D. 803], and I want to write another quartet, in fact I intend to pave my way towards grand symphony in that manner."[42] Further referencing the landmark May 1822 premiere of Beethoven's Symphony No. 9 at Vienna's Theater am Kärntnertor, Schubert's lengthy missive

[39] Grove, "Another Unknown Symphony by Schubert," 7.
[40] Grove, "Another Unknown Symphony by Schubert," 7.
[41] Grove, "Another Unknown Symphony by Schubert," 7.
[42] Deutsch, *Schubert: A Documentary Biography*, 339.

130 FORGERY IN MUSICAL COMPOSITION

to Kupelwieser sees the composer go on to ambitiously comment that "I too am thinking of giving a similar concert next year" in seeming anticipation of the completion of a "grand symphony" on a newly expansive Beethovenian scale before the end of 1825.[43] With this lofty objective in mind, the aforementioned series of large-scale chamber works written early in 1824—i.e., the Quartet in A Minor, D. 804; the "Death and the Maiden" Quartet in D Minor, D. 810; and the Octet in F Major, D. 803—appear to have been conceived as the basis on which Schubert might "pave [his] way" toward a crowning orchestral achievement the following year in ways that, crucially, would have fit the chronological profile of Grove's missing symphony to a T.[44]

Schubert's friends Joseph von Spaun and Eduard von Bauernfeld appear to have confirmed that the composer did in fact execute this artistic plan more or less as he had proposed it to Kupelwieser in the spring of 1824. Both men pointedly reference the writing of a "grand symphony" of exceptional quality in the summer of 1825 in their respective longform Schubert obituaries of 1829, with Bauernfeld going so far as to suggest that the composer "had a special liking" for this work.[45] Significantly, both Spaun and Bauernfeld further associate the composition of the "grand symphony" in question with the same geographical location—i.e., the idyllic spa town of Gastein, where Schubert had stayed in August of 1825 after passing through Steyr, Linz, Gmunden, and Salzburg on an extended four-month trip with Johann Michael Vogl described by Robert Winter as "the happiest and most productive summer of [Schubert's] short life."[46] With this final touch of biographical color, the basic mythology of the lost work explicitly referred to as the "Gastein" Symphony in Spaun's and Bauernfeld's early accounts of Schubert's life and work was set in motion, as follows: inspired by the at turns sublime and idyllic alpine and lakeside landscapes of Upper Austria and Salzburg during his restorative summer travels with Vogl in 1825, Schubert fulfilled the compositional ambition he had stated to Kupelwieser the previous spring, completing a "grand symphony" conceived on the scale of Beethoven's Symphony No. 9. The finished work was discussed favorably within Schubert's circle of friends and dedicated to the Gesellschaft der Musikfreunde in October 1826, a date that Grove believed to confirm the work's non-identity with the

---

[43] Deutsch, *Schubert: A Documentary Biography*, 339–40.

[44] A comprehensive reappraisal of the compositional ambitions expressed by Schubert in this letter to Kupelwieser can be found in John M. Gingerich, *Schubert's Beethoven Project* (Cambridge: Cambridge University Press, 2014).

[45] Joseph von Spaun, "On Franz Schubert," *Österreichisches Bürgerblatt*, March 27–April 3, 1829, reprinted in Deutsch, *Schubert: A Documentary Biography*, 865–82, at 873. Eduard von Bauernfeld, "On Franz Schubert," *Wiener Zeitschrift für Kunst*, June 9–12, 1829, reprinted in Deutsch, *Schubert: A Documentary Biography*, 885–97, at 888.

[46] Robert Winter, "Paper Studies and the Future of Schubert Research," in *Schubert Studies: Problems of Style and Chronology*, edited by Eva Badura-Skoda and Peter Branscombe (Cambridge: Cambridge University Press, 1982): 209–275, at 231.

"Great" Symphony in C Major whose manuscript was inscribed "March 1828" in the composer's own hand. Sometime after this dedication, Schubert's immense 1825 score went missing from the archival record under mysterious circumstances, abruptly casting the "Gastein" Symphony into a deep musical obscurity from which the work could, conceivably, be recovered at any moment.

For decades after Grove first stated this thesis in 1881, many Schubertians remained convinced of the idea that a lost "Gastein" Symphony was in fact still out there, somewhere, waiting to be found. The seductive idea of a coming musicological rediscovery on this monumental scale was doubtless rendered more plausible by the fact that many of the works that were ultimately to become Schubert's most influential contributions to the orchestral repertory had indeed remained unperformed, unpublished, and all but totally unknown to the musical public for decades after the composer's untimely death in 1828, notably including the "Great" Symphony, D. 944, and the "Unfinished" Symphony, D. 759, premiered, respectively, in 1839 and 1865.[47] In the wake of the latter work's belated debut in Schubert's home city, leading Viennese music critic Eduard Hanslick reflected frustratedly on the archival obscurity in which many of Schubert's most substantial compositions had been permitted to languish. Most prominently, Hanslick's 1865 review bitterly complains that the deceased musician's surviving friends had seemingly proceeded either to "calmly let Schubert's manuscripts be scattered to the winds" after his passing or else conversely remained content to "keep them locked in a trunk" in a manner that clearly implied further submerged depths of undiscovered Schubertiana still awaiting retrieval.[48] For music lovers of Hanslick's generation this lengthy process of posthumous recovery felt so revelatory yet temporally protracted that in 1862, the critic had whimsically proposed that Schubert "goes on composing invisibly" in the present, seemingly creating visionary new works from the hereafter despite the undeniable fact that "for thirty years the master has been dead."[49]

This appetite for further Schubertian rediscoveries beyond the archival horizon did not end with the nineteenth century. In preparing for the 1928 centenary of Schubert's death, Deutsch pointedly reminded new generations of Viennese newspaper subscribers that it would be "well worth the effort" to

---

[47] On the complex cultural and biographical mythology surrounding the posthumous rediscovery of such works, see, for example, Andrea Lindmayr-Brandl, "The Myth of the 'Unfinished' and the Film *Das Dreimäderlhaus* (1958)," in *Rethinking Schubert* (New York: Oxford University Press, 2016): 111–26. For an alternative thesis concerning the first performance of the "Great" Symphony in C Major, D. 944, see Otto Biba, "Die Uraufführung von Schuberts Großer C-Dur-Symphonie—1829 in Wien. Ein glücklicher Aktenfund zum Schubert-Jahr," in *Musikblätter der Wiener Philharmoniker* 51 (1997): 287–91.

[48] Eduard Hanslick, "Schubert's 'Unfinished' Symphony" [1865], reprinted in *Hanslick's Music Criticisms*, translated and edited by Henry Pleasants (London: Dover, 1988): 101–3, at 101.

[49] Eduard Hanslick, quoted in Christopher Gibbs, *The Life of Schubert* (Cambridge: Cambridge University Press, 2000), 170.

132   FORGERY IN MUSICAL COMPOSITION

"rifle through your grandparents' stacks of junk sheet music" in search of the missing "Gastein" Symphony for which Deutsch himself would later propose the cataloguing number D. 849 as an expectant canonical placeholder.[50] The international committee for the 1928 centennial commemoration went further still, offering a direct $1,500 reward in an effort to decisively coax the "Gastein" Symphony out of obscurity.[51] To be sure, Elsholz was far too late to collect this large cash prize when he reported his own archival find ahead of the next major Schubert year five decades later, in 1978. Nonetheless, by this stage, the appetite for a major archival breakthrough was both clearly palpable and ripe for exploitation. For a skilled forger familiar with Grove's century-old "Gastein" hypothesis (if not with Hanslick's romantic notion of a metaphysical Schubert who "goes on composing invisibly" in the historical present) all that would have remained was to manufacture a score carefully molded to the archival and stylistic gap that completionist Schubertians both hoped and expected to see filled.

There were, however, further hitches. By the time Goldschmidt reported Elsholz's rediscovery to the sesquicentennial Schubert Congress in 1978, the validity of Grove's "Gastein" hypothesis was crumbling under new pressure from a variety of trenchant but competing scholarly critiques that had been leveled since the end of the Second World War. In 1958, Maurice Brown had suggested that the lost "Gastein" Symphony might well have been a phantom generated, of all things, by an archival cataloguing error. The original identifying number on Schubert's covering letter of dedication to the Gesellschaft der Musikfreunde appeared to have been altered, in Brown's view—conceivably by a misguided archivist who mistakenly presumed that Schubert's dedication should correspond, chronologically, to the 100 florins given to Schubert in October of 1826.[52] If one moves the undated letter of dedication forward in the historical record to 1828 to match the date on the autograph of Schubert's "Great" Symphony in C Major, then the most important piece of evidence for Grove's "Gastein" Symphony can be seen to evaporate into thin air.[53] Shortly after the publication of Brown's book, John Reed began to put forward a similar thesis in stronger rhetorical terms, positing that the inscription of "March 1828" on

---

[50] ". . . man stöbere unter Urväter Notenkram—es lohnt sich der Mühe!" Otto Erich Deutsch, "Schuberts Gasteiner Symphonie," *Neue freie Presse*, 11 July 1925, 12. Otto Erich Deutsch, *Schubert: Thematic Catalogue of All His Works in Chronological Order* (New York: W. W. Norton, 1951), 412.

[51] *New York Herald Tribune*, "Prize of $1,500 is announced for Schubert Search," 11 March 1928, 9.

[52] "The original number on this letter has been altered, which has a faint suggestion that its position has been moved in the early files, possibly to bring it into line with the transactions over the donation to Schubert and the rumours that he intended to dedicate a symphony to the Society." Maurice Brown, *Schubert: A Critical Biography* (London: Macmillan, 1958), 357.

[53] "The undated letter . . . one feels, *must* belong to 1828." Brown, *Schubert: A Critical Biography*, 357. Emphasis from original text.

the autograph of Schubert's "Great" Symphony in C Major referred to its date of final revision (not composition), that "in spite of the date" the work "must have been the one drafted in the summer of 1825, and [thus] that the hypothesis of a missing [Gastein] symphony does not bear close examination."[54] Finally, in the 1970s, the idea of a "Gastein" Symphony distinct from the "Great" Symphony in C Major was further challenged by new source-critical lines of argument. In research first published during the year of the 1978 Schubert Congress, Ernst Hilmar asserted that generations of musicologists may have been misreading Schubert's handwriting, observing that, in manuscripts from the 1820s, the composer had developed the habit of rendering the numeric character "5" with a loop protruding above the figure and an additional stroke joining the upper crossbeam to the descender. For Hilmar, the apparent "1828" written on the autograph of the "Great" Symphony in C Major could thus plausibly be supposed to have read "1825" all along.[55]

The emerging musicological consensus around 1978 that the "Gastein" Symphony had never existed surely made Goldschmidt's declaration that the fabled work had nonetheless been recovered all the more provocative. Predictably, a number of important modifications to Grove's original thesis were necessary to keep the "Gastein" hypothesis alive. While Goldschmidt's 1978 Congress paper freely admits that the "Great" Symphony in C Major had indeed been begun in Gastein in 1825, the study goes on to claim that Schubert had drafted an additional Symphony in E Major earlier that summer at the lakeside town of Gmunden.[56] This first work—now christened the "Gmunden" Symphony by Goldschmidt—had been abandoned while still a draft in favor of the new project of a "Great" Symphony in C Major begun at Gastein and familiar to modern concert audiences as Schubert's D. 944.[57] In Goldschmidt's view it was this earlier, incomplete "Gmunden" Symphony in E Major that had resurfaced in "a deficiently and haphazardly restored" form via Elsholz, seemingly proving Grove's nineteenth-century belief in a lost "10th" Schubert symphony correct, in principle, despite the widespread backdating of the "Great" Symphony in C Major to 1825 in the years following the Second World War.[58]

---

[54] John Reed, "The 'Gastein' Symphony Reconsidered," *Music & Letters* 40, no. 4 (1959): 341–49, at 342. For further development of these ideas see John Reed, *Schubert: The Final Years* (London: Faber & Faber, 1972) and John Reed, "How the 'Great' C Major Was Written," *Music & Letters* 56, no. 1 (1975): 18–25.

[55] Ernst Hilmar, "Neue Funde, Daten und Dokumente zum Symphonischen Werk Franz Schuberts," *Österreichische Musikzeitschrift* 33 (1978): 266–76, at 273–74. On subsequent developments in the dating of the "Great" Symphony in C Major beyond 1978 see Winter, "Paper Studies," and the summary given in Mark DeVoto, *Schubert's Great C Major: Biography of a Symphony* (Hillsdale, NY: Pendragon Press, 2011), 4–5.

[56] Goldschmidt, "Eine weitere E-Dur-Sinfonie?," 79.

[57] Goldschmidt, "Eine weitere E-Dur-Sinfonie?," 105.

[58] Goldschmidt, "Eine weitere E-Dur-Sinfonie?," 107.

134   FORGERY IN MUSICAL COMPOSITION

A SYMPHONY ON TRIAL

After the 1978 Schubert Congress, Elsholz continued to send Goldschmidt materials from his historical sources for closer scrutiny. By November 1982, the orchestral parts had been made available for his consultation in their totality. Enough supporting documentation had now accumulated for the contested score to be published in a full-length edition, notably including a prefatory historical and analytical commentary on the work written by Elsholz himself.[59] The symphony's live premiere—unfeasible, to Goldschmidt's and Elsholz's regret, at the 1978 sesquicentennial Congress—was duly scheduled at the Hanover State Opera, with performances on 6 and 7 December 1982 to be preceded by a public debate about the work's authorship, on 5 December. Concert programs and publicity agnostically listed the symphony as "attributed to Franz Schubert" [Franz Schubert zugeschrieben], thereby implicitly allowing audiences to make up their own minds after hearing the relevant evidence, musical and verbal.[60] To this end, over 250 people—including a notably silent Gunter Elsholz—turned up to listen to the symphony's authenticity adjudicated by the opposing parties in the ongoing musicological controversy.[61] No live event before or since has staged an active authenticity dispute concerning a musical work in quite such a dramatically public manner. Three presentations were scheduled for the evening and published as short essays in the accompanying concert program booklet, with each speaker invoking a strikingly different methodology of authentication.

The first individual to present evidence in defense of the symphony's authenticity at the panel discussion was Reimut Vogel, chief editor at Goldoni Verlag—i.e., the publisher of the new "Gmunden" score—and a lecturer in print history at the University of Stuttgart. Having clarified that he would leave an explanation of the "musicological study of the score" to Goldschmidt, Vogel proceeded to outline the "physical and chemical" evidence in support of its sources.[62] Above all, he emphasized the forensic testimony of the Institute for Paper in Heidenau, East Germany, where—in the years since the 1978 Schubert Congress—appraisers had reportedly conducted thorough microscopic tests that indicated that the set of parts had been written "around 1880 or 1890," on "mechanically produced, unwatermarked, oblong-format pulp paper with gilt edges."[63] The argument was

---

[59] Reimut Vogel and Gunter Elsholz, *Franz Schubert Sinfonie in E-Dur 1825: Materialien, Werk und Geschichte, Partitur* (Stuttgart: Goldoni Verlag, 1982).

[60] Program booklet for *Niedersächsisches Staatsorchester Hannover '82/83, 4. Konzert, 6. und 7. Dezember '82, Opernhaus* (1982). Archive of the Neue Schubert-Ausgabe, 1393, V S 849.

[61] Walther Dürr, "Die gefälschte Schubert-Sinfonie," in *Gefälscht!* (Nördlingen: Eichborn, 1990): 410–16, at 413.

[62] Reimut Vogel, "Materialien zur E-Dur-Sinfonie," in *Niedersächsisches Staatsorchester Hannover '82/83, 4. Konzert, 6. und 7. Dezember '82, Opernhaus* (1982): 10–14, at 10.

[63] "Die Stimmen wurden um 1880 oder um 1890 mit Tinte auf maschinell hergestelltem, klangharten, wasserzeichenfreien Zellstoffpapier im Querquart-Format mit Goldschnitt-Berandung geschrieben. Das bestätigen mikroskopische Prüfungen durch das Institut für Papier in Heidenau." Vogel, "Materialien zur E-Dur-Sinfonie," 10.

that, on a purely chemical level, the rediscovered parts were entirely consistent with Goldschmidt's and Elsholz's presentations of them. This is to say that the documents were written exclusively using materials that would have been available to Gunter Elsholz's ancestors at the time when the orchestral parts were supposed to have been copied from a nineteenth-century full score that had disappeared in the immediate aftermath of the Second World War.[64]

In a second presentation, Arnold Feil recounted the Neue Schubert-Ausgabe's objections to the work, illustrating a number of technical points further documented in an essay under Dürr's name in the concert program.[65] As both Feil and Dürr explained, the source-critical evidence for forgery began with the physical descriptions and samples Elsholz had provided for the historical orchestral parts during his 1973–75 correspondence with Henle Verlag and with the Neue Schubert-Ausgabe. Even leaving to one side the issue of the forged supporting letter in "Schubert's" hand discussed earlier in this chapter, Elsholz's early accounts of the orchestral parts were fundamentally inconsistent, in a number of key details, with the material reality of the set referred to by Goldschmidt from 1978 onward.[66] For example, while Elsholz had originally described a set of orchestral parts handwritten "in pale-brown dye-based ink" on "yellowish and, in parts, very thin paper," the set referred to by Goldschmidt and Vogel was by contrast unmistakably a product of "black pigment-based ink" on "extremely high quality paper."[67] In this context Dürr and Feil aptly pointed out that late nineteenth-century copyists did not write sets of parts in "pigment-based ink" on small, musically unpractical, oblong format paper, let alone with "each staff ruled by hand" despite the ready availability, in that era, of affordable pre-ruled music stationery.[68] And while Vogel chalked up these peculiarities to the work of a passionate amateur musician in Elsholz's family untutored in the technical conventions of professionalized music copying, it remains difficult to imagine an individual musically impassioned enough to copy the immense score of a lost Schubertian "grand symphony" into sets of gilt edged orchestral parts by hand who would simultaneously have been too discreet to publicize that work's existence or to attempt to have the parts in question performed.[69] Regardless, such explanations do nothing to clarify why Elsholz had provided Henle Verlag and the Neue Schubert-Ausgabe with fundamentally inaccurate descriptions of

---

[64] Goldschmidt, "Eine weitere E-Dur-Sinfonie?," 81.

[65] Walther Dürr, "Die neue E-Dur-Sinfonie—eine Fälschung?," in *Niedersächsisches Staatsorchester Hannover '82/83, 4. Konzert, 6. und 7. Dezember '82, Opernhaus* (1982): 14–16.

[66] Many of these points are documented in detail in Dürr, "Eine gefälschte Schubert-Sinfonie."

[67] "Die Papier- und Tintenproben . . . verweisen auf gelbliches, z. T. sehr dünnes Papier. . . auf blaßbraune Tinte." "Sie sind auf weißem Papier. . . . Das Papier [ist] von ziemlich guter Qualität." Dürr, "Eine gefälschte Schubert-Sinfonie," 135–36.

[68] Dürr, "Eine gefälschte Schubert-Sinfonie," 136.

[69] Vogel, "Materialien zur E-Dur-Sinfonie," 12.

136 FORGERY IN MUSICAL COMPOSITION

his source documents in the mid-1970s if he had genuinely had access to those documents from the start. An alternative theory seemingly confirmed by Dürr's and Feil's comprehensive source-philological analysis appeared more likely: crucially, the newly accessible set of "antique" orchestral parts had "without a doubt" been based on Elsholz's transcribed score from 1973–77, and not the other way around.[70] The full score of the "Gmunden" Symphony in E Major that had emerged gradually in Elsholz's hand between 1973 and 1977 was thus implied to be fundamentally an act of composition, not transcription from pre-existing documents. With all this in mind, Dürr's program note ends by frankly asserting that "one must come to the conclusion that what is under discussion here is a forgery, albeit an artful one."[71]

Summarizing the evening's events in an extended feuilleton essay for the *Hannoversche Allgemeine Zeitung,* Rainer Wagner described the academic evidence presented for this position by the two Neue Schubert-Ausgabe scholars as "so devastating that even Franz Schubert would have had difficulty in proving his authorship of this work had he stood up in the hall and confessed to it."[72] But, crucially, Goldschmidt had not yet had an opportunity to present his defense of the symphony's authenticity. And when he did at last take the stage, he notably eschewed both chemistry and source philology, turning—for the first time that evening—to consider the artistic qualities of the composition itself at length. As Wagner observed, here Goldschmidt's key rhetorical "trump card" was that— in stark contrast to all other experts assembled in Hanover—he "finally played music examples."[73] In this vein Goldschmidt's program note for the premiere studiously avoids any extended technical description of microscopic document analysis, ink types, or source filiation, instead vouching for the aesthetic value of the work as the strongest and most decisive evidence for its authenticity: "What totally rules out any suspicion of a pastiche," he writes, "is the great breath of this symphony, the grand scale of its construction, the inexorable musical flow, all its lavish episodes, and its profoundly unusual conception."[74] This striking prose style—abundant with grammatical hypotaxis, rhetorical questions, artfully

[70] "Aus diesen Untersuchungen ergab sich zweifelsfrei, daß die neu geschriebene Partitur nicht auf die Stimmen zurückgehen kann, sondern daß umgekehrt die als alt bezeichneten Stimmen von der erst vom Finder geschriebenen Partitur abgeschrieben sein müssen." Dürr, "Die neue E-Dur-Sinfonie—eine Fälschung?," 16.

[71] Dürr, "Die neue E-Dur-Sinfonie—eine Fälschung?," 14.

[72] "Und was die beiden Schubert-Forscher da zu den Widersprüchen des Projekts anmerkten, war so vernichtend, daß selbst Franz Schubert, stünde er nun im Saale auf und würde zu diesem Werke bekennen, Schwierigkeit hätte, das zu belegen." Rainer Wagner, "Juwel, Steinbruch oder Talmi?," *Hannoversche Allgemeine Zeitung,* 8 December 1982, reprinted in *Das Orchester* 31 (1983): 261–63, at 262.

[73] Wagner, "Juwel, Steinbruch oder Talmi?," 262.

[74] "Was aber den Verdacht einer 'Stilkopie' völlig ausschließt, ist der große Atem dieser Sinfonie, die Weiträumigkeit ihrer Anlage, der unaufhaltsame musikalische Fluß bei aller verschwenderischen Episodenfülle, die großartige, absolut ungewöhnliche Konzeption." Harry Goldschmidt, Program note for *Niedersächsisches Staatsorchester Hannover '82/83, 4. Konzert, 6. und 7. Dezember '82, Opernhaus* (1982): 17–19, at 18. Archive of the *Neue Schubert-Ausgabe,* 1393, V S 849.

conceived analogies, and long chains of descriptive adjectives—is characteristic of Goldschmidt's approach to scholarly persuasion, yet worlds apart from Dürr's and Feil's comparatively concise, measured, and detail-oriented manner of communication. And it is perhaps this vivid contrast both in content and in style of delivery that Wagner sought to emphasize when he posed a rhetorical question of his own, summing up an implicit connotation of Goldschmidt's contribution to the debate by asking—in a comment presumably intended to document a subtextual snub at the Neue Schubert-Ausgabe scholars—"Who cares about paper pushers when we are talking about the sublime"?[75]

At the event's end, the audience was asked to vote on whether the symphony was genuine or not. Reportedly, in answer to the question "Do you believe that this Symphony is a work by Schubert?," 57 percent of the voting public present replied "yes."[76] And in a second round, a different question was asked, resulting in a substantially increased majority of 80 percent confirming that—regardless of whether or not it was authentic Schubert—they would be "happy to encounter the work again in a concert hall or on record."[77] Summing up his extended account of the evening's events, Wagner concluded that—even though he himself regarded "the symphony, in this form, as a forgery"—it remained important to present the arguments both for and against the contested work's authenticity to the public, since "more was learnt about Schubert and his music" in this manner "than would have been possible in the x-th performance of the 'Unfinished.'"[78] In an apparent reference to a phrase made famous at the 1967 trial of activist Fritz Teufel, Wagner goes on to add that the Schubert event in Hanover was justified because such an act of collective discussion and listening "serves the (aural) establishment of truth."[79] Nonetheless, the fundamental problem with the musical evidence presented in this case was that it could be read both ways: given the presence of clear models for many of the "Gmunden" Symphony's most convincing passages in Schubert's existing compositional corpus, "precisely the supposed proof of authenticity—the so-called 'typical passages' [of Schubert's style]—are [also] a sign of forgery."[80]

---

[75] Wagner, "Juwel, Steinbruch oder Talmi?," 262.

[76] Dürr, "Die gefälschte Schubert-Sinfonie," 413.

[77] Ludwig Flich, "Der Schubert-Krimi," *Vox* 3 (1983): 5–6 at 6.

[78] "Ich halte die Sinfonie in dieser Form für eine Fälschung." "... weil in den vielen individuellen Streitgesprächen davor und danach mehr über Schubert und seine Musik erfahren wurde, als es die x-te Aufführung einer 'Unvollendeten' möglich gemacht hätte." Wagner, "Juwel, Steinbruch oder Talmi?," 263.

[79] "... weil es der (hörenden) Wahrheitsfindung dient." Wagner, "Juwel, Steinbruch oder Talmi?," 263. After being ordered by a judge to only address topics that "serve the establishment of truth," Teufel satirically adopted this expression at his trial, notoriously declaring—for example—that he would stand up to testify only "if it serves the establishment of truth" [wenn's denn der Wahrheitsfindung dient].

[80] "Wenn es eine Fälschung ist, dann ist genau der vermeintliche Echtheitsbeweis—die 'typischen Stellen'—das Signum der Fälschung." Wagner, "Juwel, Steinbruch oder Talmi?," 263.

138 FORGERY IN MUSICAL COMPOSITION

ORIGINAL FACSIMILES

As early as the 1978 Congress, Goldschmidt had been obliged to point out at length that a large number of passages throughout the monumental Symphony in E Major bear a marked similarity to Schubert compositions already well-established in the repertory: reminiscences of *Der Wanderer*, D. 489; the Octet in F Major, D. 803; the Piano Sonata in D Major, D. 850; the String Quartet in G Major, D. 887; and the "Great" Symphony in C Major, D. 944 are all clearly and extensively audible in the score supposedly rediscovered by Elsholz, whether as direct quotations or as closely adapted musical paraphrases. Goldschmidt, of course, was outwardly unperturbed by these similarities. And Dürr and Feil generally preferred to hang their authenticating judgments on source-critical evidence, avoiding an overreliance on the questions of aesthetic and stylistic evaluation bound up in the "Gmunden" Symphony's apparent compositional borrowings, which Dürr nonetheless aptly described, in passing, as a deeply unschubertian form of "mosaic technique."[81] By comparison, critics unaffiliated with the Neue Schubert-Ausgabe were not nearly so reserved in commenting on issues of originality and musical value as such: Hartmut Lück, for instance, decried the "blank sections, banal fillers, and broken transitions" separating apparently Schubertian passages in a work that, as a whole, "oscillates strangely between brilliant ideas and mediocre hackwork."[82] Indeed, for skeptically minded listeners of this sort, Elsholz's "Schubert" Symphony in E Major evoked nothing so much as a vast orchestral potpourri assembled from shards of genuine Schubertiana by a forger skilled at the art of musical collage but ultimately powerless to create convincing new compositional material in Schubert's style.

The "Gmunden" Symphony needed a sophisticated musicological defense to overcome these charges of internal compositional derivativeness and, with them, the brand of forgery. Having rightly foreseen the danger that Elsholz's eerily familiar score would be met with open hostility, Goldschmidt took it upon himself to pre-emptively offer extensive explanations for the symphony's internal musical reminiscences of the aforementioned entries in the Schubert canon at the 1978 Congress, dividing his analysis into two large subsets determined by chronology. The first of these two analytical subsets comprises Elsholz's score's compositional similarities to those Schubert works created "between summer 1825 and 1826," after the supposed abandonment of the "Gmunden" symphonic fragment—i.e., the Piano Sonata in D Major, D. 850; the String Quartet in G Major, D. 887; and the "Great" Symphony in C Major, D. 944.[83] In what might appear to be a striking reversal of presumed causation, Goldschmidt proposed

[81] Dürr, "Die neue E-Dur-Sinfonie—eine Fälschung?," 16.
[82] Hartmut Lück, "Eine apokryphe Schubert-Sinfonie?," *Neue Musikzeitung* 32 (1983): 29.
[83] Goldschmidt, "Eine weitere E-Dur-Sinfonie?," 105.

that musicologists should reappraise these three familiar works not as the pre-existing models for a modern act of forgery, but rather as Schubert's own compositional readaptations of unpublished draft material recycled from the vast "Gmunden" symphonic fragment abandoned in the summer of 1825. Thus the striking similarities between Elsholz's rediscovered score and Schubert's Piano Sonata in D Major, D. 850, String Quartet in G Major, D. 887, and Symphony in C Major, D. 944 were reconfigured in Goldschmidt's account as instances of the routine and legitimate "borrowing" or "unconscious reuse" of sketch material from a given composer's own prior unfinished projects, rather than damning evidence of musical derivativeness on the part of some latter-day compositional forger.[84] "If Schubert left [the "Gmunden" Symphony in E Major] to the side as a draft"—asks Goldschmidt, in a characteristic rhetorical question—"why shouldn't he," after all, "have been permitted to draw on its unused material?"[85]

This rationale was all very well for works that postdated the score supposedly abandoned in the summer of 1825. Yet a second and altogether different musicological explanation was needed for Goldschmidt to account for the abandoned "Gmunden" Symphony's apparent reuse of compositional material drawn from Schubert works completed before that date. Two familiar compositions fall into this category: the Octet in F Major, D. 803, composed in 1824 and referenced prominently in Schubert's letter to Kupelwieser from March of that year; and *Der Wanderer*, D. 489, composed in 1816 and published in 1821.[86] Clearly, a "Gmunden" Symphony abandoned in 1825 could not be regarded as a precedent for these two pre-1825 Schubert compositions, by definition. Instead, Goldschmidt asserted that Schubert's reuse of material from the Octet and *Der Wanderer* in the aborted "Gmunden" fragment was not evidence of post-facto forgery but rather simply of deliberate "self-quotation" on Schubert's own part, much as the composer had practiced it in his "Death and the Maiden" String Quartet in D Minor, D. 810, or—for that matter—in the "Wanderer" Fantasy, D. 760.[87] Armed with this seductive line of argument, Goldschmidt could claim to have justified not only the fact of Schubert's reuse of pre-existing material from the Octet and *Der Wanderer* within the rediscovered Symphony in E Major, but also the more extensive and emphatic nature of that compositional reuse as a

---

[84] "Alle übrigen Parallelstellen fallen unter die Kategorie der Entlehnung oder unbewußten *Wiederverwendung*." Goldschmidt, "Eine weitere E-Dur-Sinfonie?," 105. Emphasis from original text.

[85] "Wenn Schubert sie im Entwurfszustand beiseite gelegt hat, um eine neue Sinfonie zu schreiben, weshalb sollte ihm da nicht gestattet gewesen sein, auf ihr unverwertetes Material zurückzugreifen?" Goldschmidt, "Eine weitere E-Dur-Sinfonie?," 105.

[86] After first appearing in print as the *Lied*, op. 4, no. 1, in 1821, *Der Wanderer* also served as the thematic basis for the well-known "Wanderer" Fantasy in C Major published as Schubert's op. 15 in 1823.

[87] Goldschmidt, "Eine weitere E-Dur-Sinfonie?," 104–5.

140   FORGERY IN MUSICAL COMPOSITION

deliberate focal point for what he argued Schubert might well have intended, in 1825, as a quasi-autobiographical "Wanderer Symphony."[88]

In Goldschmidt's and Elsholz's accounts, the "Gmunden" Symphony's self-quotations from pre-1825 Schubert works were thus to be understood as an intentional rhetorical strategy for the generation of richly intertextual and reflexive forms of musical meaning. Framing his exploration of the work in these terms, Goldschmidt points out that Schubert's self-quotations from the Octet and from *Der Wanderer* appear first in the Symphony in E Major's slow introduction, a formal area he understood to project "programmatic meaning" derived in part from the historical associations of the "French Overture" genre as an orchestral contextualizing device for ballet and opera, here itself troped into the putatively absolute domain of the symphony.[89] Among musicologists, Goldschmidt has by no means been alone in regarding the slow introduction as a site for the generation of narrative signification in something like this manner: in an influential 2006 study, James Hepokoski and Warren Darcy suggest the utility of analytical readings of sonata-form slow introductions as potential representations of (among other things) the "Narrator," the "Raison d'être," or the "Animating Force" for "the Tale Told" in the Allegro portion of a larger instrumental movement.[90] With these complex symbolic attitudes toward compositional form in mind, the prominent self-quotations from the Octet and *Der Wanderer* heard within the "Gmunden" symphony's slow introduction could be understood to signify with particular expressive force, appearing at the work's outer threshold as hermeneutic signposts with which to situate and decode the music to follow.

Consider example 3.1a, which shows the opening phrase from the Symphony in E Major's slow introduction, itself a derivation from Schubert's Octet. In this passage the "Gmunden" Symphony is set on its course with what Elsholz's preface describes as a "dark, downwards beseeching tremolo" in the lower strings, landing, at m. 3, on a tonic pedal E.[91] Once established, this subterranean string pedal tone is immediately supplemented by an embellishing $\frac{8-7-8}{3-3-3}$ voice-leading pattern above E in the woodwinds and trombones set in a distinctive rhythmic profile featuring prominent sixteenth-note acciaccaturas. This $\frac{8-7-8}{3-3-3}$

---

[88] "War in Analogie und Fortsetzung der Wanderer-Fantasie an eine Wanderer-*Sinfonie* gedacht?" Goldschmidt, "Eine weitere E-Dur-Sinfonie?," 88. Emphasis from original text.

[89] "Das Aufscheinen des *Wanderer*zitats an programmatisch so exponierter Stelle—seit der neueren französischen Opernouvertüre fällt Introduktionszitaten mit Vorliebe programmatische Bedeutung zu—ist konzeptionell leicht einsichtig zu machen." Goldschmidt, "Eine weitere E-Dur-Sinfonie?," 88.

[90] James Hepokoski and Warren Darcy, *Elements of Sonata Theory: Norms, Types, and Deformations in the Late-Eighteenth-Century Sonata* (New York: Oxford University Press, 2006), 304.

[91] "Ein dunkel abwärts drängendes Tremolorollen bahnt den Weg zu jener typischen Motivgebärde . . ." Gunter Elsholz, "Werk und Geschichte," in *Franz Schubert Sinfonie in E-Dur, 1825* (Stuttgart: Goldoni Verlag, 1982): 7–40, at 9.

Example 3.1a Gunter Elsholz, "Schubert" Symphony in E Major (Gmunden), "D. 849." Andante molto—Allegro—Andante molto (mvt. i), mm. 1–8

pattern is "a motivic gesture" that "functions as a fundamental formula at many points in Schubert's work" in Elsholz's own analytical account of the Symphony in E Major, appearing as "a sigh from the depths of the heart, encountered not only in the Octet, but also in the song *Schöne Welt, wo bist du?*" [i.e., *Die Götter Griechenlands*, D. 677] and "the third movement of the String Quartet in

Example 3.1b Franz Schubert, Octet in F Major, D. 803. Andante molto—Allegro—Andante molto—Allegro (mvt. vi), mm. 1–7

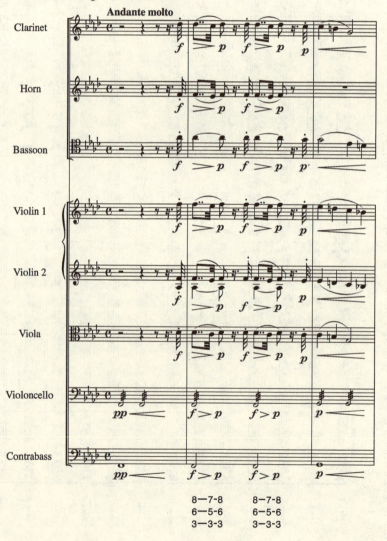

Example 3.1b Continued

A minor."[92] Indeed, the deeply expressive qualities Elsholz hears in these measures surely stem from the "sigh" gesture's unusual harmonic function: crucially, the $\begin{smallmatrix}8-7-8\\6-5-6\\3-3-3\end{smallmatrix}$ motif undermines any sense of the unadulterated root-position stability one might normatively expect from a composition's opening measures following

---

[92] "... jener typischen Motivgebärde, die in Schuberts Schaffen mehrfach die Bedeutung einer Grundformel hat, die wie ein Seufzer aus Herzensgrund anmutet und der wir sowohl im Oktett als auch in dem Lied 'Schöne Welt, wo bist du?' begegnen. Auch der dritte Satz des a-moll-Streichquartetts bringt dieses Seufzermotiv." Elsholz, "Werk und Geschichte," 9.

144 FORGERY IN MUSICAL COMPOSITION

the establishment of an apparent tonic pedal, instead producing a "haunting and strange" effect of harmonic "ambiguity between tonic and dominant," which Nicholas Temperley claims "clearly fascinated" Schubert.[93] In the passage cited in example 3.1a, the unease of the $^{8-7-8}_{5-5-5}$ $^{3-3-3}$ gesture is further heightened by the pedal passage's immediate transposition to the global subdominant at m. 7 in an ambiguous, destabilizing move suggesting that the E "tonic" established in m. 3 might possibly have been a dominant pointing forward to A from the start. While the "Gmunden" Symphony's opening Andante molto goes on to confirm E as its global tonic, this moment of diversion nonetheless aptly illustrates what Elsholz poetically envisioned as the symphony's initial "plunging" of listeners into a "dense atmosphere" populated by pervasive musical "shadows" from which the main action of the work will ultimately emerge.[94]

Example 3.1b shows the corresponding Andante molto slow introduction of the sixth and final movement from Schubert's Octet as the clear compositional source for the "Gmunden" Symphony in E Major's opening quotation as illustrated in example 3.1a. For reasons amply illuminated by a cursory comparison of these two excerpts, Goldschmidt considered the musical relationship between the Octet in F Major and the "Gmunden" Symphony to be "so close that one can truly speak of a conceptual continuation" in ways that seemingly demonstrated Schubert's own 1824 ambition to "pave [his] way towards grand symphony" in part through the composition of this large-scale chamber work.[95] The same sighing $^{8-7-8}_{5-5-5}$ $^{3-3-3}$ voice-leading pattern is set in a near identical rhythm and used to embellish the same tonic pedal with the same swelling string tremolos and the same eventual move to the global subdominant at m. 6. Yet, interesting as these surface-level resemblances may be in their own right, the similarity between the Andante molto passages cited in example 3.1a and example 3.1b ultimately extends to a structural level of organization that transcends the handful of measures excerpted here. Crucially, these uneasy opening pedals return as cyclical motto themes in the respective coda sections that conclude the finale of the Octet and the first movement of the "Gmunden" Symphony, erupting through the texture in dramatic eleventh-hour compositional breakthroughs which call back to the uneasy opening atmosphere established by example 3.1a and example 3.1b.[96]

---

[93] Nicholas Temperley, "Schubert and Beethoven's Eight-Six Chord," *19th-Century Music* 5, no. 2 (1981): 142–54, at 150, 152–53.

[94] Elsholz, "Werk und Geschichte," 9.

[95] "Die Beziehung ist so eng, daß geradezu von einer konzeptionellen Fortsetzung gesprochen werden kann." Goldschmidt, "Eine weitere E-Dur-Sinfonie?," 85. Deutsch, *Schubert: A Documentary Biography*, 339.

[96] The motif reappears at m. 415ff in the "Gmunden" Symphony's first movement and at m. 370ff in the sixth movement of Schubert's Octet. As Nicholas Temperley has observed, Schubert deploys the eight-six chord as an external framing device for the interior vocal text in something like this manner in *Die Götter Griechenlands*, D. 677. See Temperley, "Schubert and Beethoven's Eight-Six Chord," 152.

In this sense, these passages can be seen to function within the Octet and "Gmunden" Symphony as what Hepokoski and Darcy dub an "Introduction-Coda Frame"—i.e., a device in which "material from the introduction returns as all or part of the coda," with the striking effect of rendering "the sonata form proper ... an artifice that unfolds only under the prior authority of the frame."[97]

Perhaps unsurprisingly, defenders of the Symphony in E Major seem to have been well aware of the resonant hermeneutic implications of such cyclical reuse of pre-existing material. For Elsholz, the return of the Andante molto passage from example 3.1a at the end of the "Gmunden" Symphony's first movement is symbolic of nothing less than a programmatic "Idée fixe" underlying the work's symmetrical construction—i.e., "the impossibility of any true return," in which one finds oneself, fatefully, "at the goal, but not at the longed-for home."[98] In a similar narratological vein, Goldschmidt regarded the concluding "break-through of the pain-wrought introduction" from example 3.1a in the closing moments of the "Gmunden" Symphony's first movement as a key hermeneutic signifier by virtue of which "the merry wandering" of the Allegro portion of the movement is "abruptly called into question."[99] Here for Goldschmidt and Elsholz as elsewhere for Hepokoski and Darcy, "the interior sonata [form] seems subordinated to the outward container," with "introduction and coda" representing a "higher reality" dominated, in the Symphony in E Major, by a series of introspective and quasi-autobiographical Schubertian self-quotations.[100]

Example 3.2a shows the other prominent self-quotation in the "Gmunden" Symphony's slow introduction: from m. 27, a clear derivation of the lyrical second-stanza theme from Schubert's *Der Wanderer*—a melody that Elsholz himself describes as "something akin to the Leitmotiv of the entire symphony"—can be heard in the oboe, here remetered from the original simple duple into $\frac{6}{8}$.[101] Intriguingly, this particular version of the melody is a derivation of the second order, stemming not from *Der Wanderer* itself but rather from a related $\frac{2}{2}$ passage

---

[97] Significantly, Hepokoski and Darcy identify the introduction-coda frame in particular with two of Schubert's late symphonic first movements: the "Unfinished" Symphony in B Minor, D. 759, and the "Great" Symphony in C Major, D. 944, are discussed as paradigmatic examples. See Hepokoski and Darcy, *Elements of Sonata Theory*, 304–5.

[98] "Die Erregung gerade in den Phasen dieser Rückkehr wird durch die Unmöglichkeit, je wirklich zurückkehren zu können, in ihrer Aufgewühltheit so glaubwürdig. Kurz vor dem Ende des Weges kommt es tatsächlich zu einer forcierten (Allegro-molto-)Lustigkeit, die sich nach wenigen Takten in einem erneuten Andante molto gründlich bricht: am Ziel, doch es ist nicht das erstrebt Zuhause ..." Elsholz, "Werk und Geschichte," 12.

[99] "Daher bring die Koda auch keine 'zweite Durchführung' à la Beethoven, sondern ein Ereignis ganz anderer Art: Den Einbruch der schmerzgezeichneten Introduktion. ... Die gesamte freudige Wanderschaft ... erscheint—und dieses gegen Ende!—schroffstes in Frage gestellt." Goldschmidt, "Eine weitere E-Dur-Sinfonie?," 89.

[100] Hepokoski and Darcy, *Elements of Sonata Theory*, 305.

[101] "Über klopfenden Bässen entfaltet sich die tröstende Melodie, die so etwas wie das Leitmotiv der ganzen Symphonie wird." Elsholz, "Werk und Geschichte," 9.

146 FORGERY IN MUSICAL COMPOSITION

near the beginning of the *Adagio* in Schubert's "Wanderer" Fantasie, reproduced
for comparison in example 3.2b. With the exception of the change of meter and the
"Gmunden" Symphony's turn back to E major at m. 32, the melodic and harmonic
content of the two excerpts is identical down to the murmuring inner-voice figuration given to the second violins and violas. For comparison, example 3.2c shows
the original Schubert song behind the musical derivations of both example 3.2a
and example 3.2b: here, Schubert sets the second stanza from Georg Philipp
Schmidt von Lübeck's poem *Der Wanderer* with a modulating phrase beginning in C♯ minor but ending with a bittersweet and paradoxically chilling turn
to the "Gmunden" Symphony's home key of E major, cadencing there in m. 30
on a line of text that has become a familiar trope of Schubert reception in its own
right: "I am a stranger everywhere" [Ich bin ein Fremdling überall]. Expressed
in the first person, this bleak, inward-looking, proto-existentialist sentiment is
evocative of broader aesthetic, hermeneutic, and biographical ideas that have frequently been deployed in discussions of Schubert and his music, perhaps especially since the mid-twentieth century. Lawrence Kramer, for example, regards
Schubert's "predilection for evoking wanderers and other Romantic outcasts" in
songs like *Der Wanderer* as "a truism" underpinning broader critical approaches
to the composer's subjectivity, while scholars such as William Kinderman and
Charles Fisk have extended this perspective to the composer's mature music
without words, with Fisk notably confirming—with a particular eye toward the
Impromptus and Piano Sonatas of 1827–28—that "Schubert's identification
with the Fremdling wanderers of [*Winterreise* and *Der Wanderer*] links these
protagonists . . . to the instrumental music of his last year."[102] Waxing poetic, Scott
Burnham opines that Schubert "composed under the sign of the Romantic wanderer," while Jeffrey Perry goes further still in stating outright that "Schubert's
music is the music of a wanderer" as such, thereby pithily folding the composer's
style and personal identity together into this singular romantic archetype.[103]
In the specific context of what Goldschmidt hypothesized could ultimately
have been intended as a "Wanderer" Symphony in 1825, the solo oboe melody
reproduced in example 3.2a can thus arguably be heard—following Elsholz's
analysis—as a Leitmotivic musical synecdoche referring back not simply to the

---

[102] Lawrence Kramer, *Franz Schubert: Sexuality, Subjectivity, Song* (Cambridge: Cambridge
University Press, 1998), 2; William Kinderman, "Wandering Archetypes in Schubert's Instrumental
Music," *19th-Century Music* 21, no. 2 (1997): 208–22; Charles Fisk, *Returning Cycles: Contexts for the
Interpretation of Schubert's Impromptus and Last Sonatas* (Berkeley: University of California Press,
2001), 21. For extended critical discussion of "wandering" tropes in Schubert reception and analysis,
see Suzannah Clark, *Analyzing Schubert* (Cambridge: Cambridge University Press, 2011).
[103] Scott Burnham, "Landscape as Music, Landscape as Truth: Schubert and the Burden of
Repetition," *19th-Century Music* 29, no. 1 (2005): 31–41, at 40; Jeffrey Perry, "The Wanderer's Many
Returns: Schubert's Variations Reconsidered," *Journal of Musicology* 19, no. 2 (2002): 374–416,
at 374.

Example 3.2a Gunter Elsholz, "Schubert" Symphony in E Major (Gmunden), "D. 849." Andante molto—Allegro—Andante molto (mvt. i), mm. 27–34

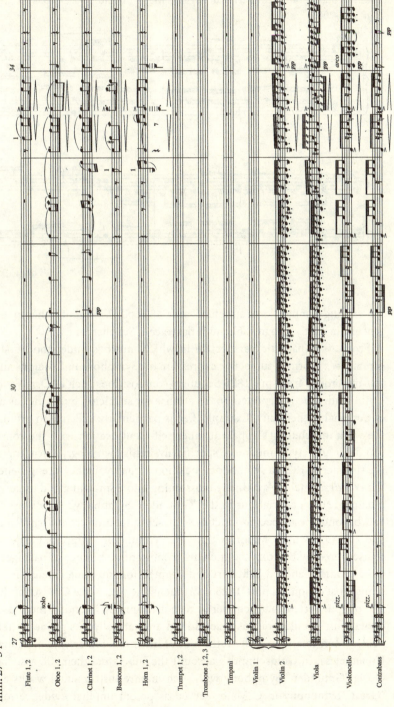

Example 3.2b Franz Schubert, Fantasy in C Major (Wanderer), D. 760 (op. 15), mm. 197–200

pre-existing compositional structures of D. 489 and D. 790, but rather to the absent and instantly recognizable authorial voice of Schubert himself.

From a sympathetic perspective in which music is understood first and foremost as a form of subjective expression the Symphony in E Major's alleged self-quotations from pre-1825 Schubert compositions such as *Der Wanderer* could readily be interpreted not as a cause for suspicion but rather as a seal of personal authenticity. Example 3.2a is particularly effective in grounding the work in Schubert's apparent inner self-identification with the romantic wanderer archetype and, more specifically, in his own biographical travels in the summer of 1825, a symbolic association arguably further strengthened by the *Wanderer* melody's ultimate blossoming into a sprawling and tonally ambulatory series of variations in the "Gmunden" Symphony's slow movement. Yet, beyond these specific junctures for self-quotation from *Der Wanderer* and the Octet in F Major within the "Gmunden" Symphony, the score rediscovered by Elsholz also includes a substantial number of passages that Goldschmidt believed Schubert had adapted for subsequent reuse in some of his most canonical post-1825 instrumental works. Since Goldschmidt and Elsholz purported that Schubert had not originally intended them as self-quotations, parallels of this second kind are naturally less prone to hermeneutic interpretations built on the idea of intentional intertextual resonance. Nonetheless, in Goldschmidt's account the subtextual thematic association of the "Gmunden" Symphony with such mature instrumental works as the "Great" Symphony in C Major served as potent implicit evidence for the

Example 3.2c Franz Schubert, *Der Wanderer*, D. 489 (op. 4, no. 1), mm. 22–30

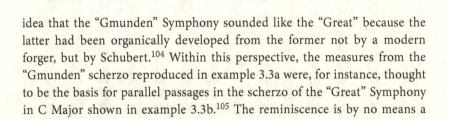

idea that the "Gmunden" Symphony sounded like the "Great" because the latter had been organically developed from the former not by a modern forger, but by Schubert.[104] Within this perspective, the measures from the "Gmunden" scherzo reproduced in example 3.3a were, for instance, thought to be the basis for parallel passages in the scherzo of the "Great" Symphony in C Major shown in example 3.3b.[105] The reminiscence is by no means a

---

[104] Goldschmidt, "Eine weitere E-Dur-Sinfonie?," 85.
[105] Goldschmidt, "Eine weitere E-Dur-Sinfonie?," 90.

Example 3.3a Gunter Elsholz, "Schubert" Symphony in E Major (Gmunden), "D. 849." Scherzo: Un poco agitato (mvt. ii), mm. 53–60

Example 3.3b Franz Schubert, Symphony No. 9 in C Major (Great), D. 944. Scherzo: Allegro vivace (mvt. iii), mm. 143–50

152   FORGERY IN MUSICAL COMPOSITION

strictly verbatim transposition; indeed, the two passages depart from each other in more melodic and harmonic details of consequence than any pair of examples discussed thus far. However, the fact remains that the fundamental musical ideas in example 3.3a and example 3.3b clearly share an identical rhythmic profile accompanied by carbon copy upper-neighbor motifs articulated in eighth notes in each example's opening measure and further augmented by similarly abrupt dynamic contrasts and playful, back-and-forth orchestral dialogue between winds and strings. In short, the differences between example 3.3a and example 3.3b are subtle enough to render the basic underlying similarity of the two passages in stark relief, thus evoking—in Goldschmidt's account—the impression of a single composer drawing from a unified thematic source at two distinct points in time.

For those adopting a more critical viewpoint, the scherzo passage reproduced in example 3.3a is also broadly illustrative of certain unidiomatic and anachronistic details of orchestration that could be seen to pose substantial challenges to the rediscovered symphony's authenticity. After m. 57, when the flutes are added to the oboes for the melody's consequent subphrase, the first flute part occupies an astonishingly high register unprecedented in Schubert's authentic orchestral music, with an Olympian apex stretching up to C♯7 in m. 59. Hector Berlioz's orchestration treatise of 1844, which lists C♯7 as the "very difficult" upper limit for modern flutes sixteen years after Schubert's death, is apt to clarify the brute historical implausibility of this C♯7 appearing in an orchestral flute part from the mid-1820s: indeed, Berlioz's 1844 treatise further adds that A♭6 had, until "very few years ago," been the highest note available from the instrument's topmost register.[106] This historical context would make the presence of C♯7 in an orchestral flute part from a work supposedly written by Schubert in 1825 highly suspicious even in the absence of the curious *piano* dynamic marking associated with the stratospheric entry ensuing from m. 57 in example 3.3a, itself a deeply questionable expressive demand for a composer to make in this context given the general incompatibility of soft dynamics with extreme upper wind registers.[107] Of course, Goldschmidt's broader thesis that the "Gmunden" Symphony was the musical equivalent of a "deficiently and haphazardly restored painting" offered him a ready explanation for such inconvenient technical solecisms: once identified as problematic, details like m. 59's C♯7 could instantaneously be reattributed from Schubert to an incompetent posthumous completer who, in taking the blame and serving as scapegoat, might nonetheless effectively

---

[106] Hector Berlioz, *Grand traité d'instrumentation et d'orchestration modernes* (Paris: Schonenberger, 1844), 151.

[107] Many further such details can be found elsewhere in the flute parts of the Symphony in E Major's score, including an additional C♯7 at m. 359 in the first movement and a D♯7 at m. 308 in the finale.

safeguard the authenticity of the work as a whole.[108] In the end, it must however be admitted that ad hoc dismissals of this sort remain inescapably circular: if any music-stylistic counterexample that might conceivably falsify Schubert's authorship of the "Gmunden" Symphony can be retroactively excluded from the limited portion of the work supposed to have been authored by Schubert in the first place, there is arguably little point in engaging with style-critical attempts to authenticate the work at all, since any potentially falsifying evidence will inevitably be defined out of the equation as such. Indeed, it would appear that no substantive proof can be provided for the attribution of any specific musical detail within the "Gmunden" Symphony to Schubert, on the one hand, or to the completer, on the other, beyond that same specific detail's perceived artistic quality as good or bad music to such an extent that aesthetic excellence and factual authenticity are ultimately rendered indistinguishable.

Conversely, the "Gmunden" Symphony in E Major's supposed status as a restored fragment also made it possible to read unorthodox details of the work's form as evidence of Schubert's authorial cultivation of an aesthetic so technically innovative and expressively potent as to be unfinishable within his lifetime. Consider example 3.4a, which shows a pivotal passage in which the first of the opening movement's three rotational statements ends by collapsing in on itself. Having established a lyrical subordinate theme in the global chromatic submediant (C Major), the orchestra halts in mid-flow after m. 153, where an A♭ pizzicato sounded *forte* in the contrabass part crashes in to disrupt the texture, "ripping the movement in two"—as Elsholz himself puts it—before giving way to an eerie general pause.[109] Strident new fortissimo material breaks the silence at the upbeat to m. 155, rushing from C major to the tritone-related active dominant of B major at m. 159. In m. 161, the timbrally uncanny timpani and pizzicato attacks that echo m. 153's A♭ can be heard to augment the overall expressive effect of a work coming apart at the seams, creating a new general pause at the barline. While the symphonic order appears to have been fundamentally fractured in this strikingly chaotic passage, the restatement of the primary theme in the global dominant (B major) that begins the second rotation at the upbeat to m. 163 sounds disconcertingly nonchalant, somehow continuing in a jovial four-square march style as if nothing unusual had happened.

Hartmut Lück was surely thinking of sections akin to that reproduced in example 3.4a when he complained about the "Gmunden" Symphony's "banal fillers" and "broken transitions" in the wake of the work's 1982 Hanover premiere.[110] Yet, from a sympathetic perspective informed by Goldschmidt's and

---

[108] Goldschmidt, "Eine weitere E-Dur-Sinfonie?," 107.
[109] Elsholz, "Werk und Geschichte," 11.
[110] Lück, "Eine apokryphe Schubert-Sinfonie?," 29.

Example 3.4a Gunter Elsholz, "Schubert" Symphony in E Major (Gmunden), "D. 849," Andante molto—Allegro—Andante molto (mvt. i), mm. 137–68

Example 3.4a Continued

Example 3.4a Continued

SCHUBERT'S UNTRUE SYMPHONY   157

Elsholz's accounts of the work, the abrupt segue from the brief violent outburst following m. 153 to the unexpected repose of m. 163 is arguably not so difficult to reconcile with the "volcanic temper" that musicians have consistently identified as a key characteristic of Schubert's mature compositional style, typified—for Hugh Macdonald—by patterns of "violence forcing itself through a calm surface" and then being suddenly "suppressed."[111] It need hardly be added that similarly overwrought patterns of rupture and repose can be identified in many of Schubert's best-known instrumental works, including the rapidly escalating and de-escalating passages on either side of the famously earthshattering *fff* diminished-seventh chord and subsequent general pause that respectively appear at m. 248 and m. 249 during the slow movement of the "Great" Symphony in C Major, shown here in example 3.4b. Biographical readings that invoke the ideology of subjective expression in the attempt to link such passages to Schubert's illness and early demise have abounded since Grove's and Hanslick's younger contemporary Hugo Wolf first described the form of the "Unfinished" Symphony in B Minor as somehow spiritually fused with "the external existence of the master, who in the flower of his life, at the height of his creative powers, was snatched away by death."[112] Considered more broadly, such perspectives on Schubert's late style are apt to show how easily moments of formal rupture and subversion can be repurposed as evidence not of compositional brokenness or banality but rather as hallmarks of the kind of radical innovation post-Enlightenment culture has habitually associated with heightened states of creative expression if not with genius itself. In sum, when coupled with the "Gmunden" Symphony's abundant quotations from genuine Schubert, the extent to which the work's more questionable passages can either be retroactively dismissed from consideration or recuperated in this way might begin to explain both the work's comparative success at the debate associated with its 1982 premiere and the corresponding difficulty involved in comprehensively debunking its authenticity in public. And from this perspective it remains telling that, when the decisive evidentiary turn came in discrediting the work once and for all, its methodological nature would be as far removed from traditional music-stylistic analysis as can possibly be imagined.

$$TiO_2$$

In 1983 the "Gmunden" Symphony controversy was further reinvigorated in the wake of an unrelated but highly publicized story that abruptly catapulted

---

[111] Hugh Macdonald, "Schubert's Volcanic Temper," *Musical Times* 119 (1978): 949–52, at 949, 951. On this aspect of Schubert's style more broadly, see Susan Wollenberg, *Schubert's Fingerprints: Studies in the Instrumental Works* (Farnham: Ashgate, 2011), 161–90.

[112] Quoted in Frank Walker, *Hugo Wolf: A Biography* (New York: Alfred A. Knopf, 1952), 150.

Example 3.4b Franz Schubert, Symphony No. 9 in C Major (Great), D. 944. Andante con moto (mvt. ii), mm. 245–56

Example 3.4b Continued

160 FORGERY IN MUSICAL COMPOSITION

issues of forgery to the forefront of German cultural consciousness. On 22 April, an ill-fated press release from the weekly news magazine *Stern* announced the shocking rediscovery—and forthcoming media syndication—of some sixty volumes of what *Stern*'s editorship claimed to be Adolf Hitler's diaries, recently purchased on their behalf by a journalist for some 9.3 million West German marks.[113] The news of this unprecedented historical find appeared on front pages worldwide with the promise of forthcoming revelations about everything from Hitler's "attitude towards Ernst Röhm and Neville Chamberlain" to "his private thoughts about the *Kristallnacht* and the Holocaust."[114] As Brian James aptly surmised for the *Daily Mail*, the affair had an aura of high drama from the start, as if "Hitler had suddenly thrust an arm out of the grave."[115] Yet, just two weeks later, on 6 May, the West German State Archives—drawing on "a short laboratory report from the Federal police"—announced the diaries to be "a crude forgery" invented by a copyist with a "limited intellectual capacity": the "paper ... binding ... glue ... [and] thread were all found to be of post-war manufacture," while the pairs of embossed gold letters "FH" affixed to each diary's cover (clumsily mistaken for the initials "AH," in gothic script, by the forger) turned out to have been "made of plastic in Hong Kong."[116] As Robert Harris's foundational account maintains, the ensuing 1983 scandal swiftly unmasked *Stern*'s Hitler diaries as "the most expensive and far-reaching fraud in publishing history" in ways that inevitably raised a host of profoundly uncomfortable and long lingering questions about the state of international journalistic and academic integrity in the face of what should always have been regarded as a blatant act of forgery.[117]

It was in this heated climate that the Neue Schubert-Ausgabe received Elsholz's orchestral parts from the "Gmunden" Symphony's publisher in July of 1984, immediately sending them to the Federal Institute for Materials Testing [Bundesanstalt für Materialprüfung], or BAM, in West Berlin.[118] Here the parts were subjected to many of the same pioneering forensic examination techniques that had so dramatically unmasked *Stern*'s forged Hitler diaries the previous year.[119] And the results were devastating: microscopic photographs taken under infrared light indicated the presence of optical brighteners such as titanium

---

[113] Robert Harris, *Selling Hitler: The Story of the Hitler Diaries* (London: Faber & Faber, 1986), 295–309, 381.

[114] Eric Rentschler, "The Fascination of a Fake: The Hitler Diaries," *New German Critique* 90 (2003): 177–92, at 178.

[115] Quoted in Rentschler, "The Fascination of a Fake," 178; Harris, *Selling Hitler*, 321.

[116] Harris, *Selling Hitler*, 24–25, 117.

[117] Harris, *Selling Hitler*, 25.

[118] Dürr, "Die gefälschte Schubert-Sinfonie," 413.

[119] A detailed technical report on this process was published as W. Dürr, W. Griebenow, B. Werthmann, and M. Ziegler, "Zur Altersbestimmung von Papier, dargestellt an Schuberts 'Unechter' in E-Dur—ein musikalisches Märchen," *Das Papier* 41, no. 7 (1987): 321–31.

dioxide not deployed in the paper manufacturing process until the 1950s, while spectroscopic analysis further revealed that a correction fluid used on the orchestral parts had a chemical composition consistent with modern consumer products such as Tipp-Ex and Wite-Out, first produced in Germany around 1970.[120] With this and other such evidence firmly in hand, the BAM analysts ultimately concluded their report by providing a damning *terminus post quem*, confirming that "the orchestral parts could have been produced in the 1960s at the earliest."[121] It need hardly be added that the problems posed by these test results were insurmountable for Elsholz and his supporters: "If the original [full] score had gone missing in 1945"—as Elsholz had always emphatically claimed— then the extant set of orchestral parts supposedly transcribed from that document "must," in Dürr's words, "have been written before 1945," at the very latest.[122] Crucially, the BAM analysis had revealed this to be objectively impossible. Like *Stern*'s phony Hitler diaries a year earlier, the "Gmunden" Symphony's orchestral parts were now exposed as a product of the post-war era on an irrevocable chemical level. In effect, the elaborate provenance narrative that Elsholz had dogmatically maintained in writing for over a decade had been demolished, utterly, from its foundation.

One might presume that this new forensic evidence left no room for any serious intellectual counterargument. Yet, when Dürr published an incisive summary of the BAM findings in response to an ongoing dialogue with Goldschmidt and Elsholz in the journal *Musica*, Reimut Vogel responded in turn by asserting that while "the test results are surely correct," it did not necessarily follow that the transcribed parts should be regarded as forgeries.[123] To resolve the matter once and for all, Vogel reported that he had enlisted the help of a third party: an unnamed "renowned historian" whose ongoing investigations into the "Gmunden" Symphony in E Major would draw on sources "as yet untapped by official Schubert research," yielding "astonishing results" to be published, by Goldoni Verlag, in the near future.[124] Vogel's "renowned historian" turned out be Werner Maser, a prominent Hitler researcher who had spoken out against the forged diaries early in the 1983 *Stern* affair, but who Robert Harris nonetheless describes as "a controversial figure" whose "bestselling biography" of the dictator was widely "regarded as having dwelt, at suspicious length, on the positive aspects of Hitler's character and achievements."[125] As Vogel projected in his rebuttal to Dürr, Maser's findings on the "Gmunden" Symphony

[120] Dürr et al., "Zur Altersbestimmung von Papier," 327–28; Dürr, "Die gefälschte Schubert-Sinfonie," 413.
[121] Quoted in Dürr, "Die gefälschte Schubert-Sinfonie," 413.
[122] Dürr, "Die gefälschte Schubert-Sinfonie," 413.
[123] Walther Dürr and Reimut Vogel, "Nochmals zu der 'gefälschten Schubert-Sinfonie': Ein Gutachten der Bundesanstalt für Materialprüfung, Berlin," *Musica* 39 (1985): 582–83, at 583.
[124] Dürr & Vogel, "Nochmals zu der 'gefälschten Schubert-Sinfonie,'" 583.
[125] Harris, *Selling Hitler*, 158.

162 FORGERY IN MUSICAL COMPOSITION

appeared swiftly enough as an extended preface to a new 1985 edition of the score.[126] Here, astonishingly, Maser once again defended the work's authenticity in strong terms and at considerable length. And in doing so, he drew on investigative methods that were and remain strikingly far removed from the established mainstream of academic Schubert research, much as Vogel had promised in his *Musica* statement:

Interviewed under hypnosis at a remote specialist clinic in the Palatinate Forest, Elsholz had confessed that he had indeed been lying about the "Gmunden" Symphony's provenance from the start. The orchestral parts tested by the BAM researchers in West Berlin had been copied from the original full score in the 1960s, not in the years before the end of the Second World War, as had always previously been maintained.[127] In 1979, Elsholz had then sent these orchestral parts to Vogel, having "unlawfully appropriated" them from the man who had apparently been their true copyist: Elsholz's uncle, Willy Henze, who had been hospitalized that year, and who had subsequently died of a chronic illness in 1982.[128] In an attempt to hide this apparent act of theft from a convalescing relative, Elsholz had reportedly invented "the most colorful stories" about his sources.[129] As to the whereabouts of the original full score copied by his uncle in the 1960s, the hypnotized Elsholz now pleaded ignorance.[130] And in response, Dürr and the BAM researchers dutifully pointed out several holes in this new story. For one thing, "if Elsholz only stole the parts in 1979, why did he invent his colorful stories in 1973, immediately after he began copying his own score?"[131] Moreover, "what was the point of copying out the parts in a calligraphic, laborious manner on old-looking paper" in the 1960s "if not to provide cover for a forgery?"[132] Yet even to politely entertain such questions after the seismic revelations of 1984 and 1985 is to lend the testimony of a self-confessed liar a degree of credibility that Elsholz had long since irretrievably lost, under hypnosis or otherwise. The conclusion should have been obvious, to Maser and to all concerned: "Even under hypnosis, Elsholz still told nothing but fairytales."[133]

With this, the "Gmunden" Symphony controversy had effectively reached a permanent impasse. At the time of his death in 1986, Harry Goldschmidt appears to have made no public comment of substance either on the BAM's forensic revelations or on Elsholz's subsequent hypnosis. With the Neue Schubert-Ausgabe's

---

[126] Werner Maser, *Armer Schubert! Fälschungen und Manipulationen: Marginalien zu Franz Schuberts Sinfonie von 1825* (Stuttgart: Goldoni Verlag, 1985).

[127] Maser, *Armer Schubert!*, 36–37.

[128] Maser, *Armer Schubert!*, 37.

[129] Maser, *Armer Schubert!*, 37.

[130] Maser, *Armer Schubert!*, 37.

[131] Dürr et al., "Zur Altersbestimmung von Papier," 328.

[132] Dürr et al., "Zur Altersbestimmung von Papier," 329.

[133] Dürr et al., "Zur Altersbestimmung von Papier," 329.

evidence well established and the work's only credible musicological advocate gone, the years to follow saw the Symphony in E Major fade precipitously from public memory. Today, the composition is generally recollected as a vaguely bewildering curiosity, if at all. Yet, as Austrian-born composer and musicologist Hans Gál wrote at the end of a long and excoriating letter to Vogel assessing the controversial symphony's authenticity as far back as 1982, even the most damning judgment meted out by the historical record might seem to leave the "Gmunden" Symphony's final riddle untouched:

> One question I freely admit I cannot resolve: how does a responsible human being come upon the idea to attribute a false work to a great man? But there is no answer. One can understand and explain what an intelligent person does, even when he is a scoundrel. But the actions of fools and obsessives are, and remain, a mystery.[134]

Gunter Elsholz died in 2004 having published a number of legitimate completions of Schubert's fragmentary works late in life.[135] Two years after his passing, a satirical set of aphorisms appeared posthumously under his name. Whimsically packaged as a self-help manual for those aspiring to overcome their "addiction" to the unspeakably dangerous drug of music, the book was marketed under the curiously punning title *Im Rausch der Töne*.[136] Its contents are devoted to Elsholz's gleefully cynical caricatures of various aspects of classical music culture, often centering on bizarre high-concept analogies that relate musical pleasure and creativity to illness and substance abuse. The potentially fatal consequences of "earworms" are lamented at length.[137] Professional music editors are accused of having been "vaccinated" against the art form's worst effects as an occupational necessity.[138] And, at every turn, the book blackly inverts the common repertory of hackneyed platitudes about music's redemptive moral and spiritual power, insisting—in contrary motion and with impeccably pessimistic bravado—that, in fact, "music makes people even worse than they already are."[139] Inscrutable irony gives way to inscrutable irony. In the end, Gál's final mystery has no more fitting resolution: "music," for Elsholz, "is just noise with nothing behind it. Except coal."[140]

---

[134] Quoted in Maser, *Armer Schubert!*, 17.

[135] On Elsholz's "reconstructions" of Schubert's fragmentary symphonies D. 708A and D. 936A see Brian Newbould, "Music Reviews," *Notes* 58, no. 2 (2001): 421–24.

[136] Gunter Elsholz, *Im Rausch der Töne*, edited by Oliver Kröker (Norderstedt: Books on Demand GmbH, 2006), 5. "Rausch" here has the same double meaning as "rush" in English, potentially connoting either a type of sound or a substance-induced high.

[137] Elsholz, *Im Rausch der Töne*, 38–39.

[138] Elsholz, *Im Rausch der Töne*, 46–47.

[139] Elsholz, *Im Rausch der Töne*, 13.

[140] Elsholz, *Im Rausch der Töne*, 29.

4
Haydn's Missing Link

On the morning of 14 December 1993, musicologist H. C. Robbins Landon stood before a crowded London press conference and announced that six Haydn keyboard sonatas (Hob. XVI:2a–e and 2g) had been rediscovered after more than 200 years (figure 4.1).[1] The response was electric: articles featuring celebratory soundbites from musicologists sprang up overnight in international news outlets, Harvard University scheduled a lecture recital for the following February, and the BBC moved to secure the first radio broadcast of the sonatas.

Earlier that winter, Landon had received an unusual package from Vienna. Sent by his colleague Eva Badura-Skoda, it contained a bulky sixty-five-page photocopy of what appeared to be a handwritten copyist's manuscript of the six Haydn scores along with a series of tapes.[2] The tapes contained audio recordings of the works performed—on a 1790 Johann Schanz fortepiano, no less—by Eva's husband, Paul Badura-Skoda, himself a well-known pianist and musicologist.[3] Playing the tapes with the scores, Landon found the music to be "extremely original, though strong influences of C. P. E. Bach and, curiously, Domenico Scarlatti could be observed."[4] The title line of his piece about the rediscovery for *BBC Music Magazine* heralded nothing less than "The Haydn Scoop of the Century."[5]

Yet all was not as it seemed. In the weeks following the December 14 press conference, the euphoria surrounding the Haydn "scoop" swiftly dissipated. As readers will have gathered, it quickly became apparent that rather than rediscovered masterpieces, the sonatas were modern forgeries—newly composed works deliberately misattributed to Haydn. But we are getting ahead of ourselves. Before unfolding the disquieting reality that lay behind these

---

[1] An article on the front page of the *Times* of London—headlined "Lost Haydn Sonatas Found in Germany"—had already alerted the public that morning. Barry Millington, "Lost Haydn Sonatas Found in Germany," *Times* (London), 14 December 1993, 1, 29.

[2] Scores of the six sonatas have since been published. Joseph Haydn, *Sechs Sonaten für Klavier*, edited and completed by Winfried Michel (Winterthur: Amadeus Verlag, BP 2557, 1995).

[3] Paul Badura-Skoda's interpretations of the sonatas were released on CD in 1995. The text on the back cover of the disc attributes the works to "Joseph Haydn (??)." Paul Badura-Skoda (fortepiano), *Six Lost Piano Sonatas by Joseph Haydn (Unauthorized Version)*, recorded October 1993, Koch International, 3-1572-2, 1995, compact disc.

[4] H. C. Robbins Landon, "A Musical Joke in (Nearly) Perfect Style," *BBC Music Magazine*, February 1994, 10.

[5] H. C. Robbins Landon, "The Haydn Scoop of the Century," *BBC Music Magazine*, January 1994, 11.

Forgery in Musical Composition. Frederick Reece, Oxford University Press. © Oxford University Press 2025.
DOI: 10.1093/9780197618332.003.0005

Figure 4.1 H. C. Robbins Landon holding photocopies of the "rediscovered" manuscripts. © Denzil McNeelance, News UK & Ireland Limited, 14 December 1993

compositions, I will first outline the musicological context for the illusion that confronted Landon when he first opened the fateful package.

HOW TO FORGE A MISSING LINK

Table 4.1 provides an overview of established chronologies for the group of Haydn's solo keyboard sonatas in Hob. XVI generally accepted to have been composed before around 1772.[6] Here we have a compelling if murky picture

---

[6] The sources collated in table 4.1 and discussed throughout this section are as follows: A. Peter Brown, *Joseph Haydn's Keyboard Music: Sources and Style* (Bloomington: Indiana University Press, 1986), 110–11, 123; Anthony van Hoboken, *Joseph Haydn: Thematisch-bibliographisches Werkverzeichnis*, vol. 1 (Mainz: B. Schott's Söhne, 1957), 733–81; H. C. Robbins Landon, *Haydn: Chronicle and Works*, vol. 1, *The Early Years, 1732–1765* (Bloomington: Indiana University Press, 1980), 224–25; H. C. Robbins Landon, *Haydn: Chronicle and Works*, vol. 2, *Haydn at Eszterháza, 1766–1790* (Bloomington: Indiana University Press, 1978), 335; László Somfai, *The Keyboard Sonatas of Joseph Haydn: Instruments and Performance Practice, Genres and Styles*, translated by László Somfai and Charlotte Greenspan (Chicago: University of Chicago Press, 1995), 353–65, originally published as *Joseph Haydn zongoraszonátái: Hangszerválasztás és előadói gyakorlat, műfaji tipológia és stíluselemzés* (Budapest: Zeneműkiadó, 1979); and James Webster and Georg Feder, *New Grove Haydn* (London: Macmillan, 2002), 126–29. Feder's invaluable work list first appeared in Stanley Sadie, ed., *New Grove Dictionary of Music and Musicians*, vol. 8: H to Hyporchēma (London: Macmillan, 1980), s.v. "Joseph Haydn."

Table 4.1 Chronologies of Haydn's Early Solo Keyboard Works from Hob. XVI

C. Landon No.	Hob. XVI No.	Feder No.	Key	Date Hoboken, 1957	Date Landon, 1978/80	Date Somfai, 1979	Date Feder, 1980	Date Brown, 1986
1	8	—	G Major	before 1766	—	probably before 1760	before 1766 (1760?)	c.1760
2	7	—	C Major	before 1766	—	probably before 1760	before 1766 (1760?)	1750s
3	9	—	F Major	before 1766	—	probably before 1760	before 1766 (1760?)	1750s
4	G1	—	G Major	—	—	probably before 1760	before 1766 (1760?)	1750s
5	11	—	G Major	before 1767	—	—	before 1767	—
6	10	—	C Major	before 1767	—	probably before 1760	before 1767 (1760?)	1750s
7	D1	—	D Major	—	—	—	1788–89	1750s
8	5	—	A Major	before 1763?	—	—	before 1763 (c.1750–55?)	c.1750–55
9	4	4	D Major	before 1760?	—	probably before 1765	c.1765?	c.1761/2–c.1767
10	1	—	C Major	before 1760	—	—	c.1750–55?	1750s
11	2	—	B♭ Major	before 1760?	—	probably c.1762	before 1760?	c.1760
12	12	—	A Major	before 1767	—	—	before 1767 (c.1750–55?)	1750s
13	6	1	G Major	before 1766	—	up to 1760	before 1766 (1760?)	c.1760
14	3	3	C Major	before 1760?	—	probably early 1760s	c.1765?	c.1761/2–c.1767
15	13	—	E Major	before 1767	—	probably early 1760s	before 1767 (1760?)	c.1760
16	14	2	D Major	before 1767	—	probably early 1760s	before 1767 (1760?)	c.1761/2–c.1767
17	Es2	—	E♭ Major	—	—	—	c.1755?	c.1750–55
18	Es3	—	E♭ Major	—	—	—	c.1764?	c.1750–55

19	—	12a	E Minor	—	—	c.1765	c.1765?	c.1765
20	18	17	B♭ Major	1767?	c.1766–67 (or later?)	c.1770–72	before 1778 (c.1771–73)	c.1767/68
—	16	—	E♭ Major	?	—	—	c.1750–55?	c.1750–55
—	17	—	B♭ Major	?	—	—	before 1768	—
21	2a	5	D Minor	before 1767?	c.1765–66(?)	—	c.1765–70?	—
22	2b	6	A Major	—	c.1765–66(?)	—	c.1765–70?	—
23	2c	7	B Major	—	c.1765–66(?)	—	c.1765–70?	—
24	2d	8	B♭ Major	—	c.1765–66(?)	—	c.1765–70?	—
25	2e	9	E Minor	—	c.1765–66(?)	—	c.1765–70?	—
26	2g	10	C Major	—	c.1765–66(?)	—	c.1765–70?	—
27	2h	11	A Major	—	c.1765–66(?)	—	c.1765–70?	—
28	5a	15	D Major	—	c.1765–66(?)	probably c.1768–69	c.1767–70	c.1767–68
29	45	13	E♭ Major	1765/67	1766	1766	1766	1766
30	19	14	D Major	1767	1767	1767	1767	1767
31	46	16	A♭ Major	1765/67	c.1767–68 (or slightly later?)	c.1768–69	before 1778 (c.1767–70)	c.1767/68
32	44	18	G Minor	1765/67	c.1768–70 (or slightly later?)	c.1771	before 1778 (c.1771–73)	c.1770
33	20	36	C Minor	1771?	1771	draft 1771 published 1780	1771	begun 1771 (finished by 1780)

■ questionable or inauthentic works ▢ missing works

168   FORGERY IN MUSICAL COMPOSITION

of a repertoire that remains contested in several important senses.[7] Consider, for example, the discrepancies between the systems of numbering—by Christa Landon, Anthony van Hoboken, and Georg Feder, respectively—listed in the three leftmost columns.[8] As one would expect, the scholarly chronologies summarized in the five rightmost columns do not offer a total consensus either. In addition to the suggested dates of composition, attributions referred to as questionable or inauthentic (where such data are provided) have been shaded in dark gray, indicating which of the studies reported the work to be suspect. The fact that—in numerous cases—Hoboken, Landon, Somfai, Feder, and Brown disagree either about the likely authenticity of the works or about their period of composition will come as no surprise to those familiar with this corpus and the challenges that it poses for musicology. Dated autograph manuscripts for Haydn's early keyboard works are scarce, necessitating a certain amount of informed estimation.[9] Moreover, for reasons involving the developing role of commercial publication in late eighteenth-century Europe and the attendant financial potential of anything associated with the booming "Haydn" brand, the composer remains—as John Spitzer has explored at length—"perhaps the most notorious [of all musical figures] when it comes to spurious works."[10]

Most striking about table 4.1 is the chronological "missing link" that disrupts this group of solo keyboard sonatas in the late 1760s. For some two centuries, the only extant evidence for the existence of the seven lost works shaded in light gray and numbered Hob. XVI:2a–e and 2g–h was a series of four-measure incipits recorded in a document known as the *Entwurfkatalog*, or "draft catalogue."[11] Around 1765 Haydn began laboriously inscribing the opening measures of his compositions in this manuscript at least in part as a means of combating opportunistic misattributions from unscrupulous eighteenth-century copyists

---

[7] Methodologies of authentication—stylistic, source-based, and otherwise—have been a point of dispute in Haydn scholarship for decades. A useful introduction to the topic may be found in James Webster, "External Criteria for Determining the Authenticity of Haydn's Music," in *Haydn Studies: Proceedings of the International Haydn Conference, Washington, D.C., 1975*, edited by Jens Peter Larsen et al. (New York: W. W. Norton, 1981): 75–80. For an extensive bibliography, see Horst Walter, "Literatur zu Echtheitsfragen bei Joseph Haydn," in *Opera incerta: Echtheitsfragen als Problem musikwissenschaftlicher Gesamtausgaben*, edited by Hanspeter Bennwitz et al. (Stuttgart: Franz Steiner Verlag, 1991): 193–204.

[8] It should be noted that Hoboken's 1957 numbering for the keyboard sonatas was itself adapted from the older system devised by Päsler for volume 14 of the Breitkopf & Härtel *Gesamtausgabe* published in 1918. For Hoboken's explanation of his relationship to Päsler and other early editions, see Hoboken, *Haydn Werkverzeichnis*, vol. 1, 733.

[9] The lack of extant autograph manuscripts from this period is sometimes speculatively attributed to the fire that destroyed Haydn's house in Eisenstadt in 1768.

[10] John Spitzer, "Authorship and Attribution in Western Art Music" (PhD diss., Cornell University, 1983), 153.

[11] As Hoboken himself noted, the Sonata Hob. XVI:2f is in fact identical with Hob. XVI:14, which is why Hob. XVI:2f is absent from most modern chronologies. See Hoboken, *Haydn Werkverzeichnis*, vol. 1, 736.

HAYDN'S MISSING LINK   169

and publishers. By the twentieth century the *Entwurfkatalog* had become one of the most important documents in Haydn source studies and chronology, offering tantalizing hints at the existence of numerous lost works that might still be "out there" waiting to be unearthed. In the 1930s, Jens Peter Larsen was able to place the seven missing sonatas later catalogued as Hob. XVI:2a–e and 2g–h "around 1767–1770" by virtue of the paper on which their undated incipits had been written.[12] In an almost-too-perfect musicological *coup de théâtre* each of the sonatas that Landon presented to the world in December 1993 opened with a phrase matching the incipit for one of these compositions. At a stroke, six of the missing puzzle pieces at the crux of Hob. XVI had slotted seamlessly into place.[13] Or so it seemed.

The style-historical significance attributed to the years around 1770 in much of the foundational Haydn scholarship from the twentieth century is difficult to overstate. For his part Larsen had asserted: "The crucial period of Haydn's development was, without argument, the years from about 1765 to 1772."[14] "Everyone who is used to regarding Haydn as the harmless personification of a traditional classicism," he wrote, "should study the works of this period to get to know him as a revolutionary."[15] The broader midcentury literature is rife with lengthy descriptions of the strikingly wide array of musical features that distinguish Haydn's so-called *Sturm und Drang* works from the implicitly unmarked "galant" compositions that preceded them: from "learned-style counterpoint," "sonata da chiesa form," and "melodic ellipsis" to "enhanced rhythmic tension," "abrupt contrast[s] of key," and "widely extended harmonic phrasing."[16]

Stylistically speaking, the Sonata in C Minor Hob. XVI:20 in particular had long been considered exceptional in a number of important ways, making its apparent date of 1771 difficult to account for in strictly teleological narratives of the

---

[12] Jens Peter Larsen, *Three Haydn Catalogues* (New York: Pendragon Press, 1979), xvii. For a more detailed account of Larsen's research on the *Entwurfkatalog*, see Jens Peter Larsen, *Die Haydn-Überlieferung* (Copenhagen: Einar Munksgaard, 1939), 209–50.

[13] Haydn did not group Hob. XVI:2a–e and 2g–h as a "set" in the *Entwurfkatalog*. The perceived appropriateness of a rediscovered group of six works is likely a result of the six-work "opus concept." See Elaine Sisman, "Six of One: The Opus Concept in the Eighteenth Century," in *The Century of Bach and Mozart: Perspectives on Historiography, Composition, Theory, and Performance*, edited by Sean Gallagher and Thomas F. Kelly (Cambridge, MA: Harvard University Press, 2008): 79–107.

[14] Jens Peter Larsen, "The Challenge of Joseph Haydn," in *Handel, Haydn, & the Viennese Classical Style*, translated by Ulrich Krämer (Ann Arbor: UMI Research Press, 1988): 95–108, at 105; first published as "Joseph Haydn, eine Herausforderung an uns," in *Bericht über den internationalen Joseph Haydn Kongress, Wien, 1982*, edited by Eva Badura-Skoda (Munich: Henle Verlag, 1986): 9–20.

[15] Jens Peter Larsen, "On Haydn's Artistic Development," in *Handel, Haydn, & the Viennese Classical Style*: 109–115, at 112; first published as "Zu Haydns künstlerischer Entwicklung," in *Festschrift Wilhelm Fischer zum 70. Geburtstag überreicht im Mozartjahr 1956*, edited by Hans Zingerle (Innsbruck: Leopold-Franzens-Universität, 1956): 123–29.

[16] Landon, *Chronicle and Works*, vol. 2, 273–77; Larsen, "The Challenge of Joseph Haydn," 105; Wilfrid Mellers, *The Sonata Principle* (London: Rockliff, 1957), 22.

170   FORGERY IN MUSICAL COMPOSITION

composer's life and work.[17] It was often held up as a strong candidate for the first composition Haydn wrote with the dynamic range of the fortepiano in mind, and it remains the earliest keyboard work that the composer himself seems to have associated with the weighty generic tag of "sonata" as opposed to "divertimento."[18] As if to sum up all this, Landon—in the 1970s—referred to Hob. XVI:20 as "Haydn's single but monumental contribution to the *Sturm und Drang* in the field of the piano sonata."[19]

Yet there is a compelling sense in which such "single monumental contributions" resist the evolutionary and teleological models of musical style popular for much of the twentieth century. "An artistic style," wrote Guido Adler in his 1911 text *Der Stil in der Musik*, "does not simply appear, like Athena from the head of Zeus, but rather develops in a calm and steady ascent."[20] Whether we speak in terms of epochs, schools, individual artists, or a particular work, for Adler, stylistic change is "based on laws of becoming belonging to the rise and fall of organic development."[21] If we take these axioms seriously (however unfashionable they may be today), then the date of 1771 for Hob. XVI:20 proposed by Landon puts a great deal of pressure on the 1767–70 missing link in Haydn's keyboard output. It is all too easy to become seduced by the idea that the lost works must hold the key, if not to "a calm and steady ascent," then at least to some form of compositional logic underlying Haydn's apparent shift of voice.[22]

Decades before the events of late 1993 and early 1994, Landon maintained that the *Entwurfkatalog* incipits alone shed significant light on Haydn's compositional development despite, in each case, consisting of no more than four measures of music. Commenting on their far-flung and minor-tinged key signatures, for example, he proposed that the lost sonatas should be considered

---

[17] More recent scholarship has revealed that the evidence dating Hob. XVI:20 to 1771 is far from conclusive. As A. Peter Brown explains, the composer's apparent inscription of the year "1771" on the autograph manuscript (F-Pn MS-133) "cannot be taken at absolute face value, for Haydn's orthography for the final numeral is not clearly written, and the autograph is incomplete." The unfinished autograph might just as well have sat around gathering dust until the work was finally completed for publication as the sixth sonata of the Auenbrugger group in 1780. See Brown, *Joseph Haydn's Keyboard Music*, 120.

[18] Concerning Haydn's use of the word "sonata" with reference to Hob. XVI:20, along with the possibility that the composer had access to a fortepiano around 1770, see Landon, *Chronicle and Works*, vol. 2, 343. The issue of Haydn's intentions regarding keyboard instruments has provoked a good deal of disagreement over the years. For a brief summary, see Howard Pollack, "Some Thoughts on the 'Clavier' in Haydn's Solo Claviersonaten," *Journal of Musicology* 9 (1991): 74–91.

[19] Landon, *Chronicle and Works*, vol. 2, 340–41.

[20] Guido Adler, *Der Stil in der Musik* (Leipzig: Breitkopf & Härtel, 1911), 14.

[21] Adler, *Der Stil in der Musik*, 13.

[22] Landon was by no means alone in subscribing to this idea. A. Peter Brown, for example, wrote in 1986: "The seven 'lost' sonatas might provide more clues to the evolution of this new style, which is hinted at in Hob. XIV:5 (*recte* XVI:5a), but there seems to be little hope for their recovery." Brown, *Joseph Haydn's Keyboard Music*, 14.

"a watershed" after which Haydn's keyboard works were no longer "teaching vehicles" but rather were "artistic forms to be developed on their own terms."[23] In an illuminating passage from volume 2 of his *Haydn: Chronicle and Works*, Landon leaned even harder on Haydn's missing link:

> The presence of the C-Minor Sonata [in 1771] is not all that unique. Alas, some of its immediate predecessors, in D minor and E minor [i.e., Hob. XVI:2a and 2e], have been irretrievably lost, but even judging from the *incipits* (especially of that in E minor) we can imagine that they must have been similar in mood, if perhaps not in perfection of language, to No. 33 [i.e., Hob. XVI:20].[24]

To adapt a now ubiquitous epistemological concept from Donald Rumsfeld, the seven missing sonatas came to function in Landon's account of Haydn's stylistic development as "known unknowns" spanning the gulf between the early keyboard works completed before 1767 and the tempestuous minor-mode sonatas composed in the early 1770s.

STYLE, CHRONOLOGY, AND PILTDOWN MAN

Historiography is replete with warnings about the dangers of speculating about such hazy "known unknown" periods. In 1912—just one year after Adler's *Der Stil in der Musik* invoked evolution as a model for musical style history—a 500,000-year-old missing link in the evolution of the human species appeared to have been unearthed by a worker in a gravel pit in East Sussex (figure 4.2). Only in 1953, after more than forty years in the British Museum, was the skull known as "Piltdown Man" definitively exposed as a forgery: the collage of a medieval human cranium, an orangutan lower jaw, and a set of fossilized chimpanzee teeth.[25] When considered alongside Piltdown Man's "ape-like" orangutan jaw, the enlarged forehead of the human skull conformed perfectly to early twentieth-century hypotheses about how the missing link in our ancestry should appear—i.e., with the prodigious brain appearing ahead of other physical features distinguishing *Homo sapiens* from their predecessors. The intellectual moral demonstrated by this bizarre object is as relevant for historians of music as it is for scientists: forgery succeeds most spectacularly when given

[23] Landon, *Chronicle and Works*, vol. 1, 225.
[24] Landon, *Chronicle and Works*, vol. 2, 335. Emphasis from original text.
[25] The evidence was swiftly made available to the public at large in *Time Magazine*, "End as a Man," 30 November 1953, 83–84. The literature that has since emerged on Piltdown Man is immense. For the classic book-length account, see J. S. Weiner, *The Piltdown Forgery* (Oxford: Oxford University Press, 1955).

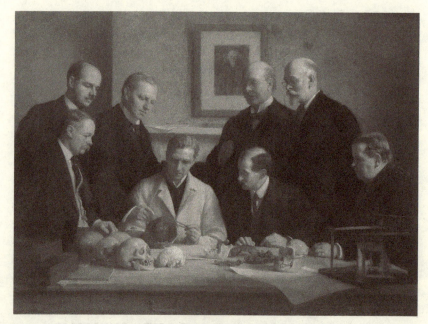

Figure 4.2 John Cooke, *Piltdown Gang* (1915)

the opportunity to provide the single absent piece of evidence necessary to bolster a cherished narrative. "Missing links" that have been subjected to years of academic speculation provide perfect openings for forgers to concoct the very things that experts expect to find.[26]

Following his press conference, Landon declared that the forged sonatas clarified "in a particularly striking way Haydn's search for a new musical language of strength and beauty," demonstrating precisely this kind of confirmation bias.[27] In his article for *BBC Music Magazine*, he went on to assert that the rediscovered works foreshadowed the composer's turn toward *Sturm und Drang* by demonstrating "an increased interest in minor keys, used in a dramatic and emotional fashion [alongside] a sharpened awareness of dynamic contrast, the use of silence, and of surprise, whether in a sudden change of key or in an

---

[26] In a poignant parallel to the Piltdown case, even Haydn's skull has been subject to counterfeiting. Shortly after his death in 1809 the composer's head was stolen from its grave by an accountant and phrenological enthusiast named Joseph Rosenbaum. When Prince Nikolaus Esterházy II pressured him for its return in 1820, Rosenbaum submitted a fake decoy. Only in 1954 was the true skull reunited with the rest of Haydn's bones (since relocated to a tomb at the Bergkirche in Eisenstadt) in an elaborate ceremony. See Davin Wyn Jones, ed., *Oxford Composer Companions: Haydn* (Oxford: Oxford University Press, 2009), s.v. "Haydn's Skull."

[27] Landon, "The Haydn Scoop of the Century," 11.

unexpected modulation."[28] It was exactly what he had predicted more than a decade earlier in volume 2 of *Haydn: Chronicle and Works.*[29]

Just as the theories that inspired Piltdown Man have little bearing on modern biology, post-Adlerian "evolutionist" accounts of style history would be considered passé by the vast majority of musicologists today. In the field of Haydn studies, James Webster's 1991 monograph on the "Farewell" Symphony has done much to debunk received wisdom about the composer's stylistic development.[30] My intention is by no means to undermine any of this important revisionist work or the modern research tradition that has emerged from it. As Webster argues, we should treat grand narratives about Haydn's musical development with suspicion, seeking instead to "interpret differences in style not teleologically, but as the display of different facets of his musical persona, as responses to differing conditions and audiences."[31] Far from seeking to revive the old evolutionist models of Haydn's development, I contend that these traditions provided fertile ground for forgery precisely because of their widely acknowledged flaws.

A MUSICAL JOKE?

At 3:38 P.M. central European time, just hours after the end of Landon's December 14 conference in London, the German press agency ddp/ADN released a report that the Joseph Haydn Institute (a Cologne-based organization engaged with the immense project of editing a Haydn *Gesamtausgabe* for G. Henle Verlag) had already examined photocopies of the sonatas and had rejected the source as a forgery on the afternoon of December 10—i.e., four days earlier.[32]

Like Landon, the Haydn Institute had received these photocopied scores from Eva and Paul Badura-Skoda, both of whom appear—like their American colleague—to have been sincerely impressed by the musical quality of the sonatas. Eva Badura-Skoda had particular musicological reasons to be excited about the rediscovery. The stylistic content of the works, including their use of a wide and expressive range of dynamics, seemed to support her pre-existing thesis that the fortepiano "existed in Vienna in the first half of the eighteenth

[28] Landon, "The Haydn Scoop of the Century," 11.

[29] Landon, *Chronicle and Works*, vol. 2, 335.

[30] James Webster, *Haydn's "Farewell" Symphony and the Idea of Classical Style: Through-Composition and Cyclic Integration in His Instrumental Music* (Cambridge: Cambridge University Press, 1991).

[31] Webster, *Haydn's "Farewell" Symphony*, 358.

[32] Markus Langer, "Ein Haydn ist ein Michel ist ein Haydn," *Frankfurter Allgemeine Zeitung*, 19 January 1994, 29.

174   FORGERY IN MUSICAL COMPOSITION

century . . . and [was] readily available from the 1760s onwards."[33] Paul, who had completed a number of Schubert's unfinished piano works for Henle, drew stylistic conclusions about the works similar to Landon's. On first encountering the "rediscovered" sonatas, he described them as being "so original and contain[ing] so many unexpected and surprising turns, that [he felt] quite sure that Haydn [was] the composer."[34]

But the story of the Haydn forgeries does not begin with the Badura-Skodas. The first package of photocopied manuscripts containing the sonatas had been delivered to them in Vienna many months earlier ("at the beginning of 1993," as Paul later recalled).[35] It had been sent by a Münster-based flutist, recorder player, and composer named Winfried Michel. In addition to authoring many original works (including compositions calling for metronomes and musical clocks alongside more conventional forces), Michel has also completed fragments as diverse as W. F. Bach's Trio Sonata in A Minor F. 49 and Glinka's Sonata for Viola in D Minor. According to his story, he had discovered the manuscript copy of the six missing Haydn sonatas in the collection of a local octogenarian woman who had possessed them for years without comprehending their true value.[36] Recognizing the composer's name and suspecting the re-emergence of the lost works for which generations of musicians had been searching, he produced a photocopy of the manuscript, promptly sending it to an expert—Paul Badura-Skoda—to solicit a second opinion. It was this same photocopied source that Landon received from Eva shortly before he announced the find to the press in December 1993.

It is important to note that Michel's putative find followed hard on the heels of a series of remarkable manuscript rediscoveries that entered musical lore after receiving significant attention in the press. As recently as September 1993 an autograph notebook containing previously unknown keyboard works by Henry Purcell had turned up in Devon.[37] Two years before that, Berlioz's *Messe solennelle*—a work that the composer claimed to have destroyed following its initial performances in the 1820s—had been recovered from an Antwerp organ loft.[38] Perhaps the most sensational of all these musical rediscoveries occurred at a Haydn festival in Melbourne in 1982. After one of the performances, an audience

[33] This research has since been published as Eva Badura-Skoda, "The Viennese Fortepiano in the Eighteenth Century," in *Music in Eighteenth-Century Austria*, edited by David Wyn Jones (Cambridge: Cambridge University Press, 1996): 249–58, at 258.

[34] Paul Badura-Skoda attributes this to a letter he wrote to Winfried Michel after receiving the photocopied scores. Quoted in Paul Badura-Skoda, liner notes to *Six Lost Piano Sonatas*, translated by Florence Daguerre de Hureaux.

[35] Paul Badura-Skoda, liner notes to *Six Lost Piano Sonatas*.

[36] Millington, "Lost Haydn Sonatas Found in Germany," 1, 29.

[37] Allan Kozinn, "Found: Unknown Music and Inkblots by Purcell," *New York Times*, 13 December 1993, C11.

[38] Hugh MacDonald, "Berlioz's *Messe solennelle*," *19th-Century Music* 16, no. 3 (1993): 267–85.

member approached conductor and musicologist Christopher Hogwood with a plastic shopping bag. In the bag were what appeared to be the missing autograph scores of the String Quartets nos. 3–6 from Haydn's op. 50 "Prussian" set. Despite the apparent improbability of these priceless manuscripts reappearing in Australia almost 200 years after their composition, the documents—like the Berlioz and Purcell scores before them—turned out to be the genuine article.[39]

Repeated often enough, rediscovery narratives like these take on lives of their own, encouraging us to imagine hidden treasures in every dusty attic. In the act of telling such stories, we often omit the painstaking process of academic authentication because it cannot match the excitement of the rediscovery itself. There is a real danger that, when a new "lost work" turns up, we remember past archival conquests and forget the questions that were asked of them. If such things were possible in the past, why couldn't six of the seven missing Haydn sonatas show up in Münster?

In this case things were not so simple. Once the Haydn Institute's repudiation of the sonatas had been made public, attempts to retrieve the original of what the German press took to calling the "Westfälische Handschrift" [Westphalian Manuscript] fell flat. It was reported that the mysterious elderly woman in Münster—apparently the only person other than Michel to have consulted the original MS—"did not want her name and address to be known" or was otherwise in a state of health too "precarious" for her to be disturbed.[40] The Badura-Skodas later printed excerpts from one of Michel's letters to Eva in which he insisted: "No-one and nothing could make me break my word, expressly given— even in the name of academia.... It is out of the question for me to disclose the name and address of the woman in possession of the manuscript."[41]

In the absence of the original source, news organizations, including those that had previously reported a genuine find, began issuing detailed retractions and clarifications as early as 16 December 1993 citing the Haydn Institute's reservations about the authenticity of the works.[42] By January 1994 a broad consensus had emerged: the find from Münster was too good to be true. Paul Badura-Skoda's Harvard lecture recital and the BBC Radio premiere of the works were swiftly and quietly canceled. While no charges were ever brought against him

[39] For a full account of the details behind this story, see W. Dean Sutcliffe, *Haydn: String Quartets Op. 50* (Cambridge: Cambridge University Press, 1992), 37–47.

[40] Joseph McLellan, "Sonata Big Deal—or Is It?," *Washington Post*, 17 February 1994, C9. Peter Lennon, "A Haydn to Nothing," *Guardian*, 4 January 1994, A3.

[41] "Niemand und nichts wird mich dazu bestimmen, ein persönliches, ausdrücklich gegebenes Versprechen nicht einzuhalten—auch nicht, wenn das im Namen der Wissenschaft geschieht.... Name und Ort der Besitzerin der Handschrift kann und werde ich nicht weitergeben." Quoted in Badura-Skoda, liner notes to *Six Lost Piano Sonatas* (translation amended).

[42] The articles about the forgeries that appeared in German media on 16 December 1993 are too numerous to list. For a representative sample, see dpa, "Wahrscheinlich eine Fälschung," *Stuttgarter Zeitung*, 16 December 1993, FEUI.

176 FORGERY IN MUSICAL COMPOSITION

(with no substantial financial gain, what would have been the crime?), the media pointed with little hesitation to Michel as the prime suspect in one of the twentieth century's most striking cases of musical forgery.[43] Landon, meanwhile, penned a follow-up to his "The Haydn Scoop of the Century" article; in the February issue of *BBC Music Magazine*, he now rebranded the sonatas as a brilliant "hoax." Attempting to defuse the situation, he concluded this new article with a quip: Haydn, one of the "greatest of musical jokers," might have "enjoyed this whole episode too."[44]

GUILT AND SHAME

The consequences of the affair are not so easily laughed off. But before we judge Landon and the Badura-Skodas too sternly, we would do well to imagine ourselves in their shoes. Stories such as this pose substantial historiographical and ethical challenges. Cases in which forgeries "ring true" under expert scrutiny are a long-neglected yet important element of our shared disciplinary history. And yet it must be acknowledged that there are some compelling reasons for this neglect. As this book's introduction has already discussed in outline, talking about such episodes is often bitterly difficult, for it involves dwelling on the mistakes and shortcomings of our peers, our predecessors, and—by implication—our discipline. In a deeply competitive academic climate that promotes the cultivation of seemingly unbroken chains of immaculate professional success, this is not a trivial problem.

Uncomfortable as it may be, our own social and institutional authority as academics remains inextricable from serious critical engagement with forged works of art. It is an ugly truth that, when cases of mistaken authentication come up for public discussion, cries that "the emperor has no clothes" are sure to follow from those keen to take the experts down a peg. As art historian Max Friedländer observed in his 1929 essay *Über Fälschung alter Bilder* [The Forgery of Old Pictures], the "errors of distinguished art scholars are welcomed by malicious lovers of sensation" in large part because they allow "the laity [to] conclude, not without satisfaction, that there is no reliable professional knowledge in the sphere of art."[45] Laymen—we are told—have "no conception" of how judgments about artistic authenticity are made, and therefore anyone claiming

---

[43] The authors of the most substantial newspaper articles about the case in English (Peter Lennon) and German (Markus Langer) both drew this conclusion. See Lennon, "A Haydn to Nothing," A3; and Langer, "Ein Haydn ist ein Michel ist ein Haydn," 29.

[44] Landon, "A Musical Joke in (Nearly) Perfect Style," 10.

[45] Max J. Friedländer, "The Forgery of Old Pictures," in *Genuine and Counterfeit: Experiences of a Connoisseur*, translated by Carl von Honstett and Lenore Pelham (New York: Albert & Charles Boni, 1930): 35–53, at 47–48; first published as "Über Fälschung alter Bilder," in *Echt und Unecht: Aus den Erfahrungen des Kunstkenners* (Berlin: Bruno Cassirer, 1929).

to be a connoisseur "comes on the scene like a magician, whom the mob, flitting from credulence to suspicion, is only too ready to expose as a charlatan."[46]

Friedländer's prose is evocative precisely because he does so little to conceal the antagonism and recrimination that forgeries tend to provoke. Unable to make informed decisions on their own, non-experts are branded a collective "mob" [Menge] the moment they question the authority of the artistic connoisseur by invoking the charge of "charlatan" [Scharlatan]. As we earlier learned from Charles Cudworth, there is another side to this story: the public, Cudworth explained, often comes to have "a sneaking admiration for [the forger], as one who has managed to hoodwink the experts, those dastardly enemies of the common man."[47] Given that forged works tend principally to harm those in positions of considerable social, institutional, or economic privilege—academics, experts, collectors, and their ilk—it is all too easy to render the art forger as a Robin-Hood-like trickster figure uniquely prepared to storm the ivory towers of authenticity and good taste.[48]

The dark side to all this has become far more readily apparent in the decades that have elapsed since the mid-twentieth-century essays on forgery penned by Cudworth, Gould, and their ilk. Yet it must be acknowledged that in the current moment of rampant climate change denial and widespread anti-vaccination movements, a cultural paradigm consistently branded "post-expert" and even "post-truth" by academics and journalists alike, Friedländer's and Cudworth's association of forgery with populist anti-intellectualism could not feel more relevant.[49] We live in an age rife with distrust in which, as Bruno Latour has written, "The smoke of the event has not yet finished settling before dozens of conspiracy theories begin revising the official account, adding even more ruins to the ruins, adding even more smoke to the smoke."[50] The oppressive fear of the "known unknown" that Donald Rumsfeld conjured up in February 2002 has become emblematic of the paranoia that besets much of modern life. If there is one thing we seem to know for certain in the new millennium—after 9/11, the War on Terror, and the COVID-19 pandemic—it is that

---

[46] Friedländer, "The Forgery of Old Pictures," 48.

[47] Charles L. Cudworth, "Ye Olde Spuriosity Shoppe, or, Put It in the *Anhang*—Part 1," *Notes* 12 (1954): 25–40, at 39–40.

[48] Countless works of popular fiction have portrayed art forgers as relatable outsiders, underdogs, or anti-heroes spurned by an oppressively elitist art world. Literary examples from the last decade alone include B. A. Shapiro, *The Art Forger* (Chapel Hill, NC: Algonquin Books, 2013); Allison Amend, *A Nearly Perfect Copy* (New York: Random House, 2013); and Michael Gruber, *The Forgery of Venus* (New York: HarperCollins Books, 2008).

[49] The Oxford English Dictionary, for example, recently declared "post-truth" its 2016 Word of the Year. The term is defined as "Relating to or denoting circumstances in which objective facts are less influential in shaping public opinion than appeals to emotion and personal belief." See *Oxford English Dictionaries Online*, s.v. "post-truth," accessed 18 September 2017, https://en.oxforddictionaries.com/definition/post-truth.

[50] Bruno Latour, "Why Has Critique Run out of Steam? From Matters of Fact to Matters of Concern," *Critical Inquiry* 30 (2004): 225–48, at 228.

178 FORGERY IN MUSICAL COMPOSITION

there are truths the experts are either unwilling or unable to tell us.[51] As discussed in the introduction of this book, philosopher and conceptual artist Jonathan Keats was writing in response to this state of affairs when he recently made the controversial assertion that "forgers are the foremost artists of our age" in no small part because their work captures the "anxious mood" of contemporary culture in ways that more conventional texts cannot.[52] "We need"—so Keats asserts in his 2013 study—"to compare the shock of getting duped to the cultivated angst evoked by legitimate art," above all as a means of recognizing "what the art establishment will never acknowledge: No authentic modern masterpiece is as provocative as a great forgery."[53]

For academics more than most, forgery is never a victimless act. When reputation and prestige are valuable commodities, one does not have to spend any money to buy into an illusion and suffer grievously for it once the veil is lifted. Consider the so-called Sokal Affair of 1996, in which physicist Alan Sokal famously succeeded in publishing a faux-postmodernist nonsense article on the "Transformative Hermeneutics of Quantum Gravity" in the prestigious cultural studies journal *Social Text*.[54] Sokal's article combined deliberately absurd algebra with baseless critical assertions, including the satirical claim that the axiom of equality was an outgrowth of set theory's "nineteenth-century liberal origins."[55] As he later explained, the parody was a politically motivated attempt to call the disciplinary authority of science studies into question and, more broadly, "to combat a currently fashionable postmodernist/poststructuralist/social-constructivist discourse . . . which is . . . inimical to the values and future of the Left."[56] We cannot "combat false ideas in history, sociology, economics, and politics," Sokal wrote, "if we reject the notions of truth and falsity."[57]

The 1990s was also the decade associated with the rise of the so-called new musicology. The story is a familiar one: traditional positivist research models that had implicitly granted "the music itself" a substantial degree of aesthetic autonomy came under increasingly heavy fire, exposing the classical canon and, in

---

[51] Numerous book-length critiques of this paradigm have been published in recent years. See, for example, Tom Nichols, *The Death of Expertise: The Campaign Against Established Knowledge and Why It Matters* (New York: Oxford University Press, 2017).

[52] Jonathon Keats, *Forged: Why Fakes Are the Great Art of Our Age* (Oxford: Oxford University Press, 2013), 3–4.

[53] Keats, *Forged*, 4.

[54] Alan D. Sokal, "Transgressing the Boundaries: Towards a Transformative Hermeneutics of Quantum Gravity," *Social Text* 46/47 (1996): 217–52; reprinted with annotations in Alan Sokal, *Beyond the Hoax: Science, Philosophy and Culture* (New York: Oxford University Press, 2008), 5–92.

[55] Sokal, "Transgressing the Boundaries," 63.

[56] Alan D. Sokal, "Transgressing the Boundaries: An Afterword," *Dissent* 43, no. 4 (1996): 93–99; reprinted in Sokal, *Beyond the Hoax: Science, Philosophy and Culture* (New York: Oxford University Press, 2008): 93–104, at 95.

[57] Alan Sokal, "A Physicist Experiments with Cultural Studies," *Lingua Franca,* May/June (1996): 62–64; reprinted in *The Sokal Hoax: The Sham that Shook the Academy* (Lincoln: University of Nebraska Press, 2000): 49–53, at 52.

particular, music theory to a series of probing cultural critiques. Writing in response to such scholarship in 1995, Pieter van den Toorn pre-empted many of Sokal's concerns about the "epistemic relativism" of cultural studies when he complained that his peers were coming to value theoretical methodologies and abstract musical structures "solely as sociopolitical comment and for the opportunity they afford for such comment."[58] If critical and analytical systems are simply mirrors of our own cultural-aesthetic prejudices, then how can we possibly discuss musical values like authenticity and originality with common standards of evidence?

This study has advanced the argument that forgeries and the debates they provoke emerge as by-products of broader anxieties about truth and ways of knowing. Clearly, such acts of deception hit hard in the academic world precisely because they can all too easily become associated with feelings of guilt and shame that carry real professional consequences. The danger, in my view, is that, by refusing to engage with subjects that trouble our authority as scholars, we condemn some of the most revealing elements of our past to be written out of the field. This book's introduction, for instance, remarked on the opening of Reinhold Brinkmann's brief but compelling outline of the neglected musicological topic of forgery, which laments: "Even within the closed walls of the academy it is possible to become trapped, stymied by a surprising discovery that undermines your confidence in the trustworthiness of your own discipline, of scholarship in general."[59] What would happen if we reappropriated these uncomfortable experiences of entrapment, lost confidence, guilt, and shame themselves as sites of self-knowledge? How might musicology address the topic of forgery if—as William Cheng has recently suggested—we were to lay aside readings that "seiz[e] critical authority to prove, persuade, and even punish," seeking instead to "defetishiz[e] control as a de facto positive value"?[60] This is by no means to suggest that scholars should abandon their commitments to truth by retreating into the kind of epistemic relativism that Sokal feared. Any awareness we might have about the potential fallibility of our discipline necessarily demands a degree of critical distance and, indeed, control. Yet there is a delicate balance to be struck. Now more than ever we need the study of forgery to highlight the valuable insights that might be gained from confronting the ways in which we—as scholars, musicians, and human beings—are led astray.

[58] Pieter C. van den Toorn, *Music, Politics, and the Academy* (Berkeley: University of California Press, 1995), 61.

[59] Reinhold Brinkmann, "The Art of Forging Music and Musicians: Of Lighthearted Musicologists, Ambitious Performers, Narrow-Minded Brothers, and Creative Aristocrats," in *Cultures of Forgery: Making Nations Making Selves*, edited by Judith Ryan and Alfred Thomas (New York: Routledge, 2003): 111–25, at 111–12.

[60] William Cheng, *Just Vibrations: The Purpose of Sounding Good* (Ann Arbor: University of Michigan Press, 2016), 42.

180 FORGERY IN MUSICAL COMPOSITION

Let us return, by way of example, to Landon's and Paul and Eva Badura-Skoda's reflections on the forged "Haydn" works, this time with the benefit of hindsight. Strikingly, all three individuals continued to insist on the reality of their aesthetic experiences even after the works were determined to be fake, maintaining their initial high regard for the musical qualities of the compositions. In February 1994, Eva Badura-Skoda gave a talk in Santa Barbara, California, in which she openly declared the Westphalian Manuscript to be "a clever forgery," arguing elsewhere that—despite any personal embarrassment the works might have caused—the six sonatas still deserved to be performed not least because "whether the music is authentic or not, everyone wants to hear it now."[61] Writing the liner notes to his own 1995 CD issue of the works more than a year after the Haydn Institute made its doubts public, Paul Badura-Skoda repeated his initial assessment that the sonatas were "not some dilettante's attempts at forgery, but precious musical works" despite numerous admittedly "unusual" passages.[62] As if to sum up, Landon commented to the press late in December 1993: "If it is a fraud it is the most brilliant fraud I've ever heard of. I don't mind being taken in by music this good."[63]

Considered seriously, these comments stake out fragile new frontiers for a discipline that has, so far, almost uniformly refused to engage with forgeries after they are exposed. Landon's admission that he was "taken in" by the quality of the music could be read as a gesture toward the "defetishization of control" that Cheng and others have begun to call for in the discipline. It might also serve as a model for engaging with forgeries as evidence of how the raw aesthetic experiences of musical compositions "take us in" as scholars wrestling with the competing claims of both historical truth and aesthetic beauty.

THE WESTPHALIAN MANUSCRIPT

More than three decades after the initial scandal, what are we to make of the Westphalian Manuscript and the sonatas that it contained as historical documents? It is significant that the works were repudiated primarily on the evidence of material anachronisms discovered by figures associated with auction houses and editorial research institutes. Consider the title page reproduced in figure 4.3a, complete with conspicuous ink blotches. In the lower right quadrant is a stamp—crossed out yet clearly visible—suggesting that the original had

---

[61] Eva Badura-Skoda's Santa-Barbara paper is discussed in Michael Beckerman, "All Right, So Maybe Haydn Didn't Write Them. So What?," *New York Times*, 15 May 1994, 33. See also McLellan, "Sonata Big Deal—or Is It?," C9.

[62] Badura-Skoda, liner notes to *Six Lost Piano Sonatas*.

[63] Quoted in Jim McCue, "Haydn Experts Say Lost Sonatas Are Clever Hoax," *Times* (London), 31 December 1993, 5.

Figure 4.3a Westphalian Manuscript, Title Page. From the H. C. Robbins Landon Collection (Box 78; Folder 11), Howard Gotlieb Archival Research Center at Boston University

182 FORGERY IN MUSICAL COMPOSITION

been in the library of an episcopal see (Eigentum des BischöflStuhles) before being moved to another collection in the mid-twentieth century (Sammlung Hegenkötter, 1956). Eva Badura-Skoda proposed an Italian provenance around 1805 after having consulted a "copy" of the watermark (which Michel supposedly traced from the manuscript hidden away in Münster).[64] Yet, when subjected to thorough interrogation, the autographic features of the scores raised the suspicions of manuscript specialists including not only Stephen Roe at London's Sotheby's (an attendee at Landon's press conference), but also the impressive group of scholars assembled by the Haydn Institute on December 10.[65]

The Haydn Institute appraisers expressed strong concerns about the presence of anachronistic textual characters in the subtitles (including a forward slash and modern quotation marks) alongside numerous other peculiarities of musical notation. As Horst Walter—the institute's then director—memorably summarized, the manuscript was "overloaded with 'antique' elements."[66] It even appeared to have been written with a steel-nibbed pen rare until decades after the "1805" date implied by the watermark.[67] Meanwhile, Roe developed his own suspicions about the source. Working from a photocopy of the opening page of the Sonata in D Minor Hob. XVI:2a that had been distributed to Landon's audience in a press pack (the same page reproduced in figure 4.3b), he observed that the rests were inscribed in a manner common in handwritten sources only after twentieth-century developments in the printing of sheet music.[68] More curious still, the German shelving mark "MS H 7[A/F], Schrank 5, Lage 4"—visible in the upper-left corner of figure 4.3b—had, bizarrely, been written in a hand identical to that of the score's notation and Italian paratext (i.e., the title "Suonata per il Cembalo solo," and name of the author, "di G. Haydn").[69] As Roe himself said when I interviewed him about the case, it is "extraordinarily unlikely" that a librarian would be the copyist of a manuscript, and even more farfetched that the same copyist would write the shelving mark in a language other than the Italian native both to the paratext and to the manuscript's country of origin.[70]

---

[64] Langer, "Ein Haydn ist ein Michel ist ein Haydn," 29.

[65] The twelve participants in the Haydn Institute's appraisal of the sources were Eva Badura-Skoda, Martin Bente, Otto Biba, Gudrun Busch, Georg Feder, Sonja Gerlach, Marianne Helms, Klaus Hortschansky, Klaus Wolfgang Niemöller, Günter Thomas, Horst Walter, and Robert von Zahn. See Horst Walter, "Eulenspiegeleien um Haydn," Haydn-Studien 6 (1994): 313–17, at 314.

[66] Walter, "Eulenspiegeleien um Haydn," 315; Robert von Zahn, "Der 'Haydn-Scoop of the Century': Qualität und Schwächen einer Fälschung," Concerto: Das Magazin für alte Musik 11, no. 90 (1994): 8–11, at 8.

[67] dpa, "Gefälscht?," Frankfurter Allgemeine Zeitung, 18 December 1993, 25.

[68] McCue, "Haydn Experts Say Lost Sonatas Are Clever Hoax," 5.

[69] For an overview of the concept of "paratext," see Gérard Genette, Paratexts: Thresholds of Interpretation, translated by Jane E. Lewin (Cambridge: Cambridge University Press, 1997); first published as Seuils (Paris: Éditions du Seuil, 1987).

[70] Stephen Roe (Head of Musical Manuscripts, Sotheby's Auction House), interview by author, Sotheby's Atlantic Avenue Branch, New York, NY, 4 June 2014, digital recording.

Figure 4.3b Westphalian Manuscript, First Page of Forged Sonata in D minor, "Hob. XVI:2a." From the H. C. Robbins Landon Collection (Box 78; Folder 11), Howard Gotlieb Archival Research Center at Boston University

184   FORGERY IN MUSICAL COMPOSITION

The final nail in the coffin came when samples of the handwriting used in the Westphalian Manuscript were compared to the MS for a keyboard sonata in F Major by the Italian composer Giovanni Paolo Tomesini that had been published in facsimile by the small Münster-based press Mieroprint Musikverlag.[71] Despite seemingly producing dozens of works for recorder, flute, violin, viola, harpsichord, and numerous combinations of the above, Tomesini never existed. Alongside another fictitious eighteenth-century composer named "Simonetti," G. P. Tomesini was an invented pseudonym under which Winfried Michel had composed an extensive collection of Baroque pastiche, publishing his works with Mieroprint and the Swiss "Amadeus" Verlag throughout the 1970s and 1980s.[72] Betraying an affection for the cryptographic, Michel even hid a clue to the shared identity behind the two pseudonyms in the construction of the names themselves: "Tomesini" and "Simonetti" are near anagrams of one another.

A less subtle hint about the authorship of the works can be found in the paratexts to editions of "Simonetti's" and "Tomesini's" music. Such publications are in fact invariably prefaced with the assurance that they have been "composed [!] and edited by Winfried Michel" [komponiert und herausgegeben von Winfried Michel]. Generally placed in small print on the title page far beneath the emboldened names of Simonetti and Tomesini, the implicit authors, this assurance is easily mistaken for any of a host of more conventional (and guileless) paratextual formulas, among them "completed and edited" [ergänzt und herausgegeben] or "arranged and edited" [bearbeitet und herausgegeben].

The glass slipper clearly fit. Because of the similarities between the textual and musical handwriting in the Tomesini facsimile and the Westphalian Manuscript, the obvious conclusion was that the latter document had not been produced by a nineteenth-century copyist—as Eva Badura-Skoda had argued—but was rather from the same twentieth-century hand that had "composed and edited" Simonetti's and Tomesini's editions.[73] Once picked up in the wider press, these new revelations quickly resolved any lingering doubts about the authenticity of the "Haydn Scoop of the Century" in the public sphere.[74]

---

[71] A description of the sources and a reproduction of the score in question can be found in Zahn, "Der 'Haydn-Scoop of the Century,'" 11.

[72] Bruce Haynes has discussed Michel's Simonetti/Tomesini works as defining examples of what he calls "period composition." See Bruce Haynes, *The End of Early Music: A Period Performer's History of Music for the Twenty-First Century* (Oxford: Oxford University Press, 2007), 210–13.

[73] In 1994, Michel had three of the forged Haydn sonatas (Hob. XVI:2a, 2b, and 2g) published independently in a small print run. The editor's foreword to this edition knowingly acknowledges that the manuscript "shows similarities in writing style and rastration to scores of Tomesini's keyboard works." See Joseph Haydn (attributed), *Sechs Sonaten für Klavier 1–3*, first edition by Winfried Michel (Münster: Urtext Edition, 1994), 4.

[74] Lennon, "A Haydn to Nothing," A3; and Langer, "Ein Haydn ist ein Michel ist ein Haydn," 29.

REVENGE OF THE ANTIQUARIANS

Having so recently declared a major academic coup, numerous media outlets struggled to backtrack in the wake of these revelations. As a result, musicology's standards of evidence and structures of accountability were suddenly cast into the limelight as subjects for the kind of public scrutiny that the discipline rarely attracts. In the *Guardian*, Peter Lennon critiqued the musicological community as one in which "the status of a document is apparently conferred not by its own antecedents so much as by the status of the messenger who delivers it."[75] While he clearly considered Landon and the Badura-Skodas to be naïve at best, much of Lennon's harshest criticism was reserved for Fiona Maddocks, the editor of *BBC Music Magazine* who had printed Landon's declaration that the forgeries constituted the "Haydn Scoop of the Century." In a particularly telling turn of phrase, Lennon portrays Maddocks as still "defending her experts against what she described scornfully as the 'antiquarians' (as distinct from music experts) who just looked at bits of paper and did not concentrate on the quality of the music."[76]

By drawing a distinction between, on the one hand, a guilty party of music experts occupied with style and cultural value and, on the other, a class of empirically minded antiquarians responsible for unmasking the truth, Lennon not only taps into conservative anxieties about the state of the humanities after postmodernism but also rehearses some of the harshest rhetoric surrounding what historians Francis Blouin Jr. and William Rosenberg have dubbed the "archival divide" in academic culture.[77] For a musicological example of this phenomenon, consider the dispute between Joseph Kerman and Edward Lowinsky that flared up following the former's address to the American Musicological Society in 1964.[78] One of Lowinsky's greatest grievances with Kerman's remarks was rooted in what he saw as a rigidly hierarchical vision of musicology in which scholarly editions, paleography, sketch studies and the like served merely to facilitate Kerman's ultimate intellectual product: a distinctly American brand of criticism. By describing Kerman's idealized critic as "the lord of the manor" to whom "lower orders" of scholars are unjustly made subservient, Lowinsky highlighted the issues of class and power that he saw in this division of labor.[79] He argued that by separating the work from the score as one separates hermeneutic data from an

---

[75] Lennon, "A Haydn to Nothing," A3.

[76] Lennon, "A Haydn to Nothing," A3.

[77] For more on the archival divide, see Francis X. Blouin Jr. and William G. Rosenberg, *Processing the Past: Contesting Authority in History and the Archives* (Oxford: Oxford University Press, 2011).

[78] The address was subsequently published as Joseph Kerman, "A Profile for American Musicology," *Journal of the American Musicological Society* 18 (1965): 61–69; reprinted in Kerman, *Write All These Down: Essays on Music* (Berkeley: University of California Press, 1994): 3–11.

[79] Edward Lowinsky, "Character and Purposes of American Musicology: A Reply to Joseph Kerman," *Journal of the American Musicological Society* 18 (1965): 222–34, at 228.

186 FORGERY IN MUSICAL COMPOSITION

empty archival vessel, musicology would risk becoming deeply imbalanced, factional, and overspecialized. The distilling and bottling of raw musical content in critical editions would have to be conducted outside of the American musicological complex by good-natured archivists "whose business it is to serve music on a silver platter ready to be criticized."[80] Yet the objection to Kerman's proposed model of musicology went further than this. As Lowinsky and those who sympathized with him saw it, focusing academic energy on the aesthetically and interpretatively interesting without due regard for the true would mean putting the critical cart before the archival horse. It would create a dangerous academic culture in which grievous factual errors could go unchallenged.

Concerns about the extent to which "criticism" entails a less thorough verification of facts have hardly gone away. Lowinsky's statements capture much of the disciplinary anxiety that was still present when news of the "Haydn Scoop of the Century" broke in the new-musicological climate of December 1993. In the eyes of commentators such as Lennon, Michel's forgeries provided a rare opportunity for the Lowinskian "antiquarians" on the wrong side of the archival divide to gloat at Kerman's "lords of the manor" when the stakes were at their highest. It was, after all, the steel-nibbed pen and the shelving number, not literary-style criticism, that won the day. Or so the argument went.

Yet Lennon's narrative of musicological incompetence and the authority of physical objects over abstract works was by no means the only way of reading the Haydn forgeries. A scholar in the early 1990s could just as well go in the opposite direction: problematizing traditional musicological axioms by suggesting that the relationships between style, authorship, and identity are not always as clear as we might like them to be. This was the position that Michael Beckerman hinted at when—looking back at the case from May 1994 in a provocative article for the *New York Times*—he dismissed the ability of musicologists to distinguish between the raw compositional content of Michel's forgeries and that of genuine Haydn works. Beckerman asserted that when it came to the Westphalian Manuscript, "not a single musician or scholar [was] willing to say for sure whether, on the basis of the score alone, these pieces are by Haydn."[81] As he saw it, unless there is "something in the music that *couldn't* be by Haydn (like five measures of Joplin or Schoenberg)," we musicologists "have no tools, theoretical or otherwise, for proving the case either way."[82] All this led Beckerman to restate what is, in essence, the same iconoclastic question that postmodernist cultural aesthetics has always asked about successful art forgeries: "If someone can write pieces that can be mistaken for Haydn, what is so special about Haydn?"[83]

[80] Lowinsky, "Character and Purposes," 228.
[81] Beckerman, "All Right, So Maybe Haydn Didn't Write Them. So What?," 33.
[82] Beckerman, "All Right, So Maybe Haydn Didn't Write Them," 33. Emphasis from original text.
[83] Beckerman, "All Right, So Maybe Haydn Didn't Write Them," 33

Strong words. Beckerman's take on the forgeries met with considerable resistance from James Webster, whose rebuke appeared in the *Times*'s letters section two weeks later.[84] Rejecting the article's argument as "misinformed," Webster cited his own low opinion of the quality of the sonatas alongside a quotation attributed to the Haydn Institute in the German press stating that the works "exhibit a host of technical faults, as well as inconsistencies in thematic construction and large-scale form . . . that arise from compositional insufficiency."[85] In his own account of the Haydn Institute's 10 December appraisal, Horst Walter declared that, in "the best philological tradition," the discussion was concerned "first and foremost with the source, with its construction, its age, and its provenance."[86] Yet Walter took pains to clarify, in tune with Webster, that the committee had also raised just as many critical objections "directed against the compositional style, against the music itself."[87]

Was Beckerman right to imply that the facts of source criticism and provenance predetermined any such objections to "the music itself"? Do we really need something as blatant as "five measures of Joplin or Schoenberg" to repudiate the sonatas on stylistic grounds? To attempt to demonstrate analytically at this stage that the works could not be by Haydn would be tautological. In the interest of not letting Michel's music fall silent I will instead do the opposite: I will attempt—counterfactually—to understand these works as if Haydn really had been the author. Unorthodox as this approach may appear, the point is dead serious. This is no trick, not a Sokal-style academic satire, but rather an earnest attempt to capture the ways in which these compositions have been intentionally designed to lead listeners and analysts astray. If I invoke the subjunctive mood here it is not an act of sarcasm but rather one of sympathy with those who were put in the position of evaluating these works without the benefit of hindsight.

AS IF

Example 4.1 shows the opening of the Sonata in D Minor Hob. XVI:2a. This is the work that Landon consistently singled out as the "particularly striking" example among six "extremely original" rediscovered compositions.[88]

---

[84] James Webster, "Haydn Forgeries: More than Sour Notes," *New York Times*, 29 May 1994, H4.

[85] Quoted in Webster, "Haydn Forgeries." See dpa, "Gefälscht?," 25. "Die Kompositionen selbst enthielten eine Fülle von satztechnischen Mängeln, Unstimmigkeiten in der Themenbildung und im formalen Aufbau."

[86] Walter, "Eulenspiegeleien um Haydn," 314.

[87] Walter, "Eulenspiegeleien um Haydn," 315. "Im Sitzungsprotokoll des 10. Dezember 1993 sind die zahlreichen kritischen Anmerkungen dokumentiert, auch die nicht minder zahlreichen Einwände, die sich gegen den Kompositionsstil, gegen die Musik selbst richteten."

[88] Landon, "A Musical Joke in (Nearly) Perfect Style," 10.

Example 4.1 Winfried Michel, "Haydn" Sonata in D Minor, "Hob. XVI:2a." Moderato (mvt. i), mm. 1–11

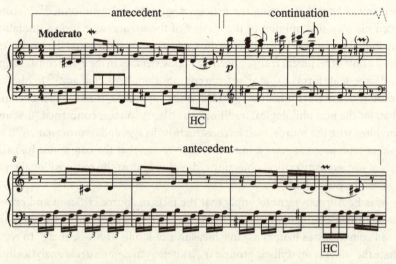

Consider the opening phrase: while the first four measures—familiar from the *Entwurfkatalog* incipit—form a well-behaved antecedent ending with a half cadence (HC), the fragmentation in m. 5 and m. 6 implies an emerging antecedent and continuation structure (or "hybrid 1," as William Caplin has called it).[89] The continuation should, conventionally speaking, close with a perfect authentic cadence (PAC) spanning mm. 7–8.[90] Yet this does not happen. The breaths of silence created by the offbeat rests in m. 7 do not lead to cadential resolution on the following downbeat but rather to a newly agitated iteration of the opening antecedent phrase. This is the iconoclastic "use of silence and of surprise" that Landon described as characteristic of Haydn's new musical language in general and the rediscovered Sonata in D Minor in particular.[91] Resisting symmetry and balance, m. 8 functions not as an ending but as a new beginning. With its thwarted unstressed dominant, the non-conclusion of the first phrase in m. 7 creates the effect of an incomplete thought that cuts itself off like a scratched record skipping backward.

---

[89] For an explanation of "hybrid" phrase structures, see William E. Caplin, *Classical Form: A Theory of Formal Functions for the Instrumental Music of Haydn, Mozart, and Beethoven* (New York: Oxford University Press, 1998), 59–63.

[90] As Caplin writes, "Unlike a sentence, [a hybrid 1 structure] almost always closes with a PAC to complement the weaker cadence ending the antecedent." William E. Caplin, *Analyzing Classical Form: An Approach for the Classroom* (Oxford: Oxford University Press, 2013), 105.

[91] Landon, "The Haydn Scoop of the Century," 11.

Example 4.2 Winfried Michel, "Haydn" Sonata in D Minor, "Hob. XVI:2a." Moderato (mvt. i), mm. 62–78

The compositional consequences of the destabilizing gesture in mm. 7–8 echo throughout Hob. XVI:2a's opening movement. As example 4.2 shows, the recapitulation of the opening phrase (beginning at m. 68) serves—if anything—to magnify the unease that characterized its expositional parallel. In contrast to the *forte* of the development that preceded it, the return of the primary subject is whispered *piano* and attenuated by the initial absence of the left hand's accompanying bass voice, here taking on an almost ghostly quality. A more timid and unsatisfying arrival could hardly be imagined. Indeed, one would be forgiven for wondering whether the mere shadow of the primary subject that emerges from the pregnant pause held in m. 67 is, in fact, the true onset of the recapitulation at all.[92]

---

[92] Haydn's proclivity for deploying the trope of "false recapitulation" in the *Sturm und Drang* years has been well documented (if inconsistently applied) since at least the era of Tovey. For a helpful overview, see Peter A. Hoyt, "The 'False Recapitulation' and the Conventions of Sonata Form" (PhD diss., University of Pennsylvania, 1999).

A more convincing dramatic high point comes at m. 74, when the sonata returns to *forte* leading into the reiteration of the primary subject at m. 75. Tellingly, the dynamic emphasis at m. 74 corresponds to the precise moment that the exposition first went awry, harking back to the fateful V chord in m. 7 that prematurely ended the opening phrase. Yet—crucially—there is no true V chord to be heard in m. 74. As if to amplify the phrase-structural interruption that set the sonata on its wayward course, the composer telescopes the Neapolitan and dominant sonorities in this measure to such an extent that ♭$\hat{2}$ and ♯$\hat{7}$ in D minor give the distinct impression of an augmented-sixth sonority resolving outward not as an intensification of the dominant, but rather as a "tritone-substituted" dominant-function chord moving directly to the tonic.[93] The *forte* emphasis on this sonority further suggests a motion that disperses into m. 75, amplifying the portentous expositional moment of phrase-structural elision in mm. 7–8 into what would have sounded—at least to Haydn's first audiences—like nothing short of a cadential train wreck.

In style-historical terms, it need hardly be noted that the implicit use of a tritone-substituted dominant at such an important structural moment is a bold gesture for the late 1760s. Conventional wisdom, after all, holds that such sonorities belong to the tonal grammar of significantly later eras.[94] Yet this spot of precocious harmonic color is not without late eighteenth-century analogs. Written a mere decade or so after Hob. XVI:2a, the closing passage of Mozart's *Idomeneo* Overture, reproduced in example 4.3, deploys—at m. 157—an augmented-sixth chord above a tonic pedal functioning in its immediate context as a dominant confirming D major as the global home key via the double leading tones ♭$\hat{2}$ and ♯$\hat{7}$.[95] It is only after the curtain goes up on act 1 that the G-minor sonority ushered in by the opening recitative retrospectively recasts the overture's final chord as a dominant in a moment of rich functional play.[96] The question of whether the rediscovered Haydn sonata might have influenced the younger man's bold harmonic choice remains a matter of historical speculation.

While Landon was right to pick up on the particularly strong presence of *Sturm und Drang* characteristics within Hob. XVI:2a, it is by no means the only

[93] On the similarities (and differences) between tritone substitutions and dominant-function augmented-sixth chords, see Nicole Biamonte, "Augmented-Sixth Chords vs. Tritone Substitutions," *Music Theory Online* 14, no. 2 (2008), accessed 21 September 2017, http://www.mtosmt.org/issues/mto.08.14.2/mto.08.14.2.biamonte.html.

[94] For an example of a putatively anachronistic "jazz-influenced" sonority turning up in an authentic Haydn composition, consider the sumptuous dominant ninth chord that appears—held by a fermata, no less—in the first movement of the Sonata in C Minor Hob. XVI:20, mm. 25–26.

[95] An extended discussion of this example can be found in Mark Ellis, *A Chord in Time: The Evolution of the Augmented Sixth from Monteverdi to Mahler* (Farnham: Ashgate, 2010), 200ff.

[96] The first movement of Hob. XVI:2a arguably engages in a similar form of play. Around m. 88, the recapitulation pivots into the subdominant, allowing the augmented-sixth chord that adopted dominant function (in D minor) at m. 74 to reappear at m. 90 in the guise of a true predominant-function chord, now in the context of G minor.

Example 4.3 W. A. Mozart, *Idomeneo*, K. 366. Piano reduction by Richard Metzdorff. Overture, mm. 156–64

work among the rediscovered sonatas to point to the harmonic language of the nineteenth century and beyond. Example 4.4 shows a particularly precocious passage from the Sonata in B Major Hob. XVI:2c, which can now take its rightful place in the repertoire alongside the Symphony No. 46 and the Baryton Trio Hob. V:5 as one of only three works that Haydn composed in this rare "enharmonic" key.

Having arrived in the expected global dominant for the subordinate subject at m. 14, the composer focuses in on its tonic pitch, F♯, which the right hand persistently intones at the top of the texture. By m. 16 modal mixture has transfigured this same F♯ into the root of a *chiaroscuro* minor sonority. At m. 17 the alberti figuration in the left hand drifts into the local chromatic submediant ♭VI as the little finger pushes m. 16's bass C♯ up to D♮. A common-tone diminished triad in m. 18 (again, supporting F♯) pulls us to B^7 at m. 19.

Here at last the F♯ spell is broken: m. 19's bass B is transformed into a leading tone tonicizing C major (i.e., local ♭V) in m. 21, now a tritone apart from the supposed key of the subordinate subject. In m. 22, ♭V's dominant, G^7, suddenly resolves back to F♯ major in another (!) tritone-substituted cadence, this time yielding the first root-position tonic chord in the subordinate key. During the six measures of music from m. 14 to m. 19, F♯ has served as the root of a major triad (F♯+); the root of a minor triad (F♯-); the chordal third of a major triad (D+); the chordal fifth of a dominant seventh chord (B^7); and as a constituent tone in a diminished triad (F♯°), all while it is emphasized in the uppermost contrapuntal voice.

Example 4.4 Winfried Michel, "Haydn" Sonata in B Major, "Hob. XVI:2c." Allegro Moderato (mvt. i), mm. 14–24

Using a single common tone to wander through so many corners of chromatic space so quickly would be striking enough in late Schubert. In an eighteenth-century keyboard sonata composed before his birth (not least one that uses the enharmonic key of B major as its tonal home), such a passage, climaxing in a tritone substitution, is beyond extraordinary. It is easy to see what Landon meant when he wrote that the rediscovered works often arouse surprise through "a

HAYDN'S MISSING LINK   193

sudden change of key or ... an unexpected modulation."[97] Even C. P. E. Bach—a frequently cited influence on Haydn in the *Sturm und Drang* years and arguably the most prominent eighteenth-century advocate of chromatic mediant relationships—might have flinched at such a passage.

DOUBLE BLUFF

Now that we know the truth, it is impossible to believe in these forged works with their stylistic sojourns to the outer limits of eighteenth-century tonal and form-functional grammar. Yet, having closed the "as if" section of this chapter, it is also hard not to sympathize with Paul Badura-Skoda when he thanked Michel for the photocopies of the Westphalian Manuscript, writing that he was "quite sure that Haydn [was] the composer" precisely because the sonatas were "so original and contain[ed] so many unexpected and surprising turns."[98] Much of today's analysis pedagogy inculcates advocacy on behalf of the composer as the overriding goal behind acts of musical observation. We do not expect geniuses to do things by the book. And so the surprising and the unexpected have slowly but surely become synonymous with the inventive and the original to such an extent that analysis is hardwired for appreciation, not authentication. A purely "descriptive" approach such as this makes sense only if we feel safe in assuming that all legitimate objects of discussion will be prima facie Great Works.[99] Analyzing a composition that deviates from stylistic norms not because it is inspired or ingenious but because it is anachronistic or just plain bad has become, broadly speaking, unthinkable.[100] From the perspective of a forger, this makes us easy marks.

None of this answers a crucial question: Why, precisely, would someone go to the trouble of producing these sonatas in the first place? Although it is possible to make money from such things, there is no substantial financial incentive to forge musical works comparable to the lucrative rewards available

[97] Landon, "The Haydn Scoop of the Century," 11.
[98] Quoted in Badura-Skoda, liner notes to *Six Lost Piano Sonatas.*
[99] "Prescriptive" music analysis has hardly disappeared, though it is now practiced primarily in the pedagogical assessment of counterpoint and model composition assignments.
[100] The history of the discipline offers us a number of telling exceptions that prove this rule. Heinrich Schenker and Hugo Riemann, for example, both published scathingly critical analyses of works by their contemporary (and Riemann's former student) Max Reger with the apparent aim of demonstrating how "bad" music might violate the laws of counterpoint and tonality. For discussion of these respective analyses, see Daniel Harrison, "A Theory of Harmonic and Motivic Structure for the Music of Max Reger" (PhD diss., Yale University, 1986), 43–61; and Alexander Rehding, *Hugo Riemann and the Birth of Modern Musical Thought* (Cambridge: Cambridge University Press, 2003), 10–14.

194 FORGERY IN MUSICAL COMPOSITION

to those who forge oil paintings.[101] This is especially true when the work in question is transmitted through a putative copyist's score like the Westphalian Manuscript rather than as a forged autograph. One possible justification is the sheer pleasure to be gleaned from immersing oneself in—and recreating—a beloved historical idiom. As Anthony Grafton wrote in an influential 1990 exploration of the topic, one might just as well be driven to forgery by love as by hate.[102] Following Landon's press conference the *Times* of London declared that the "new" Haydn sonatas were "timeproof treasure[s]" that would serve to "satisfy man's backward-looking passion and longing for basic values in a changing world."[103] Even if the objects of our "backward-looking passion" are fabricated (as such things often are), who would not want to satisfy such a longing? Yet if this were all that were going on with Michel, why take the extra step from "period composition" (Simonetti and Tomesini, in Bruce Haynes's terminology) to forgery?[104]

Another compelling possibility would be to read the forgeries as compositional critiques—whether of aesthetic snobbery, expertise, or academic authority itself. Such a reading is seductive not only because it recalls the desire to "hoodwink the experts" described by Cudworth, but also because it pins down the difference between the Westphalian Manuscript and Michel's earlier pastiche work. Beyond simply creating a work in a historical style, the act of representing the manuscript as a rediscovered copyist's score "containing the 6 Haydn sonatas"—as the Badura-Skodas always claimed Michel had done in his communications with them—surely constitutes musical forgery in the true sense of the word.[105] Moreover, if such a lauded expert as Paul Badura-Skoda took the bait, Michel's virtuosity in imitating historical styles would have passed the ultimate test. Even if they were repudiated after the fact, the forged "Haydn" works would enact a great deal of public mischief on the edifices of taste and authority that underpin modern classical-music connoisseurship, puncturing the boundary between fiction and reality in ways that Simonetti and Tomesini never could.

---

[101] This economic fact is a consequence of what Nelson Goodman has termed the "allographic" (i.e., multiple-token) nature of musical works. For an explanation of Goodman's distinction between "allographic" and "autographic" artforms, see this book's introduction and Nelson Goodman, *Languages of Art: An Approach to a Theory of Symbols* (Indianapolis: Bobbs-Merrill, 1968), 112–23.

[102] Anthony Grafton, *Forgers and Critics: Creativity and Duplicity in Western Scholarship* (London: Collins & Brown, 1990), 39.

[103] *Times* (London), "Timeproof Treasure," 14 December 1993, 17.

[104] Haynes, *The End of Early Music*, 210–13.

[105] In the letter enclosed with the photocopy of the Westphalian Manuscript sent to Paul Badura-Skoda in 1993, Michel wrote: "Es handelt sich um die Ablichtung eines MS (vermutlich einer Kopistenabschrift), das die 6 Sonaten Haydns beinhaltet, von denen meines Wissens nur die Incipits aus Haydns eigenhändigem 'Entwurfkatalog' bekannt waren." Quoted in Badura-Skoda, liner notes to *Six Lost Piano Sonatas* (translation amended).

One last musical detail illustrates this point. In producing a work to match the incipit of the Sonata in B♭ Major Hob. XVI:2d, Michel seems to have deliberately neglected to provide the retransition and the beginning of the recapitulation after m. 65. As shown in figure 4.4, page 37 of the manuscript—which follows hard on page 34—is inscribed with a note that pages 35 and 36 are "missing" [Blatt 35/36 fehlt]. Presumably the intention was to simulate a corrupted historical source, leaving Hob. XVI:2d as an artificial fragment. Stunningly, it also enabled Michel to submit a completion of his own composition when he sent the sonatas to Paul Badura-Skoda.

An excerpt from this "completion" is reproduced in example 4.5. The passage is remarkable not only because of the use of a V$^4_3$ chord to end the retransition at m. 79, but also—and more profoundly—because of the use of a subdominant recapitulation (starting at the upbeat to m. 80) that recasts the primary subject in E♭ major rather than the expected B♭ major.[106] Haydn deployed this latter technique far more sparingly than contemporaries such as Boccherini, Dittersdorf, Gassmann, and Stamitz.[107] And while Michel may simply have been unaware of this fact, it is also conceivable that the peculiarity of his completion was, on some level, deliberate.

In other words, Michel may have used the only section of the compositions marked as his own as a means of veiling his abilities as a forger, much as a pool shark might feign a lack of skill so as to divert suspicion from the greater deception.[108] If this was the intention, the gambit paid off amply when Paul Badura-Skoda wrote that Michel's reconstruction "was not really ... a convincing answer," adding that he believed his own completion to be "better and better adapted to the style of the work, whether or not it is Haydn's."[109] Michel's invention of an artificial missing link within his forgery of the missing link left by Haydn holds a peculiar power. By convincing the Badura-Skodas and Landon that his own compositions were at once not worthy of Haydn (in the case of the completion) and at the same time indistinguishable from the work of the master himself, he could assert a strong claim: it was the authorial signature on the score—not the notes on the staff—that distinguished his compositions from those of the great masters, even in the eyes of the experts.

[106] For an example of Haydn ending a retransition on an inverted dominant-seventh chord, see m. 131 from the first movement of the Sonata in E♭ Major Hob. XVI:49.

[107] On this issue see Mark Evan Bonds, "Haydn's False Recapitulations and the Perception of Sonata Form in the Eighteenth Century" (PhD diss., Harvard University, 1988), 244–46.

[108] In the 1995 "Amadeus" edition in which the sonatas were published, Michel provides a second, less extreme, completion suggestion (Ergänzungsvorschlag B) in which the recapitulation begins in the global tonic. See Haydn, *Sechs Sonaten für Klavier*, 54. Paul Badura-Skoda's completion of Hob. XVI:2d, which can be heard on his CD recording of the works, also recapitulates the primary subject in the global tonic.

[109] Badura-Skoda, liner notes to *Six Lost Piano Sonatas*.

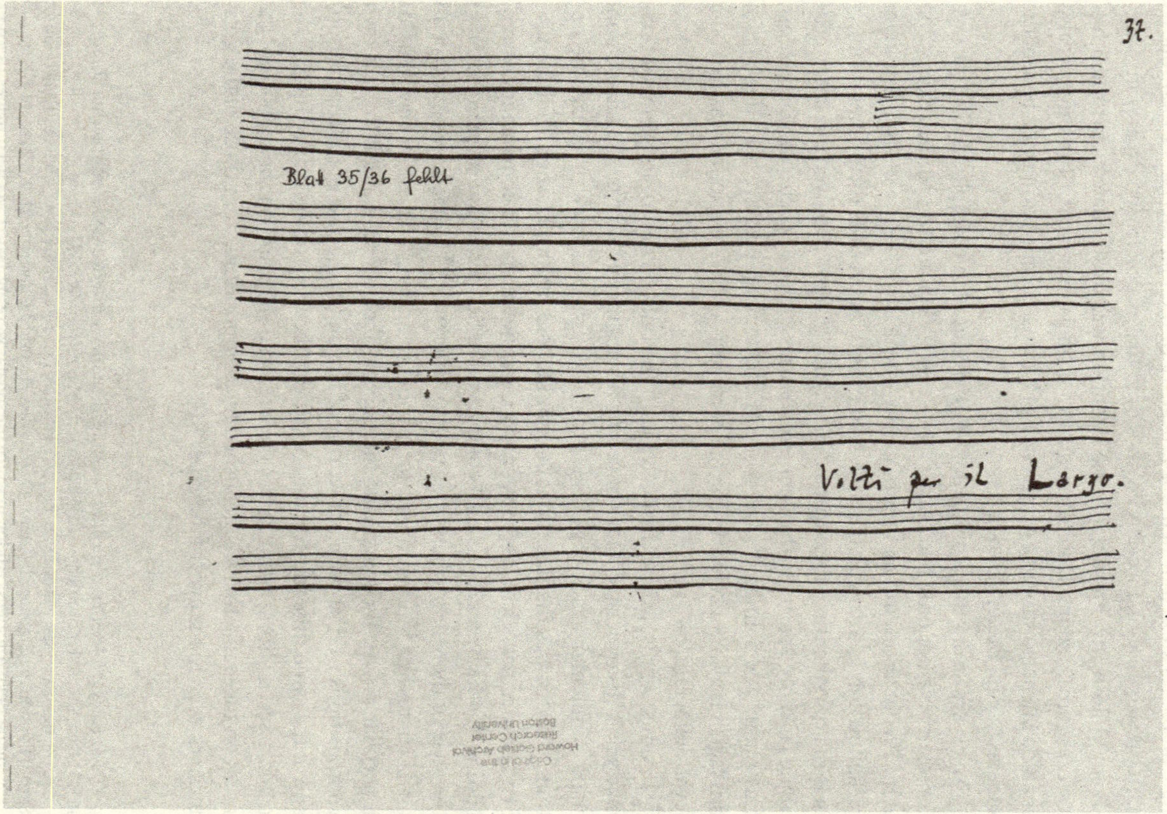

Figure 4.4 Westphalian Manuscript, page 37. From the H. C. Robbins Landon Collection (Box 78; Folder 11), Howard Gotlieb Archival Research Center at Boston University

Example 4.5 Winfried Michel, "Haydn" Sonata in B♭ Major, "Hob. XVI:2d." Allegretto (mvt. i), Michel's "completion," mm. 74–82

ART AND ITS IMPONDERABLES

Assertions about creative motivation are always difficult to adjudicate. But cases of forgery in which the author denies the act offer a special challenge. Our story resumes in winter 2015, when I succeeded in contacting Michel. The account of the sonatas that he gave me differed substantially from the press coverage of 1993 and the statements provided by the Badura-Skodas. In the course of our brief correspondence, I discovered that he is now willing to implicate himself in their composition not as "forgeries," but rather as "completions." In an attempt to do justice to his account of events here, I quote Michel at length:

> After finishing the works ... I then (in 1993?) sent the 6 keyboard sonatas in my handwritten completion to Paul Badura-Skoda in Vienna. ... Yes, the Haydn Institute pointed out that the sonatas, in their completed form, were not composed by J. Haydn, and that is of course the case! On this point the subtitle in the Amadeus edition is correct: "edited and completed by W. Michel." As regards the discussions that took place at that time, the following must be emphasized: there can, of course, be no talk of "forgeries," what we are discussing are simply "completions," as have frequently emerged in the course of the European musical tradition.[110]

[110] "Nach den oben erwähnten Werkergänzungen habe ich dann (1993?) die 6 Clavier-Sonaten in meiner handschriftlichen Vervollständigung Paul Badura-Skoda in Wien zugeschickt. ... Ja, das Haydn-Institut hat darauf hingewiesen, daß die Sonaten in ihrer vervollständigten Form nicht von

198 FORGERY IN MUSICAL COMPOSITION

This is an astonishing admission. No mention is made of the elderly woman who was supposed to have possessed the original Westphalian Manuscript according to the press coverage and the numerous statements of the Badura-Skodas. Instead, Michel explicitly refers to the document that caused so much consternation not as a historical copyist's manuscript but rather as "my handwritten completion" [meiner handschriftlichen Vervollständigung]. Needless to say, the authorial paratext "di G. Haydn," the stamp "Eigentum des BischöflStuhles," the annotation "Sammlung Hegenkötter 1956," and the shelving number "MS H 7$^{A/F}$ Schrank 5, Lage 4"—all clearly visible in figures 4.3a and 4.3b—tell a different story. So does the damning statement—in the annotation to figure 4.4—that the score for the Sonata in B♭ Major Hob. XVI:2d was missing two pages. If Michel had always intended to represent the Westphalian Manuscript simply as his own "handwritten completion," then why did he pretend that part of the source had been lost? Or give it a stamp stating that it had once been the "property of an episcopal see"? Moreover, why does Michel's name appear nowhere in the document's paratexts alongside the attribution to Haydn? For all the reasons described above, the Westphalian Manuscript was and remains a forgery. And yet today Michel is staunchly unwilling to reveal how much of the sonatas were his own compositional work:

> For me personally it is essential that those who want to play these pieces interpret them in the given form <u>as wholes</u>; that is why I do not want the material that was available to me at the time to be separated from my completion. . . . For this reason, I can and want only to confirm that enough coherent and compelling original material from Haydn was available to me that it was a simple matter to complete the sonatas in a few weeks.[111]

Despite having blatantly suggested that he had discovered a sixty-five-page historical source back in 1993, Michel was careful in his communications with me never to contradict the idea that the pre-existing material for his "completions" consisted only of the four-measure incipits from the *Entwurfkatalog*, and nothing more. Asked about this very issue in a 1994 interview with a Dutch

---

J. Haydn sind, und das ist natürlich so! Die Amadeus-Ausgabe bringt daher auch den korrekten Untertitel: 'herausgegeben und ergänzt von W. Michel.' Es muß jedoch nach der damaligen Diskussion betont werden: von 'Fälschungen' kann selbstverständlich keine Rede sein, es handelt sich schlicht um 'Werkergänzungen,' wie es sie im Lauf der europäischen Musiktradition häufig gab." Winfried Michel, letter to the author, 4 December 2015.

[111] "Mir persönlich liegt nach wie vor am Herzen, daß derjenige, der die Stücke spielen will, sie in der vorgelegten Form <u>als Ganzes</u> interpretiert; daher möchte ich nicht, daß das mir damals vorliegende Material von meiner Weiterführung separiert wird. . . . Ich kann und will deshalb nur bestätigen, daß mir zu dieser Werkgruppe soviel schlüssiges und zwingendes Originalmaterial Haydns zur Verfügung stand, daß es mir ein Leichtes war, die Sonaten in wenigen Wochen zu komplettieren." Michel, letter to the author, 4 December 2015. Emphasis from original text.

newspaper, Michel hinted that it "could well have been the case" that he was working only with the first few measures of each sonata, claiming: "With a composer of Haydn's caliber a little material is very compelling.... The notes were so strong that Haydn guided my hand as if it were his own."[112]

Laying aside Michel's deceptive statements about the authorship of the Westphalian Manuscript, the argument he advances about the act of compositional completion is revealing. A die-hard organicist with a taste for mysticism could indeed make the bizarre claim that the finished sonatas were somehow "contained within" the motivic material from Haydn's four-measure incipits such that writing down the rest would be a mere formality. If we like what we hear, Michel seems to say, we have no business asking how (or by whom) the ineffable musical sausage gets made. As he put it to the Badura-Skodas during an increasingly heated exchange of letters from 1993, our obsession with "authenticity" and "famous names" is symptomatic of the ways in which "what people choose to call academia hinders our appreciation of a work of art."[113] Michel drew on this same rhetoric of the ineffable in his correspondence with me when he closed his narrative of events with the gnomic and seemingly definitive statement that while "academia is committed to 'get to the bottom of everything': and rightly so! 'Art' has its imponderables [Unwägbarkeiten]."[114] "There are," he wrote, apparently suggesting that I not press him any further, "boundaries and points of friction that should be accepted."[115]

One urgent question remains: If the Westphalian Manuscript was always in some sense a critique, then how do we, as musicologists, respond? Are we satisfied that it was merely a well-executed joke or hoax to be laughed at and forgotten? Or does its success—however momentary—warrant a more serious reappraisal of the ways in which we hear value and authorship in organized sound, with or without consulting physical sources?

In seeking an answer, we should be in no doubt that the stakes are high. If we are indeed facing the dystopian prospect of a "post-expert" and "post-truth" age, the questions that forgery asks of us deserve serious answers. Nobody is going to die if a sonata turns out not to be by Haydn. Yet important legal and ethical ideals such as copyright and intellectual property are underpinned by a robust

---

[112] Paul Luttikhuis, *NRC Handelsblad Rotterdam*, 18 February 1994; quoted in Walter, "Eulenspiegeleien um Haydn," 316–17.

[113] "Gewiß ist das Sich-blind-Starren auf 'Echtheit' und 'berühmte Namen' ein Symptom für unsere heutige Kunstrezeption. Die sogenannte Wissenschaft verstellt dabei oft genug den Blick auf das Kunstwerk." Quoted in Badura-Skoda, liner notes to *Six Lost Piano Sonatas* (translation amended).

[114] "Die Wissenschaft ist bemüht, allem 'auf den Grund zu gehen': recht so! Die 'Kunst' hat ihre Unwägbarkeiten." Michel, letter to the author, 4 December 2015.

[115] "Das sind Grenzen und Reibeflächen [sic], die akzeptiert werden sollten." Michel, letter to the author, 4 December 2015.

200   FORGERY IN MUSICAL COMPOSITION

author concept that we abandon at our peril. As Michel wrote to me, it is indeed the business of academics to ask questions, and, where possible, to "get to the bottom of everything." The forged Haydn sonatas remind us that telling truth from falsehood in music is vital precisely because it is so difficult. It demands humility and self-knowledge. It means being prepared to resist speculation about "known unknowns," instead admitting the limits of our mastery. And it requires us to remain open to the idea that from time to time, those who seek to deceive us may know us better than we know ourselves.

Epilogue

Art forgery and art scholarship have an oddly reciprocal relationship that any lengthy academic study of the topic must ultimately confront. The deceived establishment connoisseur offers the forger a vital opportunity to gain formal accreditation. And in turn the threat of deception galvanizes criticism to trace clear outer boundaries for the authentic creative self and the meanings it purports to underpin. *Forgery in Musical Composition* has documented the remapping of these ethical, aesthetic, and epistemological borders for legitimate subjective expression in response to real and imagined acts of imposture in classical music culture over the course of two centuries. Given its exploratory breadth, the totality of the study resists neat and pithy summation. Nevertheless, a twofold core to the topic—at once urgently practical and abstrusely metaphysical—can be discerned clearly enough in the questions that musicology has habitually asked of itself whenever forgery rears its head in the light of day. Methodologically speaking, how can one claim to know who wrote what and when in music with any degree of certainty, especially in the face of outright deception? And, more philosophically, what bearing, if any, should the presumed identity and historical situatedness of the composer have on a work's value as music?

It is easier to propose concrete answers to the first question than to the second. And readers of a text on forgery in music might reasonably expect to learn how to spot such works in the present and future by observing patterns of deception ingrained in the historical past. Of course, what is to come need not necessarily resemble what has been in any easily predictable sense. The case studies explored in this book show that bygone forgers have often been highly skilled at adapting their artifices to the habits and prejudices of the moment. And it must always be remembered that the very best forgeries are impossible to examine by definition precisely because nobody recognizes them as such. All this being said, some useful principles can be synthesized from the preceding chapters. For those who wish to avoid being taken in, my recommendations are as follows:

First, beware of lost works that reappear to close chronological or stylistic gaps in the canon. Forgers have often demonstrated considerable resourcefulness in tailoring their wares to fill the historical and compositional voids that the completionist musicological impulse strives, by its nature, to eliminate. Second, deep caution should be exercised whenever the existence of a historical

202 EPILOGUE

manuscript is reported without the possibility of accessing said manuscript directly and in person. This is especially the case when the infirmity or unsociability of the owner is given as an excuse for the manuscript's inaccessibility, or when photocopies, scans, transcriptions, or facsimiles of the documents in question are distributed as an enduring substitute for the real thing.[1] Third, scholars should maintain an attitude of what I have called presumptive inauthenticity with respect to newly published works supposedly based on old sources. The naïve pre-Kreislerian assumption that "when an 'editor' claimed to have in his possession an original manuscript of the work he was speaking the truth" need not be accepted for the sake of politeness in the absence of a verifiable documentary provenance.[2] Finally, those concerned about forgery would do well to follow the post-war methodological norms established by such landmark texts as Larsen's *Die Haydn-Überlieferung* in weighing the evidence for a composition's attribution.[3] In short, this means that source-historical evidence should generally be invoked first as the most systematic, transparent, and impartial means of testing an attribution, while style-critical evidence should maintain a secondary utility in cases where a work's sources prove inconclusive. The reasons are clear: when stylistic evidence has been given free rein in matters of attribution, the historical record shows that the difference between an ingenious innovation and an amateurish solecism can too often amount to little more than the perceived identity, and talent, of the author.

I hope that readers will find these pragmatic suggestions helpful. Nonetheless, the practical fallibility of stylistic evidence lends an undeniable urgency to the second, philosophically skeptical question raised at the beginning of this epilogue. Once again: What bearing, if any, should the presumed identity and historical situatedness of the composer have on a work's value as music? There is an obvious sense in which all practical methods for attributing and authenticating musical works must inevitably rest on an underlying if often unspoken cultural presumption that attribution and authenticity are things worth having in the first place. And yet, for forgery's defenders—Gould, Kreisler, Elsholz, and Michel among them—authenticity's cultural value is impossible to justify when critics consistently fail to hear it, stylistically, in the music itself. Historically speaking, *Forgery in Musical Composition* has demonstrated that there is at least

---

[1] A whimsical rule of thumb attributed to Albi Rosenthal is particularly relevant in this context: "Never believe in the provenance of a manuscript in the possession of an old lady in the country." See Markus Langer, "Ein Haydn ist ein Michel ist ein Haydn," *Frankfurter Allgemeine Zeitung*, 19 January 1994, 29. On authenticity issues arising from "fake-similes" more generally, see Albi Rosenthal, "Facsimiles as Sources of Error," in *A Bach Tribute: Essays in Honor of William H. Scheide* (Kassel: Bärenreiter, 1993): 205–7; first published as "Faksimiles als Fehlerquellen," in *Quellenstudien I: Gustav Mahler, Igor Strawinsky, Anton Webern, Frank Martin*, edited by Hans Oesch (Winterthur: Amadeus Verlag, 1991): 235–41.

[2] Ernest Newman, "An Open Letter to Fritz Kreisler," *Sunday Times* (London), 17 March 1935, 7.

[3] Jens Peter Larsen, *Die Haydn-Überlieferung* (Copenhagen: Ejnar Munksgaard, 1939).

EPILOGUE   203

some truth to the idea that forged works do not always ring false as readily or as uncontroversially as one might hope. And, for arts scholars prepared to take the aesthetics of forgery seriously on its own terms, this state of affairs poses foundational intellectual challenges that remain, broadly, unresolved.

Here it bears repeating that my numerous exhortations to take forgery's ambiguities seriously should by no means be misunderstood as calls for music scholars to abdicate their collective responsibility to tell the truth about who wrote what and when, uncomfortable and provisional as that process may sometimes be. In this sense, meeting one's professional and ethical responsibilities to speak truthfully about an artform in which meaning and signification so often seem to transcend language can be understood to involve a delicate balance struck between two lofty conceptual antipodes dubbed the "truth of accountants" and the "truth of poets" by filmmaker Werner Herzog, who once emphatically asserted—with characteristic rhetorical flare—that the latter remains an "ecstatic truth" and "the enemy of the merely factual."[4] On the one hand, Herzog's truth of poets is a potent means of gesturing toward art's capacity for meaning beyond declarative language, beyond historical authenticity, and beyond the self as such. In these contexts forgery is uniquely apt to demonstrate that music serves not only to "mirror the reality surrounding the composer," but also—as a well-worn musicological turn of phrase has it—"to propose an alternative reality" in which conventional notions of time, identity, and signification seem utterly suspended.[5] However, it is not at all difficult to imagine ways in which an overzealous disregard for the more mundane truth of accountants could itself be subject to abuse. There are frequently good ethical reasons to call authorship to account in purely nominal terms bound to our singular reality alone. And in thus tentatively seeking out a just middle path between Herzog's aestheticist poets and historicist accountants in practice, it is well to turn upward to cosmology or inward to psychology, admitting that one cannot have an Apollo without a Hermes or an Odin without a Loki any more than a canon without forgeries. Reality seems to demand that truth and order be everywhere inextricably entwined with falsehood and flux, for better or for worse. And with all this kept in mind it should ultimately be possible to frame fakes as fakes while simultaneously endeavoring to open up new aesthetic experiences rather than foreclosing them. Forgeries can and ought to be documented and openly discussed in ways that cultivate a transformative intellectual curiosity in place of dogmatic certainty. The goal of

[4] Werner Herzog, "On the Absolute, the Sublime, and Ecstatic Truth," translated by Moira Weigel, *Arion: A Journal of Humanities and the Classics* 17, no. 3 (2010): 1–12, at 1.

[5] Carl Dahlhaus, *Foundations of Music History*, translated by J. B. Robinson (Cambridge: Cambridge University Press, 1983), 19; first published as *Grundlagen der Musikgeschichte* (Cologne: Musikverlag Hans Gerig, 1977).

204 EPILOGUE

authentication should not be to exclude or banish for its own sake but instead to suggest more intense and meaningful ways of listening to music in general.

Compelling practical models for such engagement are readily found in recent museological and art-historical work. While it may once have been true that forgeries were, as Meyer put it, routinely "banished to the basement" in the world's museums, many such institutions have endeavored to bring forgeries, replicas, and decoys out of storage in recent years, thoughtfully exhibiting them side-by-side with authentic pieces.[6] One such 2014 art show, "Intent to Deceive," saw a group of fakes by Han van Meegeren, Elmyr de Hory, Eric Hebborn, John Myatt, and Max Landis tour galleries across five US states, with the exhibits providing interactive opportunities for members of the public to test their ability to distinguish authentic artworks from known forgeries.[7] London's Dulwich picture gallery went a step further in 2015 by displaying a replica that contemporary artist Doug Fishbone had commissioned from the Meishing Oil Painting Manufacture Company based in China's Fujian province in place of one of its authentic eighteenth-century Fragonards, with the museum offering a prize to anyone perceptive enough to correctly identify which painting had been switched with an $88 copy.[8] Ultimately, the success of the Dulwich exhibition inspired a group of six British museums to replicate Fishbone's experiment on a much larger scale as part of a documentary series, *Fake! The Great Masterpiece Challenge*, televised on Sky Arts in 2017.[9] And these exhibitions would seem to be only the beginning of what remains an ongoing curatorial trend.

Encounters with forgeries in this vein invite audiences to hone their stylistic perceptions while simultaneously encouraging them to question underlying assumptions about precisely the kinds of core philosophical issues that academics often struggle to discuss beyond their extended disciplinary peer groups. It is, after all, easy to ignore the utility of looking and listening critically when museums and concert halls are presented as domains occupied exclusively by pre-authenticated masterpieces to which one owes nothing but unquestioning reverence. In their own idiosyncratic ways, commentators from Gottfried Weber

[6] Leonard B. Meyer, "Forgery and the Anthropology of Art," in *Music the Arts and Ideas: Patterns and Predictions in Twentieth-Century Culture* (Chicago: University of Chicago Press, 1994): 54–67, at 67; first published in the *Yale Review* 52, no. 2 (1963) and reprinted in *The Forger's Art: Forgery and the Philosophy of Art*, edited by Denis Dutton (Berkeley: University of California Press, 1983): 77–92.

[7] Lennie Bennet, "Ringling Show about Art Forgers Authentically Fascinating," *Tampa Bay Times*, 29 May 2014.

[8] Reportedly, 12 percent of those 3,000 members of the public who made a guess correctly identified Jean-Honoré Fragonard's *Young Woman*, c.1769, as the replica. Maggie Gray, "Made in China: The 'Fake' Fragonard that Fooled Dulwich," *Apollo*, 5 May 2015, accessed May 2021, https:// www.apollo-magazine.com/made-in-china-the-fake-fragonard-that-fooled-dulwich/. See also Winnie Wong, *Van Gogh on Demand: China and the Readymade* (Chicago: University of Chicago Press, 2014).

[9] *Fake! The Great Masterpiece Challenge*, presented by Giles Coren and Rosen Balston, aired March–May 2017.

and A. B. Marx to Ernest Newman and Glenn Gould have already imagined the starring role that compositional forgery might play in engaging the public with the questions of authenticity and value raised by truly critical listening. And if Gould was correct when he posited that civilization is on the cusp of a new dark age of anonymous and atemporal "electronic culture" for which "the role of the forger, of the unknown maker of unauthenticated goods, is emblematic," then these issues are surely more relevant now than they have ever been before.[10]

There is no reason that the curatorial approaches to forgery outlined above cannot be adapted, *mutatis mutandis*, to concert programming, lecture recitals, program notes, and other public-facing forms. Nor would the ideas discussed here be out of place in music history and theory classrooms, where an awareness of compositional forgery and the problems that it poses can often create a renewed sense of mystery, urgency, and practical relevance when core methodologies come up for discussion. However coming generations of scholars and musicians choose to approach the issue, it should be remembered that the compositional forgeries documented in this book will not be the last. As classical music culture prepares to face an uncertain future in the twenty-first century, it is time to bring these works, and the questions of authenticity which they raise, back out of the basement for good.

---

[10] Glenn Gould, "The Prospects of Recording," in *The Glenn Gould Reader*, edited by Tim Page (New York: Alfred A. Knopf, 1984): 331–53, at 343; first published in *High Fidelity*, April 1966.

Bibliography

Books and Articles

Abbate, Carolyn. "Music—Drastic or Gnostic?" *Critical Inquiry* 30 (2004): 505–36.

Abrams, M. H. *The Mirror and the Lamp: Romantic Theory and the Critical Tradition.* New York: Oxford University Press, 1953.

Adler, Guido. *Der Stil in der Musik.* Leipzig: Breitkopf & Härtel, 1911.

Adler, Guido. "Ein Satz eines unbekannten Klavierkonzertes von Beethoven." *Vierteljahrschrift für Musikwissenschaft* 4 (1888): 450–70.

Adler, Guido. *Methode der Musikgeschichte.* Leipzig: Breitkopf & Härtel, 1919.

Adler, Guido and W. Oliver Strunk. "Style-Criticism." *Musical Quarterly* 20, no. 2 (1934): 172–76.

Adler, Guido and Erica Mugglestone. "'The Scope, Aim, and Method of Musicology' (1885): An English Translation with an Historico-Analytical Commentary." *Yearbook for Traditional Music* 13 (1981): 1–21. First published as Adler, Guido. "Umfang, Methode, und Ziel der Musikwissenschaft." *Vierteljahrsschrift für Musikwissenschaft* 1 (1885): 5–20.

Adorno, Theodor W. "Bach Defended against His Devotees." In *Prisms.* Translated by Samuel and Shierry Weber. Cambridge, MA: MIT Press, 1995.

Adorno, Theodor W. *Essays on Music.* Translated by Susan H. Gillespie. Berkeley: University of California Press, 2002.

Adorno, Theodor W. "Gloss on Sibelius." Translated by Susan H. Gillespie. In *Jean Sibelius and His World.* Edited by Daniel M. Grimley. Princeton, NJ: Princeton University Press, 2011.

Adorno, Theodor W. "Stravinsky and Restoration." In *Philosophy of New Music.* Translated by Robert Hullot-Kentor. Minneapolis: University of Minnesota Press, 2019.

Agawu, Kofi. "How We Got Out of Analysis and How to Get Back In Again." *Music Analysis* 23, nos. 2–3 (2004): 267–86.

Amend, Allison. *A Nearly Perfect Copy.* New York: Random House, 2013.

Associated Board of the Royal Schools of Music. *Violin Exam Pieces: ABRSM Grade 6, 2020–2023.* London: Associated Board of the Royal Schools of Music, 2019.

Badura-Skoda, Eva. "The Viennese Fortepiano in the Eighteenth Century." In *Music in Eighteenth-Century Austria.* Edited by David Wyn Jones. Cambridge: Cambridge University Press, 1996.

Baudrillard, Jean. *Simulacra and Simulation.* Translated by Sheila Faria Glaser. Ann Arbor: University of Michigan Press, 1994. First published as *Simulacres et Simulation.* Paris: Éditions Galilée, 1981.

Barthes, Roland. "The Death of the Author." In *Image, Music, Text.* New York: Hill and Wang, 1977. First published in *Aspen* 5–6 (1967).

Bendix, Regina. *In Search of Authenticity: The Formation of Folklore Studies.* Madison: University of Wisconsin Press, 1997.

Bennwitz, Hanspeter, et al., eds. *Opera incerta: Echtheitsfragen als Problem musikwissenschaftlicher Gesamtausgaben.* Stuttgart: F. Steiner, 1991.

Bergeron, Katherine. *Decadent Enchantments: The Revival of Gregorian Chant at Solesmes.* Berkeley: University of California Press, 1998.

Berlioz, Hector. *Grand traité d'instrumentation et d'orchestration modernes.* Paris: Schonenberger, 1844.

Biamonte, Nicole. "Augmented-Sixth Chords vs. Tritone Substitutions." *Music Theory Online* 14, no. 2 (2008). http://www.mtosmt.org/issues/mto.08.14.2/mto.08.14.2.biamonte.html.

Biancolli, Amy. *Fritz Kreisler: Love's Sorrow, Love's Joy.* Portland, OR: Amadeus Press, 1998.

BIBLIOGRAPHY

Biancolli, Louis. "The Great Kreisler Hoax." *Etude* 69 (1951): 8, 56.

Biba, Otto. "Die Uraufführung von Schuberts Großer C-Dur-Symphonie—1829 in Wien. Ein glücklicher Aktenfund zum Schubert-Jahr." In *Musikblätter der Wiener Philharmoniker* 51 (1997): 287–91.

Bloom, Harold. *The Anxiety of Influence: A Theory of Poetry.* New York: Oxford University Press, 1997.

Blouin Jr., Francis X., and William G. Rosenberg. *Processing the Past: Contesting Authority in History and the Archives.* Oxford: Oxford University Press, 2011.

Blum, Susan D. *My Word! Plagiarism and College Culture.* Ithaca, NY: Cornell University Press, 2009.

Blume, Friedrich. "Requiem but no Peace." Translated by Nathan Broder. *Musical Quarterly* 47, no. 2 (1961): 147–69. Reprinted in German as "Requiem und kein Ende." In *Syntagma musicologicum.* Edited by Martin Ruhnke. Kassel: Bärenreiter, 1963.

Bohlman, Andrea F. and Peter McMurray. "Tape: Or, Rewinding the Phonographic Regime." *Twentieth-Century Music* 14, no. 1 (2017): 3–24.

Bonds, Mark Evan. *The Beethoven Syndrome: Hearing Music as Autobiography.* New York: Oxford University Press, 2019.

Bonds, Mark Evan. "Haydn's False Recapitulations and the Perception of Sonata Form in the Eighteenth Century." PhD diss., Harvard University, 1988.

Bonds, Mark Evan. *Music as Thought: Listening to the Symphony in the Age of Beethoven.* Princeton, NJ: Princeton University Press, 2006.

Botstein, Leon. "Music of a Century: Museum Culture and the Politics of Subsidy." In *The Cambridge History of Twentieth-Century Music.* Edited by Nicholas Cook and Anthony Pople. Cambridge: Cambridge University Press, 2008.

Bourdieu, Pierre. *Distinction: A Social Critique of the Judgment of Taste.* Translated by Richard Nice. Cambridge, MA: Harvard University Press, 1987. First published as *La Distinction: Critique sociale du jugement.* Paris: Les Éditions de minuit, 1979.

Breitkopf & Härtel. "Mozarts Werke." *Intelligenz-Blatt zur Allgemeinen musikalischen Zeitung* 2, no. 12 (1800): 47–48.

Briefel, Aviva. *The Deceivers: Art Forgery and Identity in the Nineteenth Century.* Ithaca, NY: Cornell University Press, 2006.

Brinkmann, Reinhold. "The Art of Forging Music and Musicians: Of Lighthearted Musicologists, Ambitious Performers, Narrow-Minded Brothers, and Creative Aristocrats." In *Cultures of Forgery: Making Nations Making Selves.* Edited by Judith Ryan and Alfred Thomas. New York: Routledge, 2003.

Brown, A. Peter. *Joseph Haydn's Keyboard Music: Sources and Style.* Bloomington: Indiana University Press, 1986.

Brown, Maurice. *Schubert: A Critical Biography.* London: Macmillan, 1958.

Bureau of Labor Statistics. *Historical Statistics of the United States from Colonial Times to the 1970,* Part I. US Government Printing Office, 1975.

Burke, Séan, ed. *Authorship: From Plato to the Postmodern.* Edinburgh: Edinburgh University Press, 1995.

Burnham, Scott. "Landscape as Music, Landscape as Truth: Schubert and the Burden of Repetition." *19th-Century Music* 29, no. 1 (2005): 31–41.

Burnham, Scott. *Mozart's Grace.* Princeton, NJ: Princeton University Press, 2013.

Caplin, William E. *Analyzing Classical Form: An Approach for the Classroom.* Oxford: Oxford University Press, 2013.

Caplin, William E. *Classical Form: A Theory of Formal Functions for the Instrumental Music of Haydn, Mozart, and Beethoven.* New York: Oxford University Press, 1998.

Casadesus, M. "Handel Concerto en si Mineur Pour Alto Avec Accompagnement d'Orchestre." *Notes* 1 (1934): 9.

Casella, Alfredo. *Music in My Time.* Translated by Spencer Norton. Norman: University of Oklahoma Press, 1955.

BIBLIOGRAPHY 209

[Chatterton, Thomas]. *Poems, supposed to have been written at Bristol, by Thomas Rowley, and others, in the Fifteenth Century.* London: T. Payne and Son, 1777.

Chaitkin, Nathaniel Jacob. "Gaspar Cassadó: His Relationship with Pablo Casals and His Versatile Musical Life." DMA diss., University of Maryland, 2001.

Cheng, William. *Just Vibrations: The Purpose of Sounding Good.* Ann Arbor: University of Michigan Press, 2016.

Christensen, Thomas. Introduction to *Cambridge History of Western Music Theory.* Edited by Thomas Christensen. Cambridge: Cambridge University Press, 2002.

Christian, Angela Mace. "The *Easter Sonata* of Fanny Mendelssohn (1828)." *Journal of Musicological Research* 41, no. 3 (2022): 182–209.

Chrysander, Friedrich. "Was Herr Prof. Hanslick sich unter 'Kunstzeloten' vorstellt." *Leipziger allgemeine musikalische Zeitung* 3 (1869): 387.

Citron, Marcia J. *Gender and the Musical Canon.* Urbana: University of Illinois Press, 1993.

Clark, Suzannah. *Analyzing Schubert.* Cambridge: Cambridge University Press, 2011.

Cook, Nicholas. *The Schenker Project: Culture, Race, and Music Theory in Fin-de-siècle Vienna.* New York: Oxford University Press, 2007.

Cowling, Elizabeth. *The Cello.* London: Charles Scribner's Sons, 1975.

Cudworth, Charles L. "Ye Olde Spuriosity Shoppe, or, Put It in the *Anhang*—Part 1." *Notes* 12, no. 1 (1954): 25–40.

Cudworth, Charles L. "Ye Olde Spuriosity Shoppe, or, Put It in the *Anhang* (Conclusion)." *Notes* 12, no. 4 (1955): 533–53.

Currie, James. "Music after All." *Journal of the American Musicological Society* 62, no. 1 (2009): 145–203.

Dahlhaus, Carl. *Foundations of Music History.* Translated by J. B. Robinson. Cambridge: Cambridge University Press, 1983. First published as *Grundlagen der Musikgeschichte.* Cologne: Musikverlag Hans Gerig, 1977.

Dahlhaus, Carl. *Nineteenth-Century Music.* Translated by J. Bradford Robinson. Berkeley: University of California Press, 1989. First published as *Die Musik des 19. Jahrhunderts.* Wiesbaden: Athenaion, 1980.

Dalchow, Johannes, Gunther Duda, and Dieter Kerner. *Mozarts Tod 1791–1971.* Pohl: Hohe Warte, 1971.

Demers, Joanna. *Steal This Music: How Intellectual Property Law Affects Musical Creativity.* Athens: University of Georgia Press, 2006.

Denman, James and Paul McDonald. "Unemployment Statistics from 1881 to the Present Day." *Labour Market Trends* 104, no. 1 (1996): 5–18.

Derrida, Jacques. *Archive Fever: A Freudian Impression.* Translated by Eric Prenowitz. Chicago: University of Chicago Press, 1996.

Derrida, Jacques. *Of Grammatology.* Translated by Gayatri Chakravorty Spivak. Baltimore: Johns Hopkins University Press, 2016.

Descartes, René. *Meditations on First Philosophy.* Translated and edited by John Cottingham. Cambridge: Cambridge University Press, 1996.

Deutsch, Otto Erich. *Mozart: A Documentary Biography.* Translated by Eric Blom, Peter Branscombe, and Jeremy Noble. London: Adam & Charles Black, 1966. First published as *Mozart: Die Dokumente seines Lebens.* Kassel: Bärenreiter, 1961.

Deutsch, Otto Erich. *Schubert: A Documentary Biography.* London: J. M. Dent, 1946.

Deutsch, Otto Erich. *Schubert: A Thematic Catalogue of All His Works in Chronological Order.* London: J. M. Dent, 1951.

Deutsch, Otto Erich. "Spurious Mozart Letters." *Music Review* 25, no. 2 (1964): 120–23.

Deutsch, Otto Erich. "Unfortunately Not by Me (Musical Spuriosities)." *Music Review* 19, no. 1 (1958): 305–10.

DeVoto, Mark. *Schubert's Great C Major: Biography of a Symphony.* Hillsdale, NY: Pendragon Press, 2011.

210   BIBLIOGRAPHY

Dolnick, Edward. *The Forger's Spell: A True Story of Vermeer, Nazis, and the Greatest Art Hoax of the Twentieth Century*. New York: Harper Collins, 2008.

Douglas, Mary. *Purity and Danger: An Analysis of Concepts of Pollution and Taboo*. London: Routledge, 2002.

Duarte, John W. "Weiss—Fiction and Fact." *BMG: Banjo, Mandolin, Guitar* 67, no. 785 (1970): 386–87.

Durkin, Andrew. *Decomposition: A Music Manifesto*. New York: Pantheon Books, 2014.

Dürr, Walther. "Die neue E-Dur-Sinfonie—eine Fälschung?" In *Niedersächsisches Staatsorchester Hannover '82/83, 4. Konzert, 6. und 7. Dezember '82, Opernhaus* (1982).

Dürr, Walther. "Die gefälschte Schubert-Sinfonie." In *Gefälscht!* Nördlingen: Eichborn, 1990.

Dürr, Walther. "Eine Gefälschte Schubert-Sinfonie." *Musica* 37, no. 2 (1983): 135–42.

Dürr, Walther and Arnold Feil. "Stellungnahme der Editionsleitung der Neuen Schubert-Ausgabe." In *Schubert-Kongreß Wien 1978*. Edited by Otto Brusatti. Graz: Österreichischen Gesellschaft für Musikwissenschaft, 1979.

Dürr, Walther and Reimut Vogel. "Nochmals zu der 'gefälschten Schubert-Sinfonie': Ein Gutachten der Bundesanstalt für Materialprüfung, Berlin." *Musica* 39 (1985): 582–83.

Dürr, W., W. Griebenow, B. Werthmann, and M. Ziegler. "Zur Altersbestimmung von Papier, dargestellt an Schuberts 'Unechter' in E-dur—ein musikalisches Märchen." *Das Papier* 41, no. 7 (1987): 321–31.

Dutton, Denis. "Authenticity in Art." In *The Oxford Handbook of Aesthetics*. Edited by Jerrold Levinson. New York: Oxford University Press, 2003.

Dutton, Denis. "Han van Meegeren." In *Encyclopedia of Hoaxes*. Edited by Gordon Stein. Detroit: Gale Research Inc., 1993.

Dutton, Denis, ed. *The Forger's Art: Forgery and the Philosophy of Art*. Berkeley: University of California Press, 1983.

Eberl, Anton. "Suum cuique." *Allgemeiner litterarischer Anzeiger* no. 136, 28 August 1798, col. 1373–75. Reprinted from *Hamburger unpartheyischer Correspondent* No. 118, 15 July 1798.

Eco, Umberto. "Fakes and Forgeries." In *The Limits of Interpretation*. Bloomington: Indiana University Press, 1990. First published as "Tipologia della falsificazione," *Fälschungen im Mittelalter* 33, no. 1 (1987): 69–82.

Ehrlich, A. *Berühmte Geiger der Vergangenheit und Gegenwart*. Leipzig: A. H. Payne, 1893.

Eibl, Joseph Heinz. "Ein Brief Mozarts über seine Schaffensweise?" *Österreichische Musikzeitschrift* 35 (1980): 578–93.

Einstein, Alfred., ed., *Chronologisch-Thematisches Verzeichnis Sämtlicher Tonwerke W. A. Mozarts*, 3rd ed. Ann Arbor: J. W. Edwards, 1947.

Einstein, Alfred. "Mozart's 'Adelaide' Concerto." In *Essays on Music*. New York: W. W. Norton, 1956.

Eliot, T. S. *Notes towards the Definition of Culture*. London: Faber and Faber, 1949.

Ellis, Katharine. *Interpreting the Musical Past: Early-Music in Nineteenth-Century France*. New York: Oxford University Press, 2005.

Ellis, Mark. *A Chord in Time: The Evolution of the Augmented Sixth from Monteverdi to Mahler*. Farnham: Ashgate, 2010.

Elsholz, Gunter. *Im Rausch der Töne*. Edited by Oliver Kröker. Norderstedt: Books on Demand GmbH, 2006.

Elsholz, Gunter. "Werk und Geschichte." In *Franz Schubert Sinfonie in E-Dur, 1825*. Stuttgart: Goldoni Verlag, 1982.

Engel, Hans. "Das angebliche Beethovensche Klavierkonzertsatz." *Neues Beethoven Jahrbuch* 2 (1925): 167–82

Feder, Georg. "Die Bedeutung der Assoziation und des Wertvergleichs für das Urteil in Echtheitsfragen." In *Report of the 11th Congress of the International Musicological Society, Copenhagen 1972*, vol. 1. Edited by Henrik Glahn et al. Copenhagen: Hansen, 1974.

BIBLIOGRAPHY   211

Feder, Georg. "Die Echtheitskritik in ihrer Bedeutung für die Haydn-Gesamtausgabe." In *Opera incerta: Echtheitsfragen als Problem musikwissenschaftlicher Gesamtausgaben.* Edited by Hanspeter Bennwitz et al. Stuttgart: F. Steiner, 1991.

Feder, Georg. "History of the Arrangements of Bach's Chaconne." In *The Bach Chaconne for Solo Violin: A Collection of Views.* Edited by Jon F. Eiche. Translated by Egbert M. Ennulat. Athens, GA: American String Teachers Association, 1985. First published as "Geschichte der Bearbeitung von Bachs Chaconne." In *Bach-Interpretationen, Walter Blakenburg zum 65. Geburtstag.* Edited by Martin Geck. Göttingen: Vandenhoeck & Ruprecht, 1969.

Fine, Abigail. *The Composer Embalmed: Relic Culture from Piety to Kitsch.* Chicago: University of Chicago Press, 2025.

Finscher, Ludwig. "Maximilian Stadler und Mozarts Nachlaß." *Mozart-Jahrbuch 1960/61* (1961): 168–72.

Fisk, Charles. *Returning Cycles: Contexts for the Interpretation of Schubert's Impromptus and Last Sonatas.* Berkeley: University of California Press, 2001.

Fleming, James M. *The Fiddle Fancier's Guide.* London: Haynes, Foucher, 1892.

Flich, Ludwig. "Der Schubert-Krimi." *Vox* 3 (1983): 5–6.

Foucault, Michel. *Discipline and Punish: The Birth of the Prison.* Translated by A. Sheridan. New York: Vintage Books, 1977. First published as *Surveiller et punir: Naissance de la prison.* Paris: Gallimard, 1975.

Foucault, Michel. "Truth and Power." In *Power/Knowledge: Selected Interviews and Other Writings, 1972–7.* Edited by Colin Gordon. New York: Pantheon Books, 1980.

Foucault, Michel. "What Is an Author?" In *Textual Strategies: Perspectives in Post-Structuralist Criticism.* Edited by Josué V. Harari. Ithaca, NY: Cornell University Press, 1979. First published as "Qu'est-ce qu'un auteur?" *Bulletin de la Société française de philosophie* 63, no. 3 (1969): 73–104.

Frary, Peter Kun. "Ponce's Baroque Pastiches for Guitar." *Soundboard* 14, no. 3 (1987): 159–63.

Fricke, Gerhard, ed. *Briefwechsel zwischen Goethe und Zelter.* Nürnberg: H. Carl, 1949.

Friedländer, Max J. *On Art and Connoisseurship.* Translated by Tancred Borenius. Boston: Beacon Press, 1960. First published as *Von Kunst und Kennerschaft.* Berlin: Bruno Cassirer, 1942.

Friedländer, Max J. "The Forgery of Old Pictures." In *Genuine and Counterfeit: Experiences of a Connoisseur.* Translated by Carl von Honstett and Lenore Pelham. New York: Albert & Charles Boni, 1930. First published as "Über Fälschung alter Bilder." In *Echt und Unecht: Aus den Erfahrungen des Kunstkenners.* Berlin: Bruno Cassirer, 1929.

Gärtner, Heinz. *Constanze Mozart: After the Requiem.* Translated by Reinhard G. Pauly. Portland, OR: Amadeus Press, 1991. First published as *Mozarts Requiem und die Geschäfte der Constanze M.* Munich: Langen Müller, 1986.

Genette, Gérard. *Paratexts: Thresholds of Interpretation.* Translated by Jane E. Lewin. Cambridge: Cambridge University Press, 1997. First published as *Seuils.* Paris: Éditions du Seuil, 1987.

Gibbs, Christopher. *The Life of Schubert.* Cambridge: Cambridge University Press, 2000.

Gingerich, John M. *Schubert's Beethoven Project.* Cambridge: Cambridge University Press, 2014.

Ginzburg, Carlo. "Morelli, Freud and Sherlock Holmes: Clues and Scientific Method." *History Workshop* 9 (1980): 5–36.

Gjerdingen, Robert O. *Music in the Galant Style.* New York: Oxford University Press, 2007.

Goehr, Lydia. *The Imaginary Museum of Musical Works.* Oxford: Oxford University Press, 1992.

Goldschmidt, Harry. "Eine gefälschte Schubert-Sinfonie? Eine quellenkritische Gegendarstellung." *Musica* 38 (1984): Beilage 1–15.

Goldschmidt, Harry. "Eine weitere E-Dur-Sinfonie? Zur Kontroverse um die 'Gmunden-Gastein'-Sinfonie." In *Schubert-Kongreß Wien 1978.* Edited by Otto Brusatti. Graz: Österreichischen Gesellschaft für Musikwissenschaft, 1979.

212 BIBLIOGRAPHY

Goldschmidt, Harry. Program note for *Niedersächsisches Staatsorchester Hannover '82/83, 4. Konzert, 6. und 7. Dezember '82, Opernhaus* (1982).

Goodman, Nelson. *Languages of Art: An Approach to a Theory of Symbols.* Indianapolis: Bobbs-Merrill, 1968.

Gould, Glenn. "Forgery and Imitation in the Creative Process." In *The Art of Glenn Gould: Reflections of a Musical Genius.* Edited by John P. L. Roberts. Toronto: Malcolm Lester Books, 1999.

Gould, Glenn. "The Prospects of Recording." In *The Glenn Gould Reader.* Edited by Tim Page. New York: Alfred A. Knopf, 1984. First published in *High Fidelity,* April 1966.

Grafton, Anthony. *Forgers and Critics: Creativity and Duplicity in Western Scholarship.* London: Collins & Brown, 1990.

Grove, George, ed. *A Dictionary of Music and Musicians.* 4 vols. London: Macmillan, 1879, 1880, 1883, 1899.

Grove, George. *Beethoven, Schubert, Mendelssohn.* London: Macmillan, 1951.

Gruber, Michael. *The Forgery of Venus.* New York: HarperCollins Books, 2008.

Guck, Marion. "Music Loving, or the Relationship with the Piece." *Journal of Musicology* 15, no. 3 (1997): 343–52.

Haberkamp, Gertraut. *Die Erstdrucke der Werke von Wolfgang Amadeus Mozart,* vol. 1. Tutzing: Hans Schneider, 1986.

Hamann, Heinz Wolfgang. "Mozarts Schülerkreis: Versuch einer chronologischen Ordnung." *Mozart-Jahrbuch 1962/63* (1964): 115–39.

Hanslick, Eduard. *Hanslick's Music Criticisms.* Translated and edited by Henry Pleasants. London: Dover, 1988.

Harris, Robert. *Selling Hitler: The Story of the Hitler Diaries.* London: Faber and Faber, 1986.

Harrison, Daniel. "A Theory of Harmonic and Motivic Structure for the Music of Max Reger." PhD diss., Yale University, 1986.

Haskell, Harry. *The Early Music Revival: A History.* London: Thames and Hudson, 1988.

Haynes, Bruce. *The End of Early Music: A Period Performer's History of Music for the Twenty-First Century.* Oxford: Oxford University Press, 2007.

Hecker, Tim. "Glenn Gould, the Vanishing Performer and the Ambivalence of the Studio." *Leonardo Music Journal* (2008): 77–83.

Hepokoski, James and Warren Darcy. *Elements of Sonata Theory: Norms, Types, and Deformations in the Late-Eighteenth-Century Sonata.* New York: Oxford University Press, 2006.

Herzog, Anton. "True and Detailed History of the Requiem by W. A. Mozart, from its inception in the year 1791 to the present period of 1839." Reprinted in Christoph Wolff, *Mozart's Requiem: Historical and Analytical Studies, Documents, Score.* Translated by Mary Whittall. Berkeley: University of California Press, 1994.

Herzog, Werner. "On the Absolute, the Sublime, and Ecstatic Truth." Translated by Moira Weigel. *Arion: A Journal of Humanities and the Classics* 17, no. 3 (2010): 1–12.

Hibberd, Sarah. "Murder in the Cathedral? Stradella, Musical Power, and Performing the Past in 1830s Paris." *Music & Letters* 87, no. 4 (2006): 551–79.

Higgins, Paula. "The Apotheosis of Josquin des Prez and Other Mythologies of Musical Genius." *Journal of the American Musicological Society* 57, no. 3 (2004): 443–96.

Hilmar, Ernst. "Neue Funde, Daten und Dokumente zum Symphonischen Werk Franz Schuberts." *Österreichische Musikzeitschrift* 33 (1978): 266–76.

Hindemith, Paul. *A Composer's World: Horizons and Limitations.* Mainz: B. Schott's Söhne, 1952.

Hoyt, Peter A. "The 'False Recapitulation' and the Conventions of Sonata Form." PhD diss., University of Pennsylvania, 1999.

Hunter, David. "Music Copyright in Britain to 1800." *Music & Letters* 67, no. 3 (1986): 269–82.

Hyde, Lewis. *Trickster Makes This World: Mischief, Myth, and Art.* New York: Farrar, Straus and Giroux, 2010.

Jacobs, Joseph, ed. *The Fables of Æsop.* London: Macmillan, 1894.

BIBLIOGRAPHY   213

Jadassohn, Salomon. *Lehrbuch der Instrumentation*. Leipzig: Breitkopf & Härtel, 1889.

Jahn, Otto. *W. A. Mozart*, vol. 3. Leipzig: 1856–59.

Jameson, Fredric. "Postmodernism and Consumer Society." In *The Anti-Aesthetic: Essays on Postmodern Culture*. Edited by Hal Foster. Seattle: Bay Press, 1983.

Johnson, Edmond T. "Revival and Antiquation: Modernism's Musical Pasts." PhD diss., University of California, Santa Barbara, 2011.

Jones, Davin Wyn, ed. *Oxford Composer Companions: Haydn*. Oxford: Oxford University Press, 2009.

Jones, Rufus M. *Studies in Mystical Religion*. London: Macmillan, 1909.

Kant, Immanuel. *Critique of Judgment*. Translated by Werner S. Pluhar. Indianapolis: Hackett, 1987. First published as *Critik der Urtheilskraft*. Berlin: Lagarde und Friedrich, 1790.

Kaufman, Gabrielle. *Gaspar Cassadó: Cellist, Composer and Transcriber*. Abingdon: Routledge, 2017.

Kawohl, Friedemann. *Urheberrechte der Musik in Preußen 1820–1840*. Tutzing: Hans Schneider, 2002.

Keats, Jonathon. *Forged: Why Fakes Are the Great Art of Our Age*. Oxford: Oxford University Press, 2013.

Keefe, Simon P. *Mozart's Requiem: Reception, Work, Completion*. Cambridge: Cambridge University Press, 2012.

Kerman, Joseph. "A Few Canonic Variations." *Critical Inquiry* 10, no. 1 (1983): 107–25. Reprinted in *Write All These Down: Essays on Music*. Berkeley: University of California Press, 1994.

Kerman, Joseph. "A Profile for American Musicology." *Journal of the American Musicological Society* 18 (1965): 61–69. Reprinted in *Write All These Down: Essays on Music*. Berkeley: University of California Press, 1994.

Kerman, Joseph. *Contemplating Music: Challenges to Musicology*. Cambridge, MA: Harvard University Press, 1985.

Kinderman, William. "Wandering Archetypes in Schubert's Instrumental Music." *19th-Century Music* 21, no. 2 (1997): 208–22.

Kopytova, Galina. *Jascha Heifetz: Early Years in Russia*. Translated by Dario Sarlo and Alexandra Sarlo. Bloomington: Indiana University Press, 2013.

Konrad, Ulrich. "Friedrich Rochlitz und die Entstehung des Mozart-Bildes um 1800." In *Mozart: Aspekte des 19. Jahrhunderts*. Edited by Hermann Jung. Mannheim: J & J, 1995.

Konrad, Ulrich. *Neue Mozart-Ausgabe* X/30/4. Kassel: Bärenreiter Verlag, 2002.

Kramer, Elizabeth. "The Idea of Transfiguration in the Early German Reception of Mozart's Requiem." *Current Musicology* 81 (2006): 73–107.

Kramer, Lawrence. *Franz Schubert: Sexuality, Subjectivity, Song*. Cambridge: Cambridge University Press, 1998.

Kramer, Lawrence. "Music Criticism and the Postmodernist Turn." *Current Musicology* 53 (1993): 25–35.

Kramer, Richard. *Unfinished Music*. New York: Oxford University Press, 2008.

Kundera, Milan. *The Curtain: An Essay in Seven Parts*. Translated by Linda Asher. New York: Harper Perennial, 2006.

Larsen, Jens Peter. "The Challenge of Joseph Haydn." In *Handel, Haydn, and the Viennese Classical Style*. Translated by Ulrich Krämer. Ann Arbor, MI: UMI Research Press, 1988. First published as "Joseph Haydn, eine Herausforderung an uns." In *Bericht über den internationalen Joseph Haydn Kongress, Wien, 1982*. Edited by Eva Badura-Skoda. Munich: Henle Verlag, 1986.

Larsen, Jens Peter. *Die Haydn-Überlieferung*. Copenhagen: Einar Munksgaard, 1939.

Larsen, Jens Peter. *Handel, Haydn, and the Viennese Classical Style*. Translated by Ulrich Krämer. Ann Arbor, MI: UMI Research Press, 1988.

Larsen, Jens Peter. "On Haydn's Artistic Development." In *Handel, Haydn, & the Viennese Classical Style*. Translated by Ulrich Krämer. Ann Arbor, MI: UMI Research Press, 1988.

214   BIBLIOGRAPHY

First published as "Zu Haydns künstlerischer Entwicklung." In *Festschrift Wilhelm Fischer zum 70. Geburtstag überreicht im Mozartjahr 1956.* Edited by Hans Zingerle. Innsbruck: Leopold-Franzens-Universität, 1956.

Larsen, Jens Peter. "Problems of Authenticity in Music from the Time of Haydn to Mozart." In *Handel, Haydn, and the Viennese Classical Style.* Translated by Ulrich Krämer. Ann Arbor, MI: UMI Research Press, 1988. First published as "Über die Möglichkeit einer musikalischen Echtheitsbestimmung für Werke aus der Zeit Haydns und Mozarts." *Mozart-Jahrbuch 1971–72* (1973): 7–18.

Larsen, Jens Peter. *Three Haydn Catalogues.* New York: Pendragon Press, 1979.

Latour, Bruno. "Why Has Critique Run Out of Steam? From Matters of Fact to Matters of Concern." *Critical Inquiry* 30 (2004): 225–48.

Lebermann, Walter. "Apokryph, Plagiat, Korruptel oder Falsifikat?" *Die Musikforschung* 20 (1967): 413–25.

Lescat, Philippe. "'Il pastor Fido', une œuvre de Nicolas Chédeville." *Informazioni e studi vivaldiani* 11 (1990): 5–19.

Lessing, Alfred. "What Is Wrong with a Forgery?" *Journal of Aesthetics and Art Criticism* 23, no. 4 (1965): 461–71. Reprinted in *The Forger's Art: Forgery and the Philosophy of Art.* Edited by Denis Dutton. Berkeley: University of California Press, 1983.

Levin, Robert D. *Who Wrote the Mozart Four-Wind Concertante?* Hillsdale, NY: Pendragon Press, 1988.

Levin, Robert D., Richard Maunder, Duncan Druce, David Black, Christoph Wolff, and Simon Keefe. "Finishing Mozart's Requiem." *Journal of the American Musicological Society* 61, no. 3 (2008): 583–608.

Levinson, Jerrold. *Music, Art, and Metaphysics: Essays in Philosophical Aesthetics.* Oxford: Oxford University Press, 2011.

Lindmayr-Brandl, Andrea. "The Myth of the 'Unfinished' and the Film *Das Dreimäderlhaus* (1958)." In *Rethinking Schubert.* New York: Oxford University Press, 2016.

Lochner, Louis. *Fritz Kreisler.* St. Clair Shores, MI: Scholarly Press, 1951.

Lowinsky, Edward. "Character and Purposes of American Musicology: A Reply to Joseph Kerman." *Journal of the American Musicological Society* 18 (1965): 222–34.

MacDonald, Hugh. "Berlioz's *Messe solennelle.*" *19th-Century Music* 16, no. 3 (1993): 267–85.

MacDonald, Hugh. "Schubert's Volcanic Temper." *Musical Times* 119 (1978): 949–52.

Macnutt, Richard. "Berlioz Forgeries." In *Berlioz: Past, Present, Future–Bicentenary Essays.* Edited by Peter Anthony Bloom. Rochester: University of Rochester Press, 2003.

Manderville, Kevin R. "Manuel Ponce and the Suite in A minor: Its Historical Significance and an Examination of Existing Editions." DMA diss., Florida State University College of Music, 2005.

Marx, Adolf Bernhard. "Nachschrift des Redakteurs." *Berliner Allgemeine musikalische Zeitung* 2, no. 46 (1825): 371–72.

Maser, Werner. *Armer Schubert! Fälschungen und Manipulationen: Marginalien zu Franz Schuberts Sinfonie von 1825.* Stuttgart: Goldoni Verlag, 1985.

Mathew, Nicholas and Mary Ann Smart. "Elephants in the Music Room: The Future of Quirk Historicism." *Representations* 132 (2015): 61–78.

Mathew, Nicholas. "Gould and Liberace, or the Fate of Nineteenth-Century Performance Culture." *Journal of Musicological Research* 39, nos. 2–3 (2020): 1–15.

Mayr, Ernst. *The Growth of Biological Thought.* Cambridge, MA: Harvard University Press, 1981.

McClary, Susan. "Terminal Prestige: The Case of Avant-Garde Music Composition." *Cultural Critique* 12 (1989): 57–81.

McLuhan, Marshall. *The Gutenberg Galaxy.* Toronto: University of Toronto Press, 1962.

McCreless, Patrick. "Contemporary Music Theory and the New Musicology: An Introduction." *Journal of Musicology* 15, no. 3 (1997): 291–96.

Melamed, Daniel R. "Who Wrote Lassus's Most Famous Piece?" *Early Music* 26, no. 1 (1998): 6–26.

BIBLIOGRAPHY   215

Mellers, Wilfrid. *The Sonata Principle*. London: Rockliff, 1957.

Meyer, Leonard B. "Forgery and the Anthropology of Art." In *Music, the Arts, and Ideas: Patterns and Predictions in Twentieth-Century Culture*. Chicago: University of Chicago Press, 1967. First published in the *Yale Review* 52, no. 2 (1963) and reprinted in *The Forger's Art: Forgery and the Philosophy of Art*. Edited by Denis Dutton. Berkeley: University of California Press, 1983.

Moberg, C. A. "Äkthets Frågor i Mozarts Requiem." *Acta universitatis upsaliensis* 4 (1960): 5–75

Mörner, C. G. Stellan. "F. S. Silverstolpes im Jahr 1800 (oder 1801) in Wien niedergeschriebene Bemerkungen zu Mozarts Requiem." In *Festschrift Alfred Orel zum 70. Geburtstag*. Edited by Hellmut Federhofer. Vienna: Rudolf M. Rohrer Verlag, 1960.

Moore, Julia. "Mozart in the Market-Place." *Journal of the Royal Musical Association* 114, no. 1 (1989): 18–42.

Mosely, Roger. "Reforming Johannes: Brahms, Kreisler Junior and the Piano Trio in B, Op. 8." *Journal of the Royal Musical Association* 132, no. 2 (2007): 252–305.

Mundy, Rachel. "Evolutionary Categories and Musical Style from Adler to America." *Journal of the American Musicological Society* 76, no. 3 (2014): 735–68.

Nelson, Devon R. "The Antiquarian Creation of a Musical Past in Eighteenth-Century Britain." PhD diss., Indiana University, 2020.

Newbould, Brian. "Music Reviews." *Notes* 58, no. 2 (2001): 421–24.

Newman, Ernest. *The Life of Richard Wagner*. 4 vols. New York: Alfred A. Knopf, 1933–46.

[Newman, Ernest]. Cecil, Hugh Mortimer. *Pseudo-Philosophy at the End of the Nineteenth Century*. London: University Press, 1897.

Nichols, Tom. *The Death of Expertise: The Campaign against Established Knowledge and Why it Matters*. New York: Oxford University Press, 2017.

Niemetschek, Franz Xaver. *Life of Mozart*. Translated by Helen Mautner. London: Leonard Hyman, 1956. First published as *Leben des K. K. Kapellmeisters Wolfgang Gottlieb Mozart, nach Originalquellen beschrieben*. Prague: Herrlischen Buchhandlung, 1798.

Nietzsche, Friedrich. *The Will to Power*. Edited by Walter Kaufmann. Translated by Walter Kaufmann and R. J. Hollingdale. New York: Vintage Books, 1968.

Oster, Ernst. "Analysis Symposium: Mozart Menuetto in D Major for Piano (K. 355)." *Journal of Music Theory* 10, no. 1 (1966): 18–52.

Parry, Charles Hubert. *Style in Musical Art*. London: Macmillan, 1911.

Perry, Jeffrey. "The Wanderer's Many Returns: Schubert's Variations Reconsidered." *Journal of Musicology* 19, no. 2 (2002): 374–416.

Phipson, T. L. *Famous Violinists and Fine Violins*. London: Chatto & Windus, 1903.

Plath, Wolfgang. "Zur Echtheitsfrage bei Mozart." *Mozart-Jahrbuch 1971/72* (1973): 19–36.

Plato. *Laws*.

Plato. *Republic*.

Pohl, C. F. *Die Gesellschaft der Musikfreunde des österreichischen Kaiserstaates und ihr Conservatorium*. Vienna: Wilhelm Braumüller, 1871.

Pollack, Howard. "Some Thoughts on the 'Clavier' in Haydn's Solo Claviersonaten." *Journal of Musicology* 9 (1991): 74–91.

Potter, Andrew. *The Authenticity Hoax: How We Get Lost Finding Ourselves*. New York: HarperCollins, 2010.

Probyn, Elspeth. *Blush: Faces of Shame*. Minneapolis: University of Minnesota Press, 2005.

Pushkin, Alexander. "Mozart and Salieri." In *Little Tragedies*. Translated by Nancy K. Anderson. New Haven: Yale University Press, 2000.

Randel, Don Michael, ed. *The Harvard Dictionary of Music*. Cambridge, MA: Belknap Press, 2003.

Reece, Frederick. "Baroque Forgeries and the Public Imagination." In *The Oxford Handbook of Public Music Theory*. Edited by J. Daniel Jenkins. New York: Oxford University Press, 2021.

Reed, John. "How the 'Great' C Major Was Written." *Music & Letters* 56, no. 1 (1975): 18–25.

Reed, John. *Schubert: The Final Years*. London: Faber & Faber, 1972.

216 BIBLIOGRAPHY

Reed, John. "The 'Gastein' Symphony Reconsidered." *Music & Letters* 40, no. 4 (1959): 334–49.

Rehding, Alexander. *Hugo Riemann and the Birth of Modern Musical Thought*. Cambridge: Cambridge University Press, 2003.

Rehding, Alexander. *Music and Monumentality: Commemoration and Wonderment in Nineteenth-Century Germany*. New York: Oxford University Press, 2009.

Rentschler, Eric. "The Fascination of a Fake: The Hitler Diaries." *New German Critique* 90 (2003): 177–92.

Rifkin, Joshua. "Problems of Authorship in Josquin." In *Proceedings of the International Josquin Symposium Utrecht 1986*. Edited by Willem Elders. Utrecht, 1991.

Robbins Landon, H. C. *Haydn: Chronicle and Works*, vol. 1, *The Early Years, 1732–1765*. Bloomington: Indiana University Press, 1980.

Robbins Landon, H. C. *Haydn: Chronicle and Works*, vol. 2, *Haydn at Eszterháza, 1766–1790*. Bloomington: Indiana University Press, 1978.

Robbins Landon, H. C. *Mozart's Last Year, 1791*. New York: Schirmer Books, 1988.

Robbins Landon, H. C. "Problems of Authenticity in Eighteenth-Century Music." In *Instrumental Music: A Conference at Isham Memorial Library, May 4, 1957*. Edited by David G. Hughes (Cambridge, MA: Harvard University Press, 1959).

Rochlitz, Johann Friedrich. "Anekdote aus Mozarts Leben." *Allgemeine musikalische Zeitung* 1, no. 12 (1798): 177–80.

Rochlitz, Johann Friedrich. "Raphael und Mozart." *Allgemeine musikalische Zeitung* 2, no. 37 (1800): 641–51.

[Rochlitz, Johann Friedrich?]. "Das Reich der Harmonie." *Allgemeine musikalische Zeitung* 12, no. 23 (1810): 353–67.

[Rochlitz, Johann Friedrich?]. "Schreiben Mozarts an den Baron von . . ." *Allgemeine musikalische Zeitung* 17, no. 34 (1815): 561–66. Reprinted in English as "Letter of W. A. Mozart, to the Baron V—." Translated by J. R. S[chult]z. *Harmonicon* 3, no. 35 (1825): 198–200.

[Rochlitz, Johann Friedrich and Christian Schwenke]. "Recension: W. A. Mozarti Missa pro Defunctis Requiem." *Allgemeine musikalische Zeitung* 4, no. 1–2 (1801): 1–11, cont. 23–31.

Rosenthal, Albi. "Facsimiles as Sources of Error." In *A Bach Tribute: Essays in Honor of William H. Scheide*. Kassel: Bärenreiter, 1993. First published as "Faksimiles als Fehlerquellen." In *Quellenstudien I: Gustav Mahler, Igor Strawinsky, Anton Webern, Frank Martin*. Edited by Hans Oesch. Winterthur: Amadeus Verlag, 1991.

Rousseau, Theodore. "The Stylistic Detection of Forgeries." *Metropolitan Museum of Art Bulletin* 26, no. 6 (1968): 247–52.

Russett, Margaret. *Fictions and Fakes: Forging Romantic Authenticity, 1760–1845*. Cambridge: Cambridge University Press, 2006.

Sadie, Stanley, ed. *New Grove Dictionary of Music and Musicians*, vol. 8, *H to Hyporchēma*, s.v. "Joseph Haydn." London: Macmillan, 1980.

Sadie, Stanley, ed. *New Grove Dictionary of Music and Musicians*." New York: Oxford University Press, 2001.

Salisbury, Laney and Aly Sujo, *Provenance: How a Con Man and a Forger Rewrote the History of Modern Art*. Penguin, 2010.

Samson, Jim. "The Great Composer." In *The Cambridge History of Nineteenth-Century Music*. Edited by Jim Samson. Cambridge: Cambridge University Press, 2001.

Schenker, Heinrich. "Ein verschollener Brief von Mozart und das Geheimnis seines Schaffens." *Der Kunstwart* 44 (1931): 660–66.

Schenker, Heinrich. *Free Composition*. Translated and edited by Ernst Oster, with commentary by Oswald Jonas. Hillsdale, NY: Pendragon Press, 1977. First published as *Der freie Satz*. Vienna: Universal Edition, 1935.

Schenkman, Walter. "Cassadó's Frescobaldi: A Case of Mistaken Identity or Outright Hoax." *American String Teacher* 28, no. 2 (1978): 26–29.

Schlichtegroll, Friedrich. *Nekrolog auf das Jahr 1791*. Gotha, 1793.

BIBLIOGRAPHY 217

Schmieder, Wolfgang. *Thematisch-systematisches Verzeichnis der Werke Joh. Seb. Bachs.* Leipzig: Breitkopf & Härtel, 1950.

Schoenberg, Arnold. "Inspiration." Translated by Wayne Shoaf. *Serial: Newsletter of the Friends of the Arnold Schoenberg Institute* 1, no. 1 (Winter 1987): 3, 7.

Shapiro, B. A. *The Art Forger.* Chapel Hill, NC: Algonquin Books, 2013.

Shields, David. *Reality Hunger: A Manifesto.* New York: Vintage Books, 2011.

Shiner, Larry. *The Invention of Art: A Cultural History.* Chicago: University of Chicago Press, 2001.

Shreffler, Anne. "Berlin Walls: Dahlhaus, Knepler, and Ideologies of Music History." *Journal of Musicology* 20, no. 4 (2003): 498–525.

Sisman, Elaine. "Six of One: The Opus Concept in the Eighteenth Century." In *The Century of Bach and Mozart: Perspectives on Historiography, Composition, Theory, and Performance.* Edited by Sean Gallagher and Thomas F. Kelly. Cambridge, MA: Harvard University Press, 2008.

Small, Christopher. *Musicking: The Meanings of Performance and Listening.* Middletown, CT: Wesleyan University Press, 1998.

Smith, Erin Elizabeth. "Mozart, Pergolesi, Handel?: A Study of Three Forgeries." MA Thesis, University of Maryland, 2014.

Sokal, Alan. "A Physicist Experiments with Cultural Studies." *Lingua Franca,* May/June (1996): 62–64. Reprinted in *The Sokal Hoax: The Sham that Shook the Academy.* Lincoln: University of Nebraska Press, 2000.

Sokal, Alan. *Beyond the Hoax: Science, Philosophy and Culture.* New York: Oxford University Press, 2008.

Sokal, Alan. "Transgressing the Boundaries: An Afterword." *Dissent* 43, no. 4 (1996): 93–99.

Solomon, Maynard. "On Beethoven's Creative Process: A Two-Part Invention." *Music & Letters* 61, nos. 3–4 (1980): 272–83.

Solomon, Maynard. "The Rochlitz Anecdotes: Issues of Authenticity in Early Mozart Biography." In *Mozart Studies.* Edited by Cliff Eisen. Oxford: Clarendon Press, 1991.

Somfai, László. *The Keyboard Sonatas of Joseph Haydn: Instruments and Performance Practice, Genres and Styles.* Translated by László Somfai and Charlotte Greenspan. Chicago: University of Chicago Press, 1995. Originally published as *Joseph Haydn zongoraszonátái: Hangszerválasztás és előadói gyakorlat, műfaji tipológia és stíluselemzés.* Budapest: Zeneműkiadó, 1979.

Spitzer, John. "Authorship and Attribution in Western Art Music." PhD diss., Cornell University, 1983.

Spitzer, John. "Musical Attribution and Critical Judgment: The Rise and Fall of the Sinfonia Concertante for Winds, K.297b." *Journal of Musicology* 5, no. 3 (1987): 319–56.

Spitzer, John. "Style and the Attribution of Musical Works." In *Rückkehr des Autors: Zur Erneuerung eines umstrittenen Begriffs.* Edited by Fotis Jannidis et al. Tübingen: Max Niemeyer Verlag, 1999.

Stadler, Abbé [Maximilian]. *Vertheidigung der Echtheit des Mozart'schen Requiem.* Vienna: Ben Tendler und von Manstein, 1826.

Stadler, Abbé [Maximilian]. *Nachtrag zur Vertheidigung der Echtheit des Mozart'schen Requiem.* Vienna: Ben Tendler und von Manstein, 1827.

Stadler, Abbé [Maximilian]. *Zweyter und letzter Nachtrag zur Vertheidigung der Echtheit des Mozart'schen Requiem.* Vienna: Ben Tendler und von Manstein, 1827.

Staehelin, Martin. "'Dank sei Dir, Herr': Zur Erklärung einer Händel-Fälschung des frühen zwanzigsten Jahrhunderts." In *Göttinger Händel-Beiträge,* II. Edited by Hans Joachim Marx. Kassel: Bärenreiter-Verlag, 1986.

Stafford, William. *Mozart's Death: A Corrective Survey of the Legends.* London: Macmillan, 1991.

Steptoe, Andrew. *The Mozart–Da Ponte Operas.* New York: Oxford University Press, 1988.

Stravinsky, Igor. *An Autobiography.* London: Simon and Schuster, 1936.

Stravinsky, Igor and Robert Craft. *Expositions and Development.* London: Faber and Faber, 1962.

218 BIBLIOGRAPHY

Sutcliffe, W. Dean. *Haydn: String Quartets Op. 50.* Cambridge: Cambridge University Press, 1992.

Süssmayr, Franz Xaver. "Letter to Breitkopf & Härtel, February 8, 1800." Reprinted in Christoph Wolff, *Mozart's Requiem: Historical and Analytical Studies, Documents, Score.* Translated by Mary Whittall. Berkeley: University of California Press, 1994. First published in [Rochlitz, Johann Friedrich and Christian Schwenke]. "Recension: W. A. Mozarti Missa pro Defunctis Requiem," *Allgemeine musikalische Zeitung* 4, nos.1–2 (1801): 1–11, cont. 23–31.

Tacconi, Marica S. "Three Forged 'Seventeenth-Century' Venetian Songbooks: A Cautionary Tale." *Journal of Seventeenth-Century Music* 27, no. 1 (2021). https://sscm-jscm.org/jscm-iss ues/volume-27-no-1/three-forged-seventeenth-century-venetian-songbooks/.

Talbot, Michael. "The Genuine and the Spurious: Some Thoughts on Problems of Authorship Concerning Baroque Compositions." In *Vivaldi Vero E Falso: Problemi di Attribuzione.* Edited by Antonio Fanna and Michael Talbot. Florence: Leo S. Olschki, 1992.

Talbot, Michael. "The Work-Concept and Composer-Centredness." In *The Musical Work: Reality or Invention?* Edited by Michael Talbot. Liverpool: Liverpool University Press, 2000.

Talbot, Michael. *Tomaso Albinoni: The Venetian Composer and His World.* Oxford: Clarendon Press, 1990.

Taruskin, Richard. *The Oxford History of Western Music,* vol. 1. Oxford: Oxford University Press, 2010.

Taruskin, Richard. "The Pastness of the Present and the Presence of the Past." In *Authenticity and Early Music: A Symposium.* Edited by Nicholas Kenyon. Oxford: Oxford University Press, 1988.

Taylor, Charles. *A Secular Age.* Cambridge, MA: Harvard University Press, 2007.

Taylor, Charles. *The Ethics of Authenticity.* Cambridge, MA: Harvard University Press, 1991.

Temperley, Nicholas. "Schubert and Beethoven's Eight-Six Chord." *19th-Century Music* 5, no. 2 (1981): 142–54.

Trilling, Lionel. *Sincerity and Authenticity.* Cambridge, MA: Harvard University Press, 1973.

Tyson, Alan. *Mozart: Studies of the Autograph Scores.* Cambridge, MA: Harvard University Press, 1987.

van den Toorn, Pieter C. *Music, Politics, and the Academy.* Berkeley: University of California Press, 1995.

van Hoboken, Anthony. *Joseph Haydn: Thematisch-bibliographisches Werkverzeichnis,* vol. 1. Mainz: B. Schott's Söhne, 1957.

van Orden, Kate. *Music, Authorship, and the Book in the First Century of Print.* Berkeley: University of California Press, 2014.

Vogel, Reimut. "Materialien zur E-Dur-Sinfonie." In *Niedersächsisches Staatsorchester Hannover '82/83, 4. Konzert, 6. und 7. Dezember '82, Opernhaus* (1982).

von Bauernfeld, Eduard. "On Franz Schubert." *Wiener Zeitschrift für Kunst,* June 9–12, 1829.

von Dadelsen, Georg. "Methodische Bemerkungen zur Echtheitskritik." In *Musicae scientiae collectanea: Festschrift Karl Gustav Fellerer zum 70. Geburtstag.* Edited by Heinrich Hüschen. Cologne: Arno-Volk-Verlage, 1973.

von Hartmann, Eduard. *Philosophie des Unbewußten,* Tenth Edition. Leipzig: Wilhelm Friedrich, 1897.

von Köchel, Ludwig Ritter. *Chronologisch-thematisches Verzeichnis sämtlicher Tonwerke Wolfgang Amade Mozarts.* Edited by Alfred Einstein. Michigan: J. W. Edwards, 1947.

von Nissen, Georg Nikolaus. *Biographie W. A. Mozart's.* Leipzig: Breitkopf & Härtel, 1828.

von Spaun, Joseph. "On Franz Schubert." *Österreichisches Bürgerblatt,* March 27–April 3, 1829.

von Zahn, Robert. "Der 'Haydn-Scoop of the Century': Qualität und Schwächen einer Fälschung." *Concerto: Das Magazin für alte Musik* 11, no. 90 (1994): 8–11.

Walton, Benjamin. "Quirk Shame." *Representations* 132 (2015): 121–29.

Watson, William and C. B. Oldman. "An Astounding Forgery." *Music & Letters* 8, no. 1 (1927): 61–72.

BIBLIOGRAPHY 219

Watt, Paul. *Ernest Newman: A Critical Biography*. London: Boydell & Brewer, 2017.

Walker, Frank. *Hugo Wolf: A Biography*. New York, 1952.

Walker, Frank. "Two Centuries of Pergolesi Forgeries and Misattributions." *Music & Letters* 30, no. 4 (1949): 297–320

Walter, Horst. "Eulenspiegeleien um Haydn." *Haydn-Studien* 6 (1994): 313–17.

Walter, Horst. "Literatur zu Echtheitsfragen bei Joseph Haydn." In *Opera incerta: Echtheitsfragen als Problem musikwissenschaftlicher Gesamtausgaben*. Edited by Hanspeter Bennwitz et al. Stuttgart: Franz Steiner Verlag, 1991.

Weber, Jacob Gottfried. "Über die Echtheit des Mozartschen Requiem." *Cäcilia* 3, no. 11 (1825): 205–29.

Weber, William. *The Rise of Musical Classics in Eighteenth-Century England: A Study in Canon, Ritual, and Ideology*. Oxford: Oxford University Press, 1992.

Webster, James. "External Criteria for Determining the Authenticity of Haydn's Music." In *Haydn Studies: Proceedings of the International Haydn Conference, Washington, D.C., 1975*. Edited by Jens Peter Larsen, Howard Serwer, and James Webster. New York: W. W. Norton, 1981.

Webster, James. *Haydn's "Farewell" Symphony and the Idea of Classical Style: Through-Composition and Cyclic Integration in His Instrumental Music*. Cambridge: Cambridge University Press, 1991.

Webster, James and Georg Feder. *New Grove Haydn*. London: Macmillan, 2002.

Weiner, J. S. *The Piltdown Forgery*. Oxford: Oxford University Press, 1955.

Werness, Hope B. "Han van Meegeren *fecit*." In *The Forger's Art: Forgery and the Philosophy of Art*. Edited by Denis Dutton. Berkeley: University of California Press, 1983.

Wilde, Oscar. *The Picture of Dorian Gray*. London: Ward, Lock & Co., 1891.

Wimsatt, W. K. Jr. and M. C. Beardsley. "The Intentional Fallacy." *Sewanee Review* 54, no. 3 (1946): 468–88.

Winter, Robert S. "Of Realizations, Completions, Restorations and Reconstructions: From Bach's 'The Art of Fugue' to Beethoven's Tenth Symphony." *Journal of the Royal Musical Association* 116, no. 1 (1991): 96–126.

Winter, Robert S. "Paper Studies and the Future of Schubert Research." In *Schubert Studies: Problems of Style and Chronology*. Edited by Eva Badura-Skoda and Peter Branscombe. Cambridge: Cambridge University Press, 1982.

Wishart, Trevor. "On Radical Culture." In *Whose Music? A Sociology of Musical Languages*. Edited by John Shepherd et al. New Brunswick: Transaction Books, 1977.

Wolff, Christoph. *Mozart at the Gateway to His Fortune: Serving the Emperor, 1788–1791*. New York: W. W. Norton, 2012.

Wolff, Christoph. *Mozart's Requiem: Historical and Analytical Studies, Documents, Score*. Berkeley: University of California Press, 1994. First published as *Mozarts Requiem: Geschichte—Musik—Dokumente—Partitur des Fragments*. Kassel: Bärenreiter Verlag, 1991.

Wolff, Christoph. "Review." *19th-Century Music* 15, no. 2 (1991): 162–65.

Wollenberg, Susan. *Schubert's Fingerprints: Studies in the Instrumental Works*. Farnham: Ashgate, 2011.

Wong, Winnie. *Van Gogh on Demand: China and the Readymade*. Chicago: University of Chicago Press, 2014.

Newspapers and Magazines

Alberge, Dalya. "The Man Whose 'Real Chagall' Could Now Be Burnt as a Fake." *The Observer*, 1 February 2014. https://www.theguardian.com/artanddesign/2014/feb/01/chagall-could-be-furnt-fortune-or-fake

B., W. E. "Fritz Kreisler." *The Musician* 14 (1909): 453.

Beckerman, Michael. "All Right, So Maybe Haydn Didn't Write Them. So What?" *New York Times*, 15 May 1994, 33.

Bennet, Lennie. "Ringling Show about Art Forgers Authentically Fascinating." *Tampa Bay Times*, 29 May 2014. https://www.tampabay.com/things-to-do/visualarts/review-ringling-show-about-art-forgers-is-authentically-fascinating/2181944/

220 BIBLIOGRAPHY

Der Spiegel. "Schwindel in D." 24 July 1977, 139–140.

Deutsch, Otto Erich. "Schuberts Gasteiner Symphonie." *Neue freie Presse*, 11 July 1925, 11–12.

Downes, Olin. "Kreisler Reveals 'Classics' as Own; Fooled Music Critics for 30 Years." *New York Times*, 8 February 1935, 1, 26.

Downes, Olin. "Kreisler's 'Classics': Story of Their Authorship—Some Rumors and Interpretations of His Course." *New York Times*, 3 March 1935, X5.

dpa. "Gefälscht?" *Frankfurter Allgemeine Zeitung*, 18 December 1993, 25.

dpa. "Wahrscheinlich eine Fälschung." *Stuttgarter Zeitung*, 16 December 1993, FEUI.

Einstein, Alfred. "The 'Adelaide' Concerto—A Question or Two for Marius Casadesus." *Daily Telegraph* (London), 3 November 1934, 9.

Ewen, David. "L'Amico Fritz." *Esquire*, August 1935, 64, 148.

G., W. "Gefälscht?" *Wochenpresse (Vienna)*, 7 June 1978, 7.

Gopnik, Blake. "In Praise of Art Forgeries." *New York Times*, 3 November 2013, 5.

Gray, Maggie. "Made in China: The 'Fake' Fragonard that Fooled Dulwich." *Apollo*, 5 May 2015. https://www.apollo-magazine.com/made-in-china-the-fake-fragonard-that-fooled-dulwich/

Grove, George. "Another Unknown Symphony by Schubert." *Times* (London), 28 September 1881, 7.

Jolley, Jennifer. "The Curious Case of Keiko Yamada." *New Music USA*, 7 November 2019. https://newmusicusa.org/nmbx/the-curious-case-of-keiko-yamada/

Kelts, Roland. "The Unmasking of 'Japan's Beethoven.'" *New Yorker*, 2 May 2014. https://www.newyorker.com/culture/culture-desk/the-unmasking-of-japans-beethoven

Kempf, Paul. "The Kreisler 'Hoax.'" *The Musician*, February 1935, 3.

Kozinn, Allan. "Found: Unknown Music and Inkblots by Purcell." *New York Times*, 13 December 1993, C11.

Kreisler, Fritz. "A Letter from Fritz Kreisler." *Sunday Times* (London), 31 March 1935, 7.

Kreisler, Fritz. "Kreisler Aroused by Critics' Taunts." *New York Times*, 18 February 1935, 19.

Kreisler, Fritz. "Mr. Kreisler's Defence." *Sunday Times* (London), 10 March 1935, 15.

Langer, Markus. "Ein Haydn ist ein Michel ist ein Haydn." *Frankfurter Allgemeine Zeitung*, 19 January 1994, 29.

Le Monde. "La paternité d'Adelaïde." 25 July 1977, 13.

Le Monde. "Qui a conçu 'Adelaïde'?" 23 July 1977, 13.

Lennon, Peter. "A Haydn to Nothing." *Guardian*, 4 January 1994, A3.

Lück, Hartmut. "Eine apokryphe Schubert-Sinfonie? Kontradiktorische Diskussion und Uraufführung in Hannover." *Neue Musikzeitung* 32 (1983): 29.

McCue, Jim. "Haydn Experts Say Lost Sonatas Are Clever Hoax." *Times* (London), 31 December 1993, 5.

McLellan, Joseph. "Sonata Big Deal—Or Is It?" *Washington Post*, 17 February 1994, C9.

Millington, Barry. "Lost Haydn Sonatas Found in Germany." *Times* (London), 14 December 1993, 1, 29.

Moore, Edward. "Kreisler Gives His Name to Classic Music." *Chicago Daily Tribune*, 17 February 1935, E3.

Musical America. "L'Affaire Kreisler." 25 February 1935, 17.

Musical Times. "Kreisleriana." March 1935, 251.

Neue freie Presse. "Eine unbekannte Sinfonie Schubert's." 1 October 1881, 2.

Newman, Ernest. "An Open Letter to Fritz Kreisler." *Sunday Times* (London), 17 March 1935, 7.

Newman, Ernest. "The Kreisler Revelations: Debit and Credit." *Sunday Times* (London), 24 February 1935, 5.

New York Herald Tribune. "Prize of $1,500 Is Announced for Schubert Search." 11 March 1928, 9.

New York Herald Tribune. "Publisher Tells Why Kreisler Hoaxed Public." 9 February 1935, 9.

New York Times. "Fritz Kreisler Back for Concert Tour." 10 January 1934, 24.

BIBLIOGRAPHY 221

New York Times. "How Kreisler Finds Musical Novelties." 8 November 1909, 7.
New York Times. "Kreisler Soloist at Philharmonic." 5 January 1908, 11.
New York Times. "Kreisler's Secret Kept by Musicians." 9 February 1935, 17.
New York Times. "Marius Casadesus Suing over Concerto 'by Mozart.'" 16 August 1977, 40.
Robbins Landon, H. C. "A Musical Joke in (Nearly) Perfect Style." *BBC Music Magazine*, February 1994, 10.
Robbins Landon, H. C. "The Haydn Scoop of the Century." *BBC Music Magazine*, January 1994, 11.
Times (London). "Timeproof Treasure." 14 December 1993, 17.
Time Magazine. "End as a Man." 30 November 1953, 83–84.
Wagner, Rainer. "Juwel, Steinbruch oder Talmi?" *Hannoversche Allgemeine Zeitung*, 8 December 1982. Reprinted in *Das Orchester* 31 (1983): 261–63.
Webster, James. "Haydn Forgeries: More than Sour Notes." *New York Times*, 29 May 1994, H4.
Webster, Paul. "Mozart's First Concerto Was a Fiddle." *Guardian*, 16 July 1977, 1.
Wine Spectator. "Rudy K's Fake Wines Get the Death Penalty." 10 December 2015. https://www.winespectator.com/articles/rudy-ks-fake-wines-get-the-death-penalty-52489

Scores

[Casadesus, Henri]. Händel, G. F. *Concerto en si mineur pour alto avec accompagnement d'orchestre.* Paris: Max Eschig, 1924.
[Casadesus, Marius]. Mozart, W. A. *Violinkonzert in D* (Adelaide-Konzert). Edited and arranged by Marius Casadesus. Mainz: B. Schott's Söhne, 1933.
[Fétis, François-Joseph]. Stradella, Alessandro. "Pietà, Signore!" In *Twenty-Four Italian Songs and Arias of the Seventeenth and Eighteenth Centuries.* New York: G. Schirmer, 1894.
[Kreisler, Fritz]. Boccherini, Luigi. *Allegretto.* Mainz: B. Schott's Söhne, 1910.
[Michel, Winfried]. Haydn, Joseph. *Sechs Sonaten für Klavier.* Edited and completed by Winfried Michel. Winterthur: Amadeus Verlag, BP 2557, 1995.
[Michel, Winfried]. Haydn, Joseph (attributed). *Sechs Sonaten für Klavier 1–3.* First edition by Winfried Michel. Münster: Urtext Edition, 1994.
Mozart, W. A. *Drei Sätze für Klaviertrio: Fragmente KV 442.* Munich: G. Henle Verlag, 2019.
Mozart, W. A. *Missa pro defunctis Requiem.* Leipzig: Breitkopf & Härtel, 1800.
Vogel, Reimut and Gunter Elsholz. *Franz Schubert Sinfonie in E-Dur 1825: Materialien, Werk und Geschichte, Partitur.* Stuttgart: Goldoni, 1982.

Recordings

Badura-Skoda, Paul (fortepiano). *Six Lost Piano Sonatas by Joseph Haydn (Unauthorized Version).* Recorded October 1993, Koch International, 3-1572-2, 1995, compact disc.
Bocelli, Andrea (tenor). *Sacred Arias.* Philips Records, 462-600-2, 1999, compact disc.
Church, Charlotte (soprano). *Voice of an Angel.* Sony Classical, B0000OI9CF, 1998, compact disc.
Primrose, William (viola). *Handel Concerto in B Minor.* RCA Victor Red Seal Records, DM1131, 1946, shellac discs.
Samuel, Gerhard (conductor), and the Cincinnati Philharmonia (orchestra). *Franz Schubert, Symphony in E Major, "1825."* Centaur CRC 2139, 2010, compact disc.
Various artists. *Baroque Masterpieces.* Sony Classical, 2110992, 2002, compact disc.

Index

For the benefit of digital users, indexed terms that span two pages (e.g., 52–53) may, on occasion, appear on only one of those pages.

Tables are indicated by an italic *t* following the page number.

Abbate, Carolyn, 27
Adler, Guido, 3–5, 16–21, 170
Adorno, Theodor, 27–28, 33–34
Albinoni, Tomaso
    Adagio in G Minor (*see under* Giazotto, Remo)
Allgemeine musikalische Zeitung, 50–51, 52–57
allographic vs. autographic art, 3–4, 12–13, 194n.101
Amadeus Verlag, 184
André, Johann, 41–44
arrangement, xviii–xix, 3–4, 78–80, 88, 98–99, 100–1, 102–4, 110–12, 184
attribution. *See* authentication
Austrian Society for Musicology 1978 Schubert Congress, 122–25, 126, 133, 138–39
authentication, 15, 175, 201–3
    source-critical, 123–24, 132–33, 134–37, 160–61, 173, 180–84
    source vs. style-critical, 16–23, 35, 36, 127, 185–87, 201–2
    style-critical, 48, 76, 136–37, 152–53
authenticity, 4–6, 10–11, 24–25, 43–44
    age of, xix–xx, 6–9
    distinct vs. indistinct problems of, 46–49
    nominal vs. expressive, 6–7, 203–4
author concept, xv–xvi, 8–9, 44–45, 90

Bach, Carl Philipp Emanuel, 164
Bach, Johann Christian, 7–8
    Viola Concerto in C Minor, (*see under* Casadesus, Henri)
Bach, Johann Sebastian, 22–23, 85–86, 88, 105–6
    The Art of Fugue, BWV 1080, 77

Partita for Violin No. 2 in D Minor, BWV 1004, 99
    St. Matthew Passion, BWV 244, 105–6
Bach, Wilhelm Friedemann
    Grave (*see under* Kreisler, Fritz)
Badura-Skoda, Eva, 164, 173–74, 180–82, 184, 194, 199
Badura-Skoda, Paul, 164, 173–74, 175–76, 180, 193, 194, 195, 197, 199
Barthes, Roland, 11–12, 29–30, 72
Baudrillard, Jean, 1–2
Bauernfeld, Eduard von, 130–31
Beckerman, Michael, 186–87
Beethoven, Ludwig van, 17n.72, 129–31
Bendix, Regina, 13–14
Berliner musikalische Zeitung, 50–51
Berlioz, Hector, 152–53, 174–75
Biancolli, Amy, 82–83, 84–85, 117–18
Blume, Friedrich, 16, 58
Boccherini, Luigi
    Allegretto (*see under* Kreisler, Fritz)
Bohlman, Andrea, 30–31
Bonds, Mark Evan, 10–12, 105–6
Breitkopf and Härtel, 41–43, 48–49, 55–57
Brinkmann, Reinhold, 13–14, 179
Burnham, Scott, 48, 145–48

Caccini, Giulio
    Ave Maria (*see under* Vavilov, Vladimir)
Cäcilia, 50–51
canon, xix–xx, 7–9, 28–29, 32, 34, 203–4
    critique of, xv–xvi, xix–xx, 5, 7–8, 23–24, 31
    forgeries in, 77, 80–81
    gaps in, 126–33, 168–73, 195, 201–2
    Mozart and, 40, 44, 46–48
    repertory versus, xixn.13, 47–48, 80–81

224 INDEX

capitalism, 12–13, 33–34, 95–96, 103–4, 115–16
Caplin, William, 187–88
Carl Fischer Music, 81–82, 88, 104–5, 106
Cartier, Jean Baptiste, 91–92, 98
   La Chasse (*see under* Kreisler, Fritz)
Casadesus family, 99–100
Casadesus, Henri, 99–100, 109–10
   "Handel" Viola Concerto in B Minor, xvi–xvii, 100
   "J. C. Bach" Viola Concerto in C Minor, 100
Casadesus, Marius, 109–10
   "Mozart" Violin Concerto in D Major (Adélaïde), K. Anh. 294a, 99–103, 104, 115–16
Casella, Alfredo, 99–100
Cassadó, Gaspar
   "Frescobaldi" Toccata, xviii–xix, 115–16
catalogue of works, 22–23, 88, 101–2, 131–32, 168–69, 170–71, 187–88, 198–99
celebrity, 82–83, 85–86
Chatterton, Thomas, 95, 97–98
Cheng, William, 27, 179, 180
complete works, 21–23, 25–26, 41–46, 48, 55, 127
composer-centeredness, 6–9, 10–11, 41, 50–51, 67, 90, 118
connoisseurship. *See* expertise
copyright, 3–4, 7–8, 87–88, 89–90, 100–1, 102–3, 199–200
Couperin, Louis, 92, 98
   Aubade Provençale (*see under* Kreisler, Fritz)
   Chanson Louis XIII and Pavane (*see under* Kreisler, Fritz)
   La Précieuse (*see under* Kreisler, Fritz)
Cudworth, Charles, 23–24, 177–78, 194
Currie, James, 24–25

Dahlhaus, Carl, 7–8, 32, 76, 203–4
d'Arányi, Jelly, 101–2
Darcy, Warren, 140, 144–45
death of the author. *See* Barthes, Roland
Deutsch, Otto Erich, 52, 53–55, 88, 131–32
Dittersdorf, Karl (Carl) D. von, 98
   Scherzo (*see under* Kreisler, Fritz)
Dossena, Alceo, 95–96
Douglas, Mary, 12–13
Downes, Olin, 78, 81–84, 90, 94–95, 104–5, 116–17

Dulwich Picture Gallery, 204
Durkin, Andrew, 27–28
Dürr, Walther, 125–26, 127, 135–37, 138, 160–62
Dutton, Denis, 6–7, 112–15

Eberl, Anton, 49–50, 51
Eco, Umberto, 18–21
Einstein, Alfred, 58, 101–2, 103, 115–16
Elman, Mischa, 84
Elsholz, Gunter, 134, 162, 202–3
   Im Rausch der Töne, 163
   "Schubert" Symphony in E Major (Gmunden [Gastein]), "D. 849," 36, 121–27, 133–63
expertise, 23–24, 176–78, 185–86, 194

Feder, Georg, 21–23, 165–68
Feil, Arnold, 125–26, 127, 135–37, 138
Fétis, François-Joseph
   "Stradella" *Pietà, Signore!*, xviii–xix
flute, 152–53
forgery 3, 4–5, 53–55, 82–83
   admiration for, 23–24, 177
   definion of, 4–5, 82–84, 86
   ethics of, 94–98, 178
   inventive vs. referential, 3, 94–95
   motivations for, 3–4, 72, 94–98, 103–4, 163, 193–200
   other terms versus, 4–5, 82–84, 86
   romantic vs. modern cultures of, 10–12, 21–22, 36, 88–89, 98, 115–17, 118, 126–27
   shame and, 12–14, 176–77, 179
fortepiano, 164, 169–70, 173–74
Foucault, Michel, 29–30, 44–45
fragments, 45–46, 48–49, 50, 68, 72–76, 77, 125, 138–40, 153, 163, 174, 195
Francoeur, François, 92, 98, 99–100
   Sicilienne et Rigaudon (*see under* Kreisler, Fritz)
Frescobaldi, Girolamo
   Toccata (*see under* Cassadó, Gaspar)
Friedländer, Max, 105–6, 112–15, 176–78

genius, 33, 39–40, 47–48, 50–51, 53, 66
   stylistic anachronism and, 19–21, 34, 190, 193
   technical incompetence versus, 67, 76, 152–57, 201–2

Gesellschaft der Musikfreunde, 128–29, 130–31, 132–33

Giazotto, Remo
"Albinoni" Adagio in G Minor, xviii–xix, 25–26

Gjerdingen, Robert, 10–11

Goehr, Lydia, 7–8

Goldoni Verlag, 134–35, 161–62

Goldschmidt, Harry, 36, 121–24, 126–27, 134, 135–37, 138, 161–63
presentation at 1978 Schubert Congress, 124–26, 132–33, 138–57

Goodman, Nelson, 3n.8, 19n.79, 48, 194n.101

Gould, Glenn, 1–2, 5–6, 15, 29–31, 202–3, 204–5
van Meegeren syndrome, 1, 5–6, 11–12, 23–24, 32–34, 36, 67, 112–15

Grove, George, 121, 127–29, 130–31, 132–33

Handel, George Friederich
Viola Concerto in B Minor (*see under* Casadesus, Henri)

Hanslick, Eduard, 99, 131

Harmonicon, 50–51

Haydn Institute, 21–23, 173–74, 175–76, 180–82, 187, 197

Haydn, Joseph, 22–23, 165–68, 169–71
Baryton Trio in B Major, Hob. V:5, 190–91
Entwurfkatalog, 168–69, 187–88, 198–99
Keyboard Sonata in C Minor, Hob. XVI:20, 169–70, 171
Keyboard Sonatas "Hob. XVI:2a–e and 2g" (*see under* Michel, Winfried)
String Quartets Op. 50 (Prussian), Hob. III:44–49, 174–75
Symphony No. 46 in B Major, Hob. I:46, 190–91

Henle Verlag, 125–27, 135–36, 173–74

Hensel, Fanny, 15n.63

Hepokoski, James, 140, 144–45

hermeneutics, 10–11, 127, 139–52

Herzog, Werner, 203–4

Higgins, Paula, 19–21

Hilmar, Ernst, 132–33

His Master's Voice (HMV), 102–3

Hitler Diaries, 157–61

hoax, 4–5, 83, 86, 117–18, 175–76, 199

Hoboken, Anthony van, 88, 165–68

intellectual property, 7–9, 51, 72, 199–200. *See also* copyright

Jameson, Frederic, 33–34

Kant, Immanuel, 33, 39

Keats, Jonathon, 5–6, 96, 177–78

Kempf, Paul, 83–84

Kerman, Joseph, 27, 80–81, 185–86

Kramer, Lawrence, 24

Kreisler, Fritz, 35–36, 80–81, 84–94, 103–5, 109–10, 115–18, 202–3
"Boccherini" Allegretto, 79t
"Cartier" *La Chasse*, 79t
as celebrity, 82–83, 85–86
Classical Manuscripts, 106
confession of forgery, 78–80, 81–82
"Couperin" *Aubade Provençaole*, 79t
"Couperin" Chanson Louis XIII and Pavane, 79t
"Couperin" *La Précieuse*, 79t, 106–7
defense of forgery, 95, 96, 97–98, 202–3
"Dittersdorf" Scherzo, 79t
"Francoeur" Sicilienne et Rigaudon, 79t
Liebesfreud, 79t, 93–94
Liebesleid, 79t, 93–94
"Martini" Andantino, 79t, 80n.11
"Martini" Preghiera, 79t
"Porpora" Allegretto in G Minor, 79t
"Porpora" Meneut, 79t
"Pugnani" Praeludium and Allegro, xviii–xix, 81, 110–12, 115
"Pugnani" Tempo di minuetto, 79t
Schön Rosmarin, 79t, 93–94
"Stamitz" Study on a Choral, 79t
"Tartini" Variations on a Theme by Corelli, 79t
"Vivaldi" Violin Concerto in C Major, RV Anh. 62, 107–9, 112–15
"W.F. Bach" Grave, 79t

Landon, Christa, 165–68

Landon, H. C. Robbins, 19–23, 36, 45, 71, 174, 185
reaction to deauthentication, 175–76, 180
reaction to Michel "Haydn" sonatas, 164, 180–82, 187–88, 192–94
on *Sturm und Drang*, 169–71, 172–73

226 INDEX

Lanner, Joseph, 93–94
  Liebesfreud (*see under* Kreisler, Fritz)
  Liebesleid (*see under* Kreisler, Fritz)
  Schön Rosmarin (*see under* Kreisler, Fritz)
Larsen, Jens Peter, 18–21, 25–27, 168–69,
  201–2
Lasso, Orlando di
  Mon coeur se recommande à vous (*see
  under* Weckerlin, Jean-Baptiste)
Latour, Bruno, 28–29, 177–78
Lavignac, Albert, 109–10
Lennon, Peter, 185–86
Lessing, Alfred, 4–5
Levinson, Jerrold, 3
Lochner, Louis, 85, 117–18
Lowinsky, Edward, 185–86

McMurray, Peter, 30–31
Maddocks, Fiona, 185
the market, 95–96, 103–5. *See also* capitalism
Martini, Giovanni Battista, 92, 98
  Andantino (*see under* Kreisler, Fritz)
  Preghiera (*see under* Kreisler, Fritz)
Marx, Adolf Bernhard, 66–67, 76, 204–5
Maser, Werner, 161–62
Meegeren, Han van, 1–2, 5, 29–30, 34, 55–57,
  112–15, 204. *See also under* Gould,
  Glenn
Mendelssohn, Fanny. *See* Hensel, Fanny
Mendelssohn, Felix, 15n.63, 99
Menuhin, Moshe, 104
Menuhin, Yehudi, 81, 102–3
Meyer, Leonard B., 31–32, 33–34, 204
Michel, Winfried, 174, 184, 197–200, 202–3
  "Haydn" Keyboard Sonata in D minor,
    "Hob. XVI:2a," 187–91
  "Haydn" Keyboard Sonata in B Major,
    "Hob. XVI:2c," 190–93
  "Haydn" Keyboard Sonata in B♭ Major,
    "Hob. XVI:2d," 195
  "Haydn" Keyboard Sonatas, "Hob.
    XVI:2a–e and 2g," 164–65, 175–76,
    180–84, 193
Mieroprint Musikverlag, 184
Misattribution. *See* authentication
missing link, 127–28, 168–73, 195, 201–2
Mozart, Constanze, 35, 41–44, 48–49, 54, 71
  finances of, 68, 72
  reputation of, 45–46, 51, 76–77
Mozart, Leopold, 101–2

Mozart, Wolfgang Amadeus 22–23, 35, 39–
  44, 48–52, 68
  creative process of, 52–55, 66
  Horn Concerto in D Major, K. 412 and
    514 (386b), 47–48
  Idomeneo, K. 366, 190
  Minuet and Trio in D Major, K. 355
    (576b), 35, 46–49, 72–76
  Piano Trio in D Minor, K. 422, 48–49
  Requiem Mass in D Minor, K. 626, 35, 46–
    48, 50, 55–58, 68–72
    Lacrimosa, 59–65
    Sanctus, 65–66
  Sinfonia Concertante for Four Winds
    in E♭ Major, K. 297b (Anh. C 14.01),
    47–48
  Violin Concerto in D Major (Adélaïde),
    K. Anh. 294a, (*see under* Casadesus,
    Marius)
  Violin Sonata in A Major, K.402, 48–49
Musical Times, 98, 115–16
music criticism, 50–51. *See also* names of
  journals and critics
The Musician, 86
music publishing, 7–8, 49–51, 78–80, 87–88,
  95, 104–5, 165–68. *See also* names of
  publishing houses
music recording, 30–31, 80–81, 102–3
music theory, 19–21, 24–25, 76, 178–79

neo-classicism, xvii
Neue Schubert-Ausgabe, 125–27, 135–36,
  138, 160–61, 162–63
Newman, Ernest, 35–36, 88–90, 97–98, 103–
  4, 105–6, 115–17, 201–2, 204–5
new musicology, 15, 24–25, 27–28, 178–79,
  185–87
New York Times, 78, 81–83, 86–87, 93–94, 95,
  104, 186–87
Niemetschek, Franz Xaver, 39–40, 48–49,
  55–57
noble lie, 54–55

objective expression. *See* subjective vs.
  objective expression
organicism, 52–53, 105–6, 199
Oster, Ernst, 72–76

paratext, xixn.11, 128–29, 180
  archival cataloguing marks, 182, 198

copyright notice, 87–88
date of composition, 68–71, 128–29
name of author, 55–57, 68–71, 104, 182, 184, 198
preface, xvi, 87–88, 100–1, 102–3, 104, 184
Pathé-Marconi, 102–3
performer-centeredness. *See* composer-centeredness
period composition, 4–5, 184, 193–94
Piltdown Man, 171–72
plagiarism, 3, 50–51, 71, 72, 94–95
Plato, 5–6, 54–55
Ponce, Manuel, xviii–xix
Porpora, Niccolo (Nicola), 92, 93–94, 98
  Allegretto in G Minor (*see under* Kreisler, Fritz)
  Menuet (*see under* Kreisler, Fritz)
positivism, 15, 24–25, 27–29, 178–79
post-truth, 177–78
presumptive inauthenticity vs. authenticity. *See* authentication
provenance, 86–87, 100–1, 121–22, 125–27, 162, 180–82, 187, 201–2
pseudonymity, 88–89, 94, 97–98, 184
Pugnani, Gaetano, 82, 91–92, 97–98
  Praeludium and Allegro (*see under* Kreisler, Fritz)
  Tempo di minuetto (*see under* Kreisler, Fritz)
Purcell, Henry, 174–75

rediscovery narratives, 174–75
Revue musicale, La, 50–51
Rifkin, Joshua, 21–22
Rochlitz, Johann Friedrich, 39–40, 47–48, 51–52, 53–57, 58–66
Roe, Stephen, 180–82
royalties, 3–4, 49–50, 84, 94–95, 102–4. *See also* copyright

Scarlatti, Domenico, 164
Schenker, Heinrich, 52, 53, 54–55
Schmidt, Leopold, 93
Schoenberg, Arnold, 91
Schott, 78–80, 87–88, 100, 101–2
Schubert Congress. *See* Austrian Society for Musicology
Schubert, Franz, 22–23, 36, 88–89, 127–33
  Der Wanderer, D. 489, 138, 139–40, 145–52

Fantasy in C Major (Wandererfantasie), D. 760, 139–40, 145–48
Octet in F Major, D. 803, 138, 139–45, 148–52
Piano Sonata in D Major, D.850, 138–39
Schöne Welt, wo bist du?, D. 677, 140–44
String Quartet in D Minor (Death and the Maiden), D. 810, 139–40
String Quartet in A Minor, D. 804, 140–44
String Quartet in G Major, D. 887, 138–39
Symphony in C Major (Great), D. 944, 125, 128–29, 131, 132–33, 138–39, 148–52
Symphony in B Minor (Unfinished), D. 759, 131
Symphony in E Major, D. 729, 121
Symphony in E Major (Gmunden [Gastein]), "D. 849" (*see under* Elsholz, Gunter)
Schumann, Robert, 99
Segovia, Andrés, xviii–xix
Sokal, Alan, 178
Spaun, Joseph von, 130–31
spuriosity, 4–5
Stadler, Maximilian, 45, 48–49, 72–73
  Minuet and Trio in D Major, K. 355 (576b) (*see under* Mozart, Wolfgang Amadeus)
Stamitz, Anton, 92, 93–94, 98
  Study on a Choral (*see under* Kreisler, Fritz)
Stradella, Antonio
  Pietà, Signore! (*see under* Fétis, François-Joseph)
Stravinsky, Igor, 11–12
Strunk, Oliver, 22–23
Sturm und Drang, 169–70, 172–73, 189n.92, 190–91, 192–93
subjective vs. objective expression, 10–12, 105–6, 118, 148–52, 153–57, 201
Sunday Times, 35–36, 88–89. *See also Times* of London
Süssmayr, Franz Xaver, 35, 45
  authorship of Mozart Requiem, 57–66
  as forger, 71
  Requiem Mass in D Minor, K. 626 (*see under* Mozart, Wolfgang Amadeus)

228 INDEX

Talbot, Michael, 6–7, 25–26, 41
Tartini, Giuseppe
  Variations on a Theme by Corelli (*see
    under* Kreisler, Fritz)
Taruskin, Richard, 4–5
Times of London, 127–29, 164n.1, 193–94.
    See also Sunday Times
Tomesini, Giovanni Paolo. *See* Michel,
    Winfried
transcription. *See* arrangement
trickster, xxn.14, 86, 177, 203–4
Trilling, Lionel, 10–11
truth, 1–2, 5–6, 10–11, 24, 25–29, 177–79,
    203–4

unfinished works. *See* fragments
urtext, 22–23, 116–17, 126–27

van Meegeren syndrome . *See under*
    Gould, Glenn
Vavilov, Vladimir,
  "Caccini" Ave Maria, xviii–xix
Vivaldi, Antonio, 91–92, 93–94, 98
  Violin Concerto in C Major, RV Anh. 62
    (*see under* Kreisler, Fritz)
Vogel, Reimut, 134–36, 161–63

Walsegg-Stupach, Count Franz von, 68, 71–72
Weber, Jacob Gottfried, 47–48, 66–67
Webster, James, 173, 187
Weckerlin, Jean-Baptiste,
  "Lasso" *Mon coeur se recommande à vous,*
    xviii–xix
Wolff, Christoph, 47–48, 50, 58, 71
work concept, 7–8